Medieval & Renaissance Literary Studies

General Editor:
Albert C. Labriola

Advisory Editor:
Foster Provost

Editorial Board:
Judith H. Anderson
Diana Treviño Benet
Donald Cheney
Ann Baynes Coiro
Mary T. Crane
Patrick Cullen
A. C. Hamilton
Margaret P. Hannay
A. Kent Hieatt
William B. Hunter
Michael Lieb
Thomas P. Roche Jr.
Mary Beth Rose
John M. Steadman
Humphrey Tonkin
Susanne Woods

Speaking Grief

Speaking Grief in English Literary Culture

Shakespeare to Milton

edited by
Margo Swiss & David A. Kent

Duquesne
University Press

Copyright © 2002 Duquesne University Press
All Rights Reserved

Published in the United States of America by

Duquesne University Press
600 Forbes Avenue
Pittsburgh, Pennsylvania 15282

No part of this book may be used or reproduced, in any manner whatsoever, without the written permission of the Publisher, except in the case of brief quotations embodied in critical articles or reviews.

Library of Congress Cataloging-in-Publication Data

Speaking grief in English literary culture: Shakespeare to Milton / edited by Margo Swiss and David A. Kent.
    p. cm. — (Medieval & Renaissance literary studies)
Includes bibliographical references and index.
    ISBN 0–8207–0330–3 (alk. paper)
1. English literature — Early modern, 1500–1700 — History and criticism. 2. Grief in literature. 3. Literature and society — Great Britain — History — 16th century. 4. Literature and society — Great Britain — History — 17th century. 5. Shakespeare, William, 1564–1616 — Views on grief. 6. Milton, John, 1608–1674 — Views on grief. 7. Loss (Psychology) in literature. 8. Death in literature. I. Swiss, Margo, 1946– II. Kent, David A., 1948– III. Medieval and Renaissance literary studies.
  PR428.G74 S64 2002
  820.9′353 — dc21
                                        2002003515

∞ Printed on acid-free paper.

In memoriam

Louis L. Martz

(1913–2001)

Contents

Acknowledgments	ix
List of Abbreviations	xi
Introduction *Margo Swiss & David A. Kent*	1
1 • Grief, Authority and the Resistance to Consolation in Shakespeare *Fred B. Tromly*	20
2 • Lyric Grief in Donne and Jonson *Robert C. Evans*	42
3 • Humourous Grief: Donne and Burton Read Melancholy *Marjory E. Lange*	69
4 • Grief, Theater and Society in Thomas Heywood's *A Woman Killed with Kindness* *Michael McClintock*	98
5 • The Action of Grief in Herbert's "The Church" *Louis L. Martz*	119
6 • Transcendence of Grief: On a Sequence by William Hammond *John T. Shawcross*	136

7 • Maternal Elegies by Mary Carey, Lucy Hastings,
Alice Thornton and Gertrude Thimelby
Donna J. Long   153

8 • An Collins and the Politics of Mourning
W. Scott Howard   177

9 • Consolatory Grief in the Funeral Sermons of
Donne and Taylor
P. G. Stanwood   197

10 • Moderate Sorrow and Immoderate Tears:
Mourning in Crashaw
Paul Parrish   217

11 • Precious Grief: Mourning and Melancholy in
Andrew Marvell's "Nymph"
Phillip McCaffrey   242

12 • Repairing Androgyny: Eve's Tears in *Paradise Lost*
Margo Swiss   261

13 • Afterword
Ralph Houlbrooke   284

Notes   303
About the Contributors   356
Index   361

Acknowledgments

The origin of this volume of essays was in "Grief Expression in Seventeenth Century English Literary Culture," a special session organized for the Modern Language Association convention in Toronto, December 1997. We wish to thank Paul Stanwood, Fred Tromly and D. R. Ewen for their advice, to acknowledge the early encouragement of Roger Reynolds and to express our gratitude to all the contributors for their cooperation. We are especially grateful to Ralph Houlbrooke for providing in his afterword an interdisciplinary perspective on this collection. Lastly, we warmly thank Marlene Caplan for her assistance in preparing the manuscript.

While this volume was being readied for publication, we were saddened to learn of Louis Martz's death. It was the unanimous wish of all the contributors that we dedicate the collection to the memory of this kind, generous and learned man.

Abbreviations

The following abbreviations have been used for sources that are frequently cited:

BMD   David Cressy, *Birth, Marriage, and Death: Ritual, Religion, and the Life-Cycle in Tudor and Stuart England* (Oxford: Oxford University Press, 1997).

DRB   Ralph Houlbrooke, ed., *Death, Ritual, and Bereavement* (London: Routledge, 1989).

DRF   Ralph Houlbrooke, *Death, Religion, and the Family in England 1480–1750* (Oxford: Clarendon Press, 1998).

DV   Gary A. Stringer et al., vol. 6 of *The Variorum Edition of the Poetry of John Donne* (Bloomington: Indiana University Press, 1995).

Elegy   G. W. Pigman III, *Grief and English Renaissance Elegy* (Cambridge: Cambridge University Press, 1985).

MB   Michael MacDonald, *Mystical Bedlam: Madness, Anxiety and Healing in Seventeenth-Century England* (Cambridge: Cambridge University Press, 1981).

Introduction

Margo Swiss & David A. Kent

I

In act 4 of *Macbeth* Malcolm challenges Macduff's reaction to news of his family's massacre, first admonishing him to "speak" his "grief" (4.3.210).[1] "Give sorrow words," exhorts Malcolm. "The grief that does not speak / Whispers the o'erfraught heart, and bids it break" (208–11). Macduff is in a state of shock; he is numbed by the news he has just heard. Nevertheless, he gradually finds words to express his devastating loss: "All my pretty ones? / Did you say all? O hell-kite! All? . . . I cannot but remember such things were, / That were most precious to me" (216–17, 222–23). Out of guilt for his absence, he assumes personal responsibility for the deaths of his wife and children. Malcolm, however, needs Macduff's military help and quickly intrudes on his expression of grief. He insists that the best way for Macduff to show his sorrow is through violent revenge: "let's make us med'cines for our great revenge / To cure this deadly grief . . . let grief / Convert to anger; blunt not the heart, enrage it" (214–15, 228–29). The stoical counsel to suppress grief — normally justified by the strict obligations of Christian faith — had been widely disseminated during the sixteenth century through such works as Erasmus's *De Conscribendis Epistolis* (1522) and *A Treatise perswadynge a man patientlye to suffre the deth of his frende* (1531) and Thomas Wilson's *The Arte of Rhetorique* (1553).[2] Malcolm's admonitions thus mark a departure from conventional advice. Armed with anger, Macduff obeys the summons: "Front to front / Bring thou this fiend of Scotland and myself; / Within my sword's length set him" (4.3.232–34).

In this brief scene, Shakespeare has provided a dramatic instance of what his audience would have recognized as "the taking of a grief." Michael MacDonald (*MB*, 158–59) informs us that this phrase in the early modern period "meant more than to have felt some sudden sorrow; it also implied that one had been assailed by a sickness or a loss" (*OED*, "grief"). After being told the dreadful news and shaking off his shock, Macduff is then seized by a mixture of guilt and anger, two characteristic elements of the experience of grief identified by modern psychology. In his *Grief and English Renaissance Elegy*, G. W. Pigman III makes a practical distinction between grief and mourning: "In everyday speech 'grief' is a synonym for 'mourning,' and some theorists prefer it as the technical term, but there are advantages to distinguishing between the two. I use 'mourning' to refer to a process and 'grief' to refer to an emotion, intense sorrow" (6). He goes on to consider the stages of mourning (which he designates as numbing, anger, despair and recovery) and to relate these to the nature and structure of elegies. The stages of mourning are not necessarily successive, however. They often overlap or occur in a different order, and psychologists have identified many subdivisions of each. In this scene from *Macbeth*, therefore, Macduff experiences grief but has almost no time for mourning.[3]

Hamlet is certainly one Shakespearean play in which the central character is in a continuing state of grief. Together with Robert Burton's *Anatomy of Melancholy* (1621), the play characterizes a cultural period that in the nineteenth century was called "the great era of melancholia."[4] From his first appearance, Hamlet's melancholic cast may be glossed by Burton's account of "*Sorrow.* An inseparable companion, *The mother and daughter of melancholy, her Epitome, Symptome, and chief cause.*" He elaborates: "*Every perturbation is a misery, but griefe a cruell torment,* a domineering passion. . . . when griefe appeares, all other passions vanish."[5] For his sorrowful demeanor Hamlet is chided by both Gertrude and Claudius "to cast [his] nighted color off" (1.2.68) since "to persever / In obstinate condolement is a course / Of impious stubbornness" and "unmanly grief / [which] shows a will most incorrect to heaven" (1.2.92–94, 94–95). Despite being assailed by the grief Burton describes as consuming in its effects, Hamlet is constrained by courtly and Christian etiquette. He concludes that he has no alternative but to restrain his grief: "It is not, nor it cannot come to good, / But break my heart, for I must hold my tongue" (1.2.158–59).

Arthur Kirsch treats Hamlet as a protagonist who successfully completes a process of mourning in the course of the play.[6] While Kirsch makes several convincing arguments and observations (such as the connections between anger and sorrow in revenge tragedy), we are less certain that Hamlet completes a satisfactory process of mourning. Like Macduff, he is called to action and lacks, for all his soliloquizing, either the time or the place in which to perform fully the ritual of "grief work." Hamlet suffers a series of bereavements, and he never recovers from one before another occurs. These successive sorrows (his father's death, his mother's rapid marriage, his mistaken killing of Polonius, his parting with Ophelia and her later suicide) cumulatively ensure that he is unable to escape his grief-stricken state. In his dying speech, although he has by this point fulfilled the ghost's commission and avenged his father's murder, he nevertheless confesses that he has no "time" to speak of what he has experienced: "You that look pale, and trouble at this chance, / That are but mutes or audience to this act, / Had I but time — as this fell sergeant, Death, / Is strict in his arrest — O, I could tell you — / But let it be" (5.2.334–38).

In contrast to Claudius's cold and false expressions of grief (4.5.151, 4.5.203), Hamlet's emotional oscillations between depression and rage are exacerbated by the additional complication that he *must* avenge his father's murder. Yet, before his final duel with Laertes, his heart wound, contained since his first speech, is reexposed in an aside to Horatio: "Thou wouldst not think how ill all's here about / my heart — but it is no matter" (5.2.212–13). Almost immediately, however, Hamlet trivializes his state as a preoccupation "as would perhaps trouble a woman" (5.2.215–16). Horatio responds with practical advice: "I will / forestall their repair hither, and say you are not fit" (217–18). This offer to disclose the incapacity of an emotionally "unfit" hero on the brink of his achievement disrupts our traditional expectations of the avenging hero.[7] Hamlet remains as he has been throughout the play — incapacitated by unresolved grief. Two allusions to grief retention, occurring as they do in his first and last appearances on stage, parenthesize all but the resolution itself. Moreover, his expressions of anger against Ophelia (3.1) and his mother (3.4) may be interpreted as his refutation of what he senses to be the womanish character of his own feelings. Further, his brute bullying of females, constituting two of the most disturbing scenes in the play, allows Hamlet to exercise the violence of his otherwise internalized grief. He acts cruelly, venting grief against Ophelia and Gertrude, each a site of his own bereavement, one of sexual fulfillment and the other of maternal comfort. In confronting these two women, once loved, now (he believes) lost, Hamlet engages in, until exhausted, the mimesis of his own grief expression. The facial contortions, tears and cries for mercy that Hamlet's rage wrings from them mirror his own powerlessness. His most aggressive act in the play, stabbing Polonius, is a spontaneous act of violence occurring during the second of the two enraged outpourings. Hamlet's grief has impaired his judgment as he precipitously kills the wrong man. Indecisive in intent and erroneous in deed, Hamlet nonetheless is, for a moment, empowered by that same principle of grief sublimation to which Macduff also obediently dedicates himself.

From *Richard II* to *King Lear*, Shakespeare dramatized crucial issues related to grief expression in theatrical representations of tragic reversals and catharsis. Monarch and pauper alike would have had numerous occasions on which to sympathize and weep as they witnessed the dramatization of that most poignant of human vicissitudes, the "taking of a grief." In *Macbeth* and *Hamlet*, unresolved personal grief intensifies the political violence and social chaos. In *Macbeth*, Scotland is a "poor country, / Almost afraid to know itself" (4.3.164–65), that "sinks beneath the yoke: / it weeps, it bleeds" (39–40). Throughout the historical period highlighted in this volume of essays, England, like Macduff's Scotland, was increasingly a state divided within itself, troubled by religious persecution, political tyranny and civil injustice. The tragic reality here, as in *Hamlet*, is that although expression is a "med'cine" for grief's deleterious effects, its discharge is also dangerous. Anne Laurence tells us that in seventeenth century England grief was "regarded as a potentially fatal affliction ... It was widely believed that grief could send people mad."[8] In her madness and subsequent suicide, Ophelia — devastated by the loss of both Hamlet's affection and by the murder of her father — is evidently one example of this phenomenon.

Among the first essays in this volume are Fred Tromly's on Shakespeare and Michael McClintock on Heywood. These studies demonstrate, as we have already suggested, that theatrical representations of grief were ways through which dramatists might "give sorrow words" both to stimulate and instruct their audiences. Before examining the social contexts within which seventeenth century writers addressed their grief, we must consider how such a powerful emotion (first uttered orally in sighs, sobs, tears and related verbal articulation) is effectively converted into a written medium. Frances Batycki's use of the term *aporia* ("difficulty, being at a loss, hesitation") as the rhetorical equivalent to grief, so helpful in discussing Rachel Speght's writing, also bridges the distance between the experience of grief and its scripted formulation.[9] During the passage from speaking to writing grief, the writer may be seen as parenthesized within an aporetic space in which she or he is compelled by reason to comprehend the loss. Since grief disrupts all routine and preconception, provoking unanswerable questions, the griever compulsively interrogates and reviews the experience, asking why the bereavement must be sustained and how its consequences are to be endured. And so, the often prolonged period of grief work begins.

Scripting grief in a formalized mode can alleviate the emotionally congested state sorrow fosters. There is evidence that early modern grievers recognized the cathartic effect of grief expression, that it was, as Malcolm has said, a "cure." The ancient principle of homeopathy, like with like, known to Aristotle and reformulated by early modern physicians in treating disease, provided a rationale for grief expression in general and grief writing in particular. The distinction between what the "heart would speake" and what "the tongue doth still discover"[10] involves the individual's heightened awareness of a dimension of experience beyond human capacities of articulation.[11] Nevertheless, through language, what Daniel Fischlin terms the "ritual of eloquence," the grief writer may actually transcend the limits of his or her own incapacities. In his *Arte of English Poesie*, George Puttenham identifies a dynamic, paradoxical relation between the grief sustained and a form of satisfaction, or "ioy," experienced in the process of expression. The resolution, which writers often articulate using

Christian topoi of consolatory joy, appears to be potentially present in the act of grieving itself: "Lamenting is altogether contrary to reioising, every man saith so, and yet it is a peece of ioy to be able to lament with ease, and freely to poure forth a mans inward sorrowes and the greefs wherewith his minde is surcharged."[12]

In the most general sense, bereavement signifies being "deprived" (*New Shorter Oxford Dictionary*), while grief is the reaction to the loss of what is valued.[13] Occasions for sorrow were to be found everywhere in early modern England. Puttenham is helpful in cataloging such circumstances:

> Nowe are the causes of mans sorrowes many:
> the death of his parents, frends, allies, and
> children . . . the ouerthrowes and discomforts
> in battell, the subuersions of townes and cities,
> the desolations of countreis, the losse of goods
> and worldly promotions, honour and good
> renowne: finally the trauails and torments of
> loue forlorne or ill bestowed, either by disgrace,
> deniall, delay, and twenty other wayes, that well
> experienced louers could recite. . . .   (1.47)

In spite of the obvious hardships of early modern culture, some modern historical commentators have been skeptical about how deeply people in the early modern period experienced sorrow. For example, Lawrence Stone has suggested that, among other factors, "high mortality rates" and Christian admonishments against excessive grieving prevented early modern folk from experiencing the intensity of grief we might expect.[14] This perspective on grief in the period has been challenged over the past two decades. One dissenting voice was Anne Laurence, who registered the following corrective opinion:

> Although many seventeenth century expressions of grief seem rather abrupt and centred upon religious concerns, they are not indicative of any less affection, rather they are indicative

of a more conscious process of withdrawal by the living person from the dying or the dead. It is this withdrawal which promoted the resignation which was essential to cultivate in an age when medical intervention was likely to precipitate rather than prevent fatalities.[15]

More recently, David Cressy has reaffirmed this view: "the bulk of evidence indicates that love, pain, and grief were deeply rooted and widely experienced in early modern England" (*BMD*, 393).

G. W. Pigman has argued that the appeal to emotional rigor, endorsed in the sixteenth century by stoically inclined writers such as Erasmus and Wilson (noted earlier), was considerably relaxed as the century turned. He points out that the early seventeenth century allowed "moderation in mourning," though rigorism still persisted in certain instances (*Elegy*, 12). Sermons, religious tracts and formularies all show a shift in thinking about grief and provide support for Pigman's thesis. Furthermore, as Raymond Anselment has shown in relation to parental bereavement in this period, diaries, memoirs and letters all offer "moving testimony to a range and complexity of grieving that defies a simple explanation."[16] This greater freedom to express grief in writing in early seventeenth century culture seems to have been encouraged by several concurrent developments. The Protestant Reformation abandoned the doctrine of purgatory, so that the faithful could no longer pray for the welfare of their loved ones. The rise of literacy and individualism encouraged self-expression, and the introspective inclinations of the Reformation and Counter-Reformation as well as the cult of melancholy heightened self-consciousness about personal experience. A new emphasis on naturalism and on psychology led to such affective manifestations as the use of inscriptions on grave markers which recorded details of the deceased and the bereaved feelings of family. The essays in this volume explore the kinds of grief expression that appeared in poetry and prose, on the stage and from the pulpit and analyze the issues of meaning and the problems of sincerity connected with the "speaking of grief."

II

In the early decades of the seventeenth century, another new emphasis gained popular currency: namely, that God himself had grieved. Burton reminds his readership that Christ was "*Vir dolorum* [a man of sorrows]" (1.2.4, 258) who had grieved openly on three occasions: at the death of a friend (John 11:35), at the prospect of Jerusalem's future (Luke 19:41), and on the brink of his own death (Hebrews 5:7). These three occasions were addressed by preachers and devotional writers of the early seventeenth century and served to legitimize the occasional grieving of Christians themselves.[17] In fact, we see in these and other grief writings how the experience of bereavement of any kind could become an opportunity for "self-fashioning" after the Christian model, whereby suffering and loss precipitate an agon in body, mind and soul, culminating often in a renewed faith.[18] Articulating complicated feelings of personal loss could temper the heartache of sorrow and ease the bereaved through a gradual procedure of healing and acceptance of loss. The scripting of grief was recognized as a legitimate therapeutic process. Puttenham actually identifies the poet as a "Phisitian" who makes "the very greef it selfe (in part) cure of the disease" (1.47). If grief were not properly dealt with, its effects could either drive one mad or cause death. In "the London Bill of Mortality for 1665," David Cressy indicates, "forty-six deaths were attributed to that cause" (*BMD*, 393).

Central to the work of grief expression were, of course, tears. As the literal and bodily expression of grief, tears were believed to alleviate the excessive pressure of the "black blood" of melancholy that congested the heart upon the "taking of a grief." In "Sorrow as a Cause of Melancholy," Burton provides the humoral explanation of intense grief. Citing Melancthon, he explains that sorrow is marked by the following physiological manifestations:

> the gathering of much melancholy blood about the heart, which collection extinguisheth the good spirits, or at least dulleth them, sorrow strikes the heart, makes it tremble and pine away, with a great paine: And the black blood drawn from the Spleene, & diffused under the ribbes, on the left side, makes those perilous hypochondriacall convulsions, which happen to them that are troubled with sorrow. (1.2.4, 258)

Like other early modern writers on the physiology of weeping, Timothy Bright identified the positive effect of tears as temporarily relieving sorrow. "Sighing," he wrote, "hath no other cause of moving then to coole and refresh the heart, with fresh breath, and pure ayre .... it easeth the heart to weep and sob.... These vapours cause that redness in the Cheekes, and about the Eares, of those that weepe, heateth the Face, and causeth the Head to ake, whereof the Heart being eased, receiveth a farther enlargement then at the beginning of the griefe, and so," concludes Bright, "enjoyeth that final comfort which weeping affordeth."[19] However medical discourses attempted to explain the phenomenon of weeping, tears remained for the Renaissance, as they do for us today, ineffable. In *Telling Tears in the English Renaissance*, Marjory Lange observes that, "[i]n their essence, tears, like all expressions of feeling, are ultimately mysterious" (2). Lange's Renaissance perspective on the mystery associated with tears aligns strikingly with Jacques Derrida's observation that tears are as "enigmatic" as the "mysterium tremendum" itself, of which "God is the cause."[20]

Derrida's existential linkage between death, grieving and faith in *The Gift of Death* delineates a continuum of like experience that was intimately part of seventeenth century culture. Ralph Houlbrooke has written of grieving in this dominantly religious age: "[O]nly if God's grace acted on the soul distressed by bereavement was a loss transformed into a blessing.... [C]hastened, cast down, and then lifted up by God's hand, some felt ultimately strengthened by the losses they had endured" (*DRF*, 244). Similarly, Bettie Anne Doebler notes that death in the period must be understood "within a process that cultivates and articulates feelings so as to move through fear, anger, grief, and hope to a sense of ultimate harmony, what the seventeenth century person would have seen as faith" (221). The spiritual progress described by both Houlbrooke and Doebler was pursued during the ritual of mourning, which usually lasted for one year but could vary considerably according to circumstances.

As a process within and through which grief is expressed, "[m]ourning is ... set in motion by the death, or sometimes by the anticipation of the death, of a person to whom the bereaved is attached" (*Elegy*, 6). The anticipatory dimension of mourning, acknowledged by the modern psychological thinking about grief, was a commonplace experience in the seventeenth century. In an age without centralized medical care, death normally occurred in the home, under the administrative vigil of family members. Serious illness, injury and the often protracted process of dying ensured that all people would from time to time literally *live with* the reality of death and its associated grief. The care of the critically ill and dying necessitated numerous preparatory arrangements that signaled the approaching death. In addition to the fact that "the process of mourning often [did] begin during the fatal illness," Anne Laurence reminds us that "[o]ne of the most important features of life in the seventeenth century was the way in which people prepared themselves for death, both their own and the death of those nearest to them" (*DRB*, 66).

Despite the increased sanction for "moderate grieving" in the earlier half of the century, rationalized by the belief that God did not turn a deaf ear to human lamentation, preachers persisted in the rubric that all were finally powerless before God. The process of grief expression seems clearly to have facilitated the bereaved's submission to this ultimate reality (*DRF*, 224). Social historians such as David Cressy and Ralph Houlbrooke present detailed discussions of the grief-inspiring conditions of life in seventeenth century England, including epidemic diseases, from residual outbreaks of the plague to the recurrence of typhus, small pox, influenza, dysentery and other potentially fatal infections that ranged widely throughout the country (*DRF*, 6–7, 11–14, 16–17). Literary accounts of the plague, according to Anselment, "illuminate not only the extreme plight of the affected but the inadequacy of all attempts to heal their physical, emotional, and spiritual suffering."[21] Recent statistical studies demonstrate the severity of the plague's impact. It has been estimated that between 1570 and 1670 some 660,000 people died of the plague in England, Scotland and Ireland. In Scotland from 1645 to 1649, 30,000 died of the bubonic plague, and in Dublin alone, 1,300 people were dying weekly in 1649–50.[22] Acute outbreaks of the plague occurred in London in 1603, killing 17.8 percent of the population; in 1625 (12.8 percent); in 1636, felling one third of the population of a town like Norwich; and in 1665–66, where London lost 12.2 percent of its population and Colchester one third of its population (*DRF*, 11; Cressy, *BMD*, 565 n. 6). Between 1540 and 1750 there were 11 years when mortality rose at least 30 percent. Four of these occurred within the general period this collection considers: 1625/6, 1638/9, 1657/8, and 1665/6 (*DRF*, 6–7).

Another occasion of loss exacerbated by the epidemic proportions of sickness was infant and child mortality, in which a number of children in a family might die within a short time. The impact of such loss is almost beyond our modern comprehension. Anne Laurence has told us that stillborn and newborn deaths would have been duly mourned and given proper funerals. The circumstances surrounding a newborn's death might even be investigated if a midwife had not been present and infanticide were suspected (*DRB*, 66). Basing his estimate on the registries of 13 parishes, Ralph Houlbrooke calculates that between one in six and one in five of all babies born died before reaching the age of one year. Life expectancy increased somewhat after the first year (*DRF*, 7). As a result of his research into diaries, memoirs, family letters and verse documenting such experiences, Raymond Anselment has affirmed that "the preoccupation with deaths of children reflects a new literary, if not, social concern."[23]

As is still the case today, the most emotionally and financially devastating of bereavements was the death of a spouse. In *Mystical Bedlam*, Michael MacDonald has noted that "[a]lmost one third of the episodes of illness, despaire and madness among Richard Napier's patients were triggered by the death of a spouse" (103). The death of a husband and father "was an economic catastrophe in most households. The death of a wife and mother was a catastrophe of a different kind, evidenced by the high rate of re-marriage" (Laurence, *DRF*, 64). There is no evidence that the comparatively higher incidence of spousal mortality in early modern England exerted any less painful effects upon the bereaved. As we might expect, human love and companionship, and the cooperative venture which marriage entails, were highly valued in seventeenth century England.

Another circumstance of death was, of course, war. For example, Houlbrooke estimates that of 50,000 English troops drafted for service abroad during the 1620s, 37,000 (74 percent) may have died (*DRF*, 24). As emotionally devastating as they were physically destructive, the civil wars produced prolonged grief among soldiers and civilians alike. Recent calculations indicate that combat claimed nearly 85,000 individuals, "of whom 34,130 were parliamentarians and 50,700 were royalists." The "bloodiest man-made event in the history of the three kingdoms" also caused an estimated 192,000 civilian deaths. This figure represents 2.5 percent of the population and may be compared with the civilian casualties of the First

World War (.36 percent of the population, most of whom died in the flu epidemic of 1918–19) and of the Second World War (.11 percent of the population, largely as a result of bombing).[24]

In response to the calamities of war, epidemic, and the persecution that religious conflict brought, Protestant divines advocated the practice of "godly sorrow," defined by Daniel Featley as "A special Law," "a duty required in the Gospel."[25] As early as 1623 William Whately admonished his parishioners concerning the political struggles already beginning. His message proclaimed the prevenient force of godly grief in averting the forces of dissension: "If enoe doe take up the task of mourning, wee may escape them in our dayes; but if we doe not preconceive them by the power of faith in Gods threats, we shall surely feele them in the execution."[26] Later, in the midst of the civil war, John Featley mourned the destructive events of the times and advocated a communal lament: "Oh, who can forbeare a *shower* of teares, that is but the least sensible of the *stormes* of our calamities? Who can choose but have *great thoughts of heart, for these divisions of Reuben*?"[27] Seventeenth century theologians repeatedly instructed the laity that the regular exercise of godly sorrow would have an efficacious effect on contemporary political affairs. There can be no doubt that the currency of such exhortations influenced many of the writers discussed in this volume.

Given the sorrowful conditions of English cultural life, it is not surprising that elegy became the dominant literary form for expressing grief. Pigman has argued that elegy enacts "an abbreviated process of mourning from praise and lament to consolation and recovery"; its poetic features are thus "psychologically coherent expressions of different parts of the process of mourning."[28] The growing acceptance of grief expression was accompanied by "an emerging ideal of sincere expression of heartfelt sorrow" as an appropriate form of mourning (*Elegy*, 92).[29] David Cressy attributes the increased popularity of elegy during the period to changes in liturgical practice under Calvinist and Arminian theologians who came to dominate the Church of England in the seventeenth century. From this perspective, it was believed that "[g]ood works during the life had limited efficacy and prayers after death had no effect at all on one's destiny, and could easily be regarded as superstitious." The influence of such beliefs encouraged a kind of severance of the dead from the living. Hence, it was assumed, there was "no sound basis for intercessory prayers for the dead." With the reduction in ritualized consolation and tribute, Cressy argues, the elegy thrived as an alternative species of grief expression (*BMD*, 387).[30]

The wide deployment of the elegy by writers of both sexes introduces one of the most controversial features of grief expression, what has come to be known as the gendering of grief. How does grief writing differ when composed by men and women? Juliana Schiesari, among others, has made us aware of the gender-specific attributes which, in early modern culture, were assigned to distinguish the nature and manner of grief as expressed by women and men. As Schiesari explains in *The Gendering of Melancholy*, "oftentimes, a woman's lament, grievance, or suffering is seen as the 'everyday' plight of the common (wo)man, a quotidian event whose collective force does not seem to bear the same weight of 'seriousness' as a man's grief. The value of 'his' grief would lie in an uncommon or unparalleled expression, which is to say, that his 'loss' is transcoded once again as a privileged suffering" (13).[31] Schiesari here distinguishes between male grief valued by early modern culture as a creative state, melancholy, and female grief as merely mourning, the ritual work of women. This evaluative difference in the gendering of grief expression explains, for example, the dismissive attitude to grief displayed by Macduff ("O I could play the woman with mine eyes" [*Macbeth* 4.3.230] and by Hamlet ("it is such a kind of gain-giving, as would perhaps trouble a woman" [*Hamlet* 5.2.215–16] in the plays discussed earlier.

In his *Anatomy*, Burton exemplifies this conception that women are rarely afflicted by melancholy and are particularly inarticulate in their grief expression: "Many of them cannot tell how to expresse themselves in wordes, or how it holds them, what ailes them, you cannot understand them, or well tell what to make of their sayings; so farre gone sometimes, so stupefied and distracted, they think themselves bewitched, they are in despaire" (1.3.4, 415). Moreover, under the duress of such cultural stereotypes it is little wonder that writers such as Carey, Hastings, Thornton, Thimelby and Collins admit being stigmatized not only by their bereavement and possible divine censure of their grief but also by their sense of womanly incompetence in formulating the experience of loss. In her study of tears in the Renaissance, Marjory Lange has countered Burton's argument about women's inability to articulate their grief. She observes the distinct absence of tears in women's grief writing and concludes that "[w]omen write to reform their reflections not to re-iterate stereotypes." The suggestion here is that women deliberately withhold tears from their discourse so as to present a more coherent account of their bereavements. Conversely, male writers, according to Lange, consciously include tears, "wield[ing] them in political-rhetorical freedom, without being stained by their moisture" (3).[32]

As these patterns of difference suggest, issues of gender are an important concern in this volume. Analyses of women's elegies strongly support Lange's argument that, in writing their grief, women wished to challenge the stereotypical view of their emotionally unbalanced nature in times of distress. Donna J. Long and Scott Howard both consider how self-consciously female elegists proceed in the articulation of their sorrow. Though invented and developed by male practitioners, elegy is innovatively used by female writers. Mary Carey, Lucy Hastings, Alice Thornton and Gertrude Thimelby's mourning of specifically infant loss and Collins's transformation of her own personal grief into political prophecy all make significant adaptations of elegiac convention.³³

Several essays in this collection indicate that many early modern male writers were also concerned with women's grief expression. According to Paul Parrish, Richard Crashaw, though highly competent in his occasional elegies, makes his more memorable contribution to grief writing when composing from the perspective of Mary, Mother of Jesus, or Mary Magdalene. It is also significant that Henry Hammond's elegies on the death of his brother were intended specifically for the personal readership of his sister-in-law, to ease her grief and provide consolation. Similarly, Fred Tromly and Michael McClintock consider, among other concerns, the exemplary nature of woman's grief in the role of Cordelia in *King Lear* and of Anne Frankford and Susan Mountford in Thomas Heywood's *A Woman Killed with Kindness*. These women stand as models of grief, potentially redemptive for male characters in the plays and edifying to their audiences. The latest writers in the period, Marvell and Milton, also chose female grievers as central foci for their poems. The closing essays illustrate how these writers recognized the vital importance of grief work and the complexities of women's grief experiences. The destructive potential of unresolved grief is well demonstrated in McCaffrey's Freudian analysis of Marvell's elegy, while in *Paradise Lost* Eve's tears, first wept in book 5 but then painfully "deferred" until book 9, are at last discharged with hysterical, nearly suicidal, consequences.

The problematic nature of writing grief, its solemnity, indeed the sacredness of its subject, makes it characteristically self-reflexive, often explicitly addressing concerns with its own legitimacy. Thus, sincerity becomes a central issue. How and why is an authentically sincere lament composed? John Shawcross's analysis of Hammond's elegies attempts to answer such crucial questions. Fred Tromly also deals with the authenticity of consolation as presented in several of

Shakespeare's plays, *King Lear* in particular. Robert Evans's examination of elegies by Donne and Jonson illustrates how these poets struggled painfully against the debilitating effects of their own aging so as to articulate the broad range of emotions evoked by death, in the end, concludes Evans, not only "to assuage grief but also to cheat death themselves."

As the cases of Donne and Jonson show, the genuineness of a writer's grief expression often appears to be rooted in his or her mortal condition and private circumstances at the time of composition. After the death of a loved one, as we might well expect, a poet may be moved to write about that loss. Donna J. Long's essay on maternal elegies, as well as most of the other essays concerned with elegy (Shawcross on Hammond, Parrish on Crashaw, Howard on Collins), all consider occasional bereavements in the lives of their poets. Grief writers lament in various forms the *lacrimae rerum* with which all human experience is fraught. P. G. Stanwood discloses the personal circumstances and sincere grief that exist within the prescribed boundaries of the eloquent funeral sermons of Donne and Taylor. Marjory Lange reminds us that Robert Burton undertook his compendious *Anatomy of Melancholy* for therapeutic reasons, diagnosing himself as a melancholic. Louis Martz and Scott Howard note that George Herbert and An Collins were both suffering from chronic illness during the writing of their poems. Personal grief seems to have acutely sensitized Herbert and Collins to "godly grief," as both struggled spiritually to transcend their condition. Herbert's use of the priestly office enabled him to fashion his own grief after Christ's own, whereas Collins adopted a prophetical persona and transformed personal grief into a political lament for England in the 1650s.

It is not an exaggeration to suggest, finally, that a poet like Milton, "blind among enemies" after the Restoration, who had literally "to speak his grief" into the sometimes confounded ears of transcribers, endured an embedded sorrow that heroically shaped his often solemn ruminations on "the ways of God." In his later years Milton suffered numerous bereavements. Not only did he witness the collapse of his ideal society but he was also bereaved of wives, children and health, including his sight. A number of scholarly accounts of the circumstances surrounding Milton's composition of *Paradise Lost* have already described the vindicating achievement of this text. Regarding Milton's Restoration stance, Steven Zwicker has argued that the "writing of *Paradise Lost* was not only an appropriation of spiritual truths...but...an appropriation of all the instruments of literary culture." He goes on to address further the grievous source of Milton's achievement: "Milton was scorned and denounced; he suffered reversal and humiliation; and although elsewhere he celebrates passivity, the recoil, the thrust of *Paradise Lost* was not passivity. Out of humiliation and political displacement, out of the need to assert the authority of *his own voice* [our emphasis] came the epic scope of this poem, an act of greater erudition, complexity, and freedom than his contemporaries had ever witnessed."[34] Zwicker's summary eloquently suggests the vocal emphasis of Milton's epic as he reverts to the oral origins of the genre. The unique "voice" Zwicker describes speaks with the righteous indignation of one deeply convinced of his own legitimate position despite compromised political and social circumstances. Such a reading returns us to the premise of "speaking grief." In Milton we have, figuratively at least, an actor on the stage of seventeenth century history from whose own harrowing drama emerges the period's ultimate grief text.

1 • Grief, Authority and the Resistance to Consolation in Shakespeare

Fred B. Tromly

(For Michael Treadwell, 1942–1999)

The final act of *Much Ado about Nothing* opens with what appears to be a throwaway exchange: Antonio warns his brother Leonato about the danger of excessive grief, and Leonato responds with one of the longest speeches in the play, a harangue against those who would give counsel to grief. These 40 lines are often cut in production, and understandably so, for the difference of opinion between the brothers does not lead anywhere, and Leonato's speech expresses an animus far exceeding its innocuous provocation. But, questionable as it may be at this moment in this play, this exchange about consolation points to an important issue in Shakespeare's work. Throughout his plays, the sense of "how hard true sorrow hits" and the corresponding need for solace are essential facts of the human condition. (The word "comfort," Shakespeare's favorite term for the alleviation of grief, is often on characters' lips, appearing some 267 times.)[1] But the exchange between Leonato and Antonio reveals more than Shakespeare's sensitivity to the importance of consolation. It also points to his characteristic inflection of the theme: the surprisingly frequent recurrence of scenes in which a character who is grieving resists the counsel that another has proffered. It is with a twist, then, that Shakespeare's plays support the Renaissance philosopher Cardano's claim that "So necessarye is this gifte of consolation, as there lyveth no man, but that hathe cause to embrace it." The dramatist's characters are more likely to reject than to embrace this necessary gift.[2]

The resistance to solace in Shakespeare can be contextualized in broad historical terms as a chapter in the much larger story of how mourning for the dead was gradually legitimated in late Elizabethan England after having been proscribed by many as un-Christian.[3] But, as both the figure of Job and our own experience remind us, the phenomenon of resisting consolation transcends historical boundaries. The rhetoricians who devised consolatory strategies had long realized that, as Thomas Wilson notes in *The Art of Rhetoric*, "all extreme heaviness and vehement sorrows cannot abide comfort, but rather seek a mourner that would take part with them." It is with this resistance to consolation in mind that Thomas More begins his *Dialogue of Comfort against Tribulation* by analyzing the various types of disconsolate people who "will seek for no comfort." That even the most artful consolation may fail is tacitly acknowledged in Angel Day's collection of model consolatory epistles, which contains "A Letter Responsorie to be conferred to an Epistle Consolatorie." In this epistle a woman thanks her brother for having sent her a letter of consolation, but also pointedly observes that the "vehemencie of a fewe speeches" cannot be sufficient to comfort her for the loss of her beloved husband.[4] As one might expect, the motif of consolation rejected also found its way onto the pre-Shakespearean stage, most notably when Sackville and Norton's King Gorboduc angrily rejects a counselor's attempt to console him for the loss of his murdered son.[5] While the motif of consolation resisted is hardly Shakespeare's invention, it recurs in his work with a frequency that suggests significance, and indeed it proves to be central to the tensions between authoritative precept and individual percept that animate his art.

To resist the canons of consolation is to open a space for both the dignity and the folly of unyielding, untutored sorrow. This two-sidedness is apparent in Leonato's long disquisition in *Much Ado about Nothing*, which mounts an articulate critique of consolatory counsel but also, between the lines, reveals a narcissism in need of counsel. Leonato's critique of consolation argues that the ability to "speak comfort" is in fact predicated on the absence of true fellow-feeling. Thus, he says that he would accept comfort if "such a one whose wrongs do suit with mine" would offer it to him:

> But there is no such man, for, brother, men
> Can counsel and speak comfort to that grief
> Which they themselves not feel, but tasting it,
> Their counsel turns to passion, which before
> Would give preceptial med'cine to rage,
> Fetter strong madness in a silken thread,
> Charm ache with air, and agony with words.
> No, no, 'tis all men's office to speak patience
> To those that wring under the load of sorrow,
> But no man's virtue nor sufficiency
> To be so moral when he shall endure
> The like himself. Therefore, give me no counsel,
> My thoughts cry louder than advertisement.
>
> (5.1.20–32)

In this view, the very fact that a person can give verbal comfort to sorrow is prima facie evidence that he is himself not feeling that sorrow. And the consolatory "counsel" that he gives is invalidated by the fact that, if the comforter himself were to "wring under the load of sorrow," he would lack the patience that he so airily enjoins. In the speech's most vivid metaphor, to give verbal comfort is merely to attempt to "patch grief with proverbs" (5.1.17).

As is usually the case with eloquent set-speeches in Shakespeare, Leonato's spirited attack on consolation loses much of its persuasiveness when it is read in its dramatic context. What suffers most is his claim to being a paragon of paternal grief. It is significant that, after an early reference, Leonato's discourse fails to mention his daughter, the slandered Hero, who is the ostensible subject of his supposedly exemplary grief. When, like Kyd's Hieronimo, he wishes that "no comforter delight mine ear / But such a one whose wrongs do suit with mine," he laments the injuries done to himself rather than to Hero. It is Leonato he mourns for. And there is something in the speech much darker than mere self-regarding, for an audience can hardly forget that only two scenes earlier Leonato had quickly and viciously sided with those who had attacked Hero's honor. In part, his rejection of comfort represents an irate resistance to self-knowledge, a problem diagnosed by the tradition he dismisses.[6] While in other Shakespearean rejections of consolation it may be more difficult to distinguish neatly between the vitally subjective and the merely solipsistic, both of these elements are usually present.

Leonato's fulmination is only nominally aimed at the brother to whom he replies. Its real target, as his repeated attacks on "preceptial med'cine" and the posturing of philosophers indicate, is the venerable literature of consolation. It would be difficult to exaggerate the moral and literary authority of the consolatory tradition that Leonato so vigorously dismisses. Not only were formal works of comfort published in a steady stream (more than 300 titles between 1478 and 1600), but arguments deriving from them furnished the stuff of innumerable sermons, letters, elegies and moral treatises.[7] Part of the authority of this discourse stems from the enormous prestige of such classical authors as Cicero, Seneca and Plutarch, all of whom wrote letters and essays that were taught as models of consolation. In Rome, moral philosophy and consolation became virtually synonymous, and Cicero declared that "the richest fruit of the whole field of philosophy is that which tends to alleviate distresses, terrors, lusts." Centuries later, when Boethius languished in his prison cell, it was Lady Philosophy herself who came to comfort him. The consolatory practice was not only limited to virtuous pagans, as Augustine and other church fathers created an insistently Christian countertradition.[8] The advent of Renaissance humanism marked a new stage of development, as Petrarch and lesser figures elegantly renewed the classical tradition and assimilated it to Christian values. It would have been virtually impossible for an advanced Elizabethan grammar school student to have escaped exposure to this tradition, and there is considerable evidence (beyond Leonato's diatribe) to indicate that Shakespeare knew it well.[9]

Despite its moral authority, or perhaps because of it, the consolatory tradition usually meets with strong opposition in Shakespeare's plays. His characters often have good reason, and much better reason than Leonato adduces, for suspecting the motives of those who offer them "preceptial med'cine." Leonato's skepticism fails to take into account a range of potential abuses of consolation, including deliberate falsehood on the part of the consoler. Throughout Shakespeare's canon, it is remarkable how frequently consolatory discourse involves the deception of the person being comforted. In many scenes of counsel, the traditional *consolatio* is delivered by a person who is literally or figuratively disguised and who stands to benefit from the sufferer's acceptance of his sage and supposedly disinterested advice. An early, simple example of devious comfort occurs in *The Two Gentlemen of Verona*, where Proteus delivers a formal consolation urging Valentine to bear his banishment from Verona and from Silvia with philosophical grace (3.1.243–58). What Proteus neglects to mention, of course, is that he is himself in love with Silvia and has in fact brought about his friend's banishment.

It is the central place of authority in consoling grief that leads to moral problems in Shakespeare. His plays explore a dark side of consolation's moon that the treatises can never afford to acknowledge: the dangerous control that the giver of comfort can all too easily wield over the needy person who suffers. As John T. McNeill notes at the close of his classic *History of the Cure of Souls*, the efficacy of spiritual counsel is in good part dependent on the authority of the healer who ministers to the sufferer.[10] Without being convinced of the comforter's authority, the person who grieves may lack the faith that allows the cure to do its work. Since those who suffer need to believe in those who would console them, the authority that the comforter represents always invites abuse. The traditional ideology and rhetoric of consolatory literature serve to maximize the authority of its message. Comfort is not only to be given, but to be conveyed as persuasively as possible.

At the core of the ancient tradition is a stoical hierarchy with manliness and rationality at the top and effeminate, slavish grief at the bottom, suggesting that the consoler is to the consoled as reason is to passion, or as man is to woman and child. The *locus classicus* for this attitude is the letter in which Plutarch attempts to console Apollonius for the death of his son by disparaging mourning as unbecoming a true man: "Yes, mourning is verily feminine, and weak, and ignoble, since women are more given to it than men, and barbarians more than Greeks, and inferior men more than better men." Very similarly, Thomas Wilson explains to the duchess of Suffolk (upon the death of her two sons) that the least rational people mourn most, "as women commonly rather than men, rude people rather than godly folk, the unlearned rather than the learned, foolish folk sooner than wise men, children rather than young men."[11]

Despite the topos that death is a leveler of social differences, consolatory literature usually curtsies to these very differences. The direction in which consolation customarily flows is downward; the office of consoling is usually discharged by a person higher on the social hierarchy than — or at the very least a peer of — the person being comforted. Thus, there is often an element of social suasion, if not blackmail, in consolations. Few consolatory letters in Elizabethan England could have carried more authority than the weightily traditional epistle that Elizabeth herself wrote to the Lady Norris on the death of her son Sir John Norris, a letter ending with the coercive wish that "the world may see, that what time cureth in weak minds, that discretion and moderation helpeth in you in this accident, where there is so just cause to demonstrate true patience and moderation."[12] The most notable exception to the social superiority of consoler to consoled occurs when the person proffering the consolation is a male who is not noble and the recipient of it is a gentlewoman.[13] The explanation for this apparent breach of social decorum lies in the venerable consolatory axiom that women are less rational than men and thus desperately in need of counsel, even from below.

In addition to these social manifestations, the idea of authority is central to the process and language of consolation. Despite various doctrinal differences, most consolatory treatises share a similar rhetorical strategy: to overcome the subjectivity of sorrow through persuasions that insist on the claim of universal laws and the truth of collective experience. The very language of consolation is insistently formulaic, as it works in terms of commonplaces, proverbs and *sententiae*, which are dutifully repeated from work to work, and indeed from generation to generation. At the outset of his "consolatory digression" in *The Anatomy of Melancholy*," Robert Burton wonders "what can any man say that hath not beene said" and then proceeds to compile a long and lively epitome of the tradition's "divine precepts." Always prominent among these gatherings of proverb and precept is the universally relevant truth that Burton calls "the first statute in *Magna Charta*, an everlasting act of Parliament, all must die."[14] When the abstractness of these commonplaces is ameliorated by reference to the specificity of human behavior, it is in the form of *exempla*, larger-than-life examples usually deriving from Greece and Rome. This insistently formulaic quality of consolatory writing accounts for one's continuous sense of déjà vu and also for the near impossibility of determining specific sources. This impersonality of consolatory rhetoric, as Shakespeare is well aware, easily can serve as a mask to conceal the comforter's true intentions.

An important function of the impersonal language of consolation is to depersonalize the grieving listener, to emphasize his or her generic identity rather than individuality. Indeed, it could be said that the very idea of consolation is predicated on convincing the sufferer that he is *not unique*. Echoing a passage from Plutarch, Cardano's treatise articulates the problem: "each man knoweth his owne evils, and is ignorant how great the greves of others be, which is the reason why eche man thinketh himselfe most unhappy."[15] It follows, then, that the sufferer may cease to think himself unhappy if he ceases to think himself unique. Or indeed if he ceases to think about himself at all.

All the dimensions of consolatory authority are mobilized and put to particularly insidious use in the formal *consolatio* that Claudius delivers to the grieving prince in the second scene of *Hamlet*. Actually, Claudius's speech is the second attempt to console Hamlet, the first being Gertrude's weak remonstrance that "Thou knowst 'tis common, all that lives must die, / Passing through nature to eternity" (1.2.72–73).

Following Hamlet's rejection ("'Tis common") of this weakly rhyming *sententia*, Claudius also stresses the "common theme" of the "death of fathers." Unlike Gertrude's, Claudius's speech forcibly expresses the (male) authority of the consolatory tradition:

> But to persever
> In obstinate condolement is a course
> Of impious stubbornness, 'tis unmanly grief,
> It shows a will most incorrect to heaven,
> A heart unfortified, or mind impatient,
> An understanding simple and unschool'd:
> For what we know must be, and is as common
> As any the most vulgar thing to sense,
> Why should we in our peevish opposition
> Take it to heart? Fie, 'tis a fault to heaven,
> A fault against the dead, a fault to nature,
> To reason most absurd, whose common theme
> Is death of fathers, and who still hath cried,
> From the first corse till he that died to-day,
> "This must be so."
>
> (1.2.92–106)

This speech draws on consolatory topoi so felicitously that some assiduous commentators, having discovered the "excellent authority" for these sentiments in Seneca and Plutarch, have allowed themselves to be convinced of the soundness of Claudius's advice.[16] But "excellent authority" is exactly the problem. Claudius speaks as if he is wisdom personified, dismissing intractable grief as insufficiently manly and rational. Not only is Claudius voicing a coldly stoical attitude, but he is also engaging in an "essential belittlement of the heartache of grief."[17] The burden of the speech is a hostility only thinly veiled as comfort, and it makes the corrective shame insinuated by Queen Elizabeth's letter look innocent by comparison. Fortunately for Hamlet, he can withstand this consolatory onslaught because he strongly senses what he will soon know: that Claudius's regal and paternal authority is a disguise.

A deeper probing of the masks and hidden motives of consolers occurs in *Measure for Measure*, a play in which the exercise of authority is always cause for suspicion. The figure in the play who is repeatedly associated with the gift of comfort is the duke of Vienna, or rather the friar whom the duke impersonates. As if his secular authority is not adequate to his needs, or is too difficult to enforce, the duke dons a religious disguise that allows him absolute spiritual authority and gives him access to the troubled souls of people on the verge of death. His friarlike duties involve the offices of consolation, and thus he is called by one woman a "man of comfort" (4.1.8) and thanked by another for "this comfort" (3.1.268) of advice. By the play's end, however, the identification of the duke as a comforter has been undercut by a good deal of irony. In part, this irony flows from the pervasive falsehood that characterizes the duke's comfortings. Not only are his actions as a friar merely an act, but also he consistently misinforms and manipulates the people to whom he ministers. By turns, he bluntly informs the pregnant Juliet that her husband-to-be (Claudio) will die on the morrow (2.3), exhorts Claudio to prepare for imminent death (3.1), insists to Barnardine that the time of his execution is (finally) at hand (4.3), and falsely tells Isabella that Claudio has been executed. Throughout the play he seems inordinately fond of telling people that their lives, or those of their loved ones, are sinful, meaningless and doomed. The comfort that the duke says he is conveying often seems less a spiritual medicine to counter the punishment that looms over the characters than a covert form of punishment in itself.

The most powerful and most disturbing of the duke's consolations is the "Be absolute for death" speech that he addresses to the imprisoned and condemned Claudio (3.1.5–41). This speech expresses very nearly the opposite of what a contemporary audience would have expected a clergyman to say to a condemned person. An Elizabethan guide for clergy on

"How to advise and comfort them that lye in prison, and be by the Magistrate iudged to dye" stresses the hope of salvation even for a criminal, and thus the comforter is to repeat the point that, while the "temporal judgment" of the law is inevitable, a delivery from the "eternal judgment" of God may be possible through prayer and contrition.[18]

In the duke's speech, however, there is no talk of salvation, and indeed its message is scarcely Christian. The closest antecedents to the duke's speech are in the Roman *consolatio* (echoes of Seneca and Cicero have been noted) and in *ars moriendi* treatises encouraging the contempt of earthly life.[19] As the countess of Pembroke's translation of a French treatise puts it, "The worlde is so full of evilles, that to write them all, would require an other worlde as great as it selfe."[20] But catalogs of the world's evils are less disconcerting than the duke's insistence on depersonalizing and even dehumanizing the sufferer:

> Thou art not thyself,
> For thou exists on many a thousand grains
> That issue out of dust. Happy thou art not,
> For what thou hast not, still thou striv'st to get,
> And what thou hast, forget'st. Thou art not certain,
> For thy complexion shifts to strange effects,
> After the moon.
>
> (3.1.19–25)

These lines, which appear to be indebted to Lucretius's atomistic philosophy, serve to atomize Claudio, as they disperse his being among a "thousand grains / That issue out of dust."[21] Even before death his life lacks all control, as it is characterized in terms of meaningless motion: striving for that which is immediately forgotten and following the changes of the moon. Insofar as this speech conveys comfort to Claudio in the face of death, it is a chilling comfort predicated on his imagined annihilation. We will not be surprised to learn that "Claudio evidently finds no consolation in the disguised

Duke's argument that, from the standpoint of atomistic philosophy, he really has no self to lose."[22]

It seems appropriate that this fraudulent friar's disquisition gains much of its power through rhetorical sleight of hand. At the outset, the duke counsels Claudio to "Reason thus with life," and he then proceeds to address life and to denigrate it: "a breath thou art," "merely, thou art death's fool," "Thou art not noble," and so on. Technically, these lines (like those quoted in the previous paragraph) are addressed to "life" rather than to Claudio. A clever grammatical slippage develops, however, as the "thou" becomes increasingly detached from "life" and attached to Claudio. By the time the duke asserts that "Friend hast thou none" and "Thou hast nor youth nor age," the force of his radical belittlement is clearly aimed at Claudio, not his nominal subject. The effect of this strategy is familiar from the treatises: to convince Claudio that his sorrows are not unique, and indeed to evacuate his sense of self. Hence, Claudio does not demur when the duke declares:

> Friend hast thou none,
> For thine own bowels, which do call thee sire,
> The mere effusion of thy proper loins,
> Do curse the gout, sapego, and the rheum
> For ending thee no sooner.
>
> (3.1.28–32)

What Claudio seems not to remember, or to dismiss as merely epiphenomenal, is that he does indeed have a "friend" in the person of Juliet, who (thanks to the "mere effusion of [his] proper loins") is great with child.[23] One of the play's iterative images is of coining, of stamping a form onto a slip of metal to make it legal tender, and it would appear that the duke has successfully imposed his design on Claudio, who weakly says, "I humbly thank you."

The speech would seem to be a triumph of the consoler's persuasive art, for at its close Claudio heroically declares that "To sue to live, I find I seek to die, / And seeking death, find life; let it come on" (3.1.41–43). But it is Isabella, not death, who immediately comes on stage. Claudio's first words to her reveal that the duke's exhortation has been less than absolutely effective: "Now, sister, what's the comfort?" (The question "what's the comfort?" could be asked of many scenes in the play, including its finale, which is comic in form but not in feeling.) Claudio's heroic resolve quickly disintegrates as he learns, despite Isabella's evasions, that life is still a possibility. Finally, the emotions which the duke had so skillfully suppressed in Claudio break out in the young man's shockingly vivid evocation of death's horrors to his sister. The effect of the duke's consolation has been not to comfort Claudio (the Elizabethans were aware that the etymological root of "comfort" is "to strengthen") but to intensify his fears. Why the duke engages in this rather abusive comforting is never really clear; he is very nearly as disguised to the audience as he is to the desperate characters whose cells he visits. Whether the duke's impulse be sadism pure and simple or some obscure need to place other people in a situation that attracts and frightens him, it is not possible to determine. What is certain, at least, is that the duke is very far from being the comforter that Leonato called for: "such a one whose wrongs do suit" with those of his listener.

King Lear, a work written soon after *Measure for Measure* and echoing it in many ways, is Shakespeare's most powerful representation of grief and also his most probing study of the methods and motives of consolation. In *King Lear* we see Shakespeare returning to *Measure for Measure* and to earlier works as well, as he intensifies the force of previous scenes and themes. One telling instance of this severe reenactment of earlier work involves *Richard II*, another play in which a deposed king discovers a world of inconsolable and hitherto unknown sorrow. More specifically, there appears to be a precedent for *King Lear* in what has been identified as a "set pattern" in *Richard II*, in which "a character is grieving, someone attempts to comfort him or her, and that attempt at consolation fails," thus creating "a sense of the awesome power and inevitability of grief."[24] *King Lear* also contains a number of sequences in which comfort is offered and fails, but to far more unsettling effect than in *Richard II*. The formal lyricism of *Richard II* always distances and softens the play's representations of grief, and Richard often laments with histrionic exaggeration, as when he declares, "I'll hate him everlastingly / That bids me be of comfort any more" (3.2.207–08). In *King Lear*, however, the extremities of suffering are brought home to the audience in harrowing fashion. To cite a single, telling parallel, the final, unconsoled expression of grief in the history play is Richard's ceremonious sorrow at parting from his wife, while the equivalent moment in the tragedy is Lear's final, wrenching grief at Cordelia's death. In a phrase from one of its central sources (Sidney's *Arcadia*), *King Lear* depicts a world where "wit but serves to have true taste of woes."[25]

If the grief in *King Lear* is extremely difficult to endure, the impulse to console that grief is uncommonly strong. As Alfred Harbage has remarked, "In every scene where there is pain, there is someone who strives to relieve that pain."[26] But this relief rarely occurs. Recognizing how hard true sorrow hits, the comforters seem to sense that verbal formulas are not adequate, that such enormous grief cannot be patched with proverbs. As a consequence, they forfeit their privilege and enter the storm of suffering in an attempt to convey a comfort that is substantial rather than merely verbal. In an attempt to console Lear, Gloucester risks and very nearly loses his life. But by the time Gloucester reaches him, Lear's wits are unsettled, and the promise of conventional comfort is not attractive to him. Ironically, Gloucester before long will find himself in a situation similar to Lear's. Soon after he is blinded, he is approached by an Old Man who offers help, but Gloucester exclaims: "Away, get thee away! Good friend, be gone, / Thy comforts can do me no good at all; / Thee they may hurt"

(4.1.15–17). Their exemplary concern notwithstanding, the consolers' attempts usually come to naught. Again and again, the play shows us the limits of good intention, the gap between the desire and the ability to comfort. In *King Lear*, even the best-intentioned attempts at consolation have a cruel edge. On more than one occasion, we are reminded of Job's outcries to his supposed consolers: "Miserable comforters are ye all" (16:2) and "Are there not mockers with me?" (17:2). It is in the company of would-be comforters that the loneliness of grief is most poignant; Gerard Manley Hopkins remembers *King Lear* when he cries out, "Comforter, where, where is your comforting?"[27]

Though many characters proffer comfort at one time or another, Edgar stands out as the figure in *King Lear* most clearly associated with the consolatory tradition. A number of Edgar's speeches contain commonplaces of stoic counsel, as William Elton observed, and these commonplaces are expressed with the kind of abstract sententiousness that provokes Leonato's attack on platitudinous comfort. With equal plausibility, it is possible to see Edgar in diametrically opposed terms. He is, on the one hand, the ideal consoler, one who has himself been brought low and who has learned to taste and share real suffering. In his own resonant description, he is "A most poor man, made tame to fortune's blows, / Who, by the art of known and feeling sorrows, / Am pregnant to good pity" (4.6.221–23). In his solicitude for suffering, he has even been identified with Christ the Consoler. On the other hand, Edgar can be seen as a near relative of the sinister duke in *Measure for Measure*, another figure who consoles in disguise (as Edgar does in the "pregnant to good pity" lines quoted above) and for his own ends. In terms of the Shakespeare canon's concern with giving comfort, Edgar is both the resolution of the problem and the problem itself.[28]

Both these sides of Edgar, or aspects of the consolation he represents, are present in his ambivalent comforting of his father, the blinded Gloucester. In one of the most elaborate consolatory strategies in Shakespeare, a scene that has elicited much conflicting commentary, Edgar elects to continue to hide his identity from his father and through a trick to convince him that there is a divine providence in which his life matters. On the heights of an imaginary Dover Cliff, Edgar stages a kind of miracle play to convince Gloucester that his attempt at suicide has been foiled by divine intervention.[29] Following this attempt to save his father from the spiritual death of despair, Edgar intervenes to rescue him from certain physical death at the hands of the despicable, bounty-seeking Oswald.

But there is a darker side to Edgar's consolation, one that connects him with Vienna's fantastical duke of dark corners.[30] Like the duke, Edgar attempts to hold himself aloof from the people he would comfort, and his detachment is deepened by the disguise he wears and the sententious language he speaks. Edgar's attempt to cure Gloucester of his despair by tricking him into thinking he has escaped certain death can be seen as a reenactment of the duke's brutal preparation of Claudio to be "absolute for death." In these two comforters, we sense the presence of unacknowledged (and therefore dangerous) impulses that underlie the motives they rehearse to themselves. Thus, the duke explains to himself that he keeps Isabella, like Claudio, "ignorant of her good, / To make her heavenly comforts of despair / When it is least expected" (4.4.109–11). And, in a similarly embarrassed aside, Edgar justifies his apparently mocking treatment of Gloucester by saying, "Why I do trifle thus with his despair / Is done to cure it" (4.6.33–34). But Edgar's avowal to himself that he is playing with his father's despair rather than with his father seems narrowly rational, a nominal distinction without a human difference. The presence of the telltale word "trifle," which contains a self-accusation, betrays his awareness that he is indeed mocking Gloucester.

We recall that, when he first sees his blinded father, Edgar hears him call out his name:

> O dear son Edgar,
> The food of thy abused father's wrath!
> Might I but live to see thee in my touch,
> I'ld say I had eyes again.
>
> (4.1.21–24)

But Edgar does not reveal his identity, and instead laments his own case: "Who is't can say, 'I am at the worst'? / I am worse than e'er I was" (4.1.25–26). There is, then, reason to wonder whether, underneath Edgar's desire to comfort his father, there is not a contrary impulse. If we remember that Gloucester had driven Edgar into the wilderness and placed a bounty on his head, we may not be surprised when, upon first seeing his father on the heath, Edgar exclaims, "This is the foul fiend Flibbertigibbet; he . . . makes the hare-lip; mildews the white wheat, and hurts the poor creature of earth" (3.4.115–19).[31]

Despite the interest of Edgar's ambivalent ministrations to Gloucester, it is King Lear himself, the person with the largest passions and greatest capacity for love and suffering, who is the focus of the play's concern with consolation. As Lear is much more complex than Gloucester, so too are the problems involved in comforting him more challenging. He is certainly a less willing pupil than the superstitious Gloucester, and his resistance to comfort has a ferocity that is new to Shakespeare's handling of the motif. For Lear the traditional politics and gendering of consolation are complicated by the fact that his most important emotional relationships are with his daughters; in his upside-down world, all the orthodoxies of consolation are inverted. His three daughters have a power to hurt him and to comfort him in ways that are not acknowledged by the male-oriented tradition. At the outset Lear insists on the maintenance of manly self-control, assuming that (in Cardano's traditional formulation) "Sorow is a womanish thing, and not fit for men." The ideal male attitude toward grief, in this view, is tersely stated in one of Gabriel Harvey's marginalia: "He bearith his misery best, that hydeth it most." In Lear we see the collapse of this idea of masculine control, which is accompanied by his humiliating acknowledgment of his need for his daughters and their comfort.[32]

Interestingly, the work of consolation that most resonates with *King Lear* is one of the rare treatises in which moral authority is vested in a female figure, the Lady Philosophy of Boethius's *The Consolation of Philosophy*.[33] As several commentators have noted, Lear shares deep similarities with the Boethius depicted in *The Consolation of Philosophy*: both are old men who have suddenly fallen from high degree and are troubled by the unacceptable and all too apparent injustice of the universe.[34] The same commentators, however, appear not to have noticed the strong Boethian echo in the scene (2.4) that propels Lear onto the heath and into madness. In this scene Goneril and Regan assault their father's dignity in a logical extension of traditional consolatory procedure: the detached consoler tells the sufferer that he is not unique. The daughters "disquantity" Lear of his servingmen, as they speedily reduce his train from a hundred to a single, superfluous man. They justify this divestiture with a thin veneer of concern for his welfare that recalls how, in the best stoic fashion, Lady Philosophy teaches Boethius about needs: "if you simply wish to satisfy the demands of nature, there is no reason why you should struggle for the superfluities of Fortune. For nature's needs are few and small. . . . Possibly you think that a large number of servants can make you happy. But if they are unreliable or dishonest, they are a pernicious influence in the house and extremely troublesome to their master."[35] In a savage parody of Lady Philosophy, Goneril and Regan profess to reduce Lear's cares by reducing his needs: *Natura contenta paucis*. Once again in Shakespeare, the platitudes of consolation serve to mask vicious self-interest.

Lear's response to this chilling comfort is perhaps the most impassioned rejection of consolation in all of Shakespeare. In lines that reflect on Lady Philosophy's values as well as those of Goneril and Regan, Lear breaks the stoics' yardstick for measuring permissible grief:

> O reason not the need! our basest beggars
> Are in the poorest thing superfluous.
> Allow not nature more than nature needs,
> Man's life is cheap as beast's.
>
> (2.4.264–67)

These resonant lines reject the imposition of consolatory formulas on suffering; to calculate legitimate needs is to diminish man, and perhaps to begin the process of denying humanity altogether. Lear makes a claim for the dignity of suffering, for (as Michael Ignatieff notes) he is essentially arguing that "To reason any man's needs . . . is to presume that he lacks the capacity to know his own mind."[36] Ultimately, it is the play's emphasis on the necessities entailed by our humanity that makes consolation so problematic an endeavor.

If Goneril and Regan represent a grotesque parody of consolation, then Cordelia contains the possibility for Lear's comfort in the play. Her very name contains a pun on "cordial," which is a medicinal, restorative drink also known as a "comfort." Unlike her sisters, who speak of the need to educate Lear by forcing him to suffer the consequences of his folly, Cordelia represents a form of healing that is (in both senses of the word) more kind. For our purposes, however, the more suggestive parallel-with-a-difference for Cordelia is Edgar, the other wronged child in the play who would give comfort. If Edgar looks attractive compared to the vicious comforting of Goneril and Regan, he looks much less attractive compared to that of Cordelia. In act 4, scenes 6 and 7, Shakespeare sets side by side two scenes in which a wrongly banished child saves from despair the parent who is responsible for the banishment. First he shows us Edgar's morality play consolation at Dover Cliff, then Cordelia's remarkably simple, unmanipulative comforting of her father. Unlike Edgar (and, before him, the duke of Vienna), she does not put ideas in the sufferer's mouth. Nor does she attempt to deceive her father by constructing a providential order where none exists. The difference between the two attitudes is pointedly conveyed by the way the two consolers attempt to guide the eye of the ailing father: whereas Edgar urges Gloucester to "Do but look up" (4.6.59), Cordelia beseeches Lear to "look upon me, sir" (4.7.56).

What is most remarkable about the scene, and the biggest difference between the two consolers, is how few words Cordelia speaks. Before Lear awakens, she exclaims "O my dear father, restoration hang / Thy medicine on my lips" (4.7.25–26). What issues from her lips is not the traditional screed of consolatory topoi that Leonato dismissed as "preceptial med'cine," but rather a kiss. Never has a consoler spoken so little or done so little to manipulate a sufferer. When, with moving hesitation, Lear progressively acknowledges her as "this lady," "my child," "Cordelia," she affirms his perception with the simplest and fullest words of the play: "I am, I am." Unlike the denial of identity and human relationship that underscores most consolations, these lines affirm. Another poignant resonance with Shakespeare's earlier consolations can be heard in the scene in Lear's repeated fear of being abused and mocked. This fear stems from his remembrance of his humiliating treatment by Goneril and Regan, and perhaps from his worry that the present moment is too good to be true. But it also reminds us of the mockery of suffering that Shakespearean consolation often (as in the previous scene) entails.

Paradoxically, the reconciliation of Lear and Cordelia reveals the limitations of the consolatory tradition more tellingly than the many scenes in Shakespeare where comfort is mocked. Instead of subverting consolatory formulas, this scene suggests their limitations by transcending them. Cordelia comforts Lear not by assuming the detached, impersonal stance of the traditional consoler, but by a complete denial of moral privilege ("No cause! No cause!"). She asks not for Lear's education and reformation, but for his benediction, and she begs him not to kneel to her. Indeed, the sense of a shared grief is so strong in the scene that the roles of comforter and comforted become fused and the conventional consolatory hierarchies dissolved. It is Cordelia whose tears are wet and Lear who implores, "I pray weep not." This scene, and perhaps this scene alone in Shakespeare, realizes Leonato's ideal of mutuality in consolation: the comforter feels and tastes the grief which she comforts.

As we all have learned to our grief, *King Lear* does not end with the comfort of the reconciliation scene. The resolution at the end of act 4, scene 7, is a false ending, a vision of what consolation could be.[37] In the play's closing moments, Shakespeare drives home the inconsolable force of loss by having Albany deliver a traditional consolatory speech, beginning: "You lords, and noble friends, know our intent. / What comfort to this great decay may come / Shall be applied" (5.3.297–99). Though Albany's "intent" is sincere enough, his resolution to apply comfort to a great decay sounds suspiciously like applying cosmetics to a festering wound. As his following lines make clear, his phrase "this great decay" refers to Lear, and the comfort Albany intends to proffer is his own abdication and the return of "absolute power" to Lear. But it is sheer delusion to speak of absolute power in a world where mankind is utterly powerless to control its fate; the irony is deepened by the close similarity of Albany's words to those of the complacent king in the play's opening scene. Worse still, his desire to restore Lear to his throne grotesquely disregards Lear himself, and Albany concludes with the hollowest assertion yet of distributing just rewards: "All friends shall taste / The wages of their virtue, and all foes / The cup of their deservings" (5.3.303–05). These are the merest of words, for Regan has already emptied the poisoned cup offered her by Goneril, and the wages of Cordelia's virtue has been death. What makes Albany's attempt to apply comfort to Lear so jarringly inappropriate is that he ignores the fact that, during his speech, Lear is holding his comfort dead in his arms.[38] For a final time in the play, the source of solace does not speak.

It is tempting to conclude a discussion of consolation in *King Lear* (and in Shakespeare) by quoting Kent's pronouncement that "All's cheerless, dark, and deadly" (5.3.291), or Gloucester's earlier cry after having been blinded, "All dark and comfortless" (3.7.85). Or, better yet, one can quote Lear's last words about Cordelia:

> And my poor fool is hang'd! No, no, no life!
> Why should a dog, a horse, a rat, have life,
> And thou no breath at all? Thou'lt come no more,
> Never, never, never, never, never.
>
> (5.3.306–09)

As William Elton points out, these lines constitute a kind of "*in-consolatio.*"[39] They echo Elizabethan characterizations of the heathen who, because they have no hope of an afterlife, despair at the death of loved ones. But, compelling as these comfortless exclamations are, they do not, I think, speak to our full experience of the play. It is true that *King Lear* takes us so far beyond the formulaic world of consolatory treatises that their prescribed methods of comfort are revealed to be woefully, even grotesquely, inadequate. And it is true that the world of the play takes its revenge upon every attempt to impose order and meaning on it. Yet *King Lear* does not deny the possibility of a painfully achieved and appallingly easily destroyed form of comfort. It suggests that meaningful consolation for suffering can be discovered only in the humanity that compels us to suffer. And, for a few precious moments, Shakespeare gives us a communion in suffering so powerful that the comfort it affords is indistinguishable from grace itself.

2 • Lyric Grief in Donne and Jonson

Robert C. Evans

John Donne and Ben Jonson wrote several of the most widely read and deeply valued poems of grief in the English language. Few readers have been immune to the power of Jonson's poem on the death of his first son, or of his great tribute to the dead Shakespeare, or of his lofty celebration of two young friends (one deceased) in the "Cary-Morison Ode." Similarly, few of Donne's poems have elicited as much commentary and admiration as his lengthy *Anniversaries*, written to commemorate the death of a patron's young daughter. Thus it is all the more striking that so many other poems of mourning composed by these two authors have been so widely ignored. Donne's shorter *Epicedes and Obsequies*, for example, have mostly been either neglected or rejected, and a similar fate has befallen Jonson's poem on the death of Lady Venetia Digby, which is not only his longest lyric but is also part of his longest sequence.[1]

Jonson's "Elegie on My Muse" is also interesting, however, for numerous other reasons: it is an intensely religious work by a poet who elsewhere makes little explicit reference to

Christian doctrine; it is one of his most impassioned works of praise; it came near the very end of his own career and thus allowed him to assess and summarize the values he considered most important; it is addressed (indirectly) to one of his most important patrons; and it is a poem whose contexts can be documented extensively (although most of the relevant evidence has received little attention). This poem's circumstances provide, in fact, one of our fullest sources of information about the potent impact of grief in early modern England. For all these reasons, then, one might expect the work to have received far more attention.

The simplest explanation for the neglect of this work and of Donne's briefer poems of mourning is also the harshest: perhaps they are simply bad *poems*. Perhaps their grief now seems contrived, their diction inept, their images impotent, their thought pedestrian, or their structures infirm. Similar charges, however, were long leveled (and sometimes still are lodged) even against Donne's *Anniversaries* (see, for example, *DV*, 281), yet the importance of those works (thanks to decades of patient analysis) now seems indisputable. Perhaps the *Epicedes and Obsequies* similarly deserve (and might also profit from) a closer look, and perhaps the same is true of Jonson's "Elegie on My Muse." Perhaps these poems will win more respect once they receive sustained attention. That, at least, is my hope, and my chief purpose here will be to argue that these poems are more successful *as poems* — and particularly as poems of grief and mourning — than has been commonly assumed.[2]

I

To deal fully with Donne's briefer poems of mourning would require a book, not an essay, so I will focus here merely (and briefly) on one representative example: the "Elegie" composed to commemorate the death in 1609 of Lady Bridget Markham, a cousin of Lucy, countess of Bedford (see *DRF*, 301). Donne had no especially close ties with the deceased, and his personal grief at her passing was probably not severe. His obligation as a poet, however, was not to feel bereaved himself but to express, in powerful and memorable language, the significance of her life and death (see, for example, Greenfield, 76). Whether he achieved these objectives is, of course, open to debate (see *DV*, 551–62). I will suggest that the poem, when examined closely, is arguably far more effective than has sometimes been claimed.[3]

The Markham elegy opens with a series of striking images:

> Man is the World, and death the Ocean,
>   To which God gives the lower parts of man.
> This Sea invirons all, and though as yet
>   God hath set markes, and bounds, twixt us and it,
> Yet doth it rore, and gnaw, and still pretend,
>   And breakes our bankes, when ere it takes a friend.
>
> (1–6)

The first four words imply human power: "World" suggests size, solidity, singularity and self-containment, and the use of four abrupt monosyllables, accented on the two key nouns, reinforces this sense of human prowess. Donne seems to compliment man's might, but this image of potency is immediately juxtaposed with (and undercut by) images of even greater, more encompassing powers. The reference to "death" as an "Ocean" implies, in both words, principles of mutability and fluidity that contradict the preceding (but very brief) assertion of firm human strength. Suddenly the singularity of the apparently self-sufficient world is supplemented, so that what had seemed at first all-encompassing now seems part of a larger, far more complex and ambiguous whole. Even the word "Ocean" (the only trisyllabic term in the entire line) both suggests and enacts the breadth and expansiveness of death — the extent to which man's comfortable little world of life is surrounded and contained by the vast unknown.

Just when Donne seems to dwell on death's omnipotence, however, the focus shifts again: line 2 shows that both man and mortality are controlled by an even greater power (God). This power "gives" death our "lower parts" as a master might feed scraps to a hungry dog, and the force of all the statements so far lies partly in their very plain diction and matter-of-fact tone. Donne implies that he is not offering opinions but is merely stating truth. Yet what seems so depressing (the idea that our "lower parts" are given to death) can also imply some hope. Lower parts, after all, necessarily imply higher parts (our reason? our soul?) that may be invulnerable to mortality. Even now, of course, Donne's rich language is not exhausted, for "lower parts" not only suggests something broadly physical or carnal (for example, the body as opposed to the spirit) but also connotes, even more specifically, our sexual and excretory organs — the "parts" we usually hide and that make persistent, insistent demands. Furthermore, "lower parts" also reinforces the imagery of shore and sea that Donne has so quickly established: the "lower parts" are the ones continually lapped by death. But there are other parts (metaphorical mountains and other higher ground) that these waters never touch. In two short lines, therefore, Donne has already created a "World" of rich poetic resonance.

The third line further extends the original conceit: the sea of death "invirons all" — that is, all of man, all men, as well as all living things. God, however, has "as yet" kept this ocean from engulfing us, but the very phrase "as yet" suggests the inevitably unstable, temporary nature of our safety as well as our utter dependence on God's grace. God has (and here Donne nicely balances contrasting pairs of nouns) "set markes, and bounds, twixt us and it," but here, for the first time, the personal implications of mortality become explicit. Heretofore the poet has spoken generally of "man" and "all" being surrounded by death, but now he refers openly to "us," thereby obviously implicating both himself and his readers. He then ratchets the tension even higher: despite God's temporary postponement of our confrontation with death, "Yet it doth rore, and gnaw, and still pretend" (5). The words "yet" and "still" can simultaneously imply such multiple meanings as "nevertheless," "even now," and "always," while the verbs "rore" and "gnaw" suggest animalistic fury even as they reinforce the established conceit of crashing waves. The verbs' very brevity emphasizes their force, while the series ("rore," "gnaw," "pretend") stresses death's relentlessness. At the same time, each verb carries its separate impact: "rore" suggests an unpleasant sound, while "gnaw" is even worse (implying fleshly pain). "Pretend," meanwhile, can imply such meanings as stretching, extending, laying claim to a right or power, purposing, designing, aspiring, and/or plotting against (*OED*). (At the same time, the word may already carry suggestions of "pretense" or "pretentiousness" — as if Donne is subtly reminding us of his earlier point that death's power is always circumscribed by God's.)

Donne then concludes the poem's second sentence (and further advances his controlling metaphor) by explaining how death "breakes our bankes, when ere it takes a friend." Here the forceful alliteration of *b* sounds, combined with the juxtaposed verb and noun phrases ("breakes our bankes" / "takes a friend"), demonstrates once more how this poem not only states meanings but *enacts* them. In addition, the word "our" again reminds us that the poem concerns not only the death of Lady Markham but also the inevitable deaths of its author and readers: the poem stresses our common interests and fates by implying our individual extinctions. For the next few lines, in fact, Donne strongly underscores this commonality of human experience by repeatedly emphasizing the word "our," even as he also continues to develop his controlling conceit:

> Then our land waters (teares of passion) vent;
>   Our waters, then, above our firmament,

> (Teares which our Soule doth for her sins let fall)
>   Take all a brackish tast, and Funerall,
> And even these teares, which should wash sin, are sin.
>   We, after Gods *Noe*, drowne our world againe.
>   (7–12)

The almost oxymoronic reference to "land waters" implies, perhaps, bursting springs, thereby associating passion with earth and with the material, corruptible body. Meanwhile, our soulful tears — the "waters . . . above our firmament" — are linked with a higher sense of spiritual unworthiness, but even these purer waters are corrupted by contact with passions and become "brackish": they are spoiled as freshwater is spoiled by the sea, becoming nauseating, distasteful and toxic. Thus "even these teares, which should wash sin, are sin." The final two words here come with sudden brevity and force, canceling any hope raised by the four words that precede them. Finally, the allusions to Genesis only implied by such earlier phrasing as "waters" and "firmament" become explicit in the reference to Noah's deluge (itself a punishment for sin) and to God's subsequent biblical promise ("Gods *Noe*") never to destroy the world again by flood. These varied allusions remind us that sin is nearly as old as humankind. They suggest that if we respond to death with uncontrolled passion, we ironically reenact the first cause of all death.

Having sustained the water metaphor for 12 skillful lines, Donne now briefly switches to new conceits, although he soon returns once more to his master trope:

> Nothing but man of all invenom'd things
>   Doth worke upon itself, with inborne stings.
> Teares are false Spectacles, we cannot see
>   Through passions mist, what wee are, or what shee.
> In her this sea of death hath made no breach,
>   But as the tide doth wash the slimie beach,
> So is her flesh refin'd by deaths cold hand.
>   (13–19)

Mankind, earlier the victim of beastly death (5), now seems almost beastly itself, yet the pains we inflict are self-destructive. Tears (originally intended to help clear our spiritual vision) now seem merely "false Spectacles" — phrasing that implies not only flawed eyeglasses but also bogus shows staged for public display. Through this "mist" of passion (more water imagery), we cannot see either ourselves or Lady Markham clearly — although Donne's poem, presumably, will help us penetrate this obscuring fog. By this point, in fact, his focus on Lady Markham has become explicit: he has moved from the generic "Man" of line 1, to the general "friend" of line 6, to the quite specific "she" of line 16. From this moment forward he will never lose sight of Lady Markham, but his thoughts about her will also have broad human significance.

The startling image comparing her flesh to a "slimie beach" washed by death seems deliberately shocking. Donne risks indecorum here, but the gamble succeeds.[4] By likening her body to slime he implies that even the best human flesh is corrupt, but he also implies that flesh itself merely temporarily obscures something far more attractive and substantial. Flesh, moreover, is easily washed away, especially by a force as powerful as death. In Donne's day, "slimie" carried many appropriate connotations: it suggested a soft, glutinous mud that stuck to (and thereby obscured and discolored) solid rocks; it suggested a viscous substance or fluid of animal or vegetable origin, such as semen or mucus (thus again suggesting corruptible flesh); it could refer disparagingly to the human body and to man in general; and it suggested anything morally filthy or otherwise disgusting (*OED*). Moreover, slime by its very nature blends solid and liquid, just as the body itself is at once alive and dying. And, just as slime can be diluted and expunged, so the body will inevitably be washed away by death. In all these ways, then, the word works, and Donne's willingness to confront so explicitly Lady Markham's fleshly corruption helps suggest the ultimate unimportance of the flesh. Donne can risk comparing her body to slime because he knows that all Christians must finally acknowledge that slime is a perfectly fitting — if momentarily shocking — analogue for the human body.

Beneath the slime of Lady Markham's flesh lie the smooth, beautiful contours of her soul and of her resurrected body. That body and that soul will, at the end of time, be irrevocably joined. Passionate tears had earlier failed to "wash sin" and had in fact been sinful themselves (11), but the great sea of death will wash Lady Markham fundamentally clean, leaving its subtle imprint on her like "embroder'd workes upon the sand" (19). Death here seems almost an artist, continually creating and re-creating, and thus seems a far cry from the earlier image of it as a threat that "rore[d]" and "gnaw[ed]" (5). In fact, the image of "embroder'd works," by implying delicate, subtle craftsmanship, prepares for the following images, in which the ideas of artistic, mystical, almost magical transformation become even more explicit:

> As men of China,'after an ages stay
>   Do take up Porcelane, where they buried Clay;
> So at this grave, her limbecke, which refines
>   The Diamonds, Rubies, Saphires, Pearles, and Mines,
> Of which this flesh was, her soule shall inspire
>   Flesh of such stuffe, as God, when his last fire
> Annuls this world, to recompence it, shall,
>   Make and name then, th'Elixar of this All.
>   (21–28)

Here the very length of the simile adds to its almost epic rhetorical force, while the combined images seem simultaneously exotic, earthy, commonplace and remote. Donne's readers would have known that porcelain is fine earthenware with a translucent body and transparent glaze (*OED*), and thus a perfect analogue for the transformed, resurrected body. That body was originally composed of "clay" — a stiff, viscous, tough, sticky and very common kind of earth often associated in the

Bible with bitumen or pitch (*OED*). Clay was often likened to mire or mud (or "slime"), and the word "clay" itself often referred to the earth covering a corpse, to earth as the original material of human flesh, and in general to the earthly part of man (*OED*). Thus in his imagery of dark, sticky clay transformed by burial into smooth, translucent porcelain, Donne hits on a masterful analogy for the spiritual transformation of corrupt human flesh. Yet he also pays Lady Markham the added compliment of suggesting that while most flesh is mere clay, hers (presumably because of her physical and spiritual beauty) was already comparable to precious jewels, even before being buried. Thus, just as common clay can be transformed into dazzling porcelain, so her even richer flesh will be transformed, almost alchemically, into something even rarer and more refined.

Donne's wit here is exemplified by such details as the claim that "her soule shall inspire / Flesh" — phrasing that recalls the common Christian idea that God originally animated man by breathing life (spirit) into his material body, just as Lady Markham's resurrected body will someday be animated (and transformed) by her own redeemed spirit. Similarly witty is his reference to the moment when God's "last fire / Annuls this world," where "Annuls" most obviously means "destroys" or "reduces to nothing," but where the word may also be a pun on "anneals" (meaning to set on fire, to kindle or inflame; to alter in any way by heating; to vitrify or glaze a surface by firing; and/or to burn in colors upon glass or earthenware [*OED*]). Such phrasing thus echoes the earlier image of clay being transformed into porcelain, even as it develops the present passage's larger trope of a process that re-creates through apparent destruction. Such transformation is cleverly emphasized again in the rest of line 27, which describes how the last fire "Annuls this word, to recompence it." Here the re-creation suggested by Donne's second verb not only cancels but also compensates for the destruction implied by his first. Such details are important because they suggest that Donne was not merely going through a series of prescribed, mechanical motions when writing this poem. Instead, his mind and wit were actively engaged in wrestling with his subject so as to wrest some larger meaning and consolation from Lady Markham's death. Through that death she will become (he prophesies) comparable to "th'Elixar of this All" — that is, the precious alchemical substance capable of transforming not only all the materials mentioned or implied in the preceding lines (clay, jewels, porcelain, gold, flesh, and so on), but also all of creation, insofar as she will have become one with God himself.

Donne now returns, if only briefly, to the image with which the poem began — the image of death as an enveloping sea:

> They say, the sea, when it gaines, loseth too;
>   If carnall Death (the yonger brother) doe
> Usurpe the body,'our soule, which subject is
>   To th'elder death, by sinne, is freed by this;
> They perish both, when they attempt the just;
>   For graves our trophies are, and both deaths dust.
> So, unobnoxious now, she'hath buried both.
>   For, none to death sinnes, that to sin is loth.
> Nor do they die, which are not loth to die,
>   So hath she this, and that virginity.
>
> (29–38)

Even the witty sound effects of phrasing such as "They say, the sea" show Donne's active mind (or creative instincts), while the clever juxtaposition of "gaines" and "loseth" mimics, in its very immediacy, the mutability this pairing describes. Similarly clever is the description of "carnell Death" as "the yonger brother," a phrase suggesting not only that sin (or spiritual death) antedates (and causes) physical death, but also that physical death is the less important of the two. Because of the primogeniture that prevailed in Donne's era, the "yonger brother" was greatly handicapped when compared to his older male sibling, just as physical death is a similar latecomer who depends on spiritual death for his meager power. For a true Christian, however, bodily death means redemption from spiritual bondage: the temporary gain of the younger brother (physical death) means a permanent loss for his older sibling (sin). Indeed, when a redeemed Christian dies, the two deaths paradoxically "perish both"; their brotherhood is forever extinguished (but also, ironically, affirmed) when they "attempt" (a word that already suggests futility or an effort doomed to fail) to test, try or attack a "just" (or justified) soul. The grave thus becomes the token or memorial of human victory over both kinds of dying (see Charmaz, 78).

By dying, Lady Markham has become "unobnoxious" — but so have both kinds of death. Typically, Donne places the key adjective so that it can apply not only to "she" but also to "both." In the first meaning, Lady Markham has now gained, through death, freedom from danger, punishment, censure, guilt, blame, dependency or the power or rule of another being (see *OED*, "obnoxious"). In the alternative application (in the note from the John Shawcross edition), "both deaths are now incapable of dealing death." Thus not only death but also the deceased become "unobnoxious." By dying and being redeemed, Lady Markham has paradoxically "buried both" physical and spiritual death, "For, none to death sinnes, that to sin is loth." In other words, no one is guilty of any mortal sin (no one sins in any eternal sense) who feels a fundamental Christian hatred for (or loathing of) sin. Likewise, no one suffers a sinful death if his or her final spiritual purity makes that person loathsome or repulsive to a personified Sin. Paradoxically, anyone truly unafraid of physical death will not die spiritually ("Nor do they die, which are not loth to die"). By the same token, anyone who feels genuine aversion to spiritual death (that is, anyone "loth to die") and who (with God's grace) attempts to combat this fate will not finally suffer such ultimate death. As always, Donne's phrasing is richly sophisticated and complex. Lady Markham thus enjoys both physical and spiritual pureness (or "virginity" — that is, preservation from the sexual connotations of the word "death").

Her purity, however, resulted less from her own efforts than from the divine intervention that makes all goodness possible:

> Grace was in her extremely diligent,
> That kept her from sinne, yet made her repent.
> Of what small spots pure white complaines! Alas,
> How little poyson breakes a christall glasse!
> She sinn'd, but just enough to let us see
> That God's word must be true, All, sinners be.
> (39–44)

The richness of this poem's diction is exemplified even by such an apparently simple word as "diligent" (which could mean constant, assiduous, industrious, attentive, careful, earnest, and persistent [*OED*]), while the poem's structural wit is typified by the second quoted line (40), which depicts Lady Markham as both free from (major) sin and yet repenting (for minor infractions). Such ironic juxtaposition is used again in the joining of the adjective-noun phrases "small spots" and "pure white," while the phrase "pure white" perhaps refers not only to Lady Markham's own conscience but also to God's strictest moral standards. Meanwhile, Donne's allusion to the common belief that "poyson cracks a christall glasse" is not only memorable itself but also contributes to the already established image pattern of liquids as corrosive and deadly. The abrupt concession that "She sinn'd" is effectively brief and enhances the poem's credibility by admitting his subject's failings, but Donne immediately manages to turn even her sin into a tribute to God's truth. He claims, moreover, that her own truthfulness was so extreme that she regarded even careless sins of omission as deliberately sinful acts (45–52). By making this claim, Donne thus uses even her own self-accusations to help praise her.

In his final lines, Donne claims he is content to tell how fit

Lady Markham was for God, if only to make death repent his "vaine" (that is, egotistical and presumptuous, but also futile and pointless) haste (54). Yet he also lists a whole host of virtues for which he will *not* praise her, lest by doing so he should make her sound older than her true age and lest he also make death "glad / Of such a prey, and to his tryumph adde" (61–62). Part of the wit of this passage, of course, is that in listing the qualities he will not praise, Donne thereby praises them, but the device also brings the poem to a cleverly abrupt conclusion by making the brevity of the ending seem due not to Lady Markham's inadequacies or to Donne's incapacity but to a desire to triumph over death by preventing it from feeling any further triumph. Yet the very last word of the lyric (which refers to death "add[ing]" to his triumph) also implicitly concedes some measure of artistic defeat, thus allowing the poem to end on a note of effective ambiguity. This final touch is just one last instance of the subtle, assured craftsmanship the poem as a whole displays.

Intellectual wit and theological subtlety of the sort Donne achieves not only here but in his other poems of mourning might strike a modern reader as among the least effective means of consolation. Instead, with our post-Romantic sensibilities, we might expect a poet to appeal empathetically to the bereaved's tender emotions, stanching grief by grieving himself. Donne's culture, however, exalted reason and condemned passion — thus anticipating the insights of modern cognitive psychology, which teaches that thoughts determine feelings, and that the best way to change emotions is to alter thinking (see Choron, 112; Rando, 108; Parkes, 31). Lawrence Babb showed long ago, for instance, that the standard Renaissance response to melancholia was to regulate passion by relying on Scripture and affable reasoning (4), and Ralph Houlbrooke notes that in the early modern period excessive grieving was often thought to demonstrate "a lack of faith, reason, self-control, and even a perverse wilfulness" (*DRF*, 221).

Appealing to reason, in fact, remains a standard method of consoling (Choron, 115), but it should hardly surprise us that this method was particularly employed during Donne's era, when reason was considered humanity's link with the divine. All of Donne's poems of mourning, as well as similar poems by many of his contemporaries, might seem more effective — both as poems and as consolations — if we could only recall that they appeal less to mere emotions than to the mind, and that in doing so they seek deliberately to master passion by controlling and redirecting thought. The intellectual maneuvers Donne undertakes in the elegy on Lady Markham, properly viewed, are not cold or self-indulgent; rather, they are attempts to engage, stimulate, and thus reorient the *thinking* of the persons pained by her loss.

II

The potentially devastating impact of early modern loss (see *BMD*, 393; *DRF*, 220; Laurence, *DRB*, 76) is illustrated by the reaction of Sir Kenelm Digby in 1633 to the sudden death of his wife, Venetia. Digby was one of Ben Jonson's most important patrons, and Jonson also seems to have been close to Lady Digby, to whom he devoted his lengthiest series of lyrics ("Eupheme"). The ninth poem, which focuses most specifically on her passing, is labeled "An Elegie on My Muse" and is particularly interesting for the grief it both expresses and addresses. Digby mourned Venetia profoundly, and his surviving letters provide one of our fullest seventeenth century records of intense grieving over death.[5] Digby suffered all the more since he and Venetia seemed finally to have found in marriage a sustained happiness missing from their long, complex courtship (see Charmaz, 282, and Amos and Sumner, 26–31). Her death at age 32, moreover, had been a complete surprise: she had gone to bed healthy but had died in her sleep. She had thus been denied the opportunity for the conventionally "good death" so valued in her culture (see Beier, 43–61). Nonetheless, her peaceful-looking corpse so astonished Digby that he asked his friend Sir Anthony van Dyke to paint its portrait — a painting that remains one of van Dyke's most intriguing (see Millar, 37–44). Her passing also, of course, provoked numerous poetic elegies, not the least of them Jonson's.

One of Digby's letters speaks of the "corrosive masse of sorrow lying att my hart wch will not be worne away vntill it haue worne me out" (121). He knows all the standard consolations but cannot profit from them:

> no balme can worke upon a mortall wound but to cause more smart; mine is not capable of cure. And for my part, I doubt much whither some great examples of constancy in like cases as mine, that are deriued downe to us from former times, haue not proceeded rather from a stupide and brutall nature then from vertue and magnanimitie: if it be vertue, I confesse not onely my stomake is too weake to digest it, but even my braine to apprehend it. (122)

Elsewhere Digby says that he would be "angry wth my heart if it were guilty of wishing for an end of that griefe that consumeth it, vntill it hath made an end of me," and he also confesses feeling "a kind of sweetenesse euen in sorrow it selfe" (137; see *BMD*, 394). Although sorrow "benumbeth and freezeth all ones spirits and faculties" (138; see Charmaz, 299), it "is not possible that time or reason can weare of [*sic*] the edge of my griefe" (141). If he were concerned with his reputation, he "should seeke now to restraine my passionate griefe or att least the expression of it from the worldes eye. But I am content to be taken for what I am, a deiected broken hearted miserable man" (447; see *DRF*, 221). Although "afflictions are to be borne by braue men with constancy and magnanimity," he is "not of that number" (449; see Houlbrooke *DRF*, 253).

In one particularly interesting letter to his brother, Digby confesses that he is "much freer in my expressions to you then I can be to any other man. In my letters to others I must haue a regarde to decency, but to you whatsoeuer commeth to my fantasie I sett it downe" (450). He notes that sometimes his "torturing smarte... stoppeth me from either writing or almost thinking" and says he sometimes cries profusely and without warning, even though he had "heretofore thought that teares misbecommed a man vpon any occasion whatsoeuer" (450). He admits to weeping for four days upon discovering Venetia, accusing himself of "a wretched impatience, despaire and womanish weakenesse, vpon which all the reason that can be suggested is lost" (450). If he ever intended "to appeare in the world againe, I would do the best I could to hide this impotency," but he foresees doing nothing now but humbly preparing for death (450).

Such themes are emphasized again in another letter: "All the Philosophy and all the constancy that it teacheth or is borne with any man, will not serue his turne when he is assaulted by a strong passion" (458). Even Cato once showed "violent and impatient affection. Why should any man then chide or admire att me?" (459). Only the prohibition against suicide has kept him from committing it (459); in the meantime, "I shall always carry my hell about with me wheresoeuer I am" (462). His "wound is so deepe and incurable, that I can not make the right and effectuall use of it that I should" (238), even though he knows a wise man should "keepe himselfe upright in affliction and crosses" (239). His brother has good "reason to chide me for my exceeding sorrow and passion" (244), but such passion is blameworthy mainly "because I trouble you and others my good frendes with the expressions of it" (244). In fact, many of his "discreetest frendes advise me ... to seeke all meanes to divert my bootelesse thoughts from this sad obiect that can never be recovered; and they chide me because I do otherwise" (248). Nevertheless, "how it becommeth me to behave my selfe with decency not to sinke in the estimation of men, truly it is not all worth a serious thought" (253). Instead, Digby expresses great gratitude to a friend from whom he had expected anger or shame but who instead "commiserated me. For I confess ingenuously I am much to blame, but God knoweth I can not help it" (254).

Although these quotations only skim the letters' surface, they do suggest some key conclusions. First, they support G. W. Pigman's claim that by the early seventeenth century, individual grief was both more keenly felt and embraced than had perhaps been previously true (*Elegy*, 27–39; see also *DRF*, 228). Digby almost takes some pleasure in his pain and sometimes actively resists others' efforts to console him when they stress the dictates of reason and constancy. Yet he also seems ashamed of his grief and recognizes the need to control it, especially in public. Ben Jonson's probable reaction to Digby's grieving might seem highly predictable, particularly since Pigman identifies Jonson as a throwback to an earlier "rigorist" position toward mourning — a position that stressed rationality and self-control. Yet Jonson's lengthy "Elegy" is far more complicated than one might at first expect.[6]

Only detailed explication could do justice to the poem, but a few comments may suggest why it deserves greater attention. Its complicated resonances begin at once:

> 'Twere time that I dy'd too, now shee is dead
>   Who was my *Muse*, and life of all I sey'd,
> The Spirit that I wrote with, and conceiv'd;
>   All that was good, or great in me she weav'd,
> And set it forth; the rest were Cobwebs fine,
>   Spun out in name of some of the old *Nine!*
>
>   (1–6)

The first line, especially, might seem merely hyperbolic (see Dennis Kay, 209–10), until we recall that Jonson at this time had already suffered two strokes, was generally unhealthy, was in eclipse at court, and in fact was recently rumored to have died (Riggs, 331). These facts give added poignancy to the words of an aged poet who eulogizes the young woman who surprisingly predeceased him. Given his own situation, his determination to celebrate Venetia at such length (and with such vigor) makes the poem all the more impressive and lends some credence to his depiction of her as a truly inspiring muse. By confronting her death, he implicitly confronts his own, including not only his literal physical demise but also potential further loss of social security. By losing Venetia he had lost not simply an imagined muse but also a real, influential patroness (one who helped "set . . . forth" his work, and one whose death, moreover, might lead Kenelm himself to retire from society and from promoting Jonson and others).[7]

When Jonson claims that it was thanks to Venetia that he "conceiv'd" (3), he credits her with almost masculine power while himself implicitly adopting a traditionally feminine role. Ambiguity of a different sort, meanwhile, appears in line 4, where the "good" and "great" qualities Venetia allegedly "weav'd" in Jonson can refer either to his poetry, or to his character, or (more likely) to both at once. In addition, the first few lines, like much of the rest of the poem, show Jonson's ability to employ subtle distinctions by exploiting balanced phrasing, including contrastive pairings. Thus he juxtaposes her real with his prospective death in line 1, calls her both his own "*Muse*" and the "life" of his writing in line 2, credits her with fashioning in him both the "good" and the "great" in line 3, and in lines 4 and 5 praises her for not only weaving his excellence but also for "set[ting] it forth." Similarly, he implicitly contrasts the works she "weav'd" with his other writings (dismissed as simply "the rest"), which were merely "Spun out in name of some of the old *Nine*." Here the phrase "Spun out" suggests a more haphazard, less careful process than weaving; "name" suggests a rather superficial, conventional connection between the poet and the muses (unlike his deeper bond with Venetia); and "old *Nine*" denies the conventional but antiquated muses even the dignity of being specified. Whereas Venetia's inspiration helped Jonson "weave" strong and lasting works, the "old *Nine*" merely spun flimsy, insubstantial "Cobwebs." But now, of course, her days as his muse seem over.

Part of the paradox of the "Elegie," however, is that the death of his supposed muse calls forth one of Jonson's most elaborate and energetic poems: just when we might have expected creative death, he displays poetic vigor. The dead muse animates his verse in spite (or perhaps because) of her passing. Any strengths the poem possesses can be credited to her influence (despite her death), while any weaknesses can be blamed on her demise. Venetia thus inspires the very work in which Jonson laments his inspiration's death. Moreover, by carrying on despite his loss he implicitly sets a good example for Kenelm and others. He transforms bereavement into creation, thus already suggesting one response to Venetia's passing.

In the next few lines, however, Jonson variously suggests his own profound loss. Even his syntax is fragmented in lines 9 and 10 (a technique he later employs often to suggest intense emotion). He effectively uses paradox by calling Venetia a "faire Cor[p]se" (11); skillfully juxtaposes near rhyme by imagining her "laid out . . . / By *Death*, on Earth" (11–12); and indicts Nature as either "Sleepie, or stupid" for allowing "that portion of her selfe to die" (14; see Sacks, 21) — a phrase that can refer to Venetia as a part of Nature and/or to Venetia's body as the physical "portion" of her earthly existence. Subsequent lines juxtapose "Nature" and "*Art*" (15–16) as well as "*Vulture death*" and the self-renewing "*Phoenix*" (18–19), and, just as Jonson began by suggesting that he himself might as well now die, so he here implies the same about nature (21–22). His tone paradoxically conveys both impotence and anger, and both emotions are implied again when he asserts that his "wounded mind cannot sustaine this stroke, / It rages, runs, flies, stands, and would provoke / The world to ruine with it" (23–25). Here the clipped, monosyllabic verbs mimic the chaos they describe, but beneath the chaos lies a subtle order. Thus "rages" contrasts with "runs," "runs" is intensified by "flies," "flies" contrasts with "stands," and "stands" contrasts with the more active "would provoke." In such phrasing Jonson achieves both apparent disorder and underlying control, and in fact this passage seems designed to evoke fiercely destructive emotions which the poet can then transform and redirect into positive, creative energies (see Sacks, 22; Schiesari, 8). Yet by imitating Digby's own grief, Jonson gives that grief its due even as he prepares to demonstrate its shortcomings. Digby was more likely to accept eventual consolation if he felt that Jonson himself shared some of his own potent sorrow.

Just as Jonson assumes the departure of Venetia's spirit, so he implies that her death has similarly affected *him*: "What's left a *Poët*, when his *Muse* is gone?" (28). In a sense, the rest of the poem will try to answer the empty despair this question raises. As if echoing his opening line, he now proclaims, "Sure, I *am* dead" (29; emphasis added), and he effectively uses enjambment, juxtaposed verbs and unexpected trochaic substitution by writing, "I feele / Nothing I doe" (29–30) and also by asserting, "My Passion / Whoorles me about, and to blaspheme in fashion!" (31–32). Yet the reference to blasphemy, ironically, implies subtle self-condemnation, signaling an imminent abandonment of despair. The phrase "in fashion" also suggests a significant shift, since although blasphemy may seem an act of extreme independence and self-assertion, Jonson depicts it as empty and imitative — a pointless if common response to painful loss. The poet even admits that he "murmure[s] against *God*, for having ta'en / Her blessed Soule, hence, forth this valley vane / Of tears, and dungeon of calamitie!" (33–35), but by the end of this sentence its opening mood has already been powerfully transformed. Thus "murmure" already suggests not only anger but also fear, perhaps even cowardice and (as with "blaspheme") self-censure, while "valley vane" suggests sorrow that is at once deep, pointless and egotistical. Even while describing his pain and frustration, then, Jonson begins to transcend them.

In a powerful series of fragments implying emotions so intense that they violate even basic syntax, Jonson now imagines Venetia's happiness, particularly her enjoyment of "the Angels amitie!" (36–38). (How typical of Jonson, who so highly prized friendship on earth, to imagine even intenser friendship in heaven; see also 184.) Yet the fragments he uses here and elsewhere to convey powerful feeling (for example, lines 59–68, 77–80, 85–96, 139–46) are also implicitly counterpointed by balanced pairings, such as "*Sheepe*" and "*Goates*" (46–47), "finall retribution" and "fleshes restitution" (49–50), "*Body* and *Spirit*" (54), "judg'd, or crown'd" (55), "guilty" and "guiltlesse" (56), "accuse, or quit" (60), "Body, and Soule" (64), "*Circle*" and "*Period*" (66) "*Hope*" and "*Faith*" (68), "tongue, or pen" (69), "spirit" and "flesh" (93), "Brother" and "Sister" (116), "Sons, and Daughters" (118), "*Union*" and "*Trinitie*" (128), "Friends" and "Foes" (139), "point" and "span" (152), and "Nobilitie" and "pride" (159–60), to mention just a few (see also 40, 41, 43, 48, 73, 109). Such counterpointings imply an active, discriminating mind — one for whom rational distinctions are crucially important for coming to terms with grief by imposing reason on it. These discriminations enact a continual, exemplary exercise of rational judgment (see McCanles, 3–45).

The "Elegie" therefore not only implies but actively demonstrates that while pained emotion is one appropriate response to Venetia's death, so are rationality and even joy. In fact, the poem shows that intense elation is a perfectly apt reaction to her passing, especially when one recalls the reason, order, justice and mercy God has built into existence. One way Jonson creates this celebrative tone, for example, is by repeating key words — as if to imply that his mind is so full of complicated thought and resonant emotion that he must constantly double back and elaborate on the rich, unfolding implications of his terms. He thus plays with the words "day" (59, 61, 63, 120–21), "Thither" and "there" (103, 108, 113, 115, 117), "*All*" (120, 122, 127) and "houre" (218–19). He similarly suggests such full and copious significance by using lists, as when he imagines Venetia among the "*Saints, Martyrs, Prophets*, with those *Hierarchies,* / *Angels, Arch-angels, Principalities,* / The *Dominations, Vertues,* and the *Powers,* / The *Thrones,* the *Cherube,* and *Seraphick* bowers" (85–88); or when he praises her as "A *Wife,* a *Friend,* a *Lady,* [and] a *Love*" (99); mentions "the *Lord* / of life, and light, the Sonne of *God,* the *Word*" (111–12); catalogs the brothers, sisters, sons, daughters and parents who will meet again in heaven (117–18; see Baumeister, 278); extols Venetia once more as "A tender *Mother,* a discreeter *Wife,* / A solemne *Mistresse,* and so good a *Friend*" (174–75); notes Christ's varied actions of "raising, judging, and rewarding" (207); speaks of Christ again as Venetia's "Judge, true *God,* true *Man,* / *Jesus,* the onely-gotten *Christ!*" (211–12), or when he mentions God's "*Power,* / His *Wisdome,* and his *Justice*" (217–18). Such lists both imply and foment excitement.

A similar technique used to convey the impression of a subject full of rich meaning is Jonson's habit of repeatedly joining closely related words (see McCanles, 3–45). By using such pairs or series, he not only suggests that no single word alone is sufficient to its descriptive task, but he also implies the subtly different meanings of related terms. He achieves this effect, for instance, when he mentions both emotional "joy" and intellectual "suretie" (61); calls heaven at once a feast, holiday and banquet (62–65); imagines desires both to "adorne" and to "compleat" (71–72); refers to both "silence, and amazement" (78); condemns "rude, / Dull, and prophane, weake, and imperfect eyes" (78–79); alludes to Kenelm's clothing of "black, or mourning" (98); celebrates Venetia's "pure, ... pretious, and exalted mind" (104); promises that she will now be even more "desir'd, and dearer" (109); foretells how dead relatives, reunited in heaven, will both "meet" and "know" one another (114–15); calls God both "all Glory" and "all Perfection" (127); alludes to a "holy, great, and glorious Mysterie" (129); explains how Christ will both "preach" and "teach" (134–35); mentions both spiritual "soules" and bodily "breath" (136); notes how Christ came both to "justifie, and quicken us" (204); or calls Christ a "Redeemer, and Repairer too" (213; see also 156, 164, 172, 179, 224).

By using such techniques of repetition and discrimination (see Sacks, 23–24), Jonson manages to create a poem that is both intensely emotional *and* intensely reasoned. The "Elegie" expresses both deep feeling and active but often subtle thought, and in its final section, especially, it rises to a pitch of emotional, rhetorical and intellectual fervor. Thus Jonson effectively uses anaphora to describe Venetia's threefold vision of her savior ("She saw . . . / She saw . . . / She saw"; 199–206) as her focus shifts from Christ's Incarnation to his Crucifixion and then to his Resurrection (see Stein, 10). Similarly, after first referring to Christ's "Power, / His *Wisdome*, and his *Justice*" (217–18), he later elaborates on each word in turn when he imagines Christ's exercise of all three capacities on the day of judgment (220–24) — the end-time that also neatly coincides with the end of the poem. Just when the "Elegie" soars to such rhetorical heights, however (that is, just when it seems to culminate in an effusive, highly ordered and highly celebratory eschatalogical revelation), it also abruptly returns to its opening mood and thought: "My *Muse* is gone" (228). These are its emphatic final syllables, and in returning to this stress on the lost Venetia after having just so powerfully envisioned the triumphant Christ, Jonson not only brings the poem full circle but also manages to reenact the quick, unforeseeable devastation associated with Venetia's death. His final four words are as shocking an ending as her death had been, and in this closing passage as indeed throughout, the "Elegie" manages to combine order and disorder, coherence and fragmentation, artistic skill and emotional power. The poem attempts to comfort Kenelm Digby's grief by appealing to both his faith and reason while never denying or minimizing his real pain and loss. It is one of Jonson's richest poems of mourning, and in its vigor perhaps it proved as much a comfort to its aging author as to the man for whom it was primarily composed (see Sacks, 2; see also Dennis Kay, 183; Smith, 21).

III

Although Jonson's "Elegie" on Venetia Digby, like Donne's on Lady Markham, deserves full appreciation as a unique and richly crafted poem, both works can also be discussed (if only briefly here) in more general terms. Thus both poems exemplify responses to grief that sometimes seem universal but also appear more specifically early modern. Most fundamentally, both poems reflect the apparently basic human instinct to treat dead people with a dignity not normally accorded to nonhuman objects (Toynbee, *passim*), and both poems exhibit a fundamental desire not to allow death to contaminate the larger community (Greenfield, 83). Both poems directly confront perhaps the most taboo of all topics, death, which Bernard Becker has called the primary human repression (96; see also Calderwood, *passim*; *Elegy*, 6; and Watson, 1), and both attempt to defeat death by using it to celebrate both divine and artistic creation. Both poems concede the loss of a valued individual while also conveying a strong sense of social continuity (see Kearl, 86; Metcalf and Huntington, 47), particularly by reaffirming their culture's most important values (Charmaz, 31; Littlewood, 21). Both elegies illustrate the standard existentialist assumption that death, by shattering the routines of life, encourages us to ponder the deeper meanings of existence (Charmaz, 45), while both poems also illustrate how death (and the art it provokes) can encourage us to search for coherent connections between past, present and future (Charmaz, 49). Both elegies also attempt to articulate the broad range of emotions that death can evoke (including not only grief but also fear, anger, frustration and others), yet both poems do so while working toward ultimate consolation (Doebler, 220–21; Haig, 10; Kearl, 178, 489; Laurence, 65; Kalish, 219; Littlewood, 14, 41; Rando, 102; Strobe and Strobe, 10–12, 56).

Both poems reaffirm the social status of the deceased (Scodel, 17) even as they both celebrate the departed's new status in heaven (Scodel, 89). Both treat death as a release from mundane burdens and as a transformation into a higher state of existence (Lifton, 253), and both seek to elevate the meaning of the deceased's, the author's and the reader's lives. The poems reflect a growing contemporary assumption that individual death was worthy of special attention (Stein, 13), and they also reflect and respond to the common need of mourners to share memories with others (Raphael, 188). Both elegies provide, in a sense, a "finished picture" of the deceased (Kearl, 95) and probably also helped to satisfy strong desires for reassurance about the fate of the departed (*DRF*, 317). The poems confront death by adopting such standard strategies as focusing on other thoughts, emphasizing positive emotions, minimizing death's importance, and/or making death seem more familiar and thus less frightening (Choron, 112–14). Both provide opportunities for (and partly enact) "memory reviews" (Haig, 24), and they imply how coming to terms with loss can help promote the psychological and spiritual growth of survivors (Haig, 13). The poems confront the lack of choice that death seems to impose, since they provide positive options of response (Charmaz, 281). In both cases, moreover, one of those positive responses involves encouraging readers to imitate the virtues of the deceased in order to prepare themselves more effectively for death (*DRF*, 317). With their heavy emphasis on religious consolation, the poems also illustrate the standard

Marxist assumption that reactions to death are always affected by the larger social structure and dominant ideology and that a culture uses important social occasions (such as death) to validate and reinforce its key beliefs (Charmaz, 38).

Both poems treat their individual subjects as symbolic beings, using these particular deaths as occasions for meditation and contemplation on death in general (Lewalski, in *DV*, 542). Both idealize the dead (see Raphael, 187) and imply that grieving is one valuable method of humbling oneself before God (*DRF*, 224), and Jonson's poem in particular illustrates the highly ritualistic quality of much elegiac rhetoric (Ochs, 8). Moreover, Jonson's poem also supports Houlbrooke's contention that in the early modern period the death of a spouse often provoked the intensest form of grief (*DRF*, 232) and that unexpected deaths often caused particularly extreme pain (*DRF*, 240; see also Rando, 116, 122; Raphael, 222–23; Spierenburg, 132). The circumstances surrounding Jonson's poem also support the argument that the death of a loved one is often interpreted symbolically as the death of oneself or of one's personal significance (Charmaz, 281), while Jonson's poem also particularly illustrates two common forms of early modern consolation: the belief that God had taken the departed to a better world, and the assumption that mourners would enjoy reunion with the dead in heaven (*DRF*, 241–42; Cole, 10). Jonson's poem also resembles many contemporary funeral sermons in its heavy reliance on scriptural teachings (for example, 199–208; *DRF*, 297, 305), in its assertion that spiritual worth is far more praiseworthy than status or birth (155–59; *DRF*, 312), in its emphasis on its subject's good works (191–98; *DRF*, 313; Kalish, 177), and in its focus on private holiness, particularly when praising women (180–90; *DRF*, 316). The Digby "Elegie," particularly in its opening section, also illustrates Dennis Kay's argument that Jonson's funeral poems increasingly came to focus on the personal reactions of the speaker (207), and indeed both Jonson's elegy and Donne's also support Kay's claim that Renaissance elegists typically defined their poetic individuality against generic norms and expectations.

Although each poet, therefore, was doing something that had been done many times before, each was also trying to write in a distinctive and memorable way. In that sense, both Donne and Jonson, merely by composing their poems about death, were trying not only to assuage grief but also to cheat death themselves.

3 • Humourous Grief
Donne and Burton Read Melancholy

Marjory E. Lange

The assertion that "such a melancholy as makes Witches, makes Papists too" may not readily impress us with the connection John Donne intended his audience to make at the Spittle on Easter Monday, 1622. "Melancholy" was an important word in Donne's homiletic vocabulary. In sermons preached during the same year, he spoke once of avoiding "Prophetical melancholy [that] thy God will overthrow this Religion," and another time urged that "to weep for sin is not a damp of melancholy, to sigh for sin, not a vapor of the spleen."[1] In each case, he drew on his culture's great variety of readings for "melancholy." He trusted they would understand that melancholic superstition and delusion connected his papists with the witches, as well as created the false fears leading to prophecies that God would abandon them, and he knew they would appreciate the distinction between a legitimate sorrow for sins committed and the false grief kindled by melancholic humours. The link between disease and sin — personal and cultural — is a key reading of the grief of melancholy in the Renaissance.

During the last two centuries, melancholy has been imprisoned within an intransigent pensiveness, noble sadness or simply depression. For Renaissance readers it covered a broader canvas: in its most current and prevailing popular unfolding, it had become one way of mapping human nature itself. Originally, and throughout the era, it named a humoural temperament expressed in diverse ways, and a disease of madness characterized by delusion, inner disorder, even despair, and manifesting symptoms across the entire spectrum of human behavior. Robert Burton expressed this last type in the *Anatomy of Melancholy* as what "[t]he common sort define . . . to be a kind of dotage without a fever, having for his ordinary companions fear and sadness, without any apparent occasion."[2] In his sermons, Donne drew on the whole array. Although he employs the word "melancholy" fewer than 40 times in his entire corpus of sermons, those applications range nearly as widely as Burton's examples, and are expressed with greater economy. Thanks to the tremendous contemporary popularity of melancholy, Donne could rely on listeners to be conversant with the varieties of interpretation being offered for religious applications, and, who, if not versed in specific medical details of melancholy, still would be able to follow a metaphoric trajectory established on that medical lore. We, on the other hand, lose much of the flavor of his writing, as well as evading the shocks he presents when, for instance, he harangues his congregation that "no man [should] think to present his complexion to God for an excuse, and say . . . My Melancholy enclined me to sadnesse, and so to Desperation, as though thy sins were medicinall sins, sins to vent humours," or when he refers to Jesus as "that melancholick man" (3:13, 286; 3:9, 220). Joining Burton in apostrophizing the whole age and race as melancholic in its superstitious running after false gods, Donne brings melancholy to the political arena and makes connections that, today, have lost most of their impact. Donne the partisan offers sufferers from disordered politics the same consolation melancholy sinners can choose to enjoy — they may turn from their wickedness and live. Otherwise, he implies, only the horrid anguish of truth recognized too late awaits them all.

Donne preaches caveats — and consolations — founded on representative ways of regarding melancholy, particularly what Robert Burton named "Religious Melancholy." Seventeenth century religious controversies had revitalized the old question of the physical body's effect on — even interference with — the soul's operations. In the ongoing debate over this crux, Donne and Burton both interpret melancholy as a danger, even a threat. Interpretation is what makes melancholy enigmatic and intricate.

Most conspicuous throughout the immense body of melancholic material is that, while melancholy readings change dramatically over the course of the early modern period, and the symptoms of melancholic diseases proliferate, contemporary understanding of the elemental content and operation of melancholy, once established, hardly shift at all. Amid the augmentations Burton incorporated into later editions of the *Melancholy*, he barely modified the physical-medical material: symptoms and varieties multiply; reputable medical authorities, prognoses and remedies endure.[3] Donne's own applications of melancholy are all well founded on the prevalent outlook, but rely on different facets of that tradition. Certain elements — most notably the problem of delusion and the ultimate goal of discovering and embracing legitimate consolation — remain consistent, but within those boundaries Donne can connect humour with politics (or with God), separate or join illness and sin, and parallel grief and deeds with the same flamboyant flexibility he achieves in his poetry, without once distorting or misrepresenting the fundamental tradition. Not a groundbreaker, he prevails as a careful and thorough reader of the grief of melancholy as it affects his listeners.

During the Renaissance, melancholy was indeed a *grief* in the older sense of the word — that is, some *thing*: a physical ailment, illness, pain, hardship or an injury received — as well as, intangibly, a kind of sorrow. Like "melancholy," "grief" was passing from its medieval roots toward its modern position as a synonym for sadness; both meanings were current and overlapped. In its relation to melancholy, Donne tended to avoid grief's modern connotations: melancholy's chimerical nature gives it only the illusion of being a grief. Therefore, although melancholy fools the sufferer into feeling sad, it cannot truly burden him: "[W]hen we conceive a sorrow in the minde, without any reall, and externall cause, without paine, or shame, or losse, this is but a melancholy, but an abundance of a distempered humour, but a naturall thing, to which some in their constitutions are borne, and to be considered but so: But when God laies his hand, and his crosses upon us, the sorrow of the wicked, conceived upon that impression, that is sorrow" (9:18, 393). Donne's use of the word "but" in this passage, as a crescendo of sadness, underscores the relationship between melancholy's illusory grief and the real sorrow that God's hand and crosses bring.

Donne's regard for melancholy is particularly useful because he uses the word *as* a word, in passing, rather than as a primary topic of discourse. Thus the word gets contextual attention and functions as part of the whole fabric. In addition, Donne's personal background put him in a position to be unusually literate about melancholy in all its manifestations. He perceived his own temperament as dominated by the melancholy humour. This understanding brought with it closer experience with that humour than, say, choler or sanguinity. A book such as the *Biathanatos*, his much-maligned investigation of suicide, clearly revealed to his contemporaries that melancholy was his dominant humour. Further, in a mature letter to his lifelong friend, Henry Goodyer, Donne wrote:

> Every distemper of the body now, is complicated with the spleen, and when we were young men we scarce ever heard of the spleen. In our declinations now, every accident is accompanied with heavy clouds of melancholy; and in our youth we never admitted any. It is the spleen of the minde, and we are affected with vapors from thence; yet truly, even this sadnesse that overtakes us, and this yeelding to the sadnesse, is not so vehement a poison (though it be no Physick neither) as those false waies, in which we sought our comforts in our looser daies.[4]

Here, as in the *Sermons*, Donne ultimately places the issue in the hands of God, urging Goodyer to pray *fiat voluntas tua* (Thy will be done). However, Donne also identifies the medical impetus of melancholy/spleen in his life, and in his friend's as well, for later the letter offers consolation against some encumbrances and distresses of fortune. Donne's contact with his stepfather, Dr. John Syminges, exposed him early to available medical perspectives on melancholy. Syminges, who married Donne's mother in 1576, and died in 1588, was in a position to influence Donne from his fourth until about his sixteenth year. Syminges had "several times been President of the Royal College of Physicians ... and [was] of considerable standing in his profession." Donne's employment of medical terminology in general is uneven: his "knowledge of disease is seldom as exact or as specific as his knowledge of anatomy and physiology." His understanding of the mind's operations, however, though not expressed directly as information so much as by implication and assumption, is considerable. His sermons indicate he fathomed the traditional operation of the humours in health and sickness; their entire vocabulary lies at his metaphoric and symbolic disposal.[5]

This essay looks first through John Donne's melancholies back toward the tradition he interprets, specifically to the growing persistence of a religious form of melancholy and to the popular accumulation of basic medical information and its "performance" through the culture. It examines some of the era's received medical knowledge and traces some of the more important developments in interpreting melancholy, particularly as readings of the discourse affected the soul. Finally, returning to Donne via Burton, it explores the pinnacle of religious melancholy's influence on the seventeenth century English soul, politically, personally and provisionally.[6]

I

All Renaissance readings of melancholy are based on a threefold understanding of the word. Its final, most complex function was to collect as "disease" the enormous array of symptoms supposedly caused by disorder or distemper in the melancholic humour. More fundamentally, melancholy characterized the person in whom the humour was naturally dominant. Originally, however, it named one of the four basic humours present in the human body: blood, phlegm, yellow bile (choler) and black bile (melan-choler). All these fluids occur in every human body. When they balance "in the proportion that nature has designed," that is, in appropriate quantities and conditions (neither too hot nor too cold), the individual is healthy. "Balance" did not mean an equal proportion of each. Every living creature had more of one humour naturally.[7]

Each humour was associated with its appropriate organ — melancholy issued from the spleen — and influenced the temperament or "complexion" of the individual. A person's temperament (we would say personality type) was named for the humour that was naturally dominant within him. Thus people were labeled sanguine, phlegmatic, choleric and melancholic depending on which humour governed when they were healthy. Often a person's temperament could be determined from his appearance and manner.[8] All the humours were elemented from the *chylus*, that is, what remained of nourishment after its digestion in the stomach (decoction). Blood was created from the most temperate part of the chylus, phlegm from the colder, choler from the hotter, and melancholy from the residue. Blood, the sanguine humour, is the basis of life itself: "bloudde hath preeminence over all other humours in susteynynge of all lyvynge creatures, for it hath more conformitie with the originalle cause of lyvynge, by reason of temperatenes in heate and moysture, alsoo nourissheth the body, and restoreth that whiche is decayed, beinge the very treasure of lyfe, by losse wherof, deathe immedyately foloweth" (Elyot, 3r).[9]

Melancholy was the thickest, coldest and driest of the four humours, the dregs of the blood after all other nourishment had been extracted, the residue of the vitality. It was the humour most like death itself, associated with the spleen, old age and the planet Saturn. Naturally melancholic individuals tended to be dry, dark visaged and desiccated in appearance. As unappetizing as melancholy appears, however, it was as necessary to health as any other humour. It cooled the (potentially excessive) heat provided by blood and choler and dried the (sometimes excessive) humidity of phlegm. Not only were those deficient in melancholy dull, foolish and forgetful, but the humour, "kepte in his temperance, profyteth moche to true jugement of the wyt" (Elyot, 72r) by cooling and drying a too-enthusiastic surplus of other humours.

Lawrence Babb refers to melancholy as a disease "fashionable" in the Renaissance, not only as a posture in literature, but as an ailment among the gentry. The same symptoms of illness would likely be called "melancholy" in a person of nobility, and "mopishness" in a person without rank.[10] Its trendiness made melancholy — humour, temperament and the disease with its plethora of causes, symptoms, remedies and repercussions — ready material for every sort of discourse. Melancholy articulated fears: fear of personal inadequacy, as found in unrequited-love lyrics; fear of appearing inadequate before God, whose mysterious providence had to be taken on faith; and the final fear, of mortality, of personal death — a fear made far more terrible as human-centered knowledge challenged traditional assumptions on every side. No great wonder that an age uncommonly eloquent about its mortality would be equally vocal about melancholy. This fashion was founded on the Renaissance tendency to perceive living in terms of performance. Thus, melancholy appears as a kind of discourse, soliloquy or dialogue, furnishing the elements of an extremely flexible emotive language. As time passed, the focus of that performance grew increasingly personal, as may be seen in an examination of the medical or religious writings, whose targets became ever narrower, even as their scope grew.

Significantly, no matter how varied the readings of melancholy grew, the basic facts of melancholy's "text" remain consistent throughout the era. The emphasis and direction of individual works changed, but Thomas Elyot, Andreas Laurentius, Timothie Bright, Robert Burton and their many medically oriented colleagues agreed on melancholy's primary attributes. Each author brought something unique to the performance. Elyot broke ground by writing in the vernacular; Bright and Laurentius made notable contributions by personalizing their discourses; and Burton, compendiously, brought biography, science, theology and extended musings to the stage.

Thomas Elyot's *Castel of Helthe* provides a clear foundation for contemporary understanding.[11] Not only is it one of the first vernacular handbooks on health, but Elyot himself epitomizes the combination of Renaissance humanist, steeped in classical culture, and English "patriot" who chose to write in English, that was paradigmatic for the kind of discourse in which melancholy best participated.[12] The *Castel* is particularly consequential for its celebrity: at least 15 editions appeared between 1539 and 1610. It underscores the rise of a literate lay readership taking increased responsibility for its own health, one of the conditions that fostered melancholy's popularity as a discourse. A well-educated amateur rather than a professional physician, Elyot was an ideal spokesman for the literate of his age. He exploited a venerable tradition to make it *popular* — in all senses of that word. This vernacular account draws on a medical inheritance unbroken (though frequently bent) since Galen, a tradition most often presented in (professional) Latin. Although Elyot simplifies many of the controversies raised over unanswerable questions, he otherwise interprets very little: his is not a casebook of behavior or personality, but instructions for a concerned readership about health issues, aimed at promoting sufferers who can better explain their symptoms to their doctors, as well as practice better habits to avoid illness.

It is important to recall that Elyot saw his topic as health, so his accounts of the melancholic temperament, melancholic disease and its treatment present the central kernel of received lore in a context of human health in its entirety. This type of larger context is typical of early Tudor writing. The flood of interest in isolated melancholy arose during Elizabeth's reign, reaching a medical and poetic crest in the 1590s, and a more explicitly religious one in the early decades of the seventeenth century. One clear measure of the popularity of medical melancholy was that no other humour ever inspired a discrete treatise: no writer produced a work on phlegm, choler or blood alone.[13]

The next generation of melancholic medical writing, represented by Timothie Bright and Andreas Laurentius, both professional physicians, shifted the context from handbooks on health per se to treatises solely on melancholy.[14] In addition, both writers adopted a new strategy of personalizing their discourse by explicitly addressing a single individual's needs, and only by publication spoke to a wider audience. Laurentius, in the *Epistle* dedicating his *Discourse* to the countess of Tonnera (whose physician he was), writes that his patient suffers from only "three ordinarie diseases, cataracts, some touches of the windie melancholie" and rheums. He continues that he has "fitted up and made readie three discourses for you, touching your three diseases." Laurentius leaves readers other than his patroness to peer over the shoulders of his defined audience.[15] Bright creates a persona, his "supposed frend *M.* not ignorant of good letters" (iiiir), whom he employs on several critical occasions throughout the *Treatise*, integrating his stylistic strategy with his presentation of material, particularly during his answers to M's request that Bright distinguish between melancholy and the tormented conscience. Bright's tone remains primarily conversational: he *speaks* from his own experience, as a physician/adviser, freed from the scholarly fetters of the Renaissance equivalent of notes.[16]

In both works, the specific audience signals a different performance strategy than had been popular 50 years earlier. The interpretive potential of melancholy has grown, putting greater emphasis on mental phenomena than on physical features. Each author is at least as concerned with the patient's psychological distress as with any physical affliction, and each provides consolation as much as physic in his remedies.[17] Addressing an individual recipient narrows and broadens the focus at the writer's will, controlling an otherwise unmanageable surfeit of potential symptoms and explanations. Both recipients are figures who fit one stereotypical need for a treatise on melancholy. Laurentius's countess is aging, although "not [yet] incombred with any of the infirmities of old age" (*Epistle*; traditionally "melancholy" and "age" were practically synonymous), and Bright's friend M. suffers from anxiety over whether he is sick with melancholy or suffers from "that heavy hande of God upon the afflicted conscience, tormented with remorse of sinne and feare of his judgement" (iiir).[18] Bright's is a new take on the basic symptoms. The writers agree that melancholic disease attacks each patient at his most vulnerable point.[19]

One of the most challenging cruxes in sorting out Renaissance melancholy lies in assessing the man of melancholic complexion — was he insane, or a genius? The controversy explains the eagerness with which many claimed to be melancholy, something that otherwise seems unaccountable. Elyot ignores the debate, which originates with Aristotle, over the nature of the genius' temperament. Many writers (particularly those, one assumes, with a tendency to melancholy, either from temperament or disease) urged that genius must be melancholic and, by corollary, that melancholics are all geniuses. Andreas Laurentius qualifies the hypothesis by arguing that it is only a natural, healthy melancholy

> mixed with a certaine quantity of blood, that maketh men wittie, and causeth them to excell others. The reasons hereof are very plaine, the braine of such melancholike persons is neither too soft nor too hard, and yet it is true, that drynes doth beare the sway therein. But *Heraclitus* oftentimes said, that a drie light did make the wisest minde ... their conceit is very deepe, their memorie very fast, their bodie strong to endure labour, and when this humour groweth hot, by the vapours of blood, it causeth as it were, a kinde of divine ravishment, commonly called *Enthousiasma*, which stirreth men up to plaie the Philosophers, Poets, and also to prophesie: in such maner, as that it may seeme to containe in it some divine parts. (85-86)

For Laurentius, the chemical combination of blood (hot and moist) with melancholy (cold and dry) produces the near ideal type for sustained creative effort, strong, sensitive and hardy. Later writers, including Donne, John Milton and John Keats, consider the implications of melancholic genius with some seriousness.[20]

Within the humoural model of health, illness resulted from distemper, when "by the increase of diminution of any of [the humours] in quantitie or qualytie, over or under their natural assignment, inequall temperature commeth in to the body" (Elyot, 3r). Practically, this resulted in identification of two varieties of each humour, natural (the healthy form) and unnatural — a humour disordered, disproportionate, or distemperate. Natural melancholy, which was "the resydence or dregges of the bloud: and therfore is colder and thycker than the bloude" (Elyot, 72v) to begin with, was particularly susceptible to becoming distemperate, or *adust* (burnt). All burnt humour is dangerous, and any humour, when burnt, becomes melancholic.[21] The symptoms attributed to diseased melancholy were numerous, varied, and often mutually contradictory: "oftentimes hevynesse of mynde, or feare without cause, slepynesse in the members, many crampes without replecion or emtynesse, sodayn fury, sodayn incontinencie of the tongue, moche solicitude of lyght thynges, with palenesse of the vysage, and fearefull dreames of terrible vysyons, dreamynge of darkenes, depe pyttes, or deathe of frendes or acqueyntance, and of all thinge that is blacke" (Elyot, 73r).[22] Elyot, unlike later writers, retains a balance between physical and mental symptoms. By the seventeenth century, mental manifestations had come to dominate, and interpretations reflect this dominance. Nearly a century later, Robert Burton produced a catalog that clearly shared the same origins, but whose weight shifted:

> The *Name* [melancholy] is imposed from the matter, and Disease denominated from the materiall cause ... from black choler ... Wee properly call that *Dotage*, as *Laurentius* interprets it, *when some one principall facultie of the minde, as imagination, or reason, is corrupted, as all Melancholy persons have.* It is without a Feaver, because the humor is most part cold & dry, contrary to putrefaction. *Feare* and *Sorrow* are the true Characters, and inseparable companions of most *Melancholy*, not all ... for to some it is most pleasant. (1.1.3.1)

Its variety made melancholy a difficult condition to treat. Elyot suggests variations in diet (by which he means not only nourishment, but habitation ["air"], and exercise); avoiding activities that dry the body — sex, strenuous activity, much study, long waking, going outdoors in heat — and eating or drinking desiccating foods; avoiding too much solitude in favor of cheerful companions; and taking various medicinals (gold or silver in wine, various flowers or herbs): "[M]ooste of all other thynges, myrthe, good companye, gladnesse, moderate exercyse, with moderate feedynge" (73r–74r). These remedies remained fairly constant over the next century. Fear, sorrow and the power of delusion over the sufferer remained totally characteristic of the disease, but were differently accounted for.

Elizabethan and Jacobean writers were more concerned than Elyot with interpretation of the melancholic discourse. Laurentius's strength is in example and anecdote. He illustrates most varieties of melancholic suffering, providing a "history" for every occasion, in a manner foreshadowing Burton's more encyclopedic endeavor. Bright's addition is more substantial. He distinguishes between melancholic disease and what might be termed a crisis of conscience: "I have layd open howe the bodie, and corporall things affect the soule, & how the body is affected of it againe: what the difference is betwixt natural melancholie, and that heavy hande of God upon the afflicted conscience, tormente with remorse of sinne, and feare of his judgement" (iiiv).[23]

This is not entirely new. Laurentius briefly discusses a melancholy provoked by religious observance: "This humour then will imprint in melancholike men the objects most answerable to their condition of life and ordinarie actions.... If [a man] be given to bee religious, he will doe nothing but mumble of his beades, and you shal never finde him out of the Church" (98).[24] Bright's most original contribution lies in asserting that all perturbations and turbulations that lack a proper foundation are melancholy: "Whatsoever molestation riseth directly as a proper object of the mind, that in that respect is not melancholicke, but hath a farther ground then fancie, and riseth from conscience, condemning the guiltie soule of those ingraven lawes of nature, which no man is voide of, be he never so laborous" (193). Thus, objectless grief and delusional sorrow are melancholic, while sin-based sadness is not. He makes the distinction explicit, and — superficially, at least — clear and unambiguous:

> [When the conscience suffers] the purities of the bloud, and the sinceritie and livelinesse of the spirits avayle nothing to mitigate the paine, but onely the expiatorie sacrifice of the unspotted lambe. On the contrarie part [when melancholy is the culprit], when anie conceit troubleth you that hath no sufficient grounde of reason, but riseth onely upon the frame of your brayne, which is subject . . . unto the humour, that is right melancholicke, & so to be accoumpted of you. (194)

Melancholic suffering always lacks "real" ground: it is delusional, chimerical. That emphasis on phantasm is fundamental to the disease as Elyot, Bright, Laurentius, Burton — and Donne — understood it. Bright, however, offers an alternative reading by insisting that a grief with its source in awareness of sin can mimic melancholy to the oblivious sufferer: "Whatsoever is besides conscience of sinne in this case, it is melancholie: which conscience terrified, is of such nature, so beset with infinite feares and distrust, that it easilie wasteth the pure spirit, congeleth the lively bloud, and striketh our nature in such sort, that it soone becommeth melancholicke, vile, and base . . . so easily is the body subject to alteration of the minde" (195). More distressingly, this misconception hinders treatment, whichever way the error runs. The grieving sinner, seeking physic, fails to confront his sin. The deluded melancholic, taking refuge in prayer, cannot find relief for his humoural imbalances. Both the physician and the divine in Bright confront this Janus-faced disorder. Whatever the patient's ultimate outcome, the healer can always send him to the priest (and vice-versa) and thus be vindicated himself — a point Burton notes with a certain irony.

The rest of Bright's argument supports this distinction. In defining melancholy, Bright places disease before humor and prepares his thesis by declaring that melancholy is "either a certayne fearefull disposition of the mind altered from reason, or else an humour of the body commonly taken to be the only cause of reason by feare in such sort depraved.... The melancholie passion is a doting of reason through vaine feare" (1). Bright's *Treatise* thus sets the stage for the contraposition of melancholy as disease and symptom of sin that figures so largely in Burton and Donne.

Robert Burton's *Melancholy*, like mercury loose upon a table, eludes capture. Teasing a single continuous meaning from the compendious text is essentially impossible; the copiousness of the *Melancholy*'s text is its strength — and the critic's despair. The only real "anatomy" is to be found in the synopsis that opens each of the three sections: these tables delineate the shape, structure and connections among Burton's many topics. Unfleshed with details, the melancholy "bones" are visible here only. In the synopsis to part 1, for instance, it is apparent that each species of melancholy has symptoms in the body distinct from those in the mind. Burton asserts that "the diseases of the mind are more grievous than those of the body"; the body of the text, however, not only buries any clear line of argument in a multiplication and exemplification of symptoms, but that particular statement is not even raised to be questioned or debated. The point is silently accepted. Offering Job (who was "even melancholy to despaire") as his example, he ignores Job's physical symptoms and tacitly privileges the mental from then on (1.4.1.1). In fact, after part 1, physical melancholy takes an inferior role, except where a remedy addresses a material symptom.

Size and detail notwithstanding, Burton's most original contribution is the section on "Religious Melancholy," in which he brings the battle to the area of his own greatest competence. Among the multitude of his cited sources, estimated at some 1,250, are fewer than 200 medical authorities.[25] This disproportion, along with Burton's own professional inclination, helps explain why the discussion of religious melancholy, like "Love Melancholy" before it, presents a disease more of the soul/mind — and society — than of the body; most of the symptoms laid out in the synopsis for love, and all for religious, are mental/psychological ones.[26] Religious melancholy is a category he claims as his own innovation: "That there is such a distinct Species of Love Melancholy no man hath ever yet doubted, but whether this subdivision of *Religious Melancholy*[27] bee warrantable, it may be controverted. . . . I have no patterne to followe as in some of the rest, no man to imitate. No Physitian hath as yet distinctly written of it as of the other, all acknowledge it a most notable Symptome, some a cause, but few a species or kinde" (3.4.1.1).

He turns from accepted love melancholy to the new religious melancholy with God as his fulcrum, human love for God. This balances the *Melancholy*'s structure; God was named the first cause of melancholy in part 1,[28] so when religious melancholy returns us to God we are brought full circle (particularly since the *Melancholy* concludes with remedies for despair, fear of God's absence). Burton presents religious melancholy primarily in terms of its societal complications, particularly those caused by superstition, until he arrives at despair. Unlike Donne, who never omits the plight of the individual soul, Burton preaches to and about the cultural predicaments of heresy, superstition and idolatry. "For methods sake," he will create "a twofold division, according to those two extreames of *Excesse* and *Defect*, Impiety and Superstition, Idolatry and Atheisme." Excess comes, not from loving God too much, but erroneously, emphasizing irrelevancies at the expense of the necessary: "We have too great opinion of our owne worth, that we can satisfie the Law. . . . Of this number are all superstitious Idolaters, Ethnickes, Mahometans, Jewes, Hereticks, Enthusiasts, Divinators, Prophets, Sectaries, and Schismatickes . . . Monkes, Hermites, &c . . . fight under this superstitious banner." Under the banner of defect "march those impious Epicures, Libertines, Atheists, Hypocrites, Infidels, worldly, secure, impenitent, unthankfull, and carnall minded men, that attribute all to naturall causes, that wil acknowledge no supreame power; that have cauterized consciences" (3.4.1.1). His lists feel oppressively long, until one realizes that no one is excluded. Burton does not acknowledge the universality of superstition until his rhetorical motion brings the attack from a variety of "thems" to a resolution on "us." "Causes" and "Symptoms" of excess happen to others, but when Burton begins to consider "Prognostickes," all are again conjoined: "Because wee are superstitious, irreligious, we doe not serve God as we ought, all these plagues and miseries come upon us" (3.4.1.4). When he turns to "defect," the discussion once more becomes adversarial, and stays that way until "despair," the core of the section on religious melancholy.

Despair causes the most difficult and acute kind of melancholy: "As Shoomakers doe when they bring home shooes, still cry, leather is dearer and dearer, may I justly say of those melancholy Symptomes; these of despaire are most violent, tragicall and grievous, far beyond the rest, not to be expressed but negatively, as it is a privation of all happinesse, not to be endured" (3.4.2.4). As mental suffering superseded the physical in part 1, now spiritual supplants mental: Burton's melancholy preserves the eternal ranking of body-mind-spirit. Despair's symptoms are identical to those of other mental melancholies — fear, sorrow, suspicion, anxiety, fearful dreams and visions — but here all are greatly magnified and exacerbated. Burton reiterates delusion's role in the sufferings of the religious melancholics, who believe "the enormity of their offenses, the intolerable burden of their sins ... [is so great] that they account themselves reprobates, quite forsaken of God, already damned, past all hope of grace" against all the evidence of faith and sound doctrine. Burton emerges as preacher. He addresses a hypothetical individual who, with his "cauterized conscience" cannot accept that his sins are not unforgivable, the sins "of an higher straine [than of common sinners], even against the Holy Ghost himselfe, irremissible sinnes, sinnes of the first magnitude." Burton offers many consolations to bring such a sufferer to repentance and finally concludes with an exceptionally brief and pithy resolution: "take this for a corollary and conclusion, as thou tenderest thine owne welfare in this, and all other melancholy, thy good health of body and minde, observe this short precept, give not way to solitarinesse and idlenesse. *Be not solitary, be not idle"* (3.4.2.6).[29] Thus, the final word on alleviating melancholy awards its readers with physical remedies, not spiritual ones, and returns them to the world, out of unproductive (or scholarly) solitude.

II

Although very different in many respects, Donne and Burton run on parallel tracks in their understanding of religious melancholy. Each of Donne's many applications of the term echoes or resonates with Burton, and thus with the tradition he has capped. Donne is the more economical of the two men: melancholy is rarely his topic, but offers support for his topics. Like Burton, he frequently appeals to the dangers of melancholically deluded superstition. Donne, however, stays with the individual's peril, more rarely harping on the threat to society at large posed by melancholy.

When Donne uses melancholy in its humoural sense, he can draw on his own temperament and the history of his illnesses. Isaac Walton, in his biography of Donne, recognized his subject's humour. When he summarized Donne's nature, he wrote: "the melancholy and pleasant humour were in him so contempered, that each gave advantage to the other, and made his company one of the delights of mankind (*The Life of John Donne* in *Devotions*, 1)." Donne himself recounts fully the course of one serious illness in *Devotions upon Emergent*

Occasions, which Walton calls "a Sacred Picture of Spiritual Ecstasies, occasioned and applicable to the emergencies of [his] sickness" (in *Devotions* xxvi). Donne not only details the course of his illness, but, in effect, traces the progress of melancholy as one repeating note in the thorough bass of his life's song — a recurrent theme in his living, a note most audible during illness. This is the melancholy of disease, not of humour, nor even the sinful tendency which he exploits in his sermons:

> As he opens his musings, Donne considers the metaphor of man as a little world, and asks:
> Is he a world to himself only therefore, that he hath enough in himself, not only to destroy and execute himself, but to presage that execution upon himself; to assist the sickness, to antedate the sickness, to make the sickness the more irremediable by sad apprehensions, and, as if we would make a fire the more vehement by sprinkling water upon the coals, so to wrap a hot fever in cold melancholy, lest the fever alone should not destroy fast enough without this contribution, nor perfect the work (which is destruction) except we joined an artificial sickness of our own melancholy, to our natural, our unnatural fever. O perplexed discomposition, O riddling distemper, O miserable condition of man! (I Meditation)

Not only the words, but the tone reverberates with melancholy. The micro/macrocosmic positioning of man, elsewhere touted as one of humanity's glories, here serves to hasten his destruction. Melancholy and fear ("sad apprehension") add to the ravages of disease. The "artificial" illness, caused by disordered spirits and an excess of the melancholic humour, supports and advances the physical fever. Melancholy makes a dangerous, potentially evil situation far worse by creating delusional worries, perilous imaginings.

Having positioned himself as a melancholy man from the outset, Donne employs melancholy as a recurring, stabilizing and focusing theme. This strategy becomes clearest in the twelfth Meditation, the structural and logical center of the

Devotions, in which Donne confronts the intangible causes of his disease — of general suffering — in "vapours." He begins by deploring the nature that lets a vapour destroy so widely, so completely. The worst of the problem is that these destructive vapours emanate *from* us; although not, of course, volitionally, or we could "divide the rebuke, and chide ourselves as much as them." Donne recognizes that intemperate behavior can cause disease — too much inappropriate food, licentiousness, "madness upon misplacing or overbending our natural faculties," and that the diseases that emerge from such conduct can be called our fault. "But," he laments, "what have I done, either to breed or to breathe these vapours? They tell me it is my melancholy; did I infuse, did I drink in melancholy into myself? It is my thoughtfulness; was I not made to think? It is my study; doth not my calling call for that? I have done nothing wilfully, perversely toward it, yet must suffer in it, die by it." The causes he lists (abundance of melancholic humour, thoughtfulness, solitary study, abuses of health) are in every respect traditional; all the sources recognize them, and Burton agrees with Donne's assessment of their influence. Donne is not, however, satisfied with this conclusion.

Crucially, while what Donne observes during the progress of the *Devotions* can be attributed to melancholy, what he *does* with the observations and the disease itself cannot be called dependent on melancholy. Throughout the meditations, expostulations and prayers, Donne looks through his melancholy, shapes and focuses his experience, even of a near-fatal illness with it. Melancholy never masters him; he applies it. Donne is not limited by his perception of his human nature.

Melancholy, the grief burden, can draw a sinner back to his sins. Donne, in an early sermon, likens temptations to arrows that God strikes us with. So far from wearing armor, the sinner is likely to "supple [himself] by provocations." Even if he tries to remove the temptation, "he that does in some measure, soberly and religiously, goe about to draw out these arrows, yet never consummates, never perfects his own work; He pulls back the arrow a little way, and he sees *blood*, and he feels *spirit* to goe out with it, and he lets it alone: He forbears his sinfull companions, a little while, and he feels a *melancholy* take hold of him, the spirit and life of his life decays, and he falls to those companions againe" (2:1, 64).[30] Donne's simile is unadorned and unambiguous — even a little obvious — but melancholy serves as the motive feeling to return the sinner to his sins.

Lady Danvers's Commemoration sermon presents a picture of a woman resistant to the allures and agonies of melancholy right to the end of her life. Magdalen Danvers (George Herbert's mother, and a steadfast friend to Donne throughout their acquaintance) was Donne's pattern for the life of a faithful Christian woman. Although, he writes, her age and illness "had opened her to an overflowing of *Melancholie*," she never let it overcome her:

> Not that she ever lay under that *water*, but yet, had sometimes, some high Tides of it; and though this distemper would sometimes cast a cloud, and some halfe damps upon her naturall cheerfulnesse, and sociablenesse, and sometimes induce darke, and sad apprehensions, *Neverthelesse*, who ever heard, or saw in her, any such effect of *Melancholy* as to murmure, or repine, or dispute upon any of *Gods* proceedings, or to lodge a Jelousie, or Suspition of his mercy, and goodnesse towards her, and all hers? . . . Occasionall *Melancholy* had taken some hold in her; *Neverthelesse*, that never Ecclipst, never interrupted her cheerfull confidence, and assurance in *God*. (8:2, 86–87)[31]

Magdalen's didactic virtue lies in her resilience to melancholy's temptations, her refusal to doubt God. Donne insists she suffered the pangs and fears without accepting their conclusions. In this she is Christlike, for, as Donne pointed out in the same year, "even Christ himself had a sad soule towards his death, and a *Quare dereliquisti*, some apprehension, that God, though his God, had forsaken him. And that therefore, no man, how righteous soever, may presume, or passe away without feare and trembling" (8:1, 45).[32] Facing death, dying daily, is the closest analogue to immortality, if one can die for Christ or in Christ. It provides no fears because in such case death has an end, and "their reward that dye for Christ, and their peace, that dy in Christ, hath no end. Therefore was not S *Paul* afraid of melancholique apprehensions, by drawing his death into contemplation, and into discourse; he was not afraid to thinke, nor to talke of his deathe" (8:6, 169).[33] This is the kind of consolation offered to the melancholic sufferer, to refocus attention away from the fear and despair toward the goal: Donne rejoices that Lady Danvers never required reminding.

Lady Danvers suffered from the disease of melancholy, but she remained undeluded by it, unafflicted in her soul. Her devotion prevailed in spite of her melancholy. Although the world will not help a person to distinguish melancholic from legitimate sorrow, it will be quick to call any devout person melancholic. In fact, to a certain segment of the world, melancholic disease and religious involvement are, effectively, synonymous: "[W]*orldly* and *carnall* men . . . were offended in Christ, that he induced an inglorious, a contemptible Religion, a Religion that opposed the *Honours* of this world; and a sooty, and *Melancholique* Religion, a Religion that opposed the *Pleasures*, and delights of this world; and a sordid, and beggerly Religion, a Religion that opposed the *Gaine*, and the Profit of this world" (9:4, 115).[34] Addressing younger members of his courtly congregation, Donne warns them that their erstwhile companions ("fellow pupils under *Gamaliel*") will "think thy present fear of God but a childishness and pusilanimity, and thy present zeal to his service but an infatuation and a melancholy, and thy present application of thy self to God . . . but an argument of thy court-dispaire, and of thy falling off from former hopes there" (8:7, 182).[35]

There are always real dangers associated with examining

one's soul and conscience. It is, according to Donne, Burton and many others, an easy path to melancholic despair because it leads to an overestimation of one's own evil and an underestimation of God's power to pardon and relieve. Donne urges his congregation to

> [n]ever consider the judgement of God for sin alone, but in the company of the mercies of Christ. It is but the hissing of the Serpent, and the whispering of Satan, when he surprises thee in a melancholy midnight of dejection of spirit, and layes thy sins before thee then; Looke not upon thy sins so inseparably, that thou canst not see Christ too: ... Even the sense and remorse of sin is a dangerous consideration, but when the cup of salvation stands by me, to keep me from fainting. (8:8, 207)[36]

Midnight has always been recognized as particularly perilous, a time especially open to dark, cold, dry, melancholic disorders leading to despair. Burton opens his discussion of the devil's role in despair by looking at the terrors that can arise then:

> Sometimes hee [the devil, with God's permission] persecutes them with that worme of conscience.... The Poets call it *Nemesis*, but it is indeed Gods just judgement, *sero sed serio*, he strikes home at last, and setteth upon them *as a theefe in the night*.... If he finde them ... *pensive and sad*, [he tempts them] *to a desperate end*.... His ordinarie engine by which he produceth this effect, is the melancholy humour it selfe, which is *Balneum diaboli*, the Divels bath.... Blacke choler is a shooing horne, a bait to allure them, in so much that many writers make melancholy an ordinary cause, and a symptome of despaire. (Burton 3.4.2.3)

Donne challenges the sufferer to resist such dark, fruitless, even deadly temptation:

> *Blessed are they that mourne*, sayes Christ: But the blessednesse is not in the mourning, but because *they shall be comforted*. Blessed am I in the sense of my sins, and in the sorrow for them, but blessed therefore, because this sorrow leads me to my reconciliation to God, and the consolation of his Spirit. Whereas, if I sinke in this sorrow, in this dejection of

spirit, though it were Wine in the beginning, it is lees, and tartare in the end; Inordinate sorrow growes into sinfull melancholy, and that melancholy, into an irrecoverable desperation. (3:12, 270)[37]

As in many other places in the sermons, Donne does not intend to cause sorrow or burden his hearers with grief for their actions so much as to provide them a sure path to consolation. Unlike many contemporary preachers, he does not measure a sinner's repentance primarily by the degree of his sorrow, but by the direction that sorrow takes, the use the sufferer makes of it. Mourning one's sins is unquestionably necessary, but if that is as far as one gets, the whole point is destroyed, and one's sadness becomes grief, an intolerable, unnecessary encumbrance.

And yet, it must be admitted, *not* to weep for one's sins creates problems, too. In a sermon on a text from Psalm 32.3–4, Donne explores the dilemma of the illacrimate, the "unable-to-weep" person, identifying one cause of this inability as melancholy. He characterizes such a sinner as dried up by sin, "his bodily moysture was wasted, literally, the sinner is sooner infirmed, sooner deformed than another man." But ordinarily a sinner also has, naturally, a "*Humidium radicale* of the soule too: A tendernesse, and a disposition to bewayle his sins, with remorsefull teares." Peter, for instance, having betrayed Christ, wept bitterly, and, as long as he could weep, "his soul was not withered, his moysture was not dryed up." Donne quotes Horace: "The learned Poet hath given some character, some expression of the desperate and irremediable state of the reprobate, when he calls *Plutonem illacrymabilem*; There is the marke of his incorrigiblenesse, and so of his irrecoverablenesse, That he cannot weepe."[38] Donne distinguishes between "just-tears" which a sinner may shed—fruitlessly, for natural sorrow — and those tears shed from repentance: "All this while the miserable *sinner* weeps not, but the miserable *man*, All this while, though he have winter in his eyes, his soule is turned into the drought of summer" [italics added]. The danger of this continued obduracy is that one stays dry and cold, melancholic. One accepts each natural loss, instead of seeing in it direction for correction. If the obdurate sinner's health fails him, he has money; if he loses that,

> he [can] take up another comfort, that though health and wealth decay, though he be poore and weake, yet he hath learning, and philosophy, and morall constancy, and he can content himselfe with himselfe, he can make his study a Court, and a few Books shall supply to him the society and the conversation of many friends, there is another worme to devour this too, the hand of divine Justice shall grow heavy upon him, in a sense of an unprofitable retirednesse, in a disconsolate melancholy, and at last, in a stupidity, tending to desperation. (9:12, 290–91, 293)[39]

God will not allow a sinner to continue comfortably sinning. If that sinner chooses to blame his sorrows on disease, or on unfaithful friends, or loss of influence, each rationalization will bear its own outcomes, but one need not endure such delusional suffering. In the sermon quoting and interpreting the Beatitude, "Blessed are they that mourne" (see above), Donne reminds his listeners that

> The Wise-men of the East, by a lesse light, found a greater, by a Star, they found the Son of glory, Christ Jesus: But by darknesse, nothing: By the beames of comfort in this life, we come to the body of the sun, by the rivers, to the Ocean, by the cheerefulnesse of heart here, to the brightnesse, to the fulnesse of joy hereafter . . . as God loves a cheerefull giver, so he loves a cheerefull taker, that takes hold of his mercies and his comforts with a cheerefull heart, not onely without grudging, that they are no more, but without jealousie and suspition that they are not so much, or not enough. (3:12, 270)

Melancholy causes one to doubt falsely and to be suspicious of the efficacy and sufficiency of mercy; melancholy offers a natural explanation for the otherwise incredible disbelief in the word of God's promises.

The union that God created between himself and humanity by becoming Jesus, and making himself one body with us, should give us complete confidence and security in God's love. And, Donne continues, we should beware of anything that divides us from that confidence, for distrust of that union would be — must be, can only be — the ultimate, incontrovertible evidence of a disordered mind:

> this were *solutio Jesus*, a tearing in peeces, dissolving of Jesus, in the worst kinde that could be imagined, if I should teare my selfe from Jesus, or by any jealousie or suspicion of his mercy, or any horror in my own sinnes, come to thinke my selfe to be none of *his*, none of *him*. . . . And shall any sad soule come hither, to gather arguments, from our preaching, to *excommunicate* it selfe, or to pronounce an impossibility upon her owne salvation? . . . Wilt thou force God to second thy irreligious *melancholy*, and to condemne thee at last, because thou hast precondemned thy selfe, and renounced his mercy? (10:4, 117)[40]

Only a deeply ill soul can make it effectively impossible for God to enact mercy. God must "second" such an individual's self-condemnation because God has given all people free will, allowing a person to judge by his own wits, however disordered.

Melancholy, however physically constituted, becomes in Donne irreligious (or in other instances sullen, sinful, rebellious, inordinate, sordid, disconsolate, desperate and hellish) when the sufferer accepts the grief without a challenge or struggle, when he turns from sound health, sound doctrine, and goes his own way. God then must support that disastrous decision. Elliptically, Donne's melancholy becomes one reliable indication of God's mercy; melancholy arises only from imbalanced humours, and creates a plethora of mental symptoms that destroy an individual's ability to think, reason, trust, pray — that is, live — well. Because it is a disease, melancholy is not as terrifying as something supernatural or unknown. The grief of melancholy is neither eternal nor incurable.

Melancholy's ability to delude is not confined to the arena of spiritual struggle. It affects perception and discretion in the sector of human interaction as well. Donne's contribution to his age's reading of the melancholic disorder is most idiosyncratic and most characteristic in the realm of political interpretation. Like Burton, Donne sees in superstition a very clear indication of unhealthy domination by melancholy. The perception that papists emphasize gloom and morbid concentration on sins allows him to use the disease to attack a popular adversary in terms none of his hearers would likely mistake: "Be not apt to think heaven is an *Ermitage*, or a *Monastery*, or the way to heaven a sullen *melancholy*" (3:4, 121).[41] Since one of the most destructive symptoms of melancholic illness is desire for unhealthy solitude, the connection between hermitages and monasteries and melancholy would be transparent. The dangers of idolatry exercised Donne: "It is not enough that the State and the Church hath destroyed Idolatry so far as we said before; still there are weeds, still there are seeds: And therefore *Cave*, Take heed. But yet it is but *take heed*. It is not, take thought. *Afflict not thy self*, deject not thy self with ominous presages, and prophetical melancholy, [that] thy God will overthrow this Religion, and destroy this work which his right hand hath been a hundred years in repairing" (4:4, 137).[42] Seeking after fearsome interpretations of texts or after preachers who prophesy undoctrinal doom is evidence of melancholy. It is also melancholic to set up one's own sins as idols — as if they were things too great for God's mercy to destroy. Donne joins Burton and many other thoughtful divines in expressing these pitfalls in political terms.

Both extremes — radical Protestants and papists — represented occasions of great melancholic peril by the errors they promulgated. Donne insists that it is better to "forbeare some things" truly commanded by God than to do things that could cause a "distempered man" to go astray. It was as impossible to complete all the practices required by the Romans as it had been to fulfill the old Law. Donne insists "that this easinesse of admitting imaginary apparitions of spirits in the Papist, and this easinesse of submitting to the private spirit, in the Schismatike, hath produced effects equally mischievous: Melancholy being made the seat of Religion on the one side, by the Papist, and Phrenzy on the other side, by the Schismatick." In the final analysis, Donne feared the Romans were more apt to induce melancholy in their followers by their "easinesse of admitting Revelations, and Visions, and Apparitions of spirits, and Purgatory of souls" (8:5, 135).[43]

Any superstition that can hinder or detour a person is threatening. There are many who will try to maneuver Christians into unhealthy paths. Each individual has received in prayer, in sermons, in Scripture, the light by which he should live; each bears a candle. What happens to a candle's light when you open the door to the street to admit a stranger? The candle can be blown out. "If you open a door to a Supplanter, an Underminer, a Whisperer against your Religion; if there be a broken window, a woman loaden with sin, as the Apostle speaks [2 Tim. 3.16], and thereby dejected into an inordinate melancholy, (for such a melancholy as makes Witches, makes Papists too) if she be thereby as apt to change Religions now, as Loves before, and weary of this God as of that man" (4:3, 108), then if you admit "her" you risk losing your light from her company. Her sins, creating her grievous burden of melancholy, will likewise cause you to fall. Donne focuses on the role of the minister in this extended metaphor of dark melancholy and true light: "we have this calling from above. First then, it must be a light; not a calling taken out of the darknesse of melancholy, or darkness of discontent, or darkness of want and poverty, or darkness of a retir'd life, to avoid the mutual duties and offices of society: it must be a light, and a light that shines" (4:3, 109). From his own background, Donne knew the dangers of melancholy on soul and body. Because he, perhaps more than many, knew the seeming arbitrariness of temperament and disease, he had an unusual compassion for those caught by their natures, their bodies, their humoural balances. At the same time, he recognized how ephemeral these issues were, and, throughout his life, strove to present a balance between the undeniable grief of melancholy and the glory possible beyond it. In this compassionate severity he represents the culmination of the tradition of melancholy as it was expressed in the English Renaissance.

4 • Grief, Theater and Society in Thomas Heywood's *A Woman Killed with Kindness*

Michael McClintock

In the *Apology for Actors* (1612), a defense of drama against the attacks of antitheatrical pamphleteers, Thomas Heywood presents an argument for the centrality of theater in early modern English society.[1] Heywood incorporates a wide range of evidence, both classical and contemporary, to demonstrate that the theater is and always has been an upholder of order rather than a promoter of vice. The contemporary benefits of the theater, for Heywood, are visible even at the level of language itself. Before the advent of the public theater in the 1570s, the English language had been "the most harsh, vneuen, and broken language of the world, . . . and indeed a gallimaffry of many [languages], but perfect in none." But with the demands of a professional, commercial theater for new plays, playwrights began to experiment with and improve the language, so that, as Heywood concludes, "you see to what excellency our refined *English* is brought, that in these daies we are ashamed of that *Euphony* & eloquence which within these 60 yeares, the best tongues in the land were proud to pronounce" (F3v). A comparison of the theatrical language, and in particular the theatrical language used to express grief, of the Jacobean public theater with the language of mid-sixteenth century English drama confirms Heywood's observation. In a mid-sixteenth century drama such as Sackville and Norton's *Gorboduc* (1560), the euphony and eloquence Heywood mentions are evident throughout the play, and in particular at the play's emotional peaks. The prominence of rhetorical amplification and figures such as alliteration, interrogatio, exclamatio and anaphora suggests that euphony and eloquence were the verbal means through which the best mid-sixteenth century tongues in the land expressed grief on stage.[2]

Shakespeare's *Hamlet*, written at the end of the sixteenth century, marks a transitional moment in the dramatic language of grief. Many of Hamlet's soliloquies, for example, represent crises both in terms of Hamlet's inwardness and in terms of the means through which intense grief can be verbalized. Kier Elam, linking changes in the art of persuasion at the start of the seventeenth century to advancements in "the psycho-semiological understanding of human disposition and behaviour," has argued that Hamlet's passionate speeches mark not a repudiation of the rhetoric that characterized earlier emotional language in drama, but rather a shift in emphasis from prominent rhetorical schemes to "unrhetorical" rhetorical figures: figures such as aporia, interjectio and aposiopesis which break up the regularity of the speaker's language and create the illusion of spontaneous utterance.[3] As Elam notes, by the early seventeenth century, "the most effective figures in the expression of the passions are not semantic figures, the tropes, nor the so-called figures of thought, but, on the one hand, those figures of orientation and appeal intimately related to the movements of the body, and, on the other, those material, phonetic, syntactic, punctuational figures classed generically as the schemes" (149–50). In this essay, I would like to focus on two works by Thomas Heywood: the *Apology* and his domestic tragedy *A Woman Killed with Kindness*. Heywood illustrates a further step in the development of theatrical representations of grief on the early English public stage, particularly in terms of figures of appeal intimately related to the body. While *A Woman Killed with Kindness* does contain some standard rhetorical expressions of grief, the crucial moments of grief in the play are primarily visual rather than verbal. My analysis of *A Woman Killed with Kindness* will be prefaced by a closer look at the *Apology for Actors*, which directly challenges the antitheatricalist claim that the emotional power of theater leads to immorality and social chaos. In the *Apology*, Heywood gives the affective power of theater a central role in his justification of theater as an agent for social stability and prosperity. Understanding Heywood's conception of theater's affective power will help locate the representations of grief in *A Woman Killed with Kindness* within the broader context of the relationship between the public theater and society in Jacobean England.

For Thomas Heywood, the theater is and has been since classical times a vital source of social stability and human progress. It takes this leading role because of its affective power: by presenting scenes of intense emotions such as grief on stage, the theater is able to reform its spectators and, in turn, improve society. Where this essay differs from most other critical studies of the emotions in early modern literature is in terms of its theatrical orientation. When emotions such as grief or melancholy are discussed, typically the critical focus is dramatic rather than theatrical. Recent studies of literary melancholy by Lynn Enterline and Juliana Schiesari, for example, take a gender-based approach to melancholy and treat it as a symptom of a character that can be discussed in terms of psychoanalytic theory.[4] Their focus is dramatic in the sense that it does not go beyond the fictional boundaries of the drama in order to consider the representation of melancholy as a theatrical event, involving both the character and the audience. The groundwork for a theatrically based discussion of grief in early English drama has been laid by Albert H. Tricomi in *Reading Tudor-Stuart Texts Through Cultural Historicism*. Tricomi calls for an approach to early modern works that values the emotional or affective dimension of these texts:

> Affectivity is one of the principal means by which the plays exert their authority. Affectivity, moreover, is part of history, part of the lived experience of the past. Playmakers, by their recourse to it, persuasively addressed issues of their time and through it solicit our attention today. Inescapably, the production of affectivity is a constitutive part of the powerful production of valuing. By treating that affectivity responsively and critically, we enlarge the range of understanding by which our cultural- historicist and feminist concerns with representation may be represented to ourselves. Simply put, the affectivity of the past is a part of our cultural identity; denial of it is a debilitating blindness.[5]

Building on Tricomi's discussion, I will treat theatrical affectivity responsively and critically in order to demonstrate that Heywood's *Apology* as well as his *A Woman Killed with Kindness* both understand theatrical affectivity as a force that integrates society (contrary to the antitheatricalists' assertions) by regulating both gender identities and familial relations.

The power of theater over spectators' passions was one of the chief criticisms leveled by Elizabethan and Jacobean antitheatrical writers. Imagining a direct and intense relation between theatrical representation and emotional response in an audience, these writers described scenes in which hundreds or even thousands of spectators would emerge from a presentation of a romantic comedy inflamed with desire. In Philip

Stubbes's *The Anatomie of Abuses* (1583), for example, Stubbes's spokesman Philoponus asks his interlocutor, Spudeus, if he can deny that public theaters

> induce whordome & vnclennes? nay, are they not rather plaine deuourers of maydenly virginitie and chastitie? For proofe wherof, but marke the flocking and ru[n]ning to Theaters & curtens, daylie and hourely, night and daye, tyme and tyde to see Playes and Enterludes, where such wanton gestures, such bawdie speeches: such laughing and fleering: such kissing and bussing: such clipping and culling: Suche winckinge and glancinge of wanton eyes, and the like is vsed, as is wonderfull to behold. Than these goodly pageants being done, euery mate sorts to his mate, euery one bringes another homeward of their way verye freendly, and in their secret conclaues (couertly) they play y^e *Sodomits*, or worse.[6]

While the dangers that theater supposedly offered to audience members may seem simplistic and overly exaggerated to modern readers, the direct and almost automatic link between sight and emotional response found in antitheatrical literature echoes explanations found in the medical literature of the period.[7] The link between the senses and the passions was a very direct one, and it was this physiological factor that made the affectivity of theatrical spectacle appear so dangerous to the antitheatrical writers.

An Apology for Actors was one of several attempts by supporters of the theater to answer the antitheatrical polemicists' attacks. In his response, Heywood counters the supposed dangers that are perceived to lie in theatrical affectivity by turning affectivity into the theater's greatest contribution to society. Against the antitheatricalists' biblically based arguments, Heywood constructs a detailed argument, drawing on a wide range of classical, biblical, patristic and humanist sources in order to demonstrate theater's significant contributions throughout human history. In one of his most important points, Heywood suggests that theatrical affectivity is the source of the heroic actions of figures such as Hercules,

Alexander the Great and Julius Caesar. Heywood constructs a line of theatrical descent, in which a theatrical representation of the deeds of a valorous ancestor moves the male spectator to perform the deeds that eventually constitute his own heroic identity. The emulative process begins with Hercules, who witnessed a theatrical presentation of the deeds of his father, Jupiter, "Which being personated with liuely and well-spirited action, wrought such impression in his noble thoughts, that in meere emulation of his fathers valour . . . he perform'd his twelue labours" (B3r). The deeds of Hercules are dramatized for Theseus, and the deeds of Theseus for Achilles; Aristotle, teaching Alexander the Great, has a performance of the destruction of Troy enacted "in which the valour of *Achilles* was so naturally exprest, that it imprest the hart of *Alexander*, in so much that all his succeeding actions were meerly shaped after that patterne, and it may be imagined had *Achilles* neuer liued, *Alexander* had neuer conquered the whole world" (B3r). The final conqueror in Heywood's sequence, Julius Caesar, is similarly inspired by a theatricalization of Alexander's deeds. The implications of Heywood's heroic genealogy are clear: theatrical affectivity, far from inducing rampant lust as Stubbes had claimed, serves to make men more manly and to inspire heroic deeds. The author of a dedicatory poem attached to Heywood's treatise expresses a similar idea:

> What profit many may attain by playes,
> To the most critticke eye this booke displaies,
> Braue men, braue acts, being brauely acted too,
> Makes, as men see things done, desire to do.
>
> (a2r)

For Heywood, though, theater's affective power is not simply a "desire to do," but instead involves an actual transformation of character: "so bewitching a thing is liuely and well spirited action, that it hath power to new mold the harts of spectators and fashion them to the shape of any noble and notable attempt" (B4r). Theater, according to Heywood, does transform identity as the antitheatricalists argued, but these transformations are presented as improvements on rather than deformations of masculine identity.

If male spectators are linked with the heroic subjects of history plays in Heywood's treatise, female spectators are linked with the affective subjects of tragedy. In this respect, Heywood's treatise is only one of several early modern discussions linking tragedy and emotions traditionally labeled feminine.[8] But in the eyes of the antitheatricalists, women were seen as facing special risk when they attended the public theater. For example, the author of *A Third Blast of Retrait from Plaies and Theaters* (1580) claims that "Some citizens wives ... have even on their deathbeds with teares confessed, that they have received at those spectacles such filthie infections, as have turned their minds from chast cogitations, and made them of honest women light huswives."[9] In a discussion of women in the public theater, Jean Howard has argued that the threat to women as perceived by antitheatricalists like the author of the *Third Blast* was less a direct physical danger than the fact that the woman became "the object of promiscuous gazing."[10] Women in the theater were in an ambiguous social and moral locale where their status (married/unmarried) and their character (good woman/whore) was not immediately apparent. Also, Howard argues (79), the woman in the theater may have been empowered to some degree by her ability to look, judge and exercise autonomy in a way that went against her subordinate status outside the theater. Heywood offers two examples of female spectators in the *Apology* that serve to allay many of the anxieties Howard finds expressed in the antitheatrical literature's discussions of women in the theater. And just as Heywood argued that the impact of theatrical affectivity on male spectators served to reinforce traditional notions of heroic masculine identity, so too do his examples of women in the theater reinforce traditional notions of feminine identity. The affective responses of both women, rather than unfixing them socially and morally, instead reveal the women's social and moral trespasses and, after their punishments, reassert the ability of a traditional patriarchal society to keep its members in place. In both of these episodes Heywood understands the affective power of theater in much the same terms as Hamlet does: theater has the power to catch the conscience, and by arousing feelings of guilt and grief it can have social benefits that extend beyond the walls of the playhouse.

Both of Heywood's female spectators, like Claudius in *Hamlet*, have committed crimes that only come to light when particularly powerful theatrical scenes provide enough of a parallel to the hidden crime that conscience is able to overcome the women's ability to keep the deeds secret. The crimes themselves — both women have murdered their husbands — are particularly suited to Heywood's polemical purpose as well, since these examples illustrate the theater's ability to regulate and punish, rather than to promote, social and sexual trespasses. In the first example, a scene in which a married woman who had murdered her husband in order to take a younger man as a lover and was visited in her chamber by the ghost of her dead husband caused a female spectator to reveal her parallel crime. She "suddenly skritched and cryd out Oh my husband, my husband! I see the ghost of my husband fiercely threatning and menacing me." She later confesses "that seuen yeares ago, she, to be possest of such a Gentleman (meaning him) had poysoned her husband, whose fearefull image personated it selfe in the shape of that ghost: whereupon the murdresse was apprehended, before the Iustices further examined, & by her voluntary confession after condemned" (G1v–2r). Heywood's second confession is triggered by a particularly brutal scene in which a character is murdered by having a nail driven through his skull. During the scene's performance, "the audience might on a sodaine vnderstand an out-cry, and loud shrike in a remote gallery, and pressing about the place, they might perceiue a woman of great grauity, strangely amazed, who with a distracted & troubled braine oft sighd out these words: Oh my husband, my husband!" This disruption remains unexplained for several days until the local Sexton visits the Churchwarden

> to tell him of a strange thing happening him in the ripping vp of a graue: see here (quoth he) what I haue found, and shewes them a faire skull, with a great nayle pierst quite through the braine-pan, but we cannot coniecture to whom it should belong, nor how long it hath laine in the earth, the graue being confused, and the flesh consumed. At the report of this accident, the woman, out of the trouble of her afflicted conscience, discouered a former murder. For 12 yeares ago, by driuing that nayle into that skull, being the head of her husband, she had trecherously slaine him. This being publickly confest, she was arraigned, condemned, adiudged, and burned. (G2r–v)

Heywood's examples of the affective power of theater are clearly designed to refute the antitheatricalists' arguments by presenting the theater in terms that make it a strong supporter of a traditional patriarchal society. Theater does not make male spectators effeminate, as some might claim; instead, it makes them more manly.[11] Theater does not drive married women from their husbands and into the arms of lovers; instead, by creating what Steven Mullaney calls a "theater of apprehension," it activates their consciences and allows their hidden crimes to be publicly revealed.[12] The affective power of theater, in other words, acts as a social regulator rather than a social disintegrator, making men more manly while chastening and subduing unruly women.

Turning from Heywood's *Apology* to his domestic tragedy *A Woman Killed with Kindness*, we can observe Heywood's theories regarding theater's affective power put into action on the public stage. Affectivity — a character's ability to project or respond to intense emotion — is one of the primary measures of moral worth in Heywood's *A Woman Killed with*

Kindness.¹³ At key moments in both the main plot and the subplot of Heywood's tragedy, the central female characters (Anne Frankford and Susan Mountford) display a strong emotional reaction to the familial crises in which they find themselves. These affective displays have an emotional and intellectual impact on the male characters who have the strongest sexual bonds with the female characters: Anne Frankford's husband, John Frankford, and Sir Francis Acton, the future husband of Susan Mountford. The ability to be moved by affective displays proves to be a token of moral growth in the male characters; conversely, characters like the villain Wendoll who remain unmoved by female tears simply confirm their status as Calvinist reprobates incapable of reform and destined for an eternity in hell. The two scenes of intense emotional display in *A Woman Killed with Kindness* present us, first in a straightforward manner and later in a more problematic manner, with an effective dramatic embodiment of the theory of affective theater outlined in Heywood's *Apology for Actors*. For the female spectators at *A Woman Killed with Kindness*, Heywood's affective spectacles present images of feminine identity defined by traditional virtues such as familial loyalty and chastity and by the ability to respond emotionally to suffering and sin. For the male spectators, Heywood offers what might be called a domestic masculine identity in which, within the context of a spousal relationship, the rigidity of masculine reason and aggression (Acton's vendetta against the Mountfords or Frankford's legal but ethically questionable punishment of Anne) is tempered by the female's traditionally superior capacity for emotion. The ultimate result of these moments of theatrical affectivity should be, according to Heywood's theory, the strengthening of the traditional social roles of husbands and wives in the society within which Heywood's theater operates.

Affectivity is introduced as the central measure of moral virtue in the play with the first entry of Susan Mountford in the third scene. In contrast to the artificial courtly melancholy that is parodied by Nick in scene 2 (24–26), the grief felt by Charles after he murders two of Acton's men and by Susan in empathy with Charles reveals the affective bond that links brother and sister. Charles's remorse over the murder of Acton's servants is presented in the religious language of sin and conscience:

> Call me a surgeon, sister, for my soul;
> The sin of murder it hath pierced my heart,
> And made a wide wound there, . . .
> . . . .
> My conscience is become my enemy,
> And will pursue me more than Acton can.
> (3.66–68, 72–73)

Susan, for her part, encourages Charles to flee in order to save his life, even though for her Charles's absence amounts to "black despair" (3.82) and will cause her to become a watery icon of grief:

> And yet to live one week
> Without my brother Charles, through every cheek
> My streaming tears would downwards run so rank
> Till they could set on either side a bank,
> And in the midst a channel; so my face
> For two salt water brooks shall still find place.
> (3.83–87)

Finally, as Charles is led away by the sheriff, the reciprocal nature of the affective bond between Susan and Charles appears. Although Susan's only words during Charles's arrest are "O God! O God!," the intensity of her grief is felt by Charles: "Sweet sister, every strain / Of sorrow from your heart augments my pain; / Your grief abounds and hits against my breast" (3.106–08). Susan's "abounding" grief picks up the earlier imagery linking grief and water, where tears grew to channels and then brooks, and takes it one step further. Here Susan's grief becomes a wave, breaking over the boundary of her character and hitting against her brother's breast. The ability of grief to break the rigid boundaries between characters and establish emotional links between them is key to the resolution of Heywood's play: Susan's grief transforms Acton from villain to a lover of virtue (and later, Susan's husband), while Anne's spectacular grief and death allows for reconciliation and forgiveness between her and Frankford at the moment of her death.

The affective bond between Susan and Charles stands in contrast to the bonds between Frankford and Anne as well as Wendoll and Anne: in the latter two cases, the bonds are notable for their absence of affection. The opening scene of the play presents the celebrations following Frankford and Anne's wedding. In this scene, Anne's relationship to Frankford is repeatedly described in material terms: Charles praises the "ornaments" (1.15) of her birth, her education and her beauty while later he compares her to "a well-made suit" and "a chain of gold" (1.59, 64). And while Charles's comments might be seen as mere flattery rather than an accurate description of Frankford and Anne's relationship, we find the same language used by Frankford himself later in the play. Discussing the happiness he feels as a result of his birth, his wealth and his education, he at last comes to the chief source of his happiness: "I have a fair, a chaste, and loving wife, / Perfection all, all truth, all ornament" (4.11–12). The play's emphasis on Anne's ornamental status suggests that her marriage to Frankford is based more on social advantage than on affection, an impression that is reinforced theatrically: unlike Susan and Charles, Anne and Frankford are never alone together on stage, and thus lack the opportunities that the Mountfords have to display affection.

The intensity of the grief projected first by Susan Mountford and later by Anne Frankford acts as a force in *A Woman Killed with Kindness* which is almost as strong as the predestination that compels Wendoll to sin.¹⁴ Susan Mountford's grief provides a model by which we can understand the final scenes of the play, in which Anne Frankford undergoes her own intense grief and dies. In those scenes in which Susan grieves, her grief is physiological rather than verbal: unlike her brother Charles or the villain/reprobate Wendoll, who are given soliloquies in which to verbalize their grief, Susan's grief is presented dramatically through a silent language of gestures and tears. This silent language is, however, a persuasive one. The sight of Susan's grief brings about what O. B. Hardison calls a moral catharsis in Sir Francis Acton, converting his malice toward the Mountfords into a love of virtue as personified in Susan; his moral cure is rewarded in social terms when he marries Susan.¹⁵ Acton's transformation is sudden and is as irresistible as Wendoll's progress toward adultery with Anne Frankford. Initially, Acton plans to continue his revenge against the Mountfords by offering to "bribe the fool [Susan] / To shame herself by lewd dishonest lust" (7.81–82). But the sight of Susan silently grieving — Malby, Acton's servant, says "See where the poor sad gentlewoman stands" (7.87) — leads to a spiritual conversion in Acton the moment he sees her:

> But stay, my heart, O what a look did fly
> To strike my soul through with thy piercing eye.
> I am enchanted, all my spirits are fled,
> And with one glance my envious spleen struck dead.
> . . . .
> She was an angel in a mortal's shape,
> And ne'er descended from old Mountford's line.
>
> (7.91–94, 100–01)

The effect of this transformation on Acton is both moral and social. Not only does he abandon his hatred of the Mountford family and restore Sir Charles to his former social station, he offers to marry Susan Mountford, thus ending her ambiguous social status. As a fatherless, unmarried young woman (7.15–26), Susan Mountford lacks a clear place in the patriarchal social order—her position is as socially unfixed as, according to Jean Howard's argument, the female public theater spectator's was. The ultimate benefit of her affective grief, then, is to reinsert her into that traditional social order in her new role as Acton's wife.

One characteristic that Susan Mountford and Anne Frankford share is the silent, iconic nature of their grief: both women have their greatest affective impact when they are silent images of grief. By contrast, masculine grief in the play is discursive rather than silent, and reflexive rather than affective. Both Sir Charles and Wendoll have scenes in which they grieve, but unlike the female characters, both male characters are given long soliloquies in which they can reflect on their condition.[16] Also, by wrestling with their grief in soliloquy, both Charles and Wendoll are represented as characters with interiority who have the ability to reform their character as a result of their inner deliberations. We saw earlier how Heywood's *Apology for Actors* suggested that the affective power of theater reinforced traditional gender roles, making men more heroically masculine and revealing the trespasses of women who stray from their subordinate role. It can be argued that *A Woman Killed with Kindness* similarly reinforces traditional models of gender in its representations of discursive masculine and silent feminine grief. Ultimately, however, Heywood places greater value on the affective and social powers of silent female grief than he does on the discursive and individuating grief of his male characters.

Anne Frankford's experience of intense grief is primarily visual rather than verbal, and the sight of her suffering brings about a moral cure in Frankford, who finally, at the moment of her death, establishes an emotional bond with her. Like Susan Mountford's grief, Anne Frankford's pathos and death also have a socially reparative role. What differentiates Anne Frankford's grief from Susan Mountford's is, as Lisa Hopkins argues, Heywood's addition of "art" to the popular domestic tragedy form.[17] In the Frankford plot, and particularly at those moments of greatest emotional intensity, Heywood invests the domestic events with extra symbolic and thematic value. Thus, for example, Wendoll's seduction of Anne is offered as a replay of the serpent's temptation of Eve, while Wendoll's betrayal of Frankford's hospitality is compared to Judas's betrayal of Christ (6.176–79; 8.106–08; 13.76–78).

Part of the symbolic heightening Heywood adds to Anne Frankford's grief scene involves the lute that her husband finds at home and sends after her.[18] When he finds the lute, Frankford transforms it, through a series of plays on words, into an emblem of the harmony that once existed in his marriage to Anne:

> Her lute! O God, upon this instrument
> Her fingers have run quick division,
> Sweeter than that which now divides our hearts.
> These frets have made me pleasant, that have now
> Frets of my heartstrings made.
>
> (15.13–17)

When Frankford's servant Nick delivers the lute to Anne, she continues the pattern of emblematization begun by her husband: "I know the lute. Oft have I sung to thee; / We are both out of tune, both out of time" (16.18–19). The symbolic weight generated by Anne's lute is carried one step further, however, when she begins to play a lament and is overheard by the hidden Wendoll. Wendoll, observing the affective power of her music on her traveling companions, compares Anne to the mythological figure Orpheus:

> She in the field laments. . . .
> So poets write that Orpheus made the trees
> And stones to dance to his melodious harp,
> Meaning the rustic and the barbarous hinds,
> That had no understanding part in them;
> So she from these rude carters tears extracts,
> Making their flinty hearts with grief to rise
> And draw down rivers from their rocky eyes.
>
> (16.51–58)

The comparison of Anne to Orpheus provides Heywood not only with a means of adding extra mythological heightening to Anne's lamentation but also with a means of highlighting his sense of the socially reparative power of affectivity in the play. The Orpheus myth told by Wendoll was frequently invoked by Renaissance rhetoricians to explain the origins of their art and of civil society. Orpheus's ability to move "the rustic and the barbarous hinds" with the affective force of his music was seen as analogy for the orator's ability to move an audience with the force of his eloquence. The myth also served to explain the origins of human civilization: just as Orpheus was able to make base matter move harmoniously to music, so the original orators used their eloquence to persuade the rustic and barbarous hinds to live in harmony.[19] By comparing the affective force of Anne's laments to the Orpheus myth, Heywood suggests not only her ability to move those not normally susceptible to emotion (the "rude carters") but also the larger reparative social role her grief will play in the interaction among the stage, the audience and society at large.

When Anne asks one of her attendants to smash the lute on her coach's wheel, she ends any possibility that her Orphic abilities might lead to a full restoration of her relationship with her husband. Instead, she adopts a silent and more iconic form of grief, which recalls Susan Mountford's earlier scene of theatrical affectivity. This physical manifestation of Anne's grief as tears, followed in the next scene by its manifestation as bodily suffering, brings about the more large-scale transformations suggested by the Orpheus analogy. Anne emphasizes the visual nature of her intense grief and asks her audience to describe the picture of her suffering body to her husband rather than attempt to put her grief itself into words:

> You have beheld the woefullest wretch on earth,
> A woman made of tears. Would you had words
> To express but what you see; my inward grief
> No tongue can utter. Yet, unto your power

> You may describe my sorrow, and disclose
> To thy sad master my abundant woes.
>
> . . . .
>
> I have no more to say. Speak not for me,
> Yet you may tell your master what you see.
>
> (16.78–83, 94–95)

Anne's Orphic, persuasive power does not lie in words, as it did for the rhetoricians who also adopted the Orpheus myth. Instead, it is her body, with its tears and suffering, which moves her companions' hearts to grief.

Just as Susan Mountford's grief led to the moral transformation of Sir Francis Acton, Anne Frankford's grief leads to the moral transformation of her husband. Before Master Frankford visits his wife on her deathbed, Heywood's audience is shown again that the index of a male character's moral worth in *A Woman Killed with Kindness* is his ability (or lack thereof) to respond to grief. When Anne presents herself to her companions and to the theater audience as "A woman made of tears" (16.79), the contrasting reactions of two minor male characters underline the moral distinction Heywood makes between them. Nick, the loyal servant who revealed Anne's adultery to her husband, is moved to tears by the spectacle of Anne's grief. He promises Anne that he will report to Frankford the affective force of the scene he has just witnessed: "I'll say you wept; I'll swear you made me sad. / Why, how now, eyes? What now? What's here to do? / I am gone, or I shall straight turn baby too" (16.67–69). The fact that Anne's grief moves Nick to tears is further proof of his good nature, just as, in an aside coming immediately after Nick's speech, Wendoll confirms his status as a reprobate by his inability to weep: "I cannot weep; my heart is all on fire. / Cursed be the fruits of my unchaste desire" (16.70–71). Anne's deathbed scene continues the affective spectacle begun in the previous scene and results in a healing of the onstage community as they unite in their tears.

At the center of the final scene of *A Woman Killed with Kindness* is the suffering body of Anne Frankford; she enters *"in her bed"* (17.38.1), and her imminent grief-induced death provides an affective focus for the audiences on and off stage. In preparation for the reformation of John Frankford, Sir Francis Acton undergoes a second moral transformation as the result of an affective spectacle. Before Anne's bedridden body enters the scene, Acton criticizes Frankford's lenient punishment of Anne. For Acton, marital transgressions deserve more violent punishments:

> My brother Frankford showed too mild a spirit
> In the revenge of such a loathed crime.
> . . . .
>
> Had it been my case
> Their souls at once had from their breasts been freed.
> Death to such deeds of shame is the due meed.
> (17.16–17, 20–22)

Acton's support for marital violence dissolves, however, when he views Anne Frankford's grieving, dying body:

> I came to chide you, but my words of hate
> Are turned to pity and compassionate grief.
> I came to rate you, but my brawls, you see,
> Melt into tears, and I must weep by thee.
> (17.63–66)

The affective spectacle of Anne's grief effectively reshapes Acton's masculine identity, replacing the rigid logic of crime and punishment ("Death to such deeds of shame is the due meed") with an emotional understanding based on "pity and compassionate grief," tears and weeping.

Frankford is the last character to arrive at Anne's deathbed and his initial cold inquiry — "How do you, woman?" (17.74) — suggests that he still holds the same dispassionate attitude toward his wife that he held when he sent her into exile earlier in the play. The "kindness" in Frankford's punishment lies in its avoidance of the physical violence endorsed by Sir Francis Acton.[20] Instead, Frankford's punishment employs psychological violence, separating Anne from her husband, her family and her home, and thereby ripping her from the social sphere that, in a patriarchal society, defined her very existence. Carried to its Acton-like logical conclusion, Anne's grief, suffering and death apart from everything that defined her domestic identity are fitting punishments for a crime (adultery) that undermines the stability of the domestic sphere.[21] But the spectacle of Anne's grief in this final scene moves Frankford from his passive notion of kindness, which involves simply eschewing violence, to a more active notion of kindness, which involves sympathy and ultimately a reparation of the psychological violence done to Anne through his punishment. Earlier, Anne's requests for pardon were rebuffed (13.80–90); in this scene, Frankford is moved not only to pardon her but also to express sympathy:

> As freely from the low depth of my soul
> As my Redeemer hath forgiven his death,
> I pardon thee. I will shed tears for thee,
> Pray with thee, and in mere pity
> Of thy weak state I'll wish to die with thee.
>
> (17.93–97)

Frankford's tears mark the first time in the play that he has expressed his emotional attachment to Anne, empathizing with her feelings rather than considering her only in relation to his own feelings. Their union in tears also recalls the earlier representation of the affective bond between Susan Mountford and her brother Sir Charles, where tears again signified a strong emotional bond. The growth of "kindness" in Frankford, in the sense of the term used by Cynthia Lewis, also marks a reformation of masculine identity in Frankford.[22] Like Acton, Frankford has his rigid logic of crime and "kind" punishment replaced by an emotionally based sense of "kindness" as empathy as a result of Anne's affective spectacle.

The conclusion of *A Woman Killed with Kindness* displays an unresolved paradox in Heywood's understanding of theater's affective power. On the one hand, Frankford's reformed masculine identity allows him to heal to a degree some of the psychological damage he inflicted on Anne by separating her from her domestic sphere. In his final speech to her, he restores the titles that define Anne's domestic identity:

> My wife, the mother to my pretty babes.
> Both those lost names I do restore thee back,
> And with this kiss I wed thee once again.
> Though thou art wounded in thy honoured name,
> And with that grief upon thy deathbed liest,
> Honest in heart, upon my soul thou diest.
>
> (17.115–20)

The affective spectacle of Anne's grief moves Frankford to repair the familial bonds that had been shattered by Anne's adultery and his subsequent punishment. In this sense, the final scene of Heywood's tragedy follows the ideas of affective theater outlined in the *Apology for Actors*, where examples of affective theatrical spectacle were introduced in order to demonstrate the ability of theatre to ultimately reinforce traditional notions of social order. At the same time, though, Heywood does not care to overturn his culture's Calvinist moral code in which the wages of sin are death. Anne's death obviously qualifies the degree to which Frankford's restoration of her domestic identity can be considered meaningful. However, given the pathos of Anne's death, Heywood can have both a strict moral lesson as well as an affective reformation of identities and reparation of the traditional social order emerge from the conclusion of his tragedy.

Grief in *A Woman Killed with Kindness* operates in the domestic sphere rather than in the cosmic realm of a tragedy like *King Lear*. But this difference in scale need not mean a difference in literary quality. Heywood's tragedy illustrates the relations among affective theater, gender and society that he treats directly in his *Apology for Actors*. Both works imagine a role for theater in society that reinforces traditional gender relations. But at the same time, this positive view of theater's affective power put Heywood at odds with antitheatrical writers, who saw the theater as a disrupter of masculine and feminine identity as well as of society as a whole. Heywood's affective tragedy does indeed, as T. S. Eliot wrote, present "a drama of common life,"[23] but in Heywood's view it is this common life, held together by affective bonds, that forms the stable base of the society in which his theater operates.

5 • The Action of Grief in Herbert's "The Church"

Louis L. Martz

Grief is a dominant theme in religious art and devotional literature of the Renaissance.[1] How could it be otherwise, when the central figure is the "servant" of Isaiah's prophecy: "A man of sorrows, and acquainted with grief," the man who, as the next verse says, "hath borne our griefs, and carried our sorrows" (53:3, 4). George Herbert uses the word in the plural when he writes to Nicholas Ferrar, saying that he has composed his notes on Valdesso with "some care, which I forbare not in the midst of my griefes."[2] He is referring to the pain and suffering of the chronic illness that caused his death only five months later. These are the physical griefs that he laments in his poems "Affliction (I)" and "The Crosse," but such pains are only the base from which another grief arises, the mental anguish that comes from the way in which his illness has prevented him from achieving his hopes for advancement in the church, a disappointment especially painful when he considers that he has given up all hope of worldly fame in order to serve the church. And now, he says in "Affliction" (I), his friends die, adding grief for them to all his other griefs:

> Thus doth thy power crosse-bias me, not making
> Thine own gift good, yet me from my wayes taking.
> Now I am here, what thou wilt do with me
>   None of my books will show.
>
>   (53–56)

None of my books? Not even the Bible? How much lower in despair can one go? But he goes one step lower: "Well, I will change the service, and go seek / Some other master out" (63–64). "Master" is capitalized in both manuscripts, thus stressing the shock that brings about an abrupt change of heart, as Chana Bloch has noted, for this is the word by which the disciples constantly address Jesus.[3] And so, in the final couplet he throws himself upon the mercy of the "deare God" (65) who has, he knows, been listening to this entire outpouring of griefs.

"Grief," then, is a complex word in Herbert's day. It can refer to a wound, or to any form of physical or mental affliction; it may also hold the meaning of a "grievance": "A wrong or injury which is the subject of formal complaint or demand for redress" (*OED*) — the very subject of the two poems of complaint that I have just mentioned. Every possible meaning of the word is implied in the first poem laid upon the altar of the broken heart in Herbert's "The Church": "The Sacrifice," where the insistent refrain, "Was ever grief like mine?," repeated in 63 stanzas,[4] brings out every nuance of the word, especially the grief that Christ feels when he considers human ingratitude for all the favors given by God. This refrain has two significant variations. The first comes at the climax of Christ's torment: "*But, O my God!, my God!* why leav'st thou me," where the refrain changes to "Never was grief like mine" (216). And then at the very end the same line is repeated:

> But now I die; now all is finished.
> My wo, mans weal: and now I bow my head.
> Onely let others say, when I am dead,
> > Never was grief like mine.
>
> (249–52)

Here, as Empson points out, the call to remember Christ's Passion is accompanied by the threat of punishment for human sin, as predicted earlier in the poem:

> Weep not, deare friends, since I for both have wept
> When all my tears were bloud, the while you slept:
> Your tears for your own fortunes should be kept:
> > Was ever grief like mine?
>
> (149–52)[5]

That cry, as applied to human grief, emphasizes the self-centered nature of such outcries, where the human sufferer, in his extremity, feels that somehow he has been singled out for torment: "Never was grief like *mine!*"

Such is the anguish that runs throughout "The Church," as the word "grief" in various forms, after "The Sacrifice," is repeated more than 60 times, supplemented and amplified by the related tears, groans, sighs and cries of pain, both physical and mental. In the final version of "The Church" these cries of grief are constantly intermingled with the memory of Christ's grief and of the opening poem in which that grief is commemorated. Thus in the third poem under the title "Affliction," the poet turns a hint of profanity into a prayer of consolation:

> My heart did heave, and there came forth, *O God!*
> By that I knew that thou wast in the grief,
> To guide and govern it to my relief
>
> . . . .
>
> Thy life on earth was grief, and thou art still
> Constant unto it, making it to be
> A point of honour, now to grieve in me,
> > And in thy members suffer ill.
>
> (1–3, 13–16)

In this way allusions to grief, in all its forms, serve to bind the poems of Herbert's "Church" into a subtle unity.

The sin of pride that lies in many of these complaints is most obviously revealed in the tautly controlled little poem headed "Submission":

> But that thou art my wisdome, Lord,
>   And both mine eyes are thine,
> My minde would be extreamly stirr'd
>   For missing my designe.
>
> (1–4)

He speaks as though both God and the reader are unaware of the poems in which he shows himself to be "extreamly stirr'd." And so he goes on blandly to suggest that God might do more for him:

> Were it not better to bestow
>   Some place and power on me?
> Then should thy praises with me grow,
>   And share in my degree.
>
> (5–8)

How generous he is to share his rewards with God! But at once he realizes the folly of this offer:

> But when I thus dispute and grieve,
>   I do resume my sight,
> And pilfring what I once did give,
>   Disseize thee of thy right.
>
> (9–12)

"Disseize" is a legal term meaning "to dispossess (a person) of his estates, etc., usually wrongfully or by force" (*OED*). "Resume" also has legal overtones, meaning "To take back to oneself (something previously given or granted)."[6] But who owns those eyes and the "sight" which this speaker says he has made as a gift to God? The second line of the poem may at first be read as a recognition that his eyes belong to God by right of Creation: "Who made the eyes but I" as the Host says in "Love (III)." But now in this stanza and the last, it would appear that God owns the eyes only by way of gift. This is a misunderstanding that the speaker takes pains to correct in "Obedience," where the earlier part of the poem may seem to imply a contract between two parties, but the seventh stanza, after the sixth has recalled the sacrifice of Christ, retracts any such inference:

> Where in the Deed there was an intimation
>   Of a gift or donation,
> Lord, let it now by way of purchase go.
>
> (33–35)

The sacrifice of Christ has made it possible for the speaker's heart "To passe it self and all it hath to thee" (8).

But now in this faulty "submission" the speaker goes on to suggest that perhaps the ways of the world are not the ways of God:

> How know I, if thou shouldst me raise,
>   That I should then raise thee?
> Perhaps great places and thy praise
>   Do not so well agree.
>
> (13–16)

However great the place, is it possible for a human creature to "raise" God? Ignoring this problem, the speaker decides that, all things considered, he will let God keep the "gift":

> Wherefore unto my gift I stand;
>   I will no more advise:
> Onely do thou lend me a hand,
>   Since thou hast both mine eyes.
>
> (17–20)

This speaker has the presumption to "advise" God. Nothing could show the hollowness of this "submission" better than this word "advise," an action which the speaker continues in the last two lines. This bleak little poem seems to live in a world without grace, without awareness of the redemption offered by Christ's sacrifice. The poem stands as a stark condemnation of the complaints against God's justice expressed in other poems.

But, in an obverse way, much the same problem appears in the more positive poem, "The Pearl," where, despite the biblical reference to the parable of the rich man in Matthew (13.45), an ominous sense of pride emerges from the speaker's long account of his knowledge of "the wayes of Learning," "the wayes of Honour" and "the wayes of Pleasure" (1, 11, 21). Can the brief declaration that closes the first three stanzas — "Yet I love thee" — outweigh the impact of this list of worldly experiences, abilities and accomplishments? Not so, as he admits in the finale:

> Yet through these labyrinths, not my groveling wit,
> But thy silk twist let down from heav'n to me,
> Did both conduct and teach me, how by it
>   To climbe to thee.
>
> (37–40)

He is the recipient of special grace, with perhaps an overtone of Calvinist election. But the calm security of this poem is immediately shattered by the poem that follows, "Affliction (IV)," one of the most violent outpourings of grief in the entire book:

> Broken in pieces all asunder,
>   Lord, hunt me not,
>   A thing forgot,
> Once a poore creature, now a wonder,
> A wonder tortur'd in the space
>   Betwixt this world and that of grace.
>
> (1–6)

But at the close his prayer for God's help restores his sense of security:

> Then shall those powers, which work for grief,
>   Enter thy pay,
>   And day by day

> Labour thy praise, and my relief;
>   With care and courage building me,
>   Till I reach heav'n, and much more, thee.
>
> (25–30)

The powers of the soul, restored by grace, can now carry on their proper work of building back the essential "me."

The recovery of that individual being is then demonstrated in the next poem, "Man," which takes such an optimistic, humanistic view of man that one may well wonder whether it really belongs in this "Church."[7] Talking with God in friendly confidence, Herbert sums up the benefits that God has showered upon man. There is no word of sin, nothing of total depravity; the poem seems to imagine man as created before the Fall. "Man is all symmetrie, / Full of proportions, one limbe to another, / And all to all the world besides" (13–15). The whole poem evokes a sense of undivided well-being. How can this comport with the religious scene set forth by Calvinism? It does not, but no matter: the poem plays its part in the immense variety of religious moods recorded in this "The Church." The poems range from the sense of utter desertion by God to the declaration of "Prayer (II)":

> Of what an easie quick accesse,
>   My blessed Lord, art thou! how suddenly
>   May our requests thine eare invade!
> To shew that state dislikes not easinesse,
> If I but lift mine eyes, my suit is made:
> Thou canst no more not heare, then thou canst die.
>
> (1–6)

How can we reconcile this with such a poem as "Deniall," where the speaker remembers the times "When my devotions could not pierce / Thy silent eares" (1–2), where he cries out in anguish for some answer, "But no hearing" — a phrase twice (15, 20) uttered? But of course no reconciliation is needed: these poems represent dramatized moments of experience, mirroring the fluctuations of the spiritual life, as well as the inconsistencies of theological doctrines. The power of the book lies in its continuous striving to comprehend opposite states of mind, just as in Herbert's day his outward church was striving to deal with its disagreements over predestination and free will, sufficient faith or need of works, real presence or symbolic witness in the sacrament of the altar. All these issues are dramatically represented in the many griefs that beset the speakers in Herbert's poetical "Church," notably the speaker who laments "Church-rents and schismes" and the controversies that currently beset "Divinitie."

A strong group of scholars, headed by Barbara Lewalski and Richard Strier, and ably supported by Ilona Bell, Gene Veith and, most recently, Elizabeth Clarke, have performed an essential service to readers of Herbert by stressing the Reformed, Calvinistic elements in Herbert's poetry.[8] I have argued elsewhere that some of the poems that clearly suggest Calvinist influence can be given alternative explanations.[9] But this does not mean that Calvinism does not operate in Herbert's "The Church." I think it is highly significant that four of the poems that most explicitly evoke Calvinist doctrine all occur in the latter part of the final version — and do not occur at all in the early Williams manuscript: "Love Unknown," "The Holdfast," "Assurance," and "The Water-course" — to name them in the order of their occurrence.

In the first of these, the naive speaker tells how his heart was saved from the furnace of affliction:

> But with a richer drug then scalding water
> I bath'd it often, ev'n with holy bloud,
> Which at a board, while many drunk bare wine,
> A friend did steal into my cup for good,
> Ev'n taken inwardly, and most divine
> To supple hardnesses.
>
> (40–45)

Evidently the service of Communion is effective only for the chosen; at least the naive speaker takes it in this way. But how can he know the inner disposition of those "many" others?

Since the treatment of this speaker is throughout broadly comic, perhaps Herbert is having his sly joke at the expense of those who take an exclusive view of the elect.

The next poem in this group, "The Holdfast," is also broadly comic and works through a naive narrator. The poem has three speakers. One is the voice of the narrator, whose story includes the voices of two other speakers. The first of these is that of a Calvinist preacher or teacher attempting to explain his doctrine to a not very apt member of his congregation:

> I threatned to observe the strict decree
> > Of my deare God with all my power & might.
> > But I was told by one, it could not be;
> Yet I might trust in God to be my light.
>
> (1–4)

The narrator thinks he gets the point: "Then I will trust, said I, in him alone." "Nay, ev'n to trust in him, was also his," insists the preacher: "We must confess that nothing is our own" (5–7). Again the narrator thinks he understands: "Then I confess that he my succour is" — only to be told, in a tone of increasing impatience, "But to have nought is ours, not to confesse / That we have nought" (8–9). "I stood amaz'd at this" (10), says the narrator, using "amaz'd" in the rich meanings of Herbert's day: "stunned or stupefied, as by a blow; out of one's wits.... Bewildered, confounded, confused, perplexed.... Struck with sudden terror" (*OED*). That is, "much troubled" by theological grief, "till I heard a friend expresse, / That all things were more ours by being his" (11–12). The friend, by his tone, seems clearly distinguished from the "one" who has brought the narrator into a state of theological fear and panic: he is the friend of the other poems in which he offers his beneficent advice or service: Christ, the friend of the gospel of John (15.12–15). As Strier points out, the "his" of the last line here makes a double reference to the God mentioned earlier, and to the friend who promises this salvation.[10]

But why are all things "more ours by being his"? The voices of the friend and the narrator seem to join in the understanding that marks the final couplet: "What Adam had, and forfeited for all, / Christ keepeth now, who cannot fail or fall" (13–14).

This sounds like a firm conclusion, but the more we ponder it, the less firm it becomes. "What Adam had" — free will — is now in the keeping of Christ. But in what sense should we read the word "keepeth"? If we take the word in the sense of "housekeeping" it means to "protect, preserve, save . . . to take care of . . . to look after, watch over . . . to preserve in being or operation" (*OED*, "keep," 2:14, 16, 23). In this sense, then, Christ is the guardian of a free will that has been restored by his sacrifice. But on the other hand, we may take the meaning "to hold in possession; to retain in one's power or control" (*OED*, "keep," 2:29). With this meaning Christ keeps all power for himself, no room is left for human agency: the Calvinist view. In that one word "keepeth" Herbert has managed to "express" the central point of controversy in his age. The poem does not take sides: the "holdfast" is an act of faith that holds both meanings in suspension.

The case is quite different in the next poem of this group, "Assurance," for which Richard Strier has given an excellent interpretation of the poem's almost desperate expression of grief (105–14). The poem opens with a revelation of the state of "amazement" induced by the fear of damnation: the first clear instance of this fear:

> O Spitefull bitter thought!
> Bitterly spitefull thought! Couldst thou invent
> So high a torture? Is such poyson bought?
>
> . . . .
>
> Thou said'st but even now,
> That all was not so fair, as I conceiv'd,
> Betwixt my God and me; that I allow
> And coin large hopes, but that I was deceiv'd:

> Either the league was broke, or neare it;
> And, that I had great cause to fear it.
>
> > And what to this? what more
> > Could poyson, if it had a tongue, expresse?
> > What is thy aim? wouldst thou unlock the doore
> > To cold despairs, and gnawing pensiveness?
>
> (1–3, 7–16)

Herbert is describing the extreme grief of "Home" or "Longing"; now at last we know the basic cause. Like a frightened child he turns to God for help: "But I will to my Father, / Who heard thee say it" (19–20). He admits that he has no powers within himself to withstand such attacks, "But thou art my desert"; the merit of Christ is imputed to me:

> And in this league, which now my foes invade,
> Thou art not onely to perform thy part,
> But also mine; as when the league was made
> > Thou didst at once thy self indite,
> > And hold my hand, while I did write.
>
> (25–30)

One may feel here a subtle pun on "indite," which may mean both to write and to indict in the legal sense: God condemned himself to death on the cross in order to create the league, the bond, the agreement that now saves the sinner. Perhaps the clause "while I did write" allows just a particle of human cooperation in this process, but one cannot insist on this. The poem is best read as a wholehearted declaration of Calvinist justification by faith alone.

But what of the fourth poem in this group, "The Watercourse," which so baldly sets forth the grim alternatives as its concluding line speaks of a God,

$$\text{Who gives to man, as he sees fit} \begin{cases} \text{Salvation} \\ \text{Damnation} \end{cases}$$

(10)

The clause "as he sees fit" may allow a slight crevice through which to escape the doctrine of absolute predestination. It suggests that God, through his foreknowledge, works by some principle of selection, perhaps not wholly unrelated to human actions. Nevertheless, Barbara Lewalski is right to see a Calvinist implication in the poem (286), strategically placed so near the end of Herbert's "The Church." The heavy stress on God's absolute power to grant salvation or damnation evokes a sense that all these many actions of grief or joy have been performed in a universe where God's power remains beyond all human understanding. As Herbert says in "The Flower," "These are thy wonders, Lord of power, / Killing and quickning, bringing down to hell / And up to heaven in an houre" (15–17).

The emergence of these poems, clearly influenced by Calvinism, is then matched in the latter part of "The Church" by the emergence of a strong emphasis upon what Herbert calls "The Holy Communion." Such references are easily found among the 76 poems added to the poems of the Williams manuscript after "Obedience." The first of these, "Conscience," may speak for them all, as the speaker addresses his troublesome thoughts:

> If thou persistest, I will tell thee,
> That I have physick to expell thee.
>   And the receit shall be
> My Saviours bloud: when ever at his board
> I do but taste it, straight it cleanseth me,
>   And leaves thee not a word;
>   No, not a tooth or nail to scratch,
>   And at my actions carp, or catch.
>
> (11–18)

From here on many allusions to the Passion,[11] including the typological poem "The Bunch of Grapes," lead on to the climactic pair of Communion poems, "The Invitation" and "The Banquet," where, in a phrase perilously close to asserting some kind of transmutation, Herbert declares, "Weep what ye have drunk amisse, / And drink this, / Which before ye drink is bloud" ("The Invitation," 10–12).

We can watch the contest between these two interrelated forms of grief — fear of damnation and its antidote, Christ's Passion — in the paired poems, "Longing" and "The Bag." "Longing" presents extreme theological anguish in unmitigated form. Its conclusion shows no sign of relief, as its stanzaform displays an unstable variation in line length:

> My love, my sweetnesse, heare!
> By these thy feet, at which my heart
>   Lies all the yeare,
>   Pluck out thy dart,
> And heal my troubled breast which cryes,
>   Which dyes.
>
>   (79–84)

The answer then comes in the firmly built stanzas of "The Bag," where the first and last lines in each stanza protrude to suggest the handles of a post-bag, a mailbag:

> Away despair! my gracious Lord doth heare,
>   Though windes and waves assault my keel,
>   He doth preserve it: he doth steer,
>   Ev'n when the boat seems most to reel.
>   Storms are the triumph of his art:
> Well may he close his eyes, but not his heart.
>
>   (1–6)

If this interpretation of the stanzaic design seems dubious, I would argue that the wit of the stanza form is quite in line with the daring and indeed outrageous familiarity with which Herbert treats the Passion in this poem. "Hast thou not heard, that my Lord Jesus di'd?" he asks (7), speaking directly to his enemy, Despair. "Then let me tell thee a strange storie" (8), which he then proceeds to tell in a mode of colloquial familiarity, as in a folk tale. "The God of power" descends from heaven, "undressing all the way,"

> And when they ask'd, what he would wear;
> He smil'd and said as he did go,
> He had new clothes a making here below.
>
> (9, 12, 16–18)

As the climax of this "strange storie" Christ himself, speaking again from the cross, offers the wound in his side as the entrance to a letter bag, by which messages may be securely transmitted to "my Fathers hands and sight" (33). And so the poem concludes with utter confidence, as the voices of Christ and the narrator coincide in the final cry: "Harke, Despair away" (42). The poem thus retells the story of "The Sacrifice" in homespun terms that even so benighted a character as Despair can understand. The poem's whimsical wit seems to express a heady sense of release into the joy of recovering the divine presence, a joy that lies at the furthest extreme from the despair expressed in "Longing."

In this contest between two modes of grief, human and divine, a pivotal moment occurs near the close of "The Church," in the group of three poems, "The Search," "Grief" and "The Crosse." The first of these is a poem of absence in which the speaker explores the vast distance between God's will and his own and pleads:

> Since then my grief must be as large,
>   As is thy space,
> Thy distance from me; see my charge,
>   Lord, see my case.
>
> (45–48)

That stanza prepares the way for the extravagant effort to develop tears in the next poem ("Grief"), which I long ago associated with the extravagance of the continental literature of tears, as represented in Tansillo's "Le Lagrime di San Pietro," and in England by Southwell's "Saint Peters Complaint" and Crashaw's "The Weeper."[12] But I missed the point that Elizabeth Clarke has recently made: that the whole poem is a brilliant parody of that continental tradition as well as a parody of the Petrarchan lover's tears (121–23). This is the point that Herbert makes at the close when he writes:

> Verses, ye are too fine a thing, too wise
> For my rough sorrows: cease, be dumbe and mute,
> Give up your feet and running to mine eyes,
> And keep your measures for some lovers lute,
> Whose grief allows him musick and a ryme:
> For mine excludes both measure, tune, and time.
>   Alas, my God!
>   (13–19)

The hollowness of this whole extravaganza is revealed by its hyperbolic wit and by the fact that the whole poem has both measure and rhyme — except for the final cry that collapses the whole fabric of parody. That final cry takes us back to the lines of "Sion": "All Solomons sea of brasse and world of stone / Is not so deare to thee as one good grone" (17–18).

Then the cry, "Alas, my God," seems to lead directly into the opening line of the next poem, "The Crosse": "What is this strange and uncouth thing?" At first the reader is likely to link the line with the title above it, taking "uncouth" in the old sense of "unusual, uncommon" (*OED*), with a reference to the mystery of the Crucifixion; but it soon appears that the "cross" is the thwarting of the speaker's ambitions by his severe illness, a double grief that in this poem leads to a violent, bitter assertion of self-will:

>   Besides, things sort not to my will,
> Ev'n when my will doth studie thy renown:
> Thou turnest th' edge of all things on me still,
>   Taking me up to throw me down:
> So that, ev'n when my hopes seem to be sped,
> I am to grief alive, to them as dead.
>   (19–24)

("Never was grief like *mine*!") But then, in Herbert's way, the last three lines of the complaint erase this entire structure of lamentation, as the higher theme implied by the title now emerges, with an allusion, not only to the Lord's Prayer, but more specifically, in this context, to the words of Christ in the Garden of Gethsemane: "nevertheless not my will, but thine, be done" (Luke 22.42):

> And yet, since these thy contradictions
> Are properly a crosse felt by thy Sonne,
> With but foure words, my words, *Thy will be done.*
>
> (34–36)

Those words, "my words," take us back to that graphic presentation of Christ's suffering in "The Agony," placed very early in "The Church," as further prologue to all the griefs that follow. With Herbert's acceptance of these words as "my words" the way is cleared for a sudden remission, as in "The Flower":

> Grief melts away
> Like snow in May,
> As if there were no such cold thing.
>
> (5–7)

Of course, the griefs return in some of the subsequent poems, but by this point in "The Church" an equilibrium has been established, as in the little poem "Bitter-sweet":

> I will complain, yet praise;
> I will bewail, approve:
> And all my sowre-sweet dayes
> I will lament, and love.
>
> (5–8)

That equilibrium has been foreshadowed in the sonnet "Josephs coat," which comes only two poems before the culminating sequence just examined. Joseph's coat of many colors was a sign of his father's favor; it brought him many griefs, but in the end it led to a happy reconciliation. So it is with the many colors of Herbert's poetical "Church":

> Wounded I sing, tormented I indite,[13]
> Thrown down I fall into a bed, and rest:

> Sorrow hath chang'd its note: such is his will,
> Who changeth all things, as him pleaseth best.
>
> . . . .
>
> I live to shew his power, who once did bring
> My *joyes* to *weep*, and now my *griefs* to *sing*.
> (1–4, 13–14)

6 • Transcendence of Grief
On a Sequence by William Hammond

John T. Shawcross

Are the words sincerely believed by the poet who mourns a death and finds that he who has died has "Weigh'd up to bliss" (poem 2, line 22)? Is it not a constant rationalization of death to invoke ascent to heaven and a God who puts his hand forth to glean the beautiful "rose"? A strain of Stoicism remains behind these attitudes, as well as a condemnation of grief, but they may also try to hide grief — real grief — for the one who has died, for another affected by that death, for the poet who measures himself against the one now gone.[1] G. W. Pigman has meaningfully analyzed psychological and literary grief, self-restraint or passionate outburst, condemnation or sympathy in some seventeenth century poetry. In what does *consolatio* inhere, and which is the more moving — expression of sorrow or suppressed grief — are the questions that he pursues. Looking only at elegy as a literary genre, and even more specifically, pastoral elegy with its long tradition, Celeste Schenck faults more general examinations (which include pastoral elegy) as confusing art and life — clearly the question of sincerity is raised — and inadequately registering "the restorative power of language to fill the palpably felt void" or its doubt that "compensation for such losses can be involved at all."[2] Funereal poems, of course, are not all elegies in literary generic terms, with form and structure and traditional elements, though they may be elegiac.

Dissimulation in literature, especially Renaissance poetry, has long been acknowledged, with a reality/biographical quotient underpinning that literature; yet questions of sincerity keep popping up, usually to discredit an author or to effect reductionism. For some critics John Donne's "Song: 'Sweetest love, I do not goe'" is biographical and that therefore is its only importance, or his analogy of the sun's disappearance "yesternight" but reappearance "here today" speciously negates the poignant potential occurrence in people's lives of separation, evoking grief. The grief expressed by the one left — "When thou weep'st, unkindly kinde, / My life's blood doth decay" — would seem, to some, to be nullified by the poet's concern for self; to some Donne is more concerned with the "decay" of his "life's blood." Or further, the significance of the fact that Mary Herbert, countess of Pembroke, translated Psalm C as a sonnet seems to have escaped such commentators: the divine world of the Bible has been united with the secular world of the poet, sincerity has been expressed within a verbal/generic dissimulation. John Milton's employment of a sonnet to explain seriously his "tardie moving" to an unknown friend concerned with his career (formerly to be the ministry) is not dissimilar: "that you may see that I am somtyme suspicious of my selfe, & doe take notice of a certaine belatednesse in me, I am the bolder to send you some of my nightward thoughts some while since since they com in fitly made up in a Petrarchian stanza" and he quotes *Sonnet 7*, "How soon hath Time" (Trinity MS, 6).

The minor poet William Hammond, whom Douglas Bush dismisses in one sentence, wrote an interesting sequence of ten poems that I want to look at here to examine the "Transcendence of Grief" in at least one seventeenth century poetic example, and to suggest that, though the poems reflect a standard vocabulary of grief and of literary expression, they are sincere in loss and grief and their restorative power of language.[3] The grief is *not* "transcended" in the sense of its being nullified or the object of grief's being forgotten, but the poet has moved into an understanding of loss that allows him to accept that loss, to overcome the outward manifestations of grief, and to express his sincerity in words that move beyond, that do indeed transcend, grief. The poet hopes that he can influence his sister's loss of her husband likewise to move beyond grief. Such is, I argue, the nature of the "transcendence of grief" in sincere elegiac poems that are not only stoic or condemnatory: there is a real grief behind the outpouring, but life, as the poems addressed to Hammond's sister admonish, must go on. The language of the poems provides restorative power.

The title of the first poem, "On the death of my dear Brother, Mr. H. S., drowned," announces the occasion (poems 2 and 3 are "On the Same"), and the title of the fourth, "To my dear Sister, Mrs. S.," moves to varying aspects of a *consolatio* (poems 5 through 10 are "To the Same").[4] Hammond's brother-in-law was Henry Sandys, the eldest son of Sir Edwin Sandys of Northbourne, the author of *A Relation of the State of Religion* (1605), *Sacred Hymns* (1615) and *Europæ Speculum* (1629). He was the husband of Hammond's older sister Margaret. (His uncle was the well-known poet George Sandys.)

Subtitles for each of the three poems on Sandys's death develop a kind of narrative: "The Tomb," "The Boat" and "The Tempers." The first (printed below), in 12 iambic pentameter couplets, asserts an elegiac intent, "I come to mourn, and not to sing his praise" (14), these being the two approaches that

Pigman elaborates in his study of elegy. The marble of the tomb "weeps," caused, perhaps, it is wondered, by Sandys's "frigid power" now dead inside against the "ambient air" in which the tomb is placed, a metaphor observing an interesting fact of natural science (condensation). But, no, the poet says in contradiction, the tears spring "from within" where the "spoil of Nature" and the "crime of destinies" are. The dead one is seen thus as Nature's (life's) and fate's victim, someone that can be and will be always sloughed off (as if Nature were a serpent, perhaps with an evil connotation) and whereby a "crime," which is against human beneficence, is committed. "Spoil" also suggests an act of stealing (one's life) and a result of war (between humankind and "nature"). The "necessity of Nature's laws" is replaced by a different kind of necessity, the unrelenting occurrence of death. The poet knows he is intruding on the "guardian angels" keeping Sandys from "the Stygian fiend," yet the appalling truth of death resists acceptance. Grief here arises because of resistance to the stoical. It is not really self-restraint, but it is not emotional outburst either; it shows sympathy and forced acceptance rather than condemnation.

However, the last ten lines of the poem do turn to praise: the dead one becomes a sun that is "past" before its meridian.[5] Sandys drowned before 1640 in the capsizing of a boat on the Thames (according to the third poem here); we do not know his age or his marriage year. Hammond's sister was born in 1610, and Sandys was the eldest son of Sir Edwin (died 1629) and his fourth wife Catherine. They had seven sons and five daughters. It thus seems possible that Sandys was in his mid-30s when he died, an age that indeed could be looked upon as not having reached his meridian.

No sun rising in the East ("orient"), the poet continues, brought a "purer" day than his "clear affections." Any "Temptuous passion" was but "physic," like the purging of air by "lightnings" (another interesting scientific metaphor); his "martial" temper was tamed by himself and "yet overcame / Others by smiles" (21–22). These aspects of Sandys's personality — affections, temptuous passion, martial temper, taming by force and the accompanying self-realization — could be negatives, but Hammond's somewhat indirect praise makes them "pure," "physic" to unrighteousness in those around him, the source of "smiles." The positive qualities lead to statements that he was "the best of man" and the "perfection" of Nature; he is construed as "the best of *man*," apparently, because, while "perfect" he also personified "integrity" and he exemplified the reputedly manly virtues of affections (friendly dispositions and influences; see line 18), and temptuous passion, and martial temper, and self- realization. "Integrity" (24) implies that Sandys demonstrated behavior that did not pursue the profitable course of action, a kowtowing to superiors, an easy path that jarred with honesty and morality. Beneath the lines of the poem is an indictment of those who did not demonstrate such behavior, and begs our placement of the persona in the poem into a contemporary, or perhaps political, setting, although we have no hint of Sandys's relation to the inexorable political maneuvers of the 1630s.

The second poem is built on the frequent analogy of a human as a boat, calling into play life as a sea, subject to changes in weather (the trials and vicissitudes of life) and ocean action (natural happenings, like tides, that are unavoidable). This "fleshy boat bears up" (5) against "The proudest storm" until "the same moisture" (9) of this "rain" that "once made thee grow" has overflowed the "Poor floating bark" (7). Youth is then addressed to observe what has transpired to Sandys, whose "emblem" the boat carried. In youth one lets out "too much sail," takes a "giddy path," and does not "ballast" oneself sufficiently, thinks one "Can shoot all cataracts, and safely steer" (15) until one reaches his fourscore years (the Bible, of course, reduces that hope: "The days of our years are threescore years and ten," Ps: 90.10). Sandys "defied / Storms, yet soon died"

(19–20), but there is consolation: the boat has "sunk downward" but Sandys has "Weigh'd up to bliss" (22). The scales of life thus introduced (Saintsbury's note is inept, at best) offer a basic thought of many elegiac poems: though the body (the boat) dies (sinks), the other side of the scale (holding the "emblem," the soul) will fly upward (to heaven, to bliss). Following those predilections of youth may prove wise in the end. The admonition to youth to "stoop thine ear" (17) counsels both the shortness of life, the need to defy its storms, and the reward for such a one as Sandys (the "only . . . difference") in salvation. The consolation is a form of the crutch that there is an afterlife for the worthy (a belief continuingly professed), and yet it champions a positive view of the active life, even though the "boat" is "brittle." The active life "scorn[s] / The proudest storm" (24) and "Grow[s]" because of "rain."

"The Tempters" are the four humours, the elements defining "man's house" and "his chiefest foes" — fire, air, earth, water — which contend to see who "shall predominate" (3–4). Each can cause a human's decay or bring him to his grave. In Sandys, however, the poet, pursuing the praise that is often the content of elegy, argues that "This war equal was in him" (13); it brought "Harmony and delight" (14) — that is, until "treacherous Thames" took water's part and tipped the fight within. There seems to be nothing of special significance for Sandys either in that harmony or in the imbalance now of water, except to pun on his death by drowning in a boat capsized in the Thames. It was unexpected (it "surpris'd") and Sandys's "open heart" (15–16) would simply seem to iterate his integrity in dealing with people and events. How much of all this praise is objective, it is impossible to judge. This poem does not seem to probe into Sandys's character: he is simply "the best of man" (poem 1, line 23).

The three-poem sequence proceeds from the fact of the death (along with praise) through the circumstance and cause of the death (and its message to youth) to the death's being unjustified, a result of "treachery" of nature. Elements cited before from Pigman's discussion of elegy emerge in these poems, but seem to be somewhere between overt grief (as in Henry King's "The Exequy") and submerged grieving (as in Milton's "Lycidas"). The dissimulation of forms and metaphors and allusions does not obviate sincerity: the shock and the loss come through, a sense of the unjust and of restraint through incomprehension, as well. The grief is transcended only in the thought that Sandys has "Weigh'd up to bliss."

The contrastive forms of these poems should be noted. While the first has a "standard" form of 24 iambic pentameter lines in couplet rhyme, it divides into six, 16, and two lines: the tomb is introduced, the person within the tomb is portrayed in the central section, and a trenchant dictum — a kind of *commiato* — concludes it. The next two poems look alike but are not. Couplet rhyme is continued, but the first in 22 lines employs pentameter and dimeter alternately and the second in 16 lines, pentameter and trimeter alternately. One poetic intention on Hammond's part was undoubtedly to offer poetic variety, and contrast may lie in the difference between dimeter and trimeter. Yet we also suspect comparison in noting that the first breaks into 16 and six lines and the second into 12 and four (totalling 16; and as noted before, the first of the three poems is six, 16, and two lines). As we have observed, in "The Boat" the metaphoric equation of boat and human being is set out, and then direct advice and the consolation that may come by following it. In "The Tempers," the settlement of the internal war by inward harmoniousness is disrupted by "treacherous Thames," who takes the side of its own singular element, water. The resolution of the previous poem seems somewhat forgotten in this indictment of external force that the "emblem" could not control. The uncontrollable in life exists as well as those things that man can attempt to conquer; the resolution in those last six lines of the middle poem does not depend upon conquering the uncontrollable in life. Sixteen lines are balanced by 16 (12 + 4) lines, but the six lines in between declaim the important message: the boat sank, the emblem "Weigh'd up to bliss."

The dimeter of "The Boat" may suggest, numerologically, connotations of the image of matter (man, the boat) which is thus not immutable (death, its capsizing), albeit eternal (the salvation of Sandys and of those who emulate him, the *consolatio* of those aforementioned important six lines, 17–22). The trimeter of "The Tempers" may contrastively suggest the presence of the godhead, who has created the elements, enabling a harmonious and delightful fight within man to make Death the Gate of Life, but allowing treachery (hinting at the debate over God's allowance of the existence of evil) from the Thames, a personification that is also literal. Rivers (and water itself) have long been seen as both the source of death — we think of John Milton's "Lycidas" or T. S. Eliot's "The Waste Land" — and the source of life and resurrection — again the same two poems. The thought was first given in lines 9–10 of "The Boat": "Now the same moisture, which once made thee grow, / doth thee o'erflow." By the Thames's exercising its amoral nature in siding with Water to unbalance the elements of God that Sandys had held in harmony, death, the inevitable, ensues. But all this is within God's purview, we are apparently to conclude, and the alteration to trimeter lines in this third poem may underscore that.

The seven further poems of the full sequence all demonstrate *consolatio*, addressed as they are to Sandys's widow, Hammond's sister: "The Chamber," "Thursday," "The Rose," "Man's Life," "The Excuse," "The Reasons" and "The Tears." The poems move from her darkened house through what come to be logical aspects to reduce her grief by the last poem when he hopes that "fortune" "Will, at last, see to recompence her pain." In the first poem (printed below), her home is "Death's shady house and household," "a dark lanthorn," "a shade," "night's dark womb," "a tomb" (2–8). Hammond is contrasting the widow's house with Sandys's tomb in the first poem of the sequence. Within her house she "shines a beauty, as of Old / Magnificent tombs eternal lamps did hold" (3–4). Her light is "In lieu of life's light"; she is a "fair taper hid," "an eye shut in's lid," "a flower," "a star," "an alabaster column" (5–8). "The Chamber" builds the radiance of his sister in this house of mourning to posit that humankind seeks out "an artificial darksome den" but does not recognize "The better part of nature [that] hidden lies" (14, 15). He is admonishing his sister not to "mask" her "better qualities" (20) by remaining in and maintaining this darkened chamber: there is enough darkness everywhere; her light should not be hidden.

Apparently her day of mourning was each Thursday, for this is the title of the next poem. Although the sun would beget seven "daughters" in the week, only six are possible because "Thursday is lost": "that day is lost in which you not appear" (8). The sun as generating force, given in human terms, contrasts with the lack of life that the darkness of his sister's home effects. Therefore, with astronomical reference to theories of differences of calendars (in the mid seventeenth century there was a discrepancy of ten days between the Gregorian and the Julian calendars, as used in England and on the Continent), he argues that in 60 years, nine years will have not existed because of the lost Thursdays. The metaphysical conceit makes her the reason that "our calculation errs" (13). The effect of such loss is to create us all old before our time, "untimely grey" (18). Her grief, which has brought on this "artificial darksome den," these lost Thursdays, will "dilate itself like day" (17). The poem attempts to turn his sister's concern for her loss and herself, one might say memories of the past, into a charitable concern for others, a solicitude for the living present.

The two poems attempt a *consolatio* by arguing that his sister's mourning should not take the form of "Death's shady home"; it will only "cheat us of our age." Her light, her presence, *unhidden* in her chamber each Thursday, will benefit others and herself. Implied is the thought that what is past is past, and life must go on, a not unusual realization that most people come to and that underlies other elegiac expression.[6] The third poem analogizes "The Rose" to a human's life (the basic image of seventeenth century *carpe rosam* poetry), reprising by its brief life the bemoaned human life that is subject of the sequence. The fourth poem expands the thought of that brevity and continues to ponder the smallness of a "Man's Life" in the full range of nature and the world. As in the earlier poem in the sequence, water in "The Rose" is both good and ill for the flower: the rain feeds the rose, adds days to its blooming, but it also "betrays" its odors, "cuts off" its days, ripens its woe. The rain droplets become tears. Urania — and the name implies not only the astrological muse governing the world (all its "roses"), but Aphrodite Urania, the goddess of wisdom and beauty — comes to gather flowers, acknowledges the contradictory effect of the rain, but then heaven, the rose so blown and washed in pearly showers, intercedes.[7] The consolation for the brief life and its cessation at its height of beauty is that "Heaven put his hand forth, and did glean" (14). Against the first two poems to Hammond's sister, this plays upon "the restorative power of language" and the rationalization that a belief in afterlife provides.

The fourth poem examines the smallness of human life: it "was once a span" but is now a mere atom, "a thing so small" that Nature doesn't even note an "emptiness," does not need to "repair" anything to remove the "vacancy" (1-6). "Death's robberies" are filled "with ample bulk" by "the swellings . . . in hearts and eyes" (7-8). Thus, attempting to argue a stanching of his sister's tears, the poet finds no reason to "weep for a thing so slight / Converting life's short day to a long night" (9-10). What may sound a note of callousness, however, is offset by a reasoned image of "Time's multiplying glass" which "is made of Tears" and which yields only "a painted perspective" (12–13). Distance makes "Grief the false light," exhorting she "dry up [her] tears" because "nought right" (14. 17–18) can materialize through the double medium of such a multiplying glass. Man's life, that is, is brief, and tears — grief — distort one's view of the heartfelt sorrow for the cessation of a life, no matter how brief, making what should be "one month seem many years" (11). These poems "To my dear Sister, Mrs. S." would seem to date their composition some month or more after Hammond's brother-in-law's drowning, a period after which passionate outburst, condemnation and suppressed grief should have run their course, yielding a confrontation with reality.

The following two poems explore the excuse that may be advanced for this continued state of mourning and then the reasons for nonremission. "The Excuse" invalidates the female "sex's easiness" in continuing profuse tears or "weeping [one's] own in others' obsequies" (1, 4). Sexual stereotyping also emerges with: "Where feminine defects are wanting, there / All feminine excuses wanting are" (6–7). Fortune controls only "material things," not "souls." An unrhymed line (13) reminds his sister that Fortune has no power over "souls," despite its control of material things like her husband's body, and does no injury to his soul. Again astrological metaphor is employed to make Hammond's point. The stars that create the music of the spheres lie above the midair where storms generate, so her "soul" should be allowed to "shine in her crystal sphere" (18), and this is above (past beyond) the sphere of the "storm" of tears.[8] (The crystalline sphere lay, according to medieval astronomy, between the Eighth Heaven — the sphere of fixed stars — and the Primum Mobile.) "They're Comets [that] in the troubled air appear" (19) and "meteors [are] but imperfect mixtures . . . / In the raw bosom of distemper'd air" (16–17).

"The Reasons" that are given for this continued mourning are insubstantial: "Is it because he died, or that his years /

Not many were, that causeth all these tears?" (1–2). The first reason should be discounted because all beings have "Prefixèd ... a necessary date" (6) and nothing mortal is permanent; the second, because "untimely deaths no windfall are" (12), pursuing an image of the human as a fruit like an apple on a Tree of Life, "ravish'd from the bough" before snows or even autumn has come. One should not wish for "a longer flame" than that of "The grand example," Jesus. Being subdued by age allows "Fortune" to pursue with rage and sin to wound a mortal worse (18–19). "To wish him long life, then," the poem concludes, "had been a curse!" (19–20). Hammond thus attempts to reverse his sister's seeming reasons for her continued mourning — her husband's death, his fewer years of life — and to console that older age can make all men subject to Fortune's rage and sin. In this there is the potential of insult to Sandys, but Hammond skirts this by the allusion to Jesus, "In virtue only old" and a "miracle of good" (13–14). Jesus' example "Newly disclos[es] man" (15), that is, depicts what manliness is in terms that had not existed before: dying bravely though young.[9]

The final poem in the sequence, "The Tears" (printed below), recapitulates the basic image of grief, but it is primarily concerned with commending the widow's tears as being bright, as a star, as "siderious rays" (10) — all to lead to an acceptance of those tears that previously have been discouraged. Grief is not transcended by the sister: it is here the symbol of true love. But "fortune passing through this rain / Will, at last, see to recompasse her pain" (27–28) and move beyond tears to transcendent acceptance. In further astronomical figuring — casting aside Copernican theory — her tears ("that water here") reflect light back to the "planets," "spots," "islands and ground" as much as those heavenly bodies reflect their light through "the water, which surrounds the earth" (5) to us. In extravagant comparison, "Her tears have, than the stars, a better right, / And a more clear propriety[10] to light"

(11–12). Stars have "borrow'd beams"; her tears "bring their own [beams] along with them," being "Born in the sphere of light" (14–15). In comparison with others who weep, his sister's tears do not "spend / The brightness of [her] eyes," for her tears "are inexhaustible." Even if, like others, "excess of tears rob her of sight" (20), still "two crystal drops" "might restor't"; after all, "our eyes / An humour watery crystalline comprise" and thus "a crystal humour" may indeed be restored (21–24). Although Hammond has tried to persuade a cessation to crying and mourning, he rationalizes his sister's situation — observing, it would seem, that cessation has not occurred over the course of his admonitory poems — by solace that her "moist sparks" will declaim their "better right" and "clear propriety to light."

The last four lines, with indentation to separate them from what has preceded and thus act as a *commiato*, accept the tears that "dew" Love's hair and "fall / A pupil in his eye, and sight recall" (25–26). The pun on "pupil" is perhaps too crass, and the possibility of sight returned to the blind Cupid through the "Two . . . moist sparks" a few lines before that "might restore" her sight is perhaps too precious. But lines 25–26 come to accept her mourning, recognizing that all grief may not be transcended although he has ranged through the frequently proffered arguments and attitudes to leave off grieving. He concludes, as noted before: "And I hope fortune passing through this rain / Will, at last, see to recompense her pain." He has failed in his aim and collapses into the hope that finally some surcease will descend, some reward will come to her, a loving widow who has not experienced the *consolatio* the sequence intends. Despite its title "To the Same," the poem has shifted addressees from his sister to "You modern Wits" (with whom he may himself have been classified), and the point of view shifts from resistance to tears to their acceptance and exaltation as magical elements. He hopes that fortune "Will, at last, *see* to recompense her pain," and if fortune does see, we must infer it will be because the "crystal humour" of her tears will, as for Cupid, bring true sight. Cupid, not blind, will be able to see true love.

But contrast is also implied in lengths and divisons in those poems: poem 1, 20 lines; 2, 18 lines; 4, eight and ten lines; 5, ten and nine lines; 6, eight and 12 lines; and 7, ten and 14 and four lines. The linkage of the first two poems presented before is strengthened by their prosodic similarity. Numbers 4, 5 and 6 link together in subject matter as well as versification, but added stress is thus placed on the unrhymed single line of poem 5: "[Fortune] There [within souls] hath no power, can do no injury," as we have seen before. It is a commanding thought for the *consolatio* poems taken together. The poet tries to separate body from soul in the bereaved's understanding of the lost one's "presence": the body dies, but the soul lives on without influence or change from Goddess Fortuna.

Poem 4, "Man's Life," is the central poem in the *consolatio* sequence and concentrates the message that tears yield only "nought right." That central position would seem calculated in this sequence and points to a dissimulation that poetry, even that of heartfelt grief, engages. Its placement is purposive; its "message" underscores a strain of stoicism and delineates literary grief that is nonetheless sincere. If numerological lore has any place in Hammond's scheme, the three poems on the death may imply the presence of a godhead controlling life and death, and the seven poems to the sister may manifest the creative act open to the sister when she acknowledges that Fortune will eventually "recompense her pain." Although the tears will yield only "nought right," they may also bring recompense, and they attest to the strength of true love. Yet, in terms of Pythagorean concepts of centrality in a group of ten being six, we should note that that position is held by "The Rose." Its prosody suggests the more usual lyric form that this variation on the *carpe rosam* theme evokes: it is in 14 lines of alternate pentameter and tetrameter in couplet rhyme. As reminiscent of love poetry, "The Rose" shifts the love from human to divine, for "Heaven put his hand forth, and did glean" (14). The final poem returns to earthly love and the expectation that Love will have his eyesight restored to see love's continuance in the grieving widow though the object of love be no more.

On the death of my dear Brother, Mr. H. S., drowned
The Tomb

Why weeps this marble? Can his frigid power
Thicken the ambient air into a shower?
Ah no; these tears have sure another cause
Than the necessity of Nature's laws;
These tears their spring have from within; there lies
The spoil of Nature, crime of destinies.
    How well this silent sadness doth become
This awful shade; the horror of the tomb
Strikes paleness through my soul; yet I must on,
And pay the rights of my devotion.
Pardon, you guardian angels, who attend
And keep his bones safe from the Stygian fiend,
That I disturb your watch with untun'd lays;
I come to mourn, and not to sing his praise.
A Sun that set in floods, but, oh sad haste,
Ere the meridian of his age was past.
A purer day the East did ne'er disclose,
Than in his clear affections orient rose.
Tempestuous passion did in him appear
But physic, as the lightnings purge the air;
Martial his temper was, yet overcame
Others by smiles, himself by force did tame.
    Here lies the best of man; Nature with thee
Lost her perfection and integrity.

To my dear Sister, Mrs. S
The Chamber

Entering your door, I started back; sure this,
Said I, Death's shady house and household is;
And yonder shines a beauty, as of old
Magnificent tombs eternal lamps did hold,
In lieu of life's light, a fair taper hid
In a dark lanthorn; an eye shut in's lid;
A flower in shade; a star in night's dark womb;
An alabaster column to a tomb.
But why this night in day? Can thy fair eye
Delight in such an Aethiop's company?
Man hath too many natural clouds: his blood
And flesh so blind his hood-wink'd soul, that good
Is scarce discern'd from bad; why should we then
Seek out an artificial darksome den?
The better part of nature hidden lies;
The stars indeed we may behold, and skies,
But not their influence; we see the fire
But not the heat; why then should we desire
More night, when darkness so o'er nature lies,
That all things mask their better qualities?

To the Same
The Tears

You modern Wits, who call this world a Star,
Who say, the other planets too worlds are,
And that the spots, that in the midst are found,
Are to the people there islands and ground;
And that the water, which surrounds the earth,
Reflects to each, and gives their shining birth;
The brightness of these tears had you but seen
Fall'n from her eyes, no argument had been,
To contradict, that water here displays
To them, as they to us, siderious rays.
    Her tears have, than the stars, a better right,
And a more clear propriety to light.

For stars receive their borrow'd beams from far;
These bring their own along with them, and are
Born in the sphere of light. Others may blind
Themselves with weeping much, because they spend
The brightness of their eyes upon their tears;
But hers are inexhaustible; she spares
Beams to her tears, as tapers lend their light;
And should excess of tears rob her of sight,
Two of these moist sparks might restore't: our eyes
An humour watery crystalline comprise:
Why may not then two crystal drops restore
That sight a crystal humour gave before?
    Love dews his locks here, woos each drop to fall
A pupil in his eye, and sight recall:
And I hope fortune passing through this rain
Will, at last, see to recompense her pain.

7 • Maternal Elegies by Mary Carey, Lucy Hastings, Gertrude Thimelby and Alice Thornton

Donna J. Long

> *What we mourn in an elegy is never simply the other but the limits of our own understanding and a loss in ourselves.*
> — W. David Shaw

"We commonly refer to the deaths of those very 'close' to us as 'losses'," Kathleen Woodward observes, and "[p]aradoxically this phrase is comforting because it allows us to foreground our role in the story . . ., to assert a relation, to refer not so much to the event of the death as to what we have suffered by that death, to speak of *our* pain, our grief."[1] In the early modern period, both women and men were expected to bear their grief within socially constructed limits. These limits differed depending on who had died. The construction of grief was also gendered, both in terms of how men and women were understood to experience it and how it was to be expressed. Women were ideally silent and nonassertive, and, as in other aspects of their lives, they were subject to chastisement for excessive grief.

In 1694 Sarah Savage thought her grief "excessive" after the death of a second infant son, and she was quick to distinguish her submission to God's will from that unruly emotion: "My *judgment* is quiet . . . but my affections are often rebelling."[2] Savage did not attend her infant's burial, which seems to have made the loss harder to bear. She "had much ado to quiet my spirit at the sight of my poor baby's grave, which I had not seen before" (70). Savage's description of seeing the grave as she entered Wrenbury Church suggests neither she nor her husband thought of visiting the site. Such a ritual seems commonplace now but may have been unacceptable for the early modern Protestant, who must believe her child resides in heaven. Once in church, Savage is both comforted and newly distressed by the sermon: "the minister was reading Isa. liii. at verse 4, *surely he bare our griefs and carried our sorrows.* Oh, sweet Scripture! . . . How dry and cold is this heart of mine in hearing, and reading of the sufferings of the blessed Jesus! When for an affliction (which comparatively is but small) I can weep floods of tears. Well may I be ashamed that thus it should be" (70–71).

Public expression of any passionate emotion by a woman was taboo, and even private tears were, for Savage, shameful behavior. Early modern women's diaries and letters reveal equanimity over child loss as often as they reveal trauma. In either case, such documents demonstrate how women were moved to mourn in socially acceptable ways, and their distress when they found social expectations difficult to meet. Perhaps the early modern woman wrote in order to remain silent, to restrain and work through grief without making that grief public.

One medium that allowed women to explore and express their complex grief over child loss was the elegy. In this essay, I look at maternal elegies by four seventeenth century women. Mary Carey, Lucy Hastings, Gertrude Thimelby and Alice Thornton seem to have little in common beyond their all-too-common experience of child loss. Each uses elegy as a way of telling her story of grief, of expressing and representing her particular loss. However, their elegies also share characteristics that allow us to consider the maternal elegy as a particular mode of the broader genre. Carey, Hastings, Thimelby and Thornton use elegy to grieve not only for individual children but for their own spiritual state. For each elegist, the attempt to reach a state of consolation is rife with ambivalence. However, as they explore the meaning of the maternal role in relation to child loss, recuperating a sense of maternal and spiritual well-being is also possible.

Much of what we know of Carey's life is from her *Meditations*, a book of prose and poetry. The daughter of Sir John Jackson of Berwick, Carey was probably born between 1608 and 1612. She first married Pelham Carey, the son of Henry, fourth Lord Hunsdon, and, according to Carey's account, her life with Pelham was "frivolous" and much time was spent in "Carding, Dice, Dancing, Masquing, Dressing, vaine Companye, going to Plays, following Fashions, & ye like." She may have met her second husband, George Payler (or Taylor, as he is named in the Meynell edition of her book), when he was garrisoned at Berwick in 1642. They were married and by July 1644 Carey was pregnant. This was one of at least eight pregnancies (the eighth ending in the miscarriage described in the poem, "Upon ye Sight of my abortive Birth"). Only two of Carey's children, Nathaniel and Bethia, lived to adulthood. Carey outlived both her husband and Nathaniel and was named executor of their estates. She died in 1680.[3]

Lucy Hastings was born in Dublin on 10 January 1612/13.[4] Her father, Sir John Davies, was a poet, lawyer and attorney general for Ireland. Her mother was Lady Eleanor Audley, whose published prophecy of the death of Charles I landed her in Bedlam Prison. Lucy married Ferdinando Hastings in 1623. Their son, Henry, died of smallpox in 1649 as negotiations for his marriage were underway. Hastings is known, as Jean Brink has shown, for her politically astute correspondence. Brink notes that Hastings's elegy for her son was written on the flyleaf of *Lachrymae Musarum*, a collection of poems commemorating Henry's death (62).

Gertrude Thimelby enjoyed a reputation as a poet among family and friends. Her body of work chronicles the happy and sad occasions of her aristocratic and close-knit community.[5] The content and tone of Thimelby's poems are at once of a woman who deeply appreciates her family and friends and one who enjoys her talent as a poet. Thimelby's range is typically domestic and familial, which may reflect in part her Catholic faith.[6] Gertrude's father was Sir Walter Aston, the patron of poet Michael Drayton. Her maternal grandfather was Sir Ralph Sadler, who had been Edward VI's treasurer general and who, according to Arthur Clifford, "had charge of" Mary, Queen of Scots, at Tutbury Castle (xxvii). In the mid-1650s, Henry Thimelby, Gertrude's husband of ten years, and their 11-month-old son died within months of one another. After the deaths of husband and son, notes Clifford, Gertrude "sought the consolations of religion in a convent of English nuns, at Louvain, in Flanders, of which her husband's sister, Winefrid Thimelby, was abbess" (xxv). Gertrude died there, having taken orders.

Alice Thornton was born in 1627. Her father, Christopher Wandesford, died young but left his wife and three children "a good estate." Thornton's financial stability and commitment to her faith made her loathe to marry, but she obeyed her mother's desire that she be "settled in the estate of marriage." Once the marriage negotiation with William Thornton was complete, Alice was "hopeful to serve God in those duties incumbent on a wife, a mother, a mistress, and governess in a family."[7] Of eight pregnancies, three children lived to adulthood. Financial difficulties plagued the Thorntons until William's death in 1669. Alice died in 1706/07. Thornton is the best known of the four elegists discussed here. Her memoirs were edited and published in 1875 by the Surtees Society.

According to Elspeth Graham, Thornton wrote her memoirs "to vindicate ... herself and her husband from accusations of financial mismanagement" and "to write [of] her husband's death."[8] Graham argues that "the death of [Thornton's] husband ... threat[ened] her identity, not only through emotional grief, but through loss of status as a wife and increased financial insecurity" (56). Graham concludes, "These crises in turn yield, in perhaps unexpected ways, moments of faltering and fragility which are equally opportunities for control and articulacy" (56–57). Like the loss of Thornton's husband, the loss of a child was both cause for "faltering," often expressed as self-chastisement, and an "opportunity" for reassessing and recuperating a woman's sense of self. In "Women's Writing and the Self," Graham argues that early modern women's writing often enabled them to explore "a variety of possibilities for establishing identity" (230–31). The maternal elegist's "story," to recall Woodward, "assert[s] not so much the event of the death as ... what [she has] suffered by that death" (93).

Grief Expression: Gender and Culture

Attempting to quantify emotions like affection and grief is a problematic endeavor. Anne Laurence begins her exploration of grief by acknowledging, "It is questionable whether grief is properly a subject for investigations by historians or whether, instead, it falls into the realm of timeless emotions unaltered by period or place." However, she recognizes "that expressions of mourning differ markedly between one culture and another." Ralph Houlbrooke's research into how Protestant reformers affected rituals of grief expression shows too that strategies for coping with grief change over time. Lucinda Beier argues that we understand less how to cope with loss now than did our early modern predecessors, who were so frequently exposed to death.[9] Their familiarity with loss and the complex means for coping with grief constructed in the period have led some scholars to suggest that early modern persons did not experience grief. In other words, the strategies for coping with grief were interpreted as no grief at all. In fact, the evidence suggests that people experienced grief and were discomforted by it, that they distinguished between kinds of losses, and that they employed a variety of social and cultural rituals to express and to control this difficult emotion. We can also consider how ritualized mourning (including elegiac tropes) may positively direct an individual's need to grieve and, at times, to restrain grief, as well as how such rituals might hinder the bereaved by orchestrating grief expression and, in doing so, may fail to recognize the scope of the loss.

There is evidence, on the one hand, for a lack of recognition of child loss by the society at large, and, on the other hand, for a specifically female recognition of maternal loss. Many of the early modern mourning rituals simply were not appropriate for infants and very young children, or were not observed when an infant or very young child died.[10] In *Death, Burial and the Individual in Early Modern England*, Clare Gittings notes Arnold van Gennep's theory of mourning as "'a transitional period for the survivors, [which] they enter . . . through rites of separation and emerge from . . . through rites of reintegration into society (rites of the lifting of mourning)'."[11] While certain "decencies," to adopt Gittings's term, were performed for the unfortunate infant, there is also evidence that child loss went unremarked by the society at large (see also Laurence, *DRB*, 66–68). Given the arguments for the importance of some mourning ritual, the frequent lack of recognition afforded infant death in the period may have left mothers feeling a lack of closure, a lack of the necessary separation from and reintegration into their social duties, and a lack of recognition for their child by the society itself. Patricia Crawford cites "the Quaker Rebecca Travers [who] testified, 'none but a tender Mother can tell what it is to have Hopeful Children so soon taken from them'."[12] Crawford suggests Travers "was right," for subsequently historians have found it hard to recognize women's grief at the deaths of their children (29). But Travers's testimony also suggests she was trying to persuade her own culture to recognize maternal grief. However, the female-centered nature of the childbirth ritual, with female friends and family members gathering to assist the midwife and to provide comfort and company to the woman in labor, suggests there was a specifically female recognition of a mother's loss. A woman whose child died at birth or shortly after would have female family and friends close at hand. It seems reasonable to argue that the potential for the newborn's demise was a secondary motive for the large attendance at a woman's childbed.

That grief was a particularly troubling emotion in the period is suggested by the many texts containing cures for it, arguments against it and directions for expressing it. For the grief- stricken, there was much at stake. To grieve over a deceased loved one was potentially dangerous to the bereaved's physical and mental health, but above all it was sinful. In her essay on seventeenth century responses to grief, Laurence notes, "bereavement was an important subject, partly because it occurred frequently, and partly because it was a spiritual trial and the purpose of such writing was usually that of spiritual self-examination" (*DRB*, 63). Constructing the grief process as a spiritual trial provided the bereaved with a specific task. The heightened rhetoric of the actual narrative, which was scripted but intense, provided an emotionally focused discharge.[13] However, it also raised the stakes for containing grief, since to fail was to sin.

On the one hand, there was a firm boundary between acceptable and unacceptable mourning in the period. David Cressy notes, "Grief was both a natural and a cultural phenomenon. It was something people felt, but also something they performed. Failure to grieve might be seen as cold and heartless, while excess grief displayed weakness and lack of control" (*BMD*, 393). To grieve excessively, that is, to grieve in a manner outside socially approved rituals, was to risk charges of impiety, insincerity or insanity. Grief proved the bereaved's "impiety, impatience, and envy" for wishing the dead back on earth, according to G. W. Pigman (*Elegy*, 93). Laurence notes, "Writers of diaries and religious testimonies tended to shun prolonged expressions of grief as being something which intruded upon God's workings," and "[b]itterness at the loss of someone was an even more reprehensible emotion" (*DRB*, 75). The belief in salvation and a better afterlife made "protract[ed] mourning" unnecessary and even wrong (Laurence, *DRB*, 66). James Fitzmaurice cites Thomas Carew's admonishment of the countess of Anglesie for "her elaborate grief . . . because the appearance of excessive mourning indicates insincerity." Laurence notes the belief that grief "could send people mad" or even prove fatal (*DRB*, 75–76). The physician Richard Napier diagnosed several of his mentally disturbed patients as suffering primarily the loss of a loved one, and certain death records in the period list grief as the cause of death. That grief expression "outside" of socially acceptable forms would be thought sinful, a sign of insanity, and potentially fatal tended to circumscribe an individual's ability to process a loss and come to terms with it.[14]

On the other hand, the boundary between acceptable and unacceptable grief was also a fluid one. Some losses were thought more cause for grief than others. Men were thought more capable of controlling their grief than were women.[15] Of course, much of the extant evidence about early modern women's grief is in the form of texts written by men chastising women for excessive grief. Whether women were in actuality more likely to grieve immoderately is unclear. That men would respond to signs of female grief with direction or chastisement seems a reasonable assumption, since men understood such supervision of female behavior to be their responsibility.[16] A husband, father or male friend also might be moved to respond to a woman's grief because it pained him to see her in pain. Further, domestic responsibilities — whether actual cleaning or cooking or the supervision of those who cleaned and cooked — were the wife's purview. Even the most understanding husband would be anxious to have his domestic partner fulfilling her role. William Temple suggested as much when he chided the countess of Essex for her grief over a daughter in 1674: "How has my Lord of Essex deserved that you should go about to lose Him a Wife?"[17]

Rather than recognize that different circumstances of loss will affect how one grieved, the objective of many grief tracts is to show that different losses *should* be treated differently. It was commonly argued that children, and especially newborns, should not be mourned. In *The Hearts Ease*, a tract promising "comforts against the loss of Children, Parents, Consorts, Friends," Simon Patrick begins with "a due consideration of what every one of them is."[18] A lost infant, according to Patrick, is "a poor little weakling newly crept into the light. And this hath the least wonder in it of all other things, that such a little spark of life should be blown out. A greater wonder," Patrick thinks, "that it was not strangled in the Gate of the Womb." He observes, in part, "[w]e were once content without [the child]; why cannot we be content without it now? It never loved us, . . . it was scarce tyed to our heart" (118). In counseling the countess of Essex, Temple maintains that yearlong mourning is appropriate "only to the loss of Parents, of Husband, or Wife. [While] to Children under Age, nothing has been allowed" (177).[19] Of course, the necessity to publicize such "guidelines" suggests grief over child loss was perceived as a problem. However, as with elegiac tropes, we can consider how such circumscribed mourning affected the bereaved in both positive and negative ways.

The variety of consolatory tropes speaks to the perceived need to direct grief expression. Temple argues the countess's current pregnancy and the promise of future fertility should console her. Patrick similarly observes, "are there not many hopes that you may have more [children]? who gave you this? cannot he give you another?" (121–22). This form of consolation requires that mourning cease: if parents refuse to submit to God's will and give up their grief, the promise of future children won't be fulfilled. The consolation of replacement suggests particularly that stillborn children and newborns who succumbed could not be recognized as significant losses.

The Maternal Elegies

Maternal elegies demonstrate that children's deaths were cause for grief. However, these elegies also show that mothers grieved for more than the loss of the individual child; that a combination of fear of grief, social pressures and religious censure often led them to repress grief; and that they suffered guilt if they could not repress their grief.[20] I suggest we see repression of grief or even apparent lack of grief not as a failing of maternal affection, but as evidence that, for early modern women, the capacity to repress grief was a necessary skill, that it was a form of grief expression.

The familiar elegiac pattern of praise, lament and consolation is revised in maternal elegies. Praise of the deceased is often either missing, metaphorical or abstract. The mother whose infant died or whose child was stillborn had no concrete praise to make. She could not fulfill the requirement of recalling and celebrating the deceased's life. In Carey's poem about her miscarriage, she recalls her five deceased children were born "all living: / Stronge, right-proportioned, lovely

Girles, & boyes" (4–5), and deems her two surviving children, "My living prety payre; Nat: & Bethia; / the Childrene deare . . ." (27–28). Thimelby distinguishes her son only as "sweet," while Thornton does not mention her son at all in the course of her poem. We might assume the youth of these children precludes praise, but even Hastings, whose son was of marriageable age when he succumbed to smallpox, leaves the praise of her son to other elegists. If these elegies are an indication, praise of one's own child may have been thought inappropriate for women. The convention of lament, too, is downplayed or absent.[21] Many elegists assumed their loss was punishment for their own sins. Carey "heare[s] Gods voyce" proclaiming "this is thy sinne; / . . . Thou often dost present me with dead frute; / Why should not my returns, thy presents sute" (37–40). Thornton warns, "Tax not thy God, / they [thy] owne defaults did urge / This toofould punishment" (1–2), while Thimelby quietly accepts, "twas thy mother's fault / So soone inclos'd thee [her son] in a vault" (1–2). Hastings's depiction of sin is worldwide. In dying, her son has left behind a place of "infectious Dust" (14).

Women understood the purpose of elegy was the achievement of, or at least the appearance of, consolation. To that end, certain of the consolatory conventions found in male-authored elegy, including familial and paternal elegy, are employed by mothers as well. They imagine the soul's transcendence; they look for comfort in the deceased's escape from the miseries of earthly existence; they speak of submission to God's will. However, knowing consolation is the goal of elegy and reaching it are not the same thing. There are some conventions found in familial and paternal elegy which maternal elegists do not use (or use with a difference): that death comes for all, that the deceased made a good end, that a short good life is preferable to a long ordinary one, that all will be reunited in heaven are not found in maternal elegy. Most maternal elegists do not use the tropes that a child's "natural" piety proved his or her fitness only for heaven, that the child's immaturity was proof of its innocence and therefore its sure salvation, or that children are only "lent" by God.[22] The maternal elegist struggles with the task of discovering consolation for herself and of "speaking" consolation to fulfill generic expectation. Perhaps the most significant aspect of the engagement of consolatory tropes is the frequency with which they fail.

Given our assumptions about the mother-child relationship, we might expect maternal elegies to reveal only stark and unrelenting sorrow. The absence of productive consolatory tropes might seem an obvious aspect for an elegy written by a mother. However, seventeenth century maternal elegists engage a range of prosodic and rhetorical strategies that enable them to recuperate, in every sense of the word, their sense of self. Even for the elegist who achieves some consolation, the emotional cost is evident. While some maternal elegists recognize their grief as inappropriate, they also recognize a uniqueness in their elegiac task that authorizes their "exploration and exploitation" of the genre's convention (see Graham, 213).

In reading Katherine Philips's elegies, Kate Lilley suggests, "Again and again women's elegies refuse the consolations we associate with elegy, to close [their poems] either by announcing the death of their writing ... or, ... their own desire to die."[23] Thimelby combines this desire with self-chastisement: "this selflove orerules me soe, / I'de have thee here, or with thee goe" (12–13). At the end of her elegy, Thimelby finds she is "Content for thee [her son], though not myselfe" (16). Thornton does not voice her wish for death, though her bleak view of life, with its promise only of "paine," implies death would be welcome. Thornton's grief encompasses the range of an early modern woman's complex sense of identity. She suffers a seeming failure to be a godly woman, wife and mother, closing her poem with the bleak sentiment, "Oh, who would droyle or delve in such a soile, / Where gaine's uncertaine, and the paine is sure" (12–13). Hastings does not so much desire to die as experience her son's death as her own: "Thus I die Living, thus alas mine Eyes, / My funerall see, since hee before me Dyes" (3–4). Hastings's closure envisions a spiritual reunion of "the Elect, / [who] Rest, and Joyfully expect / The Image of our Lords perfection, / In the approaching Resurection" (18–21). However, Hastings's abstract "Elect" potentially erases her from the gathering. The feminine ending of the final couplet may signal feminized submission, but it is also a deviation from the more typically assertive elegiac closure, and thus suggests Hastings may be speaking the strong generic sentiment with weak resolve.[24] In an elegy for her "4th, & only Child," Robert, Carey's closure reveals a desire for death:

> Tis Jesus Christ; lord I would have;
> he's thine, mine all; 'tis him I crave:
> Give him to me; and I'le reply
> Enoughe my lord; now lett me dye.
>
> (9–12)

Carey's assertion of consolation reveals a weariness with life's trials and a concern, born of the loss of her child, for her own spiritual state. In Carey's miscarriage poem, several attempts at submission and consolation are frustrated by the depth of her grief. She closes the poem by demanding that God act to sustain her faith:

> lett my walking in the Spirit say,
> I live in't; & desire it to Obey:
> And since my hart thou'st lifted up to the:
> amend it Lord; & keepe it still with thee.
>
> (89–92)[25]

In all three of her elegies, Carey negotiates with God for her obedience. In the poem for Robert, she subtly demands recompense for her submission: "But if I give my all to the / lett me not pyne for poverty" (5–6). Carey has given much: she has given birth to four children and none are living. In an elegy for Perigrene, her fifth child, Carey chastizes God, "I thought my all was given before" (1). She qualifies her consolation: "My Dearest Lord; *hast* thou fulfill'd thy will, / thy hand maid's pleas'd" (9–10; my emphasis). Finally, in her miscarriage poem, Carey warns God, "Lett not my hart, (as doth my wombe) miscarrie" (73). In the poem for Robert, she claims she is consoled but still wishes to die, while Carey's other two poems claim consolation is possible only in exchange for God's fair treatment. Carey's consolation in each of these poems is rife with ambivalence, and her grief is twofold. She grieves a lost child and she grieves her own loss of God's good will.

In the early modern period, religious discourse privileges God's right to any child. Along with religious doctrine, legal and medical discourses privilege a child's biological father over its mother. Early modern women often refer to each child as an "only" child even if they have had multiple pregnancies, suggesting deceased children cease to figure in a woman's sense of her maternal role. In this way, the identity of "mother" seems inextricable from the fact of a living child, and maternal status is represented as secondary to spiritual and earthly paternity. However, maternal elegists usually assert a claim to their maternal role, and they rarely refer to the child's biological father. Carey calls both her sons "my . . . only Child" and "my all," and she signs her name to each of her poems. Like many of the maternal elegists, Carey relates her maternal history in her poems. In "abortive Birth," she recalls, "Seven tymes I went my tyme; when mercy giving / deliverance unto me; & mine all living: / Stronge, right-proportioned, lovely Girles, & boyes" (3–5).

For Carey, God's grace is signified by full-term pregnancy, and her consolation for this loss comes not so much because the child is with God but because she created the child for God. What Carey values, at least as she expresses her values in her poem, is God's grace as evidenced by a living child. She is "please[d]" to be "instrumental" in increasing the elect (19–20), but asks,

> O Lord since I'm a Child by mercy free;
> Lett me by filiall frutes much honnor thee;
> I'm a branch of the vine; purge me therfore;
> father, more frute to bring, then heeretofore;
> A plant in God's house; O that I may be;
> more florishing in age; a grouing tree.
>
> (67–72)

Thimelby names herself "mother" and her inconsolability is initially revealed when she rejects God's will and refuses to relinquish her son: "And fathers good, that in such hast / Has *my* sweet child in heaven plac'd" (3–4; my emphasis). Thimelby is acknowledging her son's transcendence of the physical state but she does not take the conventional step of resigning herself to his absence. Thornton dedicates her poem, "Tax not thy God, they owne defaults did urge," to her son, William Thornton, who died at 14 days old, but does not name him or refer to him in the body of the poem. Her delight in her maternal role is revealed in her prose. While he lived, she writes, she "injoyed his life; and the joy of it maked me recrute faster, . . . that I might doe my duty to him as a mother" (124). Her grief is exacerbated, too, because her husband "is soe afflicted for his losse, and beeing a son he takes it more heavily, because I have not a son to live" (126). Thornton accepts that her husband's immoderate grief over William's death reflects her failure to produce a son. Her grief over this lack makes the overt absence of her son and her own maternal status in her elegy understandable and remarkable.

Like Thimelby, Hastings seems torn between claiming her son and submitting to his death. Hastings's use of the "here lies" trope is a consolatory one, as it turns her "eyes" away from the physical grave and toward her son's spiritual transcendence. The intensity of Hastings's grief in the first five lines of the poem springs from her resistance to differentiating herself from her son:

> The Bowells of the Earth my bowells [hide]
> Whilst these Dear relicks here interrd abide
> Thus I die Living, thus alas mine Eyes,
> My funerall see, since hee before me Dyes
> When [whom] I brought forth my Dear Son here he Lies.
>
> (1–5)

Hastings's imagery links her body, his body and the literal gravesite in an inappropriate, or least unconsoling, preoccupation with physical and temporal remembrance. In subtle self-reprimand for this grief, Hastings puns on the epitaphic phrase in line six: "Clear up mine eyes hee Lies not here." This self-conscious pun suggests her struggle for meaningful consolation and her recognition of the fiction of the trope. According to Joshua Scodel, the "Here lies" phrase signifies the bereaved's readiness to relinquish the deceased and "shows that the poem has shifted from . . . elegiac lament proper at a funeral to . . . brief panegyric inscription" (242). Hastings's poem demonstrates that she understands the purpose of the form, but the elegiac section of her poem, written in a stately iambic pentameter, is prematurely and emphatically shut down (see Scodel, 252–58). Hastings's relinquishing comes not through panegyric but through the promise of spiritual transcendence. Her remaining 16 lines, written in a more clipped tetrameter, envision God's special treatment of her son and assume the toxicity of life on earth:

> But meaning him a richer Case,
> To raise his Luster, not imbase,
> And knowing the infectious Dust
> Might Canker the bright piece with Rust,
> Hasted him hence, into his Treasure
> Of Blessed Spirits.
>
> (12–17)

Even though Hastings relinquishes her son's soul, the intensity of Hastings's corporeal connection with her son remains intact. The absence of consolatory phrases in maternal elegy may be partially explained in the example of Lucy Hastings. The bodily relationship with a child, so powerfully recollected in Hastings's opening internal/internment imagery, remains covertly privileged in the maternal elegy.

Maternal elegies demonstrate anxiety, a symptom of the grief process, but, for the seventeenth century woman, it is an anxiety born of a crisis of faith. In representing herself as just one more element likely to "Canker" her son's goodness, Hastings reveals her uncertainty about her own salvation. The implications of the loss of her son, William, similarly deprive Thornton of her only "sure" source of consolation: the surety of heavenly salvation. Thimelby accepts the blame for her loss, while Carey also assumes the fault for her multiple losses lies somewhere within herself. Many maternal elegists attempt to come to terms with loss through the rhetoric of the spiritual trial. The guidelines for writers of religious diaries included the necessity "to keep a strict record of all . . . sins, to account for . . . time as well or poorly spent, and to chronicle God's mercies" (Kouffman, 11). Both Thimelby and Carey engage in conscientious meditation on the state of their respective souls, while Hastings and Thornton represent their sins as inevitable and immense.

Thimelby accepts the blame for her child's death and claims consolation ("ioy") in God's goodness in taking the child to heaven. However, Thimelby's compliment on God's goodness is tempered by her complaint about his "haste." In the first six lines of the poem Thimelby (almost) dutifully speaks submission. In line seven, we have the first of four rhetorical ruptures which reveal Thimelby's approach to her loss as a spiritual trial:

> *Yet* [I] must confesse my frailty such
> My ioy by greife's exceeded much:

> *Though* I, in reason, know thy blisse
> Can not be wish'd more then it is,
> *Yet* this selfelove orerules me soe,
> I'de have thee here, or with thee goe.
> *But* since that now neyther can be.
>
> (my emphasis; 7–13)

"Yet" twice signals Thimelby's turn from consolation, while "though" and "but" return, first, to the privilege of masculine reason over feminine passion and, second, to consolation. Thimelby's appeal to rationality reveals her emotional devastation. Such an appeal is not to be devalued, even if Thimelby cannot fully embrace it. As Cynthia Pomerleau has argued, religious faith "provides an explanation" so that "[n]othing that can happen is so devastating that it cannot be justified or redeemed by being the will of God."[26] Clearly, though, Thimelby is not making a clean break but is "working through" her loss, making the process of the poem part of her mourning process.[27] A series of dramatic caesuras (lines 3, 9, 12, 15 and 16) further suggest Thimelby's struggle to make sense of her inner disruption.

Thornton's representation of her son's death as a spiritual trial is, to a greater degree than the other maternal elegists, focused on her unworthiness. Thornton's poem concentrates the most darkly cynical aspects of her prose account of William's death. Her prose account employs the self-abasing rhetoric common to godly autobiography in the period, calling herself "[God's] vilde worme and unprofitable servant" who, far from protesting his punishments, gives thanks that he has "not given [her] over to death and destruction" (125). The loss of William is, Thornton states, God's rightful curtailment of her joy over the child, "least [she] should be too much transported" (124). Thornton hopes her "soule may be bettered by all these chastisements He pleaseth to lay upon [her]" (125). She is further humiliated by her daughter Alice's observation that since her "brother is in happiness with God in heaven," Thornton herself should "be patient" (126).

Thornton writes, "I did much condemne myselfe, beeing instructed by the mouth of one of my owne children, [for] my immoderate sorrow" (126–27). Such rhetoric makes clear Thornton's desire to submit, while her detailed description of her grief makes just as clear the difficulty of achieving submission. A month after her son's death, the event is still her main chronological marker. In an entry about Charles II's coronation, Thornton begins, "Affter the Lord had taken my childe from me" (127).

Thornton's poem begins with similar self-chastising rhetoric, which she delivers in assured and not unsophisticated iambic pentameter. The speaker's sense of herself as a sinner, as deserving of punishment, is vividly rendered with images of "the mille, the scourge" upon which she will "grind" for her sins (1–4). In fact, the third-person address in the first four lines suggests the poem is a traditional admonitory elegy written for another:

> Tax not thy God, they owne defaults did urge
> This toofould punishment, the mille, the scourge,
> Thy sinns the authour of thyselfe tormenting,
> Thou grindest for sinning, scourgded for not repenting.
>
> (1–4)

Where Thornton's prose narrative returns again and again to the promise of God's goodness, her poem is unrelenting in its depiction of a harsh world and the speaker's dark view of it. After accepting that her suffering is the result of her own sin, the speaker defensively points out, "I do not begge this slender inch to while / the time away, or falsely to beguile / Myselfe with joys" (5–7). The "slender inch," or the briefness of a human life, suggests Thornton, is not something we choose but something that is thrust upon us.[28]

The controlled meter and vivid imagery of Thornton's opening lines (including judicious use of enjambment and feminine endings) suggest the short and darkly cynical lines which follow are self-consciously clipped and meant to express frustration and anger over the suffering she is required to endure:

> Heere's nothing worth a smile.
> What's Earth, or in it,
> That longer then a minuite
> Can lend a free delight?
>
> (8–11)

The last lines of this short poem revert to the confident pentameter of the beginning, but they do not, as might be expected, revert to self-reproach. Instead the speaker demands the reader acknowledge the harshness of her lot: "Oh, who would droyle or delve in such a soile, / Where gaine's uncertaine, and the paine is sure" (12–13). The reference to "such a soile" recalls God's punishment of Adam, requiring man "to til the ground from whence he was taken," and makes "uncertaine" God's forgiveness. Ending with the word "sure" emphasizes the speaker's resoluteness that mortal life entails "paine" and suggests Thornton's ambivalence over submission. Like her use of meter, Thornton's rhyme scheme is quirky but seems more controlled than not. She begins with a regular scheme but at line seven she introduces a new terminal sound that is not picked up until line 12 ("joys" / "soile"). Line seven is the shortest line of the poem and the line that discloses the speaker's cynicism; deferring the fulfillment of this rhyme until nearly the close of the poem acts to retain the tense mood through to the end of the poem.

The rhetoric of the spiritual trial assumes individual sin. The engagement of a spiritual trial narrative enabled the sinner to accept her sin. Both Thornton and Hastings end their elegies on images of uncertainty. In other words, if they make any assumption about their spiritual state, it is that they must rely on a just and forgiving God. Hastings may not envision herself as a member of the elect, but she knows there is one; Thornton's suffering in this earthly life implies the possibility, if not the promise, of a better (after)life.

Carey engages the spiritual trial rhetoric in a way that enables the recuperation of her maternal self. She defines her spirituality through the physical act of childbearing, which allows her to privilege her biological role as a means for recuperating subjectivity. Carey's prosodic shaping of particularly her miscarriage poem negotiates the grief she feels over child loss and over her own loss of God's good will. Her use of the present tense provides the poem with immediate and "realistic" imagery, as well as a "plain" style which would have been appropriate both to her sex and to her Calvinism. Carey accepts responsibility for the miscarriage in a dialogue with God, where he chastises her for her devotional "dead frute." Calvinism's emphasis on individual conscience is apparent in Carey's lines, "Methinkes I heare Gods voyce, this is thy [the] sinne; / And Conscience justifies [the] same within" (37–38). Carey's location of her conscience "within" parallels the site of fetal nurture; thus "conscience" for Carey may be read as spiritual and physical, just as she represents her relationship with God. Carey's God explains that his "returns" (dead children) only suit her "presents" to him.[29] Carey's choice of the noun "presents" echoes her signification of a child as gift and as a member of the elect for God, but also as a sign of election for a mother. Carey makes effective use of repetition of key words like "nothing" and "quickening" that suggest a need for "conscientious meditation" on submission, and, by implication, the depth of her grief, and four other word choices — "frute," "expectation," "presents" and "miscarrie" — that reflect consideration of connotative and double meanings. Carey's dialogue with God is a familiar trope, but in it she not only compels God to chastise, she compels his forgiveness as well: "Mend now my Child, & lively frute bring me; / so thou advantag'd much by this wilt be" (51–52). The doubling of "frute" as devotion and promise of pregnancy allows Carey to recuperate maternal power and spiritual assurance.

The occasion of "On the Death of her only Child" is a wholly personal one since, already a widow, Thimelby is both poet and recipient of the poem. This duality enables Thimelby to step outside elegiac expectations. We recognize the split, possibly before Thimelby does herself, as the title and first lines of the poem refer to Thimelby in the third person: "Deare infant, O twas thy mother's fault / So soone inclos'd thee in a vault." As a whole, the poem is formally restrained, even plain: just 16 lines, most of them end-stopped iambic tetrameter. Each of the four conjunctive ruptures registers subjectivity:

> Though I, in reason, know thy blisse
> Can not be wish'd more then it is,
> Yet this selfelove orerules me soe,
> I'de have thee here, or with thee goe.
>
> (9–12)

Thimelby's reference to her "selfelove" demonstrates that, at this moment in the poem, her sense of self is inextricable from her role as mother. Her inability to differentiate leads to a desire to escape her self, to "goe," to give up her life if she must live without her child. The final lines suggest Thimelby's discovery of the discomforting split in her sense of self, of the differentiation she initially resisted but which will enable her to live on. Like other maternal elegists, Thimelby's negotiation of elegiac convention produces a specifically female "poetics of tension," to recall Stanley Fish, born of a continuing social repression of immoderate grief and a need to express emotion over her loss. What is remarkable here is that Thimelby discovers a sense of self that she chooses to acknowledge and recuperate.

Thimelby accepts blame for the loss, chastises herself for feeling unreasonable grief, and equates her desire to have her child back with an egotistical "selfelove." But she also recuperates herself and rejects her death wish by recognizing a sense of self apart from "mother" and "mourner" and resolving to make "vertue of necessitie":

> But since that now neyther can be,
> A vertue of necessitie
> I yet may make, now all my pelf
> Content for thee, though not myselfe.
>
> (13–16)

In contrast to conventional elegy, Thimelby refuses consolation, but she does not end hopelessly. Thimelby's distinction is between "all my pelf" (or her "property, possession, goods, gear" according to the *OED*) which is "Content," and her "selfe" which is not. That she closes the poem at the moment of recognition, ending on "myselfe," suggests her ambivalence at discovering the "possibilities for establishing identity," as Graham phrases it. Thimelby becomes her own "subject in discourse," a "desiring, mourning, writing subject" (Lilley, 72), a position typically unavailable to women and one that Thimelby seems both to fear and embrace. The moment of separation in Thimelby's elegy is at once threatening and liberating: threatening in how undefined and discontented the self is, signified by Thimelby's closure at the moment of recognition, and liberating in that it seems also the impetus for her decision to recuperate this self.

Conclusion

Elegizing a child allowed the early modern mother not only an opportunity to recognize herself as a mother, but also the opportunity to recognize the child's death. Elegy signals a shift in a woman's relationship with a deceased child. It provided a space in which a woman recognized the child as no longer her husband's and not yet God's but as her own. It further provided women with a meditative place in which to reconstruct their own sense of identity, to discover the means to live on. If, as David Shaw, has suggested, "[w]hat we mourn in an elegy is never simply the other but the limits of our own understanding and a loss in ourselves," the seventeenth century maternal elegist was able to accept those limits of understanding and to recognize herself in a new way.[30]

Reconstructing the experience of early modern maternal grief is always only an exercise in interpretation. Even if we have a text describing a specific loss and its aftermath and we are able to place that text within certain historical contexts, we still have only a partial story. Reading the early modern capacity for coping with grief as a lack of grief or an inability to express grief, both considered "pathological" in modern psychology, may reveal our own subconscious suspicion of the mother who does not exhibit grief over the loss of a child.

8 • An Collins and the Politics of Mourning

W. Scott Howard

> And lastly in regard of any one,
> Who may by accident hereafter find,
> This, though to them the Auther bee unknown,
> Yet seeing here, the image of her mind;
> They may conjecture how she was inclin'd:
> And further note, that God doth Grace bestow,
> Vpon his servants, though hee keeps them low.
> — An Collins, "The Discourse"

An Collins (?–1653?) may appear to be "in most respects a poet nearly anonymous," but her readers are intimate companions.[1] In what is perhaps her best known work, "The Discourse," Collins imagines her future anonymity and directly challenges her audience to see beyond that veil to "the image of her mind." Collins reveals precious little about herself in the one extant copy of her only known work, *Divine Songs and Meditacions*, which was printed and published in 1653 by Richard Bishop.[2] Even her most autobiographical texts (such as the opening prose address, "To the Reader," and the poems,

"The Preface" and "The Discourse") continue to yield only provisional claims from critics and scholars about Collins's personal life.[3] An Collins's religious beliefs have been variously defined as anti-Puritanical, Calvinist, Catholic, anti-Calvinist and Quaker. Her politics have likewise been described in a number of ways: critical of sectaries and Independents, pro-Commonwealth, opposed to the radical wing of Parliament, anti-Commonwealth, and royalist.[4]

Within this context of conflicting interpretation, there is agreement upon at least one defining characteristic of *Divine Songs and Meditacions*: the central role of physical and spiritual affliction in Collins's devotional poetics. Devotional writing by seventeenth century English women consistently demonstrates an acute awareness of the female body. Devotional works by male contemporaries, of course, illustrate similar concerns with relationships between body and soul, but a combination of long-established and (at midcentury) prevalent tenets in Christian thought would have heightened that sensitivity for women writers: the sinful weakness of the flesh; associations of the feminine with body rather than mind; definitions of women according to their biological reproductive functions; and identifications of feminine desire with Eve and original human corruptibility.[5] In her poems An Collins intimates often that she endured chronic physical suffering, although she does not specify either the cause or course of her illnesses.[6] She also frequently articulates her spiritual anguish, which shapes her search for "inward grace" (57). Her poems record the transformation of bodily pain, or "outward Crosse" (48), into "Internall Peace and Consolacion" (57); of her soul's distress, or "fruitlesse greife" (47), into "joy Celestiall" (58). *Divine Songs and Meditacions* thus constitutes a work of mourning through which Collins turns private losses into spiritual gain, revealing God's pattern for her own life.[7]

Since 1815 *Divine Songs and Meditacions* has been classified and interpreted as either a spiritual autobiography, a conversion narrative, or a collection of devotional verse.[8] However, Collins's work has not yet been considered in relation to the tradition of poetic elegy despite the importance of that genre in her volume.[9] I will argue that, for An Collins, the elegy facilitates not only her personal expression of grief, but her construction of mourning as a devotional practice of articulating redemptive self-scrutiny and social criticism. Through the devotional capacities of poetic elegy, Collins fashions her own mourning as a model for her reader's spiritual conversion and social commitment to the ongoing work of true Reformation.[10]

One poem, "A Song composed in time of the Civill Warr, when the wicked did much insult over the godly," best exemplifies the poet's sacred and secular concerns and will therefore occupy the center of this essay. Collins's elegy upon the civil war (written, I believe, in response to the Engagement Oath of January 1650) poignantly appraises the corrupt politics of Parliament and the Council of State through a mournful renunciation of "the seeds of Error" (line 35) that yields a defense of "The *Cause* that's now derided so" (79) together with an apocalyptic consolation that "Truth will spread and high appear, / As grain when weeds are gon, / Which may the Saints afflicted cheare / Oft thinking hereupon" (97–100). In this and the majority of elegies in the first section of *Divine Songs and Meditacions*, which will provide a context for my argument, Collins establishes a relationship between poetry, private grief expression, public mourning and politics. The five elegies that conclude the *Divine Songs* section of Collins's book embody that correlation and enact, through their consequent arrangement, what I wish to call a "politics of mourning."

"Another Song (The Winter of my infancy)" articulates a transition from Collins's earlier elegies in the volume that posit spiritual consolation within a sacred transcendental horizon to those concluding poems that place consolation within secular contexts of virtuous human action. This first elegy in the sequence of five formulates, through godly grief, a critique of spiritual knowledge that Collins elaborates through the following four poems, progressively extending her practice of mourning from the personal to the public spheres. "Another Song (Having restrained Discontent)" and "Another Song (Excessive worldly Greife the Soule devouers)" dramatize a defense of "saving Knowledge" (58) that informs Collins's attack against "the Foes of Truth" (61) in the fourth elegy in the sequence, "A Song composed in time of the Civill Warr." In turn, her political views in that work culminate in the following poem, "Another Song (Time past we understood by story)," that declares an imperative vision of redemptive history: "Now God to manifest his Glory / The truth hereof did let us taste" (3–4). These five elegies ground the book's devotional poetics in a politics of mourning that hinges upon a trope of spiritual conversion, by which Collins extends to her imagined reading audience of "Saints" a quietist prophecy of devotion and dissent. For An Collins, the poetic elegy shapes the occasions for her own private worship and her readers' concomitant turnings toward active faith and political change.

A Fruit Most Rare

An Collins's physical suffering and withdrawal from the public realm defined much of her life. She often tells us that she endured chronic afflictions, the etiology of which she does not specify.[11] Collins attributes her bodily distress to God's providential workings upon her soul, thus linking her inward grief to grace.[12] Her first of two prefaces to *Divine Songs and Meditacions*, "To the Reader," begins with the following confession: "I inform you, that by divine Providence, I have been restrained from bodily employments, suting with my disposicion, which enforced me to a retired Course of life" (1). In the book's first poem, and second preface, aptly titled "The

Preface," Collins indicates further that "through weakness" she was "to the house confin'd" (line 1). Collins often metaphorically describes her bodily pains as "crosses," as in the following stanza from "The Discourse":

> Even in my Cradle did my Crosses breed,
> And so grew up with me, unto this day,
> Whereof variety of Cares proceed,
> Which of my selfe, I never could alay,
> Nor yet their multiplying brood destray,
> For one distemper could no sooner dy,
> But many others would his roome supply.
>
> (57–63)

An Collins may have been chronically ill, perhaps homebound, even bedridden. Some critics have advanced diagnoses for her physical distress.[13] Her withdrawal from the world and avowed celibacy may have been dictated by her physical condition; or perhaps her seclusion was, to some degree, her own choice. Until scholarship presents new evidence, the life record of An Collins will be left to the critic's conjecture.[14]

Because Collins did experience persistent physical illness, her deliberate use of the spiritual anguish topos as a literary and cultural form of mourning bears uncommon fruit. Themes of spiritual deprivation inform much of the devotional poetry and prose from sixteenth and seventeenth century England. Devotion and meditation have been widely discussed by Renaissance scholars as secular practices of religious mourning by which a writer purges the soul's imperfections in order to achieve spiritual enlightenment.[15] Collins's poems, although written in private, give voice to her suffering not only for her own benefit, but primarily for the consolation of those Christian readers who have similarly struggled through a period of spiritual crisis and seek compassionate guidance, as she tells us in "To the Reader":

> Witnesse hereof, this Discourse, Songs and Meditacions, following; which I have set forth (as I trust) for the benifit, and

comfort of others, Chiefly for those Christians who are of disconsolat Spirits, who may perceive herein, the Faithfullnesse, Love, & Tender Compassionatness of God to his people, in that according to his gracious Promise, *He doth not leave nor forsake them. Heb. 13.5. But causeth all things to work for theyr good. Rom. 8.28.* (1)

On a personal level, her "Saving Faith" (24) grants her own inward consolation; on a public level, her account of that spiritual knowledge would deliver "the manifestacion of Divine Truth, or rather the Truth it self" (1). Collins thereby invests her articulation of grief with a principle of conversion that may bring forth her reader's "spirituall calmnesse" (1) and enlarged understanding that, as she notes above, through suffering God "*causeth all things to work for theyr good.*" Devotion thus enables An Collins to translate her private experience of grief into a public practice of sympathetic mourning. Her tribulations and seclusion were certainly defining experiences, but those constraints, I will argue, did not preclude her social criticism through verse.

Many critics and scholars have held that, during the late sixteenth and early seventeenth centuries in England, mourning became an increasingly public act marked by a rise in compassionate consolation; however, that paradigm measures somewhat inconsistently against the diversity of early modern mourning practices that recent studies in the field have brought to light.[16] Lawrence Stone, Philippe Ariès, Clare Gittings and Sara van den Berg, for example, link an advance in public ceremony and compassionate consolation with the rise of individualism and an attendant need to assuage new subjective anxieties about death and the afterlife, which emerge in response to the decreasing presence of the church and the expanding role of government in the regulation of death and burial.[17] Michael Neill also underscores the individual's augmented anxiety concerning death, reasoning that the "extraordinary burgeoning of tragic drama in late Elizabethan and

Jacobean England was a crucial part of this secularizing process" by which mourning customs were reinvented.[18] G. W. Pigman, on the other hand, claims that the rhetoric of bereavement undergoes a shift from rigorism, "which prohibits and condemns all grief," toward more sympathetic forms of consolation that illustrate "a decided reduction of anxiety about mourning" (*Elegy*, 27, 67).

Ralph Houlbrooke, Anne Laurence and David Cressy hesitate to posit a paradigmatic improvement of the English emotional climate during the seventeenth century. Houlbrooke links increased compassion in funeral sermons with the abolition of the doctrine of purgatory, though not necessarily with a consequential diminishment of the individual's anxiety about death and grief (*DRB*, 36). Laurence charts a pervasive feeling of abruptness and resignation in expressions of grief, which does not simply indicate a lack of affection, but rather "a more conscious process of withdrawal by the living person from the dying or the dead," necessitated in part by the popular belief that prolonged outpourings of grief could lead to fatal illness. Laurence notes further that devotional writers tended not to elaborate upon grief that "intruded upon God's workings" (*DRB*, 74, 75). Cressy confirms the importance of moderation in godly grief, but also remarks that, by "the end of the Stuart era it was not thought improper to observe formal mourning for a year" (*BMD*, 439). Although these interpretations conflict, they nonetheless all underscore important social implications of private grief expression in early modern England. That is, mourning undergoes a decisive shift through the personal to the public sphere of discourse, and that transition, in turn, reveals a growing secularity of consolation.

An Collins's grief is godly. As a work of mourning, her verse moves from the personal to the public realm of discourse in order to serve "as a corrasive to mortifie / And kill the power of inniquity" (28). Through the testament of her own struggle to attain personal spiritual knowledge, Collins joins her devotional poetics to the ongoing manifestation of God's work in the secular realm; her mourning thereby yields a call for political and social reform: "To stop the Course of Prophanacion / And so make way for Reformacion" (63). The poetic elegy plays a central role in Collins's politics of mourning during the early 1650s. An elegy typically begins with a private utterance of grief and the particularization of loss, then incorporates a combination of voices and perspectives into the poem's mourning procession, and concludes with a consolation linking the public recognition of loss with universal principles.[19] The genre's conventional rhetorical progression from lament to praise to consolation thus provides Collins with a pattern for translating her own physical pain and spiritual strife into "saving Knowledg" (58), for a public defense of "the Light of Truth" (65). The elegy was widely employed by Collins's contemporaries not only for devotional purposes, but also as a means of moving from the personal to the public sphere of discourse.[20] Kate Lilley asserts that early modern English women's elegies are "unusually mobile" and disrupt "the putative divisions between high and low culture, literary and nonliterary... private and public, occasional and nonoccasional writing" (72). However, the transition from private to public speech was often intractable for women writers because the public realm was culturally constructed as a male domain; the private as female. Reading, writing and publishing were subversive acts for women and were commonly troped as signs of disease, madness and promiscuity.[21] In most cases, a woman's entrance into public discourse through either speech or print necessitated an eclipse or change of identity in order to retain her proper Christian virtues of silence, chastity and obedience.[22]

For An Collins, who figures herself in verse as a bride of Christ, the elegy facilitates not only her expression of grief, but her construction of mourning as a devotional practice of self-abnegation in the service of Christian morality. Devotional mourning purges her body and mind of suffering, her poetic persona of hubris. Collins's text thereby garners the virtue of anonymity for her reader's spiritual benefit. Nearly all of Collins's critics have maintained that such anonymity and Christian charity underscore the poet's withdrawal from religious and political debate.[23] However, it is my contention that Collins turns her gendered constraints into enabling conditions for political criticism through the poetic elegy. Despite the quietism that her devotional poetry suggests, Collins engages in subtle critiques of her own art and moment in time through her works' crafted disengagements from politics. Collins's physical and spiritual crises thus serve as elegiac pretexts engendering self-scrutiny, spiritual affirmation and social critique in her writing.

Many critics have praised "Another Song (The Winter of my infancy)," making it the fifth most frequently cited of Collins's poems or prose works.[24] Stanley Stewart holds that this elegy illustrates Collins's retreat from the public sphere to seek private consolation for her physical pain and spiritual crisis. The elegy's *hortus conclusus* topos and conversion theme therefore signify the poet's turning away from timely affairs of church and state to meditate timeless spiritual truths:

> Yet as a garden is my mind enclosed fast
> Being to safety so confind from storm and blast
> Apt to produce a fruit most rare,
> That is not common with every woman
> That fruitfull are.
>
> (26–30)

This elegy and the whole of *Divine Songs and Meditacions*, reasons Stewart, therefore conforms to the pattern of a Christian spiritual autobiography recorded by a devotional poet compelled by "the flame of conscience" to seek spiritual consolation and maturation through an exchange of timely concerns for timeless illumination. Concluding his reading of "Another Song (The Winter of my infancy)," Stewart claims that through "her denial of the body and of the world, the speaker conveys with the image of the enclosed garden the figure of 'heavenly blis,' which marks exactly that departure from the bounds of time."[25]

Such transcendental, apolitical interpretations work extremely well for some, but not most, of the devotional elegies in the first section of *Divine Songs and Meditacions*. Twelve of the 15 poems in the *Divine Songs* section of Collins's book are elegies; of those 12, five articulate mystical unions between the poet's soul and God that transcend time. "Another Song (The Winter of my infancy)" initiates a key transition to the book's latter elegies, which place consolation within contexts of human time and action. Stewart's reading of the elegy under question here does not account for the important conceit in the poem's two concluding stanzas. Within a sacred space of consolation, Collins situates the profane forces of politics:

> But evil mocions, currupt seeds, fall here also
> whenc springs prophanesse as do weeds where flowers grow
> Which must supplanted be with speed
> These weeds of Error, Distrust and Terror,
> Lest woe succeed
>
> So shall they not molest, the plants before exprest
> Which countervails these outward wants, & purchase rest
> Which more commodious is for me
> Then outward pleasures or earthly treasures
> Enjoyd would be.
>
> (36–45)

Although this elegy's final lines concern the poet's desire to meditate upon her soul's transcendence of timely affairs, that consolation turns upon the conversion of "prophanesse" into "rest," a rhetorical principle that reveals at once the poem's sacred and secular dimensions. This devotional elegy serves Collins as a vehicle for both private meditation and social criticism through a crafted withdrawal from worldly concerns. The poem's defense of the poet's spiritual understanding — "a fruit most rare" — extends to the reader a converting critique of knowledge that calls for virtuous action in the public sphere: "But evill mocions, currupt seeds, fall here also / whenc springs prophanesse as do weeds where flowers grow / Which must supplanted be with speed." As an aesthetic mode, devotional mourning voices dissent, although in a reactionary fashion. Collins builds similar indirect formulations in "To the Reader" (1), "The Discourse" (106–12, 407–13), "A Song composed in time of the Civill Warr" (57–64, 81–88), and "Another Song (Time past we understood by story)" (8–14). In each of these cases, as in the above concluding stanzas, Collins's mourning underscores the paradox that "These weeds of Error, Distrust and Terror" condition the possibility of political reform.

Of Devotion and Dissent

"A Song composed in time of the Civill Warr, when the wicked did much insult over the godly" mourns the political climate of the early 1650s, attacking the Engagement Oath, and defends the work of true Reformation as a consolation for the current state of religious and political chaos. In 1961 Stanley Stewart judged this poem not "representative of [Collins's] work as a whole" (iii), choosing to omit the elegy from his photographic facsimile selected edition of *Divine Songs and Meditacions*, despite his stated recognition of the work's involvement with political controversy (iv n. 6). Since then readers have noted this particular elegy's political import, but only recently have critics begun to grant the poem a sustained analysis within the larger context of Collins's book.[26] An Collins's elegy on the civil war, I believe, establishes a relationship between private grief, poetry, public mourning and politics that turns upon a devotional topos of conversion, thereby investing consolation with the promise of social change.

This elegy has a three-part structure: first an opening

section in which Collins explores possible rhetorical contexts and poetic personae for the work's design and social critique (1–24); second a catalog of the enemies of true Reformation (25–64); and last an invocation of an impending apocalypse (65–104). Collins begins by juxtaposing overdetermined objects of knowledge (that is, prophecies) against particular, historically situated, discrete insights, or what she calls "mentall mocions" and "free / Conceptions of the mind":

> With Sibells I cannot Devine
> Of future things to treat,
> Nor with Parnassus Virgin's Nine
> Compose in Poems neat
> Such mentall mocions which are free
> Conceptions of the mind,
> Which notwithstanding will not be
> To thoughts alone confind.
>
> (1–8)

The poem's first section confronts a problem: how to begin an elegy that directly addresses (from the inside out) a moment of political crisis. As the title explains, this work does not have the benefit of hindsight, but offers a song of protest "composed in time of the Civill Warr." Through these two tropes (that is, "mentall mocions" and "free / Conceptions"), Collins critiques reified false virtue and defends her own personal spiritual knowledge. Her subject in this elegy "will not be / To thoughts alone confind"; this poem, as these lines affirm, will not retreat from political controversy.

After distinguishing herself from false prophets and poets, Collins ironically invokes Deborah (the biblical prophetess of Judges 4 and 5) in the following stanza. Collins qualifies her alignment with this figure — "twere joy to sing" — at the same time that she appropriates Deborah's triumph as a remedy for England's present turmoil:

> With Deborah twere joy to sing
> When that the Land hath Rest,

> And when that Truth shall freshly spring,
> Which seemeth now deceast,
> But some may waiting for the same
> Go on in expectation
> Till quick conceipt be out of frame,
> Or till Lifes expiracion.
>
> (9–16)

Collins's two tropes for redemptive spiritual knowledge from the first stanza return here in the form of "quick conceipt," underscoring both the prophetic force of Deborah's song and Collins's own sense of urgency. Just as Deborah's song praises triumphant godly acts in times of religious and political crisis, Collins's own "quick conceipt" defends God's truth in the public sphere. The third stanza fully articulates this rhetorical movement, concluding the poem's first section.

The elegy's second section presents a mournful catalog of "the Foes of Truth" (25). As Gottlieb observes, Collins begins writing this list of enemies in the conventional language of moral allegory and satire, representing her adversaries as followers of Satan who oppose truth, corrupt the souls of the godly and violate the Scriptures.[27] These satirical formulations serve two purposes: they link Collins's previous invocation of Deborah to a similarly allegorical level of discourse that acts as a metapoetic frame for the elegy's social critique; and they also provide Collins with a layer of aesthetic distance from the more explicit political accusations that follow:

> And to bind Soul and Body both
> To Sathans service sure
> Therto they many ty by Oath,
> Or cause them to endure
> The Losse of lightsom Liberty
> And suffer Confiscacion,
> A multitude they force therby
> To hazard their Salvacion.
>
> (41–48)

Throughout 1649 and 1650 propagandists for the parliamentary government encouraged the swearing of oaths of allegiance; such enforcement generated strong opposition. The Engagement Oath of January 1650 illustrates the culmination of this parliamentary movement, which has come to be called the "Engagement Controversy." In the above stanza, Collins clearly levels a strong charge against that unpopular oath. Such pledges of allegiance were resisted not only by Royalists, but also by a diversity of religious and political groups, including Levellers, Quakers, Independents, Millenarians and both General and Particular Baptists.[28] Opponents of the oath indeed faced "The Losse of lightsom Liberty," as Collins asserts above, by imprisonment and torture. Collins's apt use of the word "Confiscacion" may indeed refer to the Rump Parliament's segregation of royalists' estates between 1649 and 1653, though not only royalists were required to pay for unpopular religious and governmental services.[29]

Because there was such widespread resistance to these parliamentary infringements upon liberty, it is difficult to link Collins to a single religious or political group. Since 1961 critics have offered conflicting views of Collins's religious and political inclinations. I propose an alternative view that, I believe, resolves many of those interpretive contradictions. Rather than a Quaker, as many have supposed, An Collins was most likely a Particular Baptist who may have also been sympathetic toward the Fifth Monarchist movement. The two groups were closely linked during the early 1650s. Collins's poems consistently exhibit a constellation of tendencies that would have been central concerns for a Particular Baptist at midcentury. Those tenets, as the following catalog illustrates, underscore important affinities with, and differences from, Quakerism: a strong belief in an elect society of Saints who will complete the task of true Reformation together with an equally strong dislike of religious hierarchy and dogma; an understanding of some principle of the inner light, but not a firm association with a larger society of Friends; both a solid belief in the personal revelation of divine truth through the interpretation of Scripture and a complementary, deep suspicion of church and civil government structures; a conviction that faith alone is not sufficient, but must be made manifest through godly works; a conservative and reactionary view of Parliament, one that would call for its reform while also defending the "Cause" in its pure sense of regenerating society at every level; hostility toward all ungodly sects; ambivalence over the role of prophecies together with a millenarian, apocalyptic outlook; an allegorical rather than a strictly literalist reading of Scripture; a firm belief in the coming kingdom of Jesus; both a hesitancy to speak in public and a defense of women's public speech; an exhortation of both personal spiritual knowledge and a woman's right to publish her devotional writing; an unfailing concern with personal salvation; and a distrust of historical precedent together with a positive belief in the redemption of humanity by the return of Jesus to govern England through the efforts of the godly Saints.[30] Collins was no Fifth Monarchist herself, but, as Capp's landmark study would confirm, she could have held strong millenarian views without being an active Fifth Monarchist (20). *Divine Songs and Meditacions* was published in 1653, the year of the Barebones Parliament and the apex of the Fifth Monarchists' religious and political influence. Collins probably composed her poems between 1649 and 1653; the book may have gone to press during the rise of Fifth Monarchist propaganda (1650–53) prior to the Rump's dissolution by Cromwell on 20 April 1653.[31]

All of these equivocal motivations accord with Collins's attack — set forth in a register of "the seeds of Error" (35) — upon a diversity of religious sects and political factions that she calls "Enimies / To Lady Verity" (49–50). The central paradox of her elegy upon the civil war, however, turns upon such widespread religious and political criticism. For the "Foes of

Truth" (25) currently wield religious and political power and must ironically play a central role in the restoration of order, as Collins asserts:

> Yet these are they, as some conceit,
> Who must again reduce,
> And all things set in order strait
> Disjoynted by abuse,
> And wakeing witts may think no lesse
> If Fiends and Furies fell,
> May be suppos'd to have successe
> Disorders to expell.
>
> (57–64)

Collins's earlier tropes for her defense of personal spiritual knowledge in stanzas 1 and 2 (that is, "mentall mocions," "free / Conceptions" and "quick conceipt") return here as a "conceit" held by "some" who understand this central paradox. Collins thereby underscores as well the wayward processes of mourning for political reform. While this stanza appears to level a strong charge, Collins concludes the poem's second section by again ironically qualifying her assertion's prophetic strain: "May be suppos'd to have successe / Disorders to expell." Although necessary agents in the true Reformation's current phase, the "seeds of Error" will only temporarily triumph. Their purported success concerns only their own "Disorders to expell." After that overturning, implies Collins, the godly Saints will complete the work of true Reformation.

Collins stresses this sequence of events in the elegy's final section (65–104), which opens with a defense of Truth. Truth might be threatened, "Yet can shee never fall" (66); although "Her Friends . . . may seem wasted all" (67–68), a "holy Seed [will] remain / The Truth to vindicate, / Who will the wrongeds Right regain / And Order elevate" (69–72). Collins links herself and her readers with this holy remnant that will persist through the chaos of England's civil war to actualize the true Reformation of society. Collins predicts that "perfect Day"

(76), but tempers the poem's prophetic registers since the elegy's mourning concerns the difficulty of the imagined political present. Through her elegy's subtle qualifications, however, Collins constructs an immanent/imminent apocalypse visible as the imagined present. The Reformation's historical immanence hinges upon the presence of spiritual knowledge already dwelling within the individual Saints; the Reformation's political imminence turns upon the paradox that "Prophanesse must be fully grown" (81) in order for the Saints' devotional mourning to engender social change. This twofold formulation conditions the possibility of her elegy's religious and political criticism as well as Collins's vision of redemptive time.

Collins's millenarian rhetoric crests between the elegy's third- and second-to-last stanzas: Jesus, "the Son of wished peace" (87), will return to govern England through the work of the godly Saints; "the Gospels splendant rayes / Must shine the World throughout" (91–92) in order to achieve the conversion of the Jews, the fall of "The Man of Sin" (94), and the destruction of "New Babell" (95). Collins posits the future historical unfolding of the apocalypse, however, within the potential of the imagined political present. Through the saving knowledge of the Saints and the converting force of devotional mourning, she asserts, the work of true Reformation has already begun: "*That there are* such auspicious dayes / To come, we may not doubt" [my emphasis] (89–90). In the elegy's final stanza Collins again emphasizes these sacred and secular relationships; personal spiritual knowledge yields a converting and redemptive power that will become manifest because the Saints are already engaged in a process of religious and political transformation:

> Then Truth will spread and high appeare,
> As grain when weeds are gon,
> Which may the Saints afflicted cheare
> Oft thinking hereupon;
> Sith they have union with that sort

> To whom all good is ty'd
> They can in no wise want support
> Though most severely try'd.
>
> (97–104)

Collins's imagined audience already possesses the consoling wisdom that will regenerate England; "the Saints" are already "Oft thinking hereupon; / Sith they have union with that sort / To whom all good is ty'd." Here Collins's choice of the word "Sith" is particularly apt. According to the *Oxford English Dictionary*, between 1520 and 1670 "sith," as an adverb, commonly held the following connotations: then, thereupon, afterwards, subsequently, continuously, ago and before now. As a preposition, "sith" signified continuously and during (a certain period of time); as a conjunction: from, subsequent to, since (a particular time), during and seeing that. In each of these cases "sith" carries a doubled temporality that invokes the presentness of the past as well as the pastness of the future. Collins's employment of "Sith" therefore reveals her elegy's quietist prophecy: the Saints will prevail to renew society at every level because, through their devotional mourning for true Reformation, they are already engaged in a critique of personal spiritual knowledge that brings forth virtuous political action. Although facing formidable challenges, "They can in no wise want support / Though most severely try'd." For An Collins and the Saints, the apocalypse is both historically immanent and politically imminent.

Mourning, Conversion and Reform

The poetic elegy and elegiac mode shape Collins's devotional practice of transforming physical suffering and spiritual strife into redemptive knowledge that grounds her religious and political critiques. Collins's private mourning thus engenders both her quietism and the quickening of her own virtue that would convert and thereby move her readers to effect social reform, as "The Preface" affirms:

> So sorrow serv'd but as springing raine
> To ripen fruits, indowments of the minde,
> Who thereby did abilitie attaine
> To send forth flowers, of so rare a kinde,
> Which wither not by force of Sun or Winde:
> Retaining vertue in their operacions,
> Which are the matter of those Meditacions.
>
> (106–12)

The matter of her poems, explains Collins, is the work, or "operacions," of the godly virtue that they effect in the world on both personal and public levels. An Collins's physical and spiritual crises — the experiential conditions of her own enclosed garden — provide an elegiac pretext of suffering and loss within which she seeks, finds and offers to her readers the consolation of her own spiritual knowledge. Those fruits and flowers "of so rare a kinde" signify the religious and political dimensions of her consoling wisdom.

Collins deliberately employs the rhetoric of the enclosed garden topos to political ends. In two memorable stanzas from "The Preface," she figures herself as a "Bee" who, through a practice of mourning for the true Reformation, converts spiritual and social sufferings into "sweetnesse, fit for some good end" and thereby countervails the "vennom so compacted" of a "spider generacion" (115, 114):

> So shall they not the humble sort offend
> Who like the Bee, by natures secret act
> Convert to sweetnesse, fit for some good end
> That which they from small things of worth extract,
> Wisely supplying every place that lackt,
> By helping to discover what was meant
> Where they perceive there is a good intent.
>
> (120–26)

The bee was a common conceit in devotional writing of the sixteenth and seventeenth centuries, signifying the manner by which a true and pure meditative soul extracts the essence of spiritual wisdom from either sacred or secular exemplars, improving those sources of inspiration in the process of reflection.[32] However, another connotation of the bee conceit has thus far escaped scholarly attention in relation to An Collins. "Bee" is the namesake of Deborah.[33] If the biblical prophetess Deborah embodies the public spirit of godly political protest in "A Song composed in time of the Civill Warr," here the bee serves as a private trope for An Collins's politics of mourning. Like the bee, this devotional elegist would, from the flowers of her own suffering, gather the essence of God's true intentions, delivering "strong perfumes" (94) to "some good end," excoriating the ungodly — the "spider generacion" — in defense of the true Reformation.

Rather than recording the withdrawn, apolitical life of a nearly anonymous, mid-seventeenth century woman of Christian virtue, An Collins's elegies articulate both devotion and dissent, praise and protest grounded in the poet's conversion of physical and spiritual strife into redemptive knowledge.

9 • Consolatory Grief in the Funeral Sermons of Donne and Taylor

P. G. Stanwood

Funeral sermons occupied an important place in seventeenth century discourse, and there are many examples in the preaching of the period. Although only a few reached the printed state, our knowledge of this form can be well and predictably illustrated.[1] Of the 200 or so sermons published in the first half of the century by Anglicans and nonconformists alike, hardly any are as well composed and moving as those by John Donne (1572–1631) and Jeremy Taylor (1613–67). Like their contemporaries, both men preached for many kinds of occasions, to a variety of congregations, generally constructing their sermons according to the familiar patterns inherited from classical oratory, including the disposition of a text into several branches and a final summing up in a timely conclusion and application. The funeral sermon, however, required a somewhat different method, where the text of the sermon served also as the "text" of the deceased, usually some notable person, whom the preacher eulogizes within, or most commonly following, a lengthy meditation on the divine order. Donne's funeral sermons show these qualities, yet Taylor's even more so, in whose hands the sermon becomes an eloquent, rather formal oration. Donne and, to a somewhat lesser extent, Taylor offer small consolation to the bereaved, but this is not really their first purpose; for they are able to gather sorrow into the contemplation of grief, of misery and of the death that leads to resurrection.

In spite of the common occurrence of funeral sermons in the early church, the Reformation occasioned much criticism of them from such militant protestants as John Knox, Thomas Cartwright and others, who complained of their supposed lack of scriptural authority, their evident origin in classical oratory and panegyric, and their lavish praise of sometimes unworthy persons. These reformers were inclined to see the funeral sermon as a kind of replacement of the Roman Catholic intercessory Mass for the dead. Moreover, the deceased person should be known as he was, they held, and not be praised for virtues perhaps hardly possessed in life. But clerical practitioners of early modern English funeral sermons, partly in response to these criticisms, developed what would become the usual pattern for this kind of discourse: praise was to be greatly tempered by instruction.

One of the most influential of all homiletic textbooks was by Andreas Hyperius, called *The Pathway of Preaching*, translated into English in 1577 by John Ludham, and widely used for many decades thereafter by a huge variety of preachers of varying theological views. Hyperius notes that funeral orations are to "be ordeyned to the comfort of them that be alive." Nor should one miss the fact that "some thinges which the auncient writers have published touching the pacient suffering of martyrdome, are put foorth, partely to the consolation, partely to the confirmation of the faithfull." Hyperius writes this advice at the close of his fourteenth chapter, on

"Consolatory, or Comfortative" sermons. He is much more expansive and detailed on the subject of funeral sermons in the preceding chapter, on sermons "Corrective." He is hopeful that "the ecclesiasticall Teachers" who give funeral sermons "handle not prayses curiouslye contriued and couched togyther, but other places much more holesome and fitte for the enformation of the hearers, such as are these":

> of preparation unto death, that death is the penaltye of sinne, of the miseries of mannes lyfe, of the delyueraunce from them by death, of the contempt of the world and all earthely things, of desiring the felicitie of the lyfe to come, of the immortalytye and eternall blessednes of sowles, of the resurrection of bodyes, of the last judgement, how an accompt is to be made therin of all the life past, of Gods mercy open to all sinners if they repent but euen at the last gaspe, againe that the deade are not immoderately to be bewayled or lamented, but that GOD rather is to be thanked, which hath deliuered them out of the most filthy prison of theyr body, that the death of the sayntes is pretious in the lordes sight, that they are all happye and blessed, to whom it is giuen to sleepe in the LORDE, that is to saye, in the confession of a true fayth, and who is able to recken uppe the residewe?

Only after the preacher has dealt with these concerns may he then properly turn to the eloquent testimony of death lying before him — the body of the deceased — by adding something briefly on the kind of life the person lived and how devoutly he served God.[2]

Henry King (1592–1669) preached the funeral sermon for Brian Duppa, bishop of Winchester, in Westminster Abbey on 24 April 1662, on Psalm 116.15, "Pretious in the sight of the Lord is the death of his saints." King's sermon, while offering textual analysis followed by a eulogy for the deceased, yet comes close to the patristic panegyric that makes little distinction between meditation on mortality at large and on the life of the deceased in particular. King refers twice in his sermon to Saint Gregory of Nazianzen's "Oratio in Laudem

Patris," an oration for his own father given in the presence of Basil, which is a well-sustained description of the father's life and deeds and at the same time a reflection on the fragility of life and the passing of time and the world. King applies to Duppa "that Eulogy which Nazianzen bestowes upon His Father: He was *alwaies so faithfull to God in the service of His Church*, wherein He liv'd, that He never receded from His first Principles in any slackness either toward Hir Doctrine or Hir Discipline." Earlier in the sermon he has told of the despair of this world which Duppa was able to assuage, citing also Saint Gregory of Nazianzen: "The World is now in its Dotage, Creepled and Bed-rid, In the last and worst Age.... Whensoever then a Good man dyes, a Shore of the declining world is taken away, and a *Pillar of the Church*, threatning a Ruine to that part where the Stay was broken out."[3]

Henry King, son of John King, the bishop of London who ordained Donne in 1615, helps to remind us of the "consolatory" sermons of Donne and Taylor while recalling us to remember the double influence on them of patristic authors and also the demands of the late Renaissance "on framing of divine sermons," especially for funerals. By placing the funeral sermons of Donne and Taylor in conjunction, one may see textual explication, celebration and, above all, the means for dealing with public mourning being worked out over the period of two generations during the golden age of English pulpit oratory.

Some consideration of Basil should be helpful in displaying the kind of patristic influence that touches such preachers as Donne and Taylor. These seventeenth century divines fashioned much of their panegyrical and funerary sermonic mode from richly suggestive patristic homilies, drawing inspiration especially from the Cappadocian Fathers, notably Saint Basil of Caesarea (c. 330–79) and Saint Gregory of Nazianzus (c. 329/30–389/90). Basil's two great themes concern our common life, of all who live in the homocentric universe that God created especially for our use, and of God's identifying himself with us for the sake of our redemption. Basil's great homily "In Martyrem Julittam" expresses well these themes; and this homily was to become, with those of other of the Greek Fathers (and of the Latin Fathers, too, particularly Saint Ambrose [c. 339-97], and much later of Saint Bernard of Clairvaux [1090-1153]), one of the greatest of all literary influences on seventeenth century homilists — a touchstone both for subject and technique. Donne mentions Basil, or quotes from him, over 100 times in his 160 surviving sermons, referring to a wide range of his works. Likewise, Jeremy Taylor makes similarly frequent use of Basil. A characteristic statement from Basil's homily is this one that reveals his awe when contemplating the Creation and the Incarnation:

> *What shall I render unto the Lord for all his benefits toward me?* From the cheerless gloom of nonexistence He waked us into being; He ennobled us with understanding; He taught us arts to promote the means of life; . . . He bade the animals to own us as their lords. For us the rains descend, for us the sun diffuses his creative beams; the mountains rise, the valleys bloom, affording us a grateful habitation and a sheltering retreat. For us the rivers flow; for us the fountains murmur; the sea spreads wide its bosom to extend our commerce; the earth exhausts its precious stores; each new object presents a new enjoyment; all nature pouring her treasures at our feet through the boundless grace of Him Who wills that all is ours!
>
> But why do I descant on lesser subjects, when nobler themes should grace the preacher's tongue? For us God dwelt with man! . . . For sinful, perishable flesh *The Word was made flesh, and dwelt among us.* . . . The benefactor tarried with the ungrateful; the deliverer came unto the captives; in the realms of benighted man arose the orb of righteousness. . . . He, who was exempt from suffering was stretched upon the cross; immortality was wedded to death; light descended into darkness. . . . He rose again for those who had fallen; He sent forth the spirit of adoption; He diffused the celestial grace. . . . He

accomplished all that angels can conceive, and more than man can utter.⁴

Donne powerfully recalls and enlarges these lines in his invitation that we should learn to live by hanging "upon *him* that *hangs* upon the *Crosse*, there *bath* in his *teares*, there *suck* at his *woundes*, and *lye downe in peace* in his *grave*" (10.248).

These are the final words from the last of his sermons, generally styled "Death's Duell," which was, says Donne's contemporary biographer Izaak Walton, "his own Funeral Sermon"; but this is a highly subjective, even sentimental account, not a properly descriptive one. The great sermon on John 11.35, "Jesus wept," is similarly concerned with "compassion and passion" and the joy of "holy tears." Indeed, Donne preached on many occasions; but of his extant sermons, only five are directly related to funeral occasions; of these I wish to consider the two that seem to me most traditionally and eloquently designed.⁵ Let us consider first of all the sermon preached on 12 December 1626 "at the funerals of Sir William Cokayne Knight, Alderman of London," on the text in John 11.21, the words of Martha to Jesus after the death of Lazarus, "Lord, if thou hadst been here, my brother had not died." Donne organizes his sermon in the way characteristic of such discourses, adapting the rhetorical principles of classical oratory; but Donne also, and especially Taylor after him, further adapts these oratorical forms for such special occasions as funerals in a direction that Basil and other fathers of the church pointed to. While Basil might combine panegyric and scriptural or theological analysis, Donne, characteristic of his time, tends to divide carefully these two concerns: first, there is instruction, then a eulogy. The result may sometimes produce a kind of formality that hardly seems to be consoling. Yet the exceptions to this general pattern are the more striking for their rarity, and Donne, followed by Taylor, is able to identify grief, if not quite to shed tears.

Donne's theme in this sermon for Cokayne is mankind's

impermanence and wavering faith, but also the certainty and amplitude of God's generosity through the Resurrection. The text is divided in order to reveal this theme: Martha's words offer evidence that "there is nothing, no spirituall thing, perfect in this world; Nothing, no temporall thing, permanent and durable; And these two Considerations shall be our two parts" (7.259). From this division, we discover branches. From the first part, on spiritual inadequacy, we consider, "The weaknesse of Mans best actions; And secondly, . . . The weaknesses in *Martha's* Action; And yet, in a third place, the easinesse, the propensnesse, the largenesse of Gods goodnesse towards us." From the second part, on temporal insecurity, there hang similar branches: "the fluidnesse, the transitorinesse of all such temporall things; And then, . . . in Gods Master-piece, amongst mortall things, the body of man, That even that flowes into putrefaction; And then lastly, returne to that, in which we determined the former part, The largenesse of Gods goodnesse to us, in affording even to mans body, so dissolved into putrefaction, an incorruptible and a glorious state."

Martha and her companions lacked faith, Donne says, by suggesting that Christ needed to be sent for: "they solicited not Christ in person" (7.269). Even in their hope and charity, there was insufficiency: "Not to hope well of him that is gone, is uncharitablenesse; and at the same time, when I beleeve him to be better, to wish him worse, is uncharitablenesse too. And such weaknesses were in those holy and devout Sisters of *Lazarus*." Likewise, Donne discovers defects in temporal things, above all in the decay of "Gods noblest piece in Nature, The body of man." Yet even as he, through Christ, is ready to "cherish their piety" in the midst of the sisters' feeble petitions and spiritual desires (and by extension, of ours), so also God rescues Lazarus (and us) from deadness; "so we shall . . . conclude that, with this goodnesse of God, that for all this dissolution, and putrefaction, he affords this Body a Resurrection" (7.272).

In an ingenious shift, Donne inverts his text: *Not*, "Lord, if thou hadst been here, my Brother had not died," a passionate but untimely expostulation; *rather*, "Lord, because thou wast here, our Brother is not dead," a joyful reckoning. The sermon moves now into its commemorative half by turning to the life of the deceased Sir William Cokayne. Donne cites Cokayne's several accomplishments, remarking that "his crosses, as well as his blessings established his assurance in God," thus proving that throughout all his life "*The Lord was here*, and therefore *our Brother is not dead*; not dead in the evidences and testimonies of life; for he, whom the world hath just cause to celebrate, for things done, when he was alive, is alive still in their celebration" (7.275). The dead man lives still, Donne reminds his auditory, just as we all are alive "in the presence of God . . . In the power of God . . . In the person of Christ," already risen. These consolatory words see no grief but only joy; yet they are powerful in assuaging grief because they urge one not to send for help, or to hope that help may come, or that help may be too late. The right understanding of the scriptural text may indeed be Donne's interpretation of it, that is, there is sorrow in falsely grieving, but not in grief itself, for it is a reminder of the presence of Christ with us, and with "our Brother who is not dead."

Donne indeed emphasizes the feebleness of human actions and the capaciousness of God's goodness toward us all, and his willingness to accept our imperfect "sacrifices." While the body decays and "flows into putrefaction," God is nevertheless granting to it a glorious state. The balancing between two states, between decay and revival, between wretchedness and glory, and between the visible and invisible worlds thus characterizes much of Donne's homiletic oratory — and above all his funeral orations. The second of these he preached on 1 July 1627, on the death of the Lady Danvers, George Herbert's mother and "*late Wife of Sir Iohn Danvers . . . at Chilsey, where she was lately buried*" (8.61). Donne was unable to be present at the burial itself, which occurred on 8 June, on account of "*Pre-obligations* and *Pre-contracts*, in the services of mine own Profession, which could not be excused, nor avoided"; but his sermon in Chelsea Church is clearly a performance intended for Magdalen Herbert's obsequies, and it was soon afterwards published as *A Sermon of Commemoration of the Lady Danvers . . . with other Commemorations of her*, a work accompanied by a number of elegiac poems, some in Greek, and some in Latin, by George Herbert, under the general title *Memoriae Matris Sacrum*.

This splendid — and unusually long — sermon is on the text from 2 Peter 3.13: "Nevertheless we, according to his promise, look for new heavens and a new earth, wherein dwelleth righteousness." Yet Donne regards the whole of this final chapter of 2 Peter, which is notable throughout for its apocalyptic theme, for its warnings against the last day and its promises of restoration to the diligent, the watchful and the godly. Donne's purpose is "*To instruct the Living,* and then *To commemorate the Dead*," the appropriate and usual concerns and divisions of funeral sermons at this time; and to his congregation he says that he would wish "to assist the Resurrection of your soules . . . And to assure the Resurrection of your bodies" (8.63). Descriptions of the Judgment Day, a time certain to arrive, will always be accompanied by "*Scorners, Iesters, Scoffers*, and *Mockers* at *Religion*" (8.65), referred to in 2 Peter 3.3, and this forms a first consideration in Donne's sermon. Then come "terrors" (verse 10), and next advice about how all "*persons*" should await the last day (verse 11); but the text offers "promises," and Donne now begins to close up the first instructive half of the sermon with a summary: "If *God* will have us stay a little longer, it is but for a few *minutes*; for, this is our *last houre*. Wee feele *scornes*, wee apprehend *terrours*, *Neverthelessse we, we* rooted in his *promises*, doe *expect*, we are not at an end of our desires, and with an holy *impatience* that he would give us, and yet with a holy *patience* till he be pleas'd to give us *New Heavens and new Earth, wherein dwelleth Righteousness*" (8.80).

With "New Heavens" and "new Earth," reached through the bridge of "Nevertheless," Donne puts forth both the "instruction" and the "commemoration" of the text, from the Book of Life to the Book of Death:

> But when *all we*, shall have beene mellow'd in the earth, many yeeres, or chang'd in the *Aire*, in the twinkling of an eye, (*God* knowes which) That *body* upon which you tread now, That *body* which now, whilst I speake, is mouldring, and crumbling into lesse, and lesse dust, and so hath some *motion*, though no *life*, That *body*, which was the *Tabernacle* of a *holy Soule*, and a *Temple* of the *holy Ghost*, That *body* that was eyes to the blinde, and hands, and feet to the lame, whilst it liv'd, and being dead, is so still, by having beene so *lively* an example, to teach others, to be so, That *body* at last shall have her last expectation satisfied, and dwell *bodily*, with that *Righteousnesse*, in these *new Heavens*, and *new Earth*, for *ever*, and *ever*, and *ever*, and *infinite*, and *super-infinite evers*. (8.92)

The old world and the new one which is, and is already come, Donne here balances, negotiating between them. The scriptural text that looks promisingly, and *nevertheless*, to the new heavens is descriptive of life that overwhelms death, for immortality joins death while light scatters darkness. In a similar way, Donne's sermon on "Jesus wept" emphasizes the rightness of tears for "the sinnes of all the world," through which all life may be secured, and toward which all the world tends (4.338).

Of the three funeral sermons by Jeremy Taylor, the earliest and probably most impressive was preached in 1650 for the Lady Frances, countess of Carbery; I shall discuss this last, after some comments about the sermon for Sir George Dalstone (1657) and for archbishop John Bramhall (1663). Through these sermons of Taylor, we enter a world of oratorical splendor and richness that even so skillful a homilist as Donne only modestly suggests. Of all English sermons, Taylor's alone can be compared to the great French orations of Bossuet; they are much more formal than Donne's, for they celebrate by means of extended meditations the issues of mortality and resurrection, with little close examination of the sermon text, but with a separate, final consideration of the life of the person he is commemorating, told often in a glorious though perhaps slightly detached manner. The funeral oration for Queen Henrietta Maria on 16 November 1669, for example, is a notable and famous example of Bossuet's remarkable skill in this mode.[6]

Grief in Taylor's sermons is an extraordinary occasion for general consolation. While there is obvious concern for the deceased whose life is broadly described and eulogized, the sermons have the much larger purpose of theological reflection and comment on secular affairs. In this way, Taylor, even more than Donne, reminds us of the funeral addresses of Basil and Gregory Nazianzen. For example, in the panegyric "In Martyrem Julittam," from which I quoted earlier, Basil urges patience in a lengthy and eloquent passage, commending especially the efficacy of "prayer without ceasing." In a section notable for its rhetorical skill and reflective quality, Basil recommends facing adversity with thanksgiving for every act, every part and moment of our life. And when the day is done, we should "give thanks to Him Who has given us the sun for our daily work.... [So let us] divide the time of night between sleep and prayer. Nay, let thy slumbers be themselves experiences in piety; for it is only natural that our sleeping dreams should be for the most part echoes of the anxieties of the day.'"[7] Gregory Nazianzen, indeed, in his funeral sermon for Basil, remembers that "Basil's beauty was virtue, his greatness theology, his course the perpetual motion reaching even to God by its ascents, and his power the sowing and distribution of the Word."[8] And Gregory himself elsewhere writes, as Basil so often did, of the inestimableness of God and the mysterious conjunction of Spirit and flesh in the Incarnation.[9] And

Taylor, preaching and writing some 20 years after Donne, is better able to combine such large theological issues with the personal and public grief in the general misery and loss that surrounds him. He has, after all, lived through the terror of the civil wars, and he suffered experiences that may have affected his sensibility.

The funeral sermon for Sir George Dalstone is based on the text from 1 Corinthians 15.19, "If in this life only we have hope in Christ, we are of all men most miserable"; but the text seems nearly to disappear in Taylor's wide-ranging exposition. While he finds three propositions in the text for three large branches of his sermon, these are occasions not for analysis but for luxuriant rumination, filled with classical and patristic references, exquisitely balanced phrases, with *isocola* and antitheses, and rich imagery. The scriptural text, Taylor notes, contains three propositions which he will "consider": the first declares that "the servants of God in this world are very miserable, were it not for their hopes of what is to come hereafter," and under this heading Taylor says:

> In this world men thrive by villainy, and lying and deceiving is accounted just, and to be rich is to be wise, and tyranny is honourable; and though little thefts and petty mischiefs are interrupted by the laws, yet if a mischief become public and great, acted by princes and effected by armies, and robberies be done by whole fleets, it is virtue and it is glory; it fills the mouths of fools that wonder, and employs the pens of witty men that eat the bread of flattery. How many thousand bottles of tears and how many millions of sighs does God every day record, while the oppressed and the poor pray unto Him, worship Him, speak great things of His holy name, study to please Him, beg for helps that they may become gracious in His eyes, and are so, and yet never sing in all their life, but when they sing God praises out of duty, with a sad heart and a hopeful spirit, living only upon the future, weary of to-day, and sustained only by the hope of to-morrow's event? and after all, their eyes are dim with weeping and looking upon distances, as knowing they shall never be happy till the "new heavens and the new earth" appear. (8.547–48)

In the second proposition, Taylor discovers a further contrast in the limitation of uninformed hope and the "vast joys of a certain intuitive hope" that shall be known in the life to come. Finally, in the third proposition, we as God's servants shall see all miseries turned into glories in the newness of the general resurrection: "In the day of felling timber, the shrub and the bramble are better than the tallest fir, or the goodliest cedar.... [T]he day of judgment will come, and it shall appear to all the world that they whose joys were not in this world, were not of all men most miserable, because their joys and their life were hid with Christ in God" (8.563).

The sermon that Taylor preached at the funeral of John Bramhall (1594–1663), archbishop of Armagh, opens with a sustained and plangent meditation on mortality:

> The condition of man in this world is so limited and depressed, so relative and imperfect, that the best things he does he does weakly, and the best things he hath are imperfections in their very constitution.... And truly what is the hope of man? It is indeed the resurrection of the soul in this world from sorrow and her saddest pressures, and like the twilight to the day, and the harbinger of joy; but still it is but a conjugation of infirmities, and proclaims our present calamity, only because it is uneasy here, it thrusts us forward toward the light and glories of the resurrection. (8.395)

The text from 1 Corinthians 15.23 is useful, but analyzed and developed very loosely and somewhat repetitively — repetition of principal ideas and phrases being a feature of this kind of discourse: "[E]very man in his own order: Christ the first fruits; afterward they that are Christ's at His coming." After his splendid introduction, Taylor regards the three divisions of his text: "1. That Christ who is the first-fruits ... is already risen from the dead. 2. We shall all take our turns, we shall all die, and ... rise again; and, 3. This very order is effective of the thing itself.... If Christ be the first-fruits, we are the whole vintage ... but Christ first, then they that are Christ's: that's the order" (8.397–98).

Taylor hovers over and plays with his text, vividly imagining beginnings and endings, illustrating death and resurrection. He demonstrates his partiality for ripe metaphor in such passages as the following:

> Night and day, the sun returning to the same point of east, every change of species in the same matter, generation and corruption, the eagle renewing her youth, and the snake her skin, the silk-worm and the swallows, the care of posterity and the care of an immortal name, winter and summer, the fall and spring, the Old testament and the New, the words of Job [19.26], and the visions of the prophets, the prayer of Ezekiel [37] for the resurrection of the men of Ephraim, and the return of Jonas from the whale's belly, the histories of the Jews and the narratives of Christians, the faith of believers and the philosophy of the reasonable; all join in the verification of this mystery. (8.403)

The periodic statement points, of course, once more to the "mystery" of the text and the fulfillment of this meditation on the resurrection — incomplete as such reflection must inevitably remain. From these considerations, Taylor moves to the particular "story" that lies before him, for here is the dead body of Bramhall. Yet "all men bear mortality about them, and the cabinet is not so beauteous as the diamond that shines within its bosom; then we may without interruption pay this duty to piety and friendship and thankfulness, and deplore our sad loss by telling a true and sad story of this great man, whom God hath lately taken from our eyes" (8.408).

Taylor speaks sympathetically though also rather formally of Bramhall; he reviews his career, especially of his excellence as an episcopal overseer in a troubled country and time: but "he stood up in public and brave defence for the doctrine and discipline of the church of England" (8.416). In a remarkable display of classical, patristic and contemporary allusions, lively illustrations, extended analogies and ready metaphors, Taylor sums up his grand eulogy by invoking, among others, Horace, Melanchthon, Luther, Hooker, Jewel, Andrewes, Saints

Athanasius, Chrysostom and Jerome — all within a short space, and all with indubitable relevance and advantage:

> For in him was visible the great lines of Hooker's judiciousness, of Jewel's learning, of the acuteness of bishop Andrewes. He was skilled in more great things than one; and as one said of Phidias, he could not only make excellent statues of ivory, but he could work in stone and brass; he shewed his equanimity in poverty, and his justice in riches; he was useful in his country, and profitable in his banishment; for as Paraeus was at Anvilla, Luther at Wittenberg, S. Athanasius and S. Chrysostom in their banishment, S. Hierome in his retirement at Bethelehem, they were oracles to them that needed it; so was he in Holland and France, where he was abroad. (8.422–23)

Almost as an epitaph, Taylor wittily concludes his eulogy: "He wrote many things fit to be read, and did very many things worthy to be written" (8.423).

One may discover little cause for grief and the shedding of tears in such a carefully wrought composition as this one, or in any of those works we have considered, even in Donne's sermon on the Lady Danvers, an individual for whom he must have personally grieved.[10] Yet in such artful discourse there exists a channel for grief to discover its own consolation; for great feeling may be contained in the familiarity of common ideas, expressed in conventional forms that generalize universal feelings. Set prayers possess this merit; and in the same way also does the traditional funeral oration function, which Taylor inherited from earlier ages, and, most magnificently of all English preachers, appropriated for his own time, advancing it beyond the best expression of Donne. Taylor seems to have had a particular fondness for the elegiac and melancholy, and, like Sir Thomas Browne, he writes often of temporality and loss. The dominant theme is of decay, or of fleeting scenes of earthly joy that fade into oblivion, into the unsteadiness of "Time which antiquates Antiquities, and hath an art to make dust of all things."[11] Taylor's fascination with the inevitable ruin that awaits all humanity may be a commonplace of funereal discourse and of an age that was deeply conscious of life's tenderness; but the genius of Taylor elevates ordinary truths into unforgettable phrases.

So to turn finally to Taylor's sermon "preached at the obsequies of . . . the Lady Frances, Countess of Carbery" we reach the apogee of his funeral oratory and of his elegiac style, which has probably never been surpassed in English writing. As a member of the Carbery household in Golden Grove, Carmarthenshire, Taylor knew well the subject of this sermon, which has a special poignancy because Taylor's own wife also died shortly before Lady Carbery. Taylor refers to this painful conjunction of woe in his prefatory epistle to the earl of Carbery, Richard, Lord Vaughan: "[I]t is a sad office to be the chief minister in a house of mourning, and to present an interested person with a branch of cypress and a bottle of tears" (8.427). Similarly, Taylor writes of this double loss in the "Dedicatory Epistle" to his *Holy Dying* (1651), which Lady Carbery had requested he write along with *Holy Living* (1650). But she died too soon; nevertheless, "since her work is done and God supplyed her with provisions of his own . . . it is necessary to present to your Lordship those bundles of Cypresse [that is, *Holy Dying*] which were intended to dresse her Closet, but come now to dresse her Hearse. . . . Both your Lordship and my self have lately seen and felt such sorrows of death, and such sad departure of Dearest friends, that it is more than high time we should think our selves neerly concerned in the accidents."[12]

Since *Holy Dying* and the Carbery sermon are so closely related on account of their occasion and their mood, we should reflect briefly on the somber and speculative tone of the treatise, and especially on its treatment of grief and deep sorrow, attitudes that inform both works. Taylor wrote *Holy Dying* in order to give advice on how we should let life anticipate death, and to prepare us for the concerns of an imminent death. This he does by general preparatory directions, consisting mainly of meditations on the brevity and sadness of life, the varieties of temptations that beset all persons, and their several curatives, and finally considerations and prayers for the visitation of the sick, the dying and the dead. In the last section, which is of particular interest to this discussion of grief and mourning, Taylor writes a long peroration "concerning the contingencies, and treatings of our departed friends after death, in order to their will and buriall" (225–36).

Taylor begins this concluding section by advising his readers to follow the "seasonable" counsel of Syrach: "Weep bitterly and make great moan" (Ecclus. 38.17), but for a time only, "For if the dead did die in the Lord, then there is joy to him, and it is an ill expression of our affection and our charity to weep uncomfortably at a change that hath carried my friend to the state of a huge felicity" (226). Weep, and weep copiously. Taylor would wish "to *dye a dry death*," but he would not wish to have "a *dry funeral*: some flowers sprinkled upon my grave would do well and comely; and a soft shower to turn those flowers into a springing memory or a fair rehearsal, that I may not go forth of my doors as my servants carry the entrails of beasts" (227). But the grief must not be "immoderate" or "unreasonable."[13] After one has wept for a while, it is time to compose the body for burial; and against this final disposition, Taylor gives much practical advice, including the need for an honest and appropriate funeral sermon. One must not tell lies or make reproaches over the dead; nor should one make "a great flame from a heap of rushes and mushrooms, and Orations crammed with the narrative of little observances and acts of *civil*, and *necessary*, and *externall religion*" (233). It is much better to do something of "proper advantage," to perform the unfinished acts and to pay the debts of those who have left us behind. Herein lies real gratitude, virtue and charity; and it is clear that Taylor regarded *Holy Dying* as a reverent offering to Lady Carbery. With the same disposition, he conceived and spoke his funeral sermon for her, with a fineness of restraint and also of very deep and personal participation in her loss — and also of his own wife. I can think of no funeral sermon of the early modern period that manages to be so poignant and also so universal in its treatment of sorrow.

Like Donne's funeral sermons, Taylor's also, and most especially this one, accommodate grief through the consolation afforded by the general calamity of life and the refinement of death. Both preachers appear to stand some emotional distance from the subjects of their discourse, for their grief, to be consoling, requires the poise of detachment, a quality that we should naturally expect in their oratory. Taylor manages, however, with extraordinary dignity, to intimate his deep sense of personal loss for Lady Carbery, and, while he speaks of her, he is implicitly and simultaneously grieving for his own wife. Of all these funeral orations under consideration, this one is thus the most moving because it succeeds in being both distant and familiar.[14]

Taylor's chosen text for the Carbery sermon is from 2 Samuel 14.14 — "For we must needs die, and are as water spilt on the ground, which cannot be gathered up again; neither doth God respect any person; yet doth He devise means that His banished be not expelled from Him" — a text that allows him large opportunities for rumination about grief. The difficulty of living obviously lies in the challenges of life itself and the omnipresence of death by accident, by disease, by secret or hidden terrors:

> In all the process of our health we are running to our grave: we open our own sluices by viciousness and unworthy actions. . . . [W]e make ourselves like water spilt on the ground; . . . we let our years slip through our fingers like water; and nothing is to be seen, but like a shower of tears upon a spot of ground; there is a grave digged, and a solemn mourning, and a great talk in the neighbourhood, and when the days are finished, they shall be, and they shall be remembered, no more: and that's like water . . . when it is spilt. . . . There is no redemption from the grave. (8.433)

Thus the first half of the sermon contemplates the shortness of life, the nearness of death and the necessity "to secure our state by holy living" so that when we are banished from the world, "we may not be expelled from God . . . but that from our beds of sorrows our souls may pass into the bosom of Christ" (8.442). The sermon so far corroborates in epitome the themes of the complementary books intended also for Lady Carbery, that is, *Holy Living* and *Holy Dying*.

Now Taylor speaks a further sermon; but his general reflections on mortality and immortality lead easily into his specific panegyric for Lady Carbery, for she realized a life of "affections swelled up into a religion," fitting herself in every good respect for a holy death. In an extended metaphor, characteristic of Taylor's exuberant style, we learn that "she had a strange evenness and untroubled passage, sliding toward her ocean of God and of infinity with a certain and silent motion":

> So have I seen a river deep and smooth passing with a still foot and a sober face, and paying to the *fiscus* [the imperial treasury], the great exchequer of the sea, the prince of all the watery bodies, a tribute large and full: and hard by it a little brook skipping and making a noise upon its unequal and neighbour bottom: and after all its talking and bragged motion, it payed to its common audit no more than the revenues of a little cloud, or a contemptible vessel. (8.447)

The countess of Carbery, however, "did not believe that religion was intended to minister to fame and reputation," but to make ready for the days of death and judgment. She is like the deep river, quietly moving toward the great ocean, "and all her humility and arts of concealment, made the virtues more amiable and illustrious."

> But so it was, that the thought of death dwelt long with her, and grew from the first steps of fancy and fear, to a consent, from thence to a strange credulity and expectation of it; and without the violence of sickness she died, as if she had done it

voluntarily, and by design, and for fear her expectation should have been deceived, or that she should seem to have had an unreasonable fear, or apprehension; or rather (as one said of Cato) *sic abiit e vita ut causam moriendi nactam se esse gauderet,* "she died, as if she had been glad of the opportunity." (8.448)

As Taylor nears the end of his sermon, seeming to swallow the tears of his grief, he speaks with consoling simplicity and affection, surpassing the ordinary limitations of the funeral oration by lifting it further than any of his predecessors, even Donne himself, had managed. "She lived as we all should live, and she died as I fain would die"; and so "they that mourn sadly, think they can never commend sufficiently" (8.450). With these final words, Taylor portrays the grief that gladdens sorrow.

10 • Moderate Sorrow and Immoderate Tears
Mourning in Crashaw

Paul Parrish

In his study of mourning and grief expression in the early modern period, G. W. Pigman persuasively argues that literature of mourning from the early sixteenth through the mid-seventeenth century reveals a gradual (though not always consistent) progression from what he terms "rigorism" to sympathetic mourning. More specifically, he finds during the period three alternative modes of responding to death: (1) "inhuman insensitivity" or "rigorism," (2) moderate grief, and (3) immoderate mourning (*Elegy*, 27–28). The first receives its primary impetus from church teachings and develops from the belief that, since the deceased has gone on to a better world, there is no need — indeed, it is possibly even a sign of weak faith — to mourn.

In the midst of the increasing acceptance in the late sixteenth and early seventeenth century of both the legitimacy and the worth of overt expressions of grief, Ben Jonson is a curiously insistent rigorist, determined not to give into the softer expressions of grief but to stand in the tradition of what Pigman calls the "angry consoler," one who would chide mourners for weakness and lack of faith (*Elegy*, chapters 1 and 6). For Jonson, it is not, however, merely faith that demands resistance to grief; "manliness" also requires resistance to the enervation of unreserved mourning. Faith should hold sway over grief, reason should rule passion, and masculine rigor should be superior to feminine mourning. Jonson's pride over "manly accomplishments" makes genuine grief expression quite unacceptable, a sign of weak faith and feeble masculinity.

This perceived connection between mourning and gender figures importantly in other studies of the practice of mourning in general and its literary expression in the elegy. Drawing from Freud's classic treatise on "Mourning and Melancholia" (1917) and focusing on the modern elegy, Jahan Ramazani makes a distinction between two dominant modes of mourning: "the normative (i.e., restitutive, idealizing) and the melancholic (violent, recalcitrant)."[1] There is, he further argues, a tension between the consolatory aim, the "psychological propensity of the genre to translate grief into consolation," and the anticonsolatory inclination, a "melancholic" mourning that resists consolation and that remains unresolved, ambivalent or even violent (3-4). Complicating this tension is the traditional "feminization of grief," the perception that weeping, mourning and grieving are women's work, not the business of men. For someone like Jonson, this meant suppressing and denying grief. A number of modern poets, Ramazani argues, take a different stance. Public expression of grief might be perceived as dangerously feminine, but poetry allowed such expression in a kind of subterfuge. The funeral elegy, he suggests, "afforded male poets the exploration of feelings publicly marked as unavailable and alien, permitting the social mask of the griefless male to slip a little." The literary tradition of the elegy becomes itself a convenient and "safe" context within which "men could enact a psychological work that in extraliterary practices might have been more dangerously feminizing," for as traditional male elegists "guardedly associated their laments with nymphs and muses," so modern elegists such as Hardy, Frost and Stevens often cast the "most despondent" mourners in their poems as women. Both older elegists and more modern ones, in short, link "femininity with mourning" (20).

Juliana Schiesari's *The Gendering of Melancholia*, as its title makes clear, is even more overtly and more thoroughly concerned with gender and mourning, with what she calls the "gendered politics of melancholia and lack."[2] Schiesari argues that male "melancholy" (with Hamlet as the quintessential example) has been honored, while female "depression" is dismissed and denigrated (3–4). Citing the work and observations of Elaine Showalter, she notes that male melancholy is seen as intellectual and creative, while its female counterpart is emotional and biological (10 n. 23). As a consequence of these value-laden judgments, a woman's "lament, grievance, or suffering" is typically seen as an everyday occurrence, "a quotidian event whose collective force does not bear the same weight of 'seriousness' as a man's grief" (13). Even in such instances as those alluded to by Ramazani, where a male poet takes on the guise of "feminine" sensitivity in an expression of grief or mourning, a gendered hierarchy is, to Schiesari, implicit: "any ambiguity of gender turns out to be recuperated by male power as individual triumph in the guise of moral conscience, artistic creativity, or heightened sensitivity, and the melancholic thus stands both in reaction to and in complicity with patriarchy" (14).

These compelling observations about measures of grief, gender and mourning provide an instructive context within which to consider grief expression in the poetry of Richard Crashaw. There are two radically different sorts of occasions for mourning in Crashaw. Their range is considerable, and while terms such as "rigorism," on the one hand, or "melancholic," on the other, are not particularly satisfactory when applied to Crashaw, his poetic expressions of sadness — his literary responses to death or loss — encompass the quite mundane, obligatory and controlled reaction to the death of a distant acquaintance (poems written more or less as "performance," as Peter Sacks defines the term), as well as more compelling, emotionally evocative responses to deeply anguishing moments.[3] Moreover, the voices Crashaw adopts include those of the ritualistic and uninvolved observer, the more tender and expressive witness to death, and the passionate, tearful mourner. All of the poems appropriately described in the first two ways are about the deaths of men (the one partial exception being a poem on a married couple) and written as if by a male witness or acquaintance; the poems of the last sort ("The Tear," "Sancta Maria Dolorum" and "The Weeper") all convey the response of a woman mourner, a feminine figure with whom Crashaw identifies and through whom he expresses deeper and more genuine grief. The example of Crashaw complicates the arguments of Ramazani and Schiesari, each of whom sees an otherwise (apparently comfortable) "masculine" poet using the occasion for mourning to "enact a psychological work" that, outside literary expression, "might have been more dangerously feminizing" (Ramazani) or to create an apparent "ambiguity of gender" that at once stands "in reaction to and in complicity with patriarchy" (Schiesari). But for Crashaw the feminine is neither dangerous nor appropriated only for the "safe" act of mourning.

As has been argued often in recent years, Crashaw, both in his poetry and in his life, aligns himself with the feminine and "feminine" perspectives, and he frequently challenges the hierarchy of masculine values. That his most profound attachments and insights are those that would traditionally be judged "feminine" is confirmed in his poetry of mourning, but that truth is evident elsewhere as well — in his poems on Saint Teresa, in poems such as "Deaths Duell" and many of the epigrams, in his extraordinary attachment to Mary Collet.[4] In his sacred verse it is especially noteworthy that Crashaw is moved to love, admiration, wonder or tears by his imaginative recollection of female religious figures. Saints recollected in contemplation and devotion typically energize and excite Crashaw more than do contemporary acquaintances or events. Crashaw is a particularly fitting practitioner of what Anthony Low, following Augustine Baker, calls "sensible devotion." "Sensible devotion" or "sensible affection," as different from Ignatian meditation, puts less emphasis on rational and intellectual apprehension of its object, arises from what Baker describes as an "abundance of affections in the Heart," and yields a more evident outpouring of emotion and sensation. "There is no lack of intellectual activity in his poems," Low wisely reminds us, "yet the affections seem to flow spontaneously, to require no promptings from reason or discursive imagination."[5]

Crashaw's poems evoking a biblical scene of feminine mourning provide powerful evidence of the "abundance of affections" that moves the poet to recall and to mourn with weeping women. Either unmoved or not deeply moved in his poetry by occasions of death in his immediate surroundings, Crashaw responds to the biblical death of Jesus and the grief of mourners with heightened imagination and emotion. The death is moving, and more moving still are the mourners themselves: Mary the mother of Jesus and Mary Magdalene. Images of feminine mourning evoke in Crashaw the kind of grieving that is rare when he responds in his own voice to a death of his time. Grief expression in Crashaw is, in short, most powerful when the occasion is remembered, imagined and filled with feminine presences and responses.

I

Crashaw wrote 18 poems in response to the death of acquaintances, 12 in English and six in Latin. There is no evidence that Crashaw was closely associated with any of the subjects of his funeral verse; they are, in the main, scholars and fellows at Cambridge University, and Crashaw's verses are often emotionally uninvolved, the response of a student to persons who mattered to him almost exclusively in an academic context. Several of these poems are quite conventional, exhibiting only modest wit within a usually short commemoration; other poems are more elaborate, and more witty, though they remain largely intellectual and academic exercises; and a final group is both more expressive and more often characterized by imagery of grief and tears.

The most conventional poems take advantage of traditional images and responses but exhibit little sentimentality or sorrow. "An Epitaph Upon Mr. Ashton a conformable Citizen," perhaps the only commemorative poem Crashaw wrote before his university years, describes a modest and admirable man of London whose death was as gentle as his life. His exemplary life will be kept alive in two ways, both of them utterly predictable: through the "life" of the poem and through the imitative lives of others: "So while these Lines can but Bequeath / A Life perhaps unto his Death, / His better Epitaph shall bee, / His Life still kept alive in Thee" (35–38).[6] Crashaw wrote two epitaphs, one in English and one in Latin, for Samuel Brooke, master of Trinity College, who died only about two months after Crashaw's matriculation in July 1631. The English version takes advantage of an easy and uninspired pun on Brooke's name ("A *Brooke* whose streame so great, so good, / Was lov'd, was honour'd as a flood" [1–2]), leading to a remote and mythologized evocation of tears. This "Brooke," once so great a stream, "Here at length, hath gladly found / A quiet passage under ground; / Meane while his loved bankes now dry, / The Muses with their teares supply" (5–8). The Latin poem gives praise to Brooke's learning, to his fame in letters ("literarum fama") and allows that his life seemed so calm that it is hard to believe he is dead ("Et hunc mori credis?").

Other elegiac poems of this sort include "Upon the death of a freind" and "An Epitaph upon a Young Married Couple." The poems are not without their interest and wit, but the interest is limited and the wit largely of one note. The "freind" was a musician, and Crashaw plays constantly with that fact. His death is "harsh" (1) music, bringing on "Discord" (3) and a lack of "Harmony" (6). In coming so soon, Death keeps "false time" (9) and causes the very world to be "out of tune" (15). Even the expected "he is dead, but continues to live" motif is cast in musical terms: "And though that Musick of his life be still / The Musick of his name yett soundeth shrill" (21–22). The epitaph on the young married couple similarly calls attention to a single element: the couple died and were buried together, thus affording them a "second Marriage-bed." In this instance, readers are urged explicitly *not* to weep, as the poem advances its dominant image of the death as a second marriage.

The most instructive set of elegies written in response to the death of friends or acquaintances consists of the several poems on William Herrys, Fellow of Pembroke College, who died on 15 October 1631, less than four months after Crashaw's arrival. As with the two poems on Samuel Brooke, one would not expect to see evidence of personal grief for surely there was none, but in response to Herrys's death Crashaw wrote seven poems — the Latin epitaph for the memorial to Herrys in Pembroke and six other poems of varying lengths and effects. Whether Crashaw wrote several poems and, as a consequence, was honored by being named to write the memorial epitaph, or, perhaps, positive response to the epitaph led to his writing additional poems, we do not know, but the situation suggests that Crashaw was, or quickly came to be, recognized for his poetic talents, and that he was still finding his way as a poet (he was, after all, not yet 20), taking the occasion of a death to "try out"and experiment with different responses, moods and images. Dennis Kay has suggested that the funeral elegy was a form that encouraged "emulation and competition," that it was a kind of "laboratory" in which "writers of all ages and abilities" could experiment and imitate, offering them the opportunity to understand "the components of art and the disciplines of the craft."[7] Crashaw's elegies taken as a whole testify to the significance of Kay's observations, and they are particularly apposite with respect to these several poems on Herrys.

Crashaw's English "Epitaph" and his Latin "Epitaphium" on Herrys are structurally similar, though the latter — the text of the commemorative tablet at Pembroke College — is more concerned with details and facts, pointing to Herrys's association with Essex, his years as a student at Christ's College and as a fellow at Pembroke, and the occasion of his death on 15 October 1631. In the context of the usual trilogy of themes in a commemorative poem — praise, lament and consolation — both poems give their attention to praising the accomplishments of Herrys, noting (in the English poem) that the "splendor of his Birth and Blood / Was but the Glosse of his owne Good" (23–24) and (in the Latin poem) that he excelled in oratory, poetry, philosophy and, especially, the Christian virtues of faith, hope, charity and humility.[8]

The two poems handle the occasion of death and Herrys's burial somewhat differently. In the "Epitaphium" it provides further evidence of his humility as the great Herrys is buried under so small and so modest a monument ("tantillo marmore" [54]). The "Epitaph," having just indulged in descriptions of Herrys's many talents and virtues, notes the sudden and premature onslaught of Death, the "rush of Death's unruly wave" that "Swept him off into his Grave" (47–48). The most evident link between the two poems is that each begins as if by stopping a passerby (a "Passenger" or "viator") who may or may not be aware of the person whose grave is near. The "Epitaphium" largely abandons this initial motif but the English poem comes back to it to create a more effective close. The "Epitaphium," no doubt influenced by its placement on the memorial tablet, ends by noting the day of Herrys's death and its aptness in light of the liturgical reading assigned for that day; the "Epitaph" returns to the passerby who has been stopped, urging that as he continues on he keep Herrys "entomb'd, but in thy Heart" (52).

As a transition to those poems on Herrys that are more openly expressive, we should consider two shorter Latin poems, one of which appears to be closely associated with the "Epitaphiuim." The first, "In Eundem Scazon" (A Scazon on the Same), follows, in the 1648 *Steps to the Temple*, one of the English poems on Herrys ("Upon the Death of Mr. Herrys"); the second, "Elegia," also appears in the 1648 *Steps*, and, in the 1670 edition, it follows the "Epitaphium" and is said also to be about Herrys. What is significant about each brief response (the "Scazon" is only seven lines, the "Elegia" is 12) is its more evident mourning, as if the fuller and more descriptive poem with which each is associated is a prelude to lament. Each is filled with tears, uninhibited in their expression:

> Huc hospes, oculos flecte, sed lacrimis coecos,
> Legit optime haec, Quem legere non sinit fletus.
>
> ("Scazon," 1–2)

> [Hither, O guest, turn your eyes, but blind with tears,
> he reads these best whom weeping does not let read.]

> Ite meae lacrymae (nec enim moror) ite. Sed oro
>   Tantùm ne miserae claudite vocis iter.
>
> ("Elegia," 1–2)

> [Go my tears go, for I do not delay (you). But I pray
> only do not bar the path of my sad voice.]

Of the three further poems on Herrys, each is substantial (42, 62 and 76 lines) and two of them, in particular, show Crashaw more directly and more emotionally involved in his response to death. Gone is the more restrictive format of the epitaph, gone is the pretense of addressing a passerby. These poems speak more fully and more poetically to Herrys's qualities, or challenge Death more directly, or urge lament for the death of one who lived an exemplary life. They can also, I believe, be read profitably in the context of several other of Crashaw's funeral elegies: his two poems on the death of James Stanenough (or Stanninow), and his poems on a "Gentleman" (Michael Chambers of Queens' College) and George Porter.

"Upon the Death of Mr. Herrys" and the two poems on Stanenough share several qualities, and each reveals an interest in exploring and elaborating on a theme while maintaining evident control of grief and tears. The Herrys poem, in fact, reads much as an extension and elaboration of the English epitaph. The "passenger" reappears, though here only in the closing lines ("Meane while who e're thou art that passest here, / O doe thou water it [Herrys's grave] with one kind Teare" [41–42]), and, as in the epitaph, the impact of this account is heightened by the early description of Herrys's youthful and vibrant activities, activities that are, almost three-fourths of the way through the poem, cut short by the ravages of Fate and Time. Early on even Time itself was an ally, or appeared to be, as with the promise shown by the young Herrys: "Glad Time [begins] to ripen expectation" (22). As with all such poems on the death of the young, this expectation is disappointed, as Time, now allied with Fate, "the dire rage / Of a mad storme these bloomy joyes all tore, / Ravisht the Maiden Blossoms, and downe bore / The trunke" (32–35). No opportunity is urged or allowed for grief as the transition to an expectation that will not be realized is immediately signaled by "Yet": "Yet in this ground his pretious Root / Still lives" (35–36). Time, once apparently allied with the young man, then cast, with Fate, as his adversary, is ultimately humbled as "weake Time" (36) that gives way to and is swallowed up by Eternity.

"Upon the Death of Mr. Herrys" is structured so as nearly to disallow grief and mourning. Hyperbolic praise of Herrys through nearly 29 lines gives way to the event (his death) that might otherwise evoke grief, but the event is followed immediately by consolatory rhetoric of resurrection. The "Elegy upon the death of Mr. Stanninow" varies this structure, inviting the reader to be aware of a disorder in nature and an occasion for grieving before attention is called to the "prime flowre of youth" that has died. Stanenough was buried on 5 March 1635, near the transitional time between winter and spring. The first 14 lines of the poem speak to that seasonal event, to the joy and anticipation and new life signaled by the flight of "aged winter" (1). In defiance of the hope of spring, "shoures of teares" (16) and "Cataracts of greife" (17) result from the untimely departure of the young Stanenough, caused not by winter's "rage" but by "old doting Death." The considerable mourning that is suggested by these images is, however, never realized, and the poem closes on a modest note that echoes the end of the Herrys poem just discussed. There, following images of resurrection and eternity, the passerby is urged to water the grave of the young Herrys "with one kind Teare" (42); here, also following images of resurrection and eternity ("A golden summer, an aeternall spring" [54]), a "courteous teare" is urged: "Now that his root such fruit againe may beare, / Let each eye water't with a courteous teare" (55–56).

"Old doting Death" makes a more pronounced and prolonged appearance in the second poem on Stanenough, "Death's Lecture at the Funeral of a Young Gentleman." The poem is, indeed, cast in the form of a moral lecture delivered by Death over the body of the young Stanenough; in most respects, in fact, it is only nominally a funeral elegy. There is no hint of Stanenough himself, no allusions to his accomplishments or to the nature of his death. Rather, the death is universalized, an inevitability for all made more poignant because of the youth of the deceased.

Whereas, in the "Elegy" on Stanenough, the destruction of the "prime flowre of youth" was a cause for sorrow and tears, here it is, more bluntly, a lesson to be learned. Only once is the youthfulness itself identified, as Death summons "YOUTH, BEAUTY, and blood" (7) as witnesses to the funeral. Seen from the vantage point of Death, however, these qualities, otherwise so often praised and desired, are mere "soft powres, / Whose sylken flatteryes swell a few fond howres / Into a false aeternity" (8–10). The appropriate response to this death is neither a suppression of grief nor an outpouring, but a stark realization of the brevity of life and the irrelevance of otherwise valued niceties such as "Proud lookes" (21), "lofty eyliddes" (21) and "painted" faces (24). Human life is here reduced to "Hyperbolized NOTHING!" (11), a "wild circle" collapsed to a "Point" (15). Death's emphasis on the nothingness of humankind is relentless and unyielding, unmitigated and unsoftened by any other perspective. In all of his other commemorative poems, even those most conventional and impersonal, Crashaw urges sorrow, appreciation, emulation, kindness or courtesy, and there is at least some recognition of the individual who has died. Here, Death is given the first and last word, and Stanenough largely disappears except as he is present as a corpse. Implicitly taking his words to a wider audience, Death explicitly addresses the bones and body, the "Reliques of a dislodg'd Soul" (1), that reside in the funeral coffin, leading them, and the reader, to a bleak understanding of human worth and of the transparent foolishness of pride in appearance or accomplishment. The lesson is, finally, "dust to dust, and ashes to ashes," for Death's lecture is, fundamentally, a lecture on the truth of death, a truth that is more powerful than superficial appearances of life: "All-daring dust and ashes! only you / Of all interpreters read Nature True" (31–32).

Four remaining funeral elegies, a final two on Herrys and the ones on George Porter and Michael Chambers, more consistently and more fully urge mourning, grief and tears. "Feare not to dy with greife" (43), Crashaw says in the poem on Porter, and the four poems generally confirm the importance of eloquent grieving — in words, in silence and in tears. The overly pronounced stresses and the too familiar and unvarying rhythm of "Upon the Death of the most desired Mr. Herrys" ("Death, what dost? ô hold thy Blow, / What thou dost, thou dost not know" [1–2]) belie the expression of regret and grief that is more pronounced than in most other poems on Herrys. Challenging and addressing Death directly, the speaker spends much of the poem describing the rare figure here praised, "Natures choycest Jewell" (4), emphasizing, as do other poems, his youth and his expectations of maturity and achievement. As in "Upon the Death of Mr. Herrys," images from nature abound; the youthful Herrys cut down in his prime is as a "hopefull bud, / Of a ruddy Rose" (31–32) that shows itself only to be rudely blasted by Auster, the South Wind, or as the bright sunshine of early morning cut short by the "scoule" of a "ruddy storme" (51). In the former poem, the "mad storme" that tore and destroyed Herrys's "bloomy joyes" (33) succeeded only to be followed immediately by the poet's awareness of new life and eternity. Here, the transition to hope is not nearly so sudden or so complete. Seeming not yet to accept the reality of death, the speaker plaintively appeals to Death not to act ("Spare him Death, ô spare him then" [59]), but such pleas are, of course, unanswered, and the poem closes with darkness and loss. Consolation is not offered, only a hope that the pain and anguish of his death will be kept hidden. The death of this exemplar of virtue, "Natures choycest Jewell," would affect most deeply his "mother," Nature, and it is from her that his death must be kept, "Lest for Griefe his losse may move, / All her Births abortive prove" (75–76).

The poem headed simply "Another" continues the portrait of Herrys's distinctive worth, arguing that "If ever Pitty were acquainted / With sterne Death" (1–2), it would have affected Death's action here; if ever the Fates were inclined to relent, they would have done so here. Tears flow more abundantly in this poem: Herrys's "pretious memory, / Bathes in Teares of every eye" (7–8); the Fates, had they relented, would have "learnt to beare, / The soft tincture of a Teare: / Teares would now have flow'd so deepe, / As might have taught Griefe how to weepe" (19–22). The tears are at once human tears of sadness and grief over Herrys's death and tears evoked in Death, the Fates and destruction, who come to be softened by their realization of his worth.

Crashaw's argument here is the argument Donne makes, more elaborately and with much greater complexity, in the Anniversary poems, and this poem shows the influence, in thought and in language, of Donne's poetic tribute to Elizabeth Drury. Both William Herrys and Elizabeth Drury are cast as distinctly virtuous figures, figures the world should have fought to save but did not. Elizabeth Drury's exemplary virtues and the consequent impact of her death are cited repeatedly in the eulogies and refrains of *The First Anniversarie* (for example, "She to whom this world must it selfe refer, / As Suburbs, or the Microcosme of her, / Shee, shee is dead; shee's dead: when thou knowst this, / Thou knowst how lame a cripple this world is" [235–38]; "Shee, after whom, what forme soe're we see, / Is discord, and rude incongruitee, / Shee, shee is dead, shee' s dead; when thou knowst this, / Thou knowst how vgly a monster this world is" [323–26]).[9] Herrys's life is also exemplary, a "fairer Text" in the Book of Life (52):

> In briefe, if any one were free,
> Hee was that one, and onely he.
>   But he, alas! even hee is dead
> And our hopes faire harvest spread
> In the dust.
>
>   (53–57)

As with a number of the poems we have considered, Crashaw here shows little interest in consolation, of a Christian or other sort. Rather, the ending retains the emphasis on the certainty of death and the grief of the living:

> Pitty now spend
> All the teares that griefe can lend.
> Sad mortality may hide,
> In his ashes all her pride;
> With this inscription o're his head
> *All hope of never dying, here lyes dead.*
>
> (57–62)

Grieving — abundant, consistent and eloquent grieving — is urged in each of the final two funeral elegies to be considered here, the poems on Michael Chambers and George Porter, but the poetical contexts and the nature of the grief experience are quite different. "Upon the Death of a Gentleman [Chambers]" opens in a manner that is reminiscent of Crashaw's poems that chastise Death; the speaker's antagonist here is "Faithlesse and fond Mortality" (1) that has dashed the hopes of those who looked to Chambers's future with anticipation. The poem plays off the fact that Chambers was apparently known for his eloquent speaking, but is now mute. The speaker turns that absence of verbal eloquence into a plea for eloquent (but silent) grief. With Chambers's death the "Mouth of Eloquence" (18) is silenced, but eloquence finds a new form of speech in the "sad language of our eyes": "We are contented: for then this / Language none more fluent is. / Nothing speakes our Griefe so well / As to speake Nothing" (24–28).

The final ten lines of the poem repeatedly call for mourning, but in a manner that effectively summons both verbal eloquence and eloquent mourning and that may, once again, develop from Chambers's oratorical skills. Honoring Chambers, who was gifted with words, is best done by uttering only two words ("*Hee's Dead*" [38]) and letting tearful silence represent the depth of one's grief: "Eyes are vocall, Teares have Tongues, / And there be words not made with lungs; / Sententious showers, ô let them fall, / Their cadence is Rhetoricall" (31–34).

In the poem on Chambers, tears of mourning are urged in response to the action of "Faithlesse and fond Mortality" and as a kind of eloquent replacement for the words of grief that cannot be uttered. In the poem on Porter, tears and weeping are invited throughout, made more available and integral to the poem in that it is addressed to the river Cam which, as early as line 3, is told not to hasten to the sea but to "Fixe heere thy wat'ry eyes upon these towers" (3) in Cambridge. Brief comments, no more than four lines, allude to Porter's university appointment as Regius Professor of Civil Law, and they are ended abruptly: "Enough is said" (19). In fact, not much has been said about Porter, but the speaker's interest is in the river and the opportunity that image affords to heighten the sadness and mourning the occasion demands. All of nature participates in a kind of mourning procession, not in Cambridge but on the banks of the river as it winds its way to the sea. Birds will sing "their saddest Dir'ges" (29); rocks and stones will "melt in gentle drops" (33); grief will be so intense that resistant nature will itself be moved to "chant an Elegie" (36).

There is a consistency of imagery and perspective in this poem, but it comes at a cost. There is even less evidence of the subject, Porter, than is the case in most other commemorative poems, and little attention is given to human mourners until near the end. Cam itself weeps abundantly, and in lines that anticipate the liquefaction that has so often been seen to characterize the Baroque Crashaw, the poem brings together a "sea of teares," "a bright Christall tide," "mines of Nectar" and "sweet fountains" in a tearful procession of nature's mourners (37–42). The excess of nature's mourning, suggested throughout the poem and made explicit in the final 15 lines, is, finally, matched by human mourners. Cam need not fear its "death" through an outpouring of watery grief for tearful eyes of mourners will replenish its loss: "Feare not to dy with greife; all bubling eyes / Are teeming now with store of fresh supplies" (43–44).

Crashaw's funeral elegies taken as a whole are marked by considerable variety in perspective, theme and emphasis. They reveal a poet experimenting with different forms and modes, achieving varying degrees of success. They never resist or speak against the importance and legitimacy of mourning, though among them are poems such as "Upon the Death of Mr. Herrys" or "Deaths Lecture" that give almost all of their attention to other responses to death, such as praise of the deceased or a challenge to death itself.

Given the number of Crashaw's commemorative poems, one might wonder why Crashaw does not appear in important book-length discussions of the Renaissance and early modern elegy. None of Crashaw's elegies is discussed nor is he given more than passing mention, at most, in the studies of Sacks, Pigman, Kay and Schiesari noted earlier. It might be argued that the quality of the poems does not merit attention, but that seems to me both wrong and inadequate. It is perhaps more likely that, if considered at all, they are regarded as poetic exercises of a young university student intent less on grieving than on engaging in literary practice, death conveniently providing a number of occasions for such efforts. Crashaw is not unconcerned with mourning, as I believe I have shown, but neither is that necessarily the principal concern of these poems.

II

There is more decisive grief expression in Crashaw, however, in poems that are not usually viewed as commemorative or elegiac. These poems — "The Teare," "Sancta Maria Dolorum" and "The Weeper" — respond both to the reality of death and to the grief of those still living. The first and the last of these are Crashaw's representations of Mary Magdalene's tears, typically understood to be her tears of repentance, prompted by her recognition of Jesus and by her awareness of her own sins. This event is recorded in Luke 7.37–38, and while the "sinner" who stands, kneels and weeps before Jesus and who washes his feet with her tears and dries them with her hair is never named, tradition has long held that she is Mary Magdalene. Acknowledging the likely connection between this biblical account and "The Teare" and "The Weeper," I nonetheless believe that the associations and contexts are more complex. The tears of repentance of the Mary Magdalene of tradition are offered in the presence of the living Jesus, but the tears of mourning of the biblical Magdalene are offered in the presence of the dying Christ. A more inclusive reading of both poems thus embraces the death of Jesus, a death that prompts the weeping of both Mary Magdalene and the other Mary, the mother of Jesus, in "Sancta Maria Dolorum." Thus, I believe that all three poems speak importantly and distinctively to the issues and concerns raised in this volume, revealing Crashaw most intimately and emotionally involved in grief expression, seeing and weeping for death through the eyes of two of the women whose lives and faith moved him most deeply.

"Sancta Maria Dolorum" is Crashaw's free translation of the Latin "Stabat Mater," and as has often been observed, only the subject of the poem and the Latin hymn are similar; in every other way Crashaw personalizes and embellishes the original, transforming it into an emotional and sensuous response both to Christ's death and blood and to Mary's sorrow and tears.[10] The grieving first described is that of Mary, "SORROW'S MOTHER" (4), observing "Her's, and the whole world's joyes, / Hanging torn" (6–7) on the cross. As early as the second stanza, the poet's participation in the mourning is foreseen, though not yet expressed. Who could look on such a scene and not be moved, he says; who could not, in fact, "keep such noble sorrowes company" (14) with his own grieving. Weeping and bleeding join in a "faithfull, mutuall, floud" (19), inviting the speaker both to recall the event and to experience it as a participant. The grieving and weeping that is anticipated in stanza 2 is made explicit from stanza 5 to the end. Although the scene is the death of Christ, the poem is more frequently about Mary, and it is to her that the speaker pleads "That these dry lidds might borrow / Something from thy full Seas of sorrow!" (43–44). The "faithfull, mutuall, floud" of tears and blood that makes the weeping of Mary and the bleeding of Jesus virtually indistinguishable the speaker seeks for himself: "O teach those wounds to bleed / In me" (51–52); "Yeild something in thy sad praerogative / (Great Queen of greifes) and give / Me too my teares" (57–59).

Ultimately, Crashaw's speaker seeks a full absorption into the scene of death at the cross and, simultaneously, a kind of transcendent ecstasy beyond the moment until he becomes "A lost Thing to the world, as it to me" (104). The emotional fervor of the desire to be fully in the scene, to witness the death and to experience the sorrow, is captured most powerfully in stanza 8 in lines addressed to the wounded Lord and sorrowing mother:

> O you, your own best Darts
> Dear, dolefull hearts!
> Hail; and strike home and make me see
> That wounded bosomes their own weapons be.
> Come wounds! come darts!
> Nail'd hands! and peirced hearts!
> Come your whole selves, sorrow's great son and mother!
> Nor grudge a yonger-Brother
> Of greifes his portion, who (had all their due)
> One single wound should not have left for you.
>   (71–80)

The closing stanzas continue to merge speaker, mother and son, blood and tears, sorrow and wounds, all held together by the speaker's desire to experience what he describes. Tears are more attainable than blood, however, grieving with Mary more galvanizing than being wounded with Christ:

> Flow, tardy founts! And into decent showres
>   Dissolve my Dayes and Howres.
> And if thou yet (faint soul!) deferr
> To bleed with him, fail not to weep with her.
>
> (96–99)

Much of the emotional power of this poem comes from the speaker's appeals to and identification with the grieving Mary. The poem celebrates the efficacy of the divine intoxication that comes through understanding and experiencing the meaning of the Crucifixion. As Crashaw puts it:

> O let me suck the wine
> So long of this chast vine
> Till drunk of the dear wounds, I be
> A lost Thing to the world, as it to me.
>
> (101–04)

It is, nonetheless, the Mother of Sorrows with whom he imaginatively casts himself during most of the poem and it is she who moves him most deeply. The "Great Queen of greifes" is an unassailable example for Crashaw of one whose mourning is both openly displayed and compellingly right. The result is an uninhibited participation in witnessing, reflecting and grieving.

Mary Magdalene was also witness to the death and Resurrection of Jesus, and this event is, in fact, one of only two occasions when she is identified by name. Although the Gospel writers differ in the details when they describe the women who were followers of Jesus at the Crucifixion and who were later witnesses to the empty tomb and Resurrection, each of them names Mary Magdalene at this momentous occasion. She is, furthermore — and especially in the versions offered by Mark and John — the focus of highly individualized attention as a follower and mourner of the crucified Christ. The only other mention of Mary Magdalene identifies her as the woman out of whom Jesus had cast seven demons (Mark 16.9, Luke 8.2).

Of these two occasions, only the events at the Crucifixion and Resurrection are given much attention, and they offer an important and highly focused portrait of Mary Magdalene. The woman of the biblical account and the woman of tradition are, however, quite different, a difference Susan Haskins succinctly captures in her study of the myth and the metaphor of the Magdalene:

> The predominant image we have of her is of a beautiful woman with long golden hair, weeping for her sins, the very incarnation of the age-old equation between feminine beauty, sexuality and sin. For nearly 2,000 years, the traditional conception of Mary Magdalen has been that of the prostitute who, hearing the words of Jesus Christ, repented of her sinful past and henceforth devoted her life and love to him. She appears in countless devotional images, scarlet-cloaked and with loose hair, kneeling below the cross, or seated at Christ's feet in the house of Mary and Martha of Bethany, or as the beauteous prostitute herself sprawled at his feet, unguent jar by her side, in the house of the Pharisee. Her very name evokes images of beauty and sensuality, yet when we look for this creature in the New Testament, we look for her in vain.[11]

The Mary of tradition, in short, has been conflated with other biblical women in accounts that never bear her name but that, nonetheless, contribute to her image as the penitent sinner. She has been identified as the woman whom Luke describes as a "sinner" and who washes the feet of Jesus with her tears, wiping them with her hair, kissing them and anointing them with oil (Luke 7.36–50), and tradition also merges her with Mary of Bethany who, in Luke's brief account (10.38–42), sits at the feet of Jesus while her sister Martha serves the guests. John's much longer account of Mary and Martha focuses on the death and restoration of their brother Lazarus (John 11.1–44). John alludes briefly to Mary's previous action of anointing and wiping Jesus' feet, much as does Luke's "sinner." But Mary appears more fully in John's account as a mourner, one who weeps over the death of her beloved brother.

Understanding the different images that emerge from the biblical accounts, on the one hand, and from longstanding tradition, on the other, is important because it puts in greater relief Mary Magdalene's significance as a witness to Christ's death and as a faithful mourner at the Crucifixion. For most Gospel writers that is her one role. She is not, in those accounts, the weeping and penitent sinner; she is the weeping and grieving mourner, witnessing the death of someone she loves and follows. In Crashaw's poems on the weeping Mary she is, I believe, both the penitent sinner and the grieving mourner. If tradition offers the first, Gospel writers stress the second, and those accounts, featuring faithful, mourning women, often named, would surely have spurred Crashaw's imagination. The mourning Mary is given singular attention, especially in John's version of the events. There, it is she alone who goes to the tomb and it is she who is weeping when the resurrected Christ appears to her. In "The Teare" and "The Weeper," repentant sinner and grieving friend merge to produce an outpouring of emotion and tears.

Whether "The Teare" is, as George Walton Williams suggests, a "preliminary sketch" that led to "The Weeper," or, as proposed by L. C. Martin, "material not used in the longer poem," the relationship between the two poems is evident.[12] The extraordinary focus on the tears of Mary Magdalene is unwavering in each poem, as each yields to a superfluity of weeping. In the shorter poem the tear is a "moist sparke" (3), a "watry Diamond" (4), the "eyes Jewell" (12), a "Pearle" (19), a "watry Blossome" (29); it is a "Faire Drop" (31) that angels will carry upward to heaven to be among the "bright *Chorus*" (42). Images pile on top of each other, confirming the worth and transcendence of each teardrop. But the value of the tear is ultimately confirmed, not through metaphor, but through association with the woman who weeps. Given the opportunity to be carried upward into heaven, to be "an eye of Heaven" (47), the tear would, the speaker suggests, no doubt prefer to remain where it is, to "shine here / In th' Heaven of *Mary's* eye, a *Teare*" (47–48).

Sustaining a focus on tears over 48 lines is one kind of challenge; to do so over the 31 stanzas and 186 lines of "The Weeper" is a different experience altogether. The longer poem is equally insistent on representing the eyes and tears of Mary, but, much more than "The Teare," "The Weeper" moves beyond the face to probe meaning and context. The shorter poem twice mentions Mary's eyes, but there is otherwise little to identify the occasion for, or cause of, sadness and weeping. Sadness and grief are given more careful attention in "The Weeper," and the language of the poem confirms the proximity of death and sorrow. Much is cast in metaphor, as the "evening's eyes" grow red with weeping "For the Sun that dyes," but the story of Mary and the causes of her weeping evoke a different and more compelling death and thus a greater cause for sorrow:

> Not in the evening's eyes
> When They Red with weeping are
> For the Sun that dyes,
> Sitts sorrow with a face so fair,
> No where but here did ever meet
> Sweetnesse so sad, sadnesse so sweet.
>
> When sorrow would be seen
> In her brightest majesty
> (For she is a Queen)
> Then is she drest by none but thee.
> Then, and only then, she weares
> Her proudest pearles; I mean, thy TEARES.
>
> (31–42)

Stanza 19, which has evoked the harshest criticism because it casts the weeping eyes as "two faithfull fountaines; / Two walking baths; two weeping motions; / Portable, and compendious oceans" (112–14), is, at the same time, a stanza that speaks to the role the biblical and the mythical Mary played as witness to and follower of Christ as he "strayes, / Among the Galilean mountaines, / Or more unwellcome wayes" (109–11). In its attention to both Jesus and a weeping woman, "The Weeper" is more like "Sancta Maria Dolorum" than "The Teare." Mother and son are intricately entwined in "Sancta Maria Dolorum"; in "The Weeper," master and follower mutually reinforce and support each other. She is her "lord's faire store" (115); the "rich and rare expenses" of her abundant tears are a kind of wealth that is as "the wealth of Princes" (116–18). He is, in turn, her "King," the recipient of her constant attention and devotion.

Overwhelmingly, of course, "The Weeper" is about Mary Magdalene and her tears, but both weeper and lord appear together again at the end of the poem. The tears themselves are given voice to identify their destination: "We goe to meet / A worthy object, our lord's FEET" (185–86). The occasion remembered here is surely, at the most obvious level, the scene from Luke 7.38, where the "sinner" washes the feet of Jesus with her tears and wipes them with her hair. It also captures, I believe, the biblical scene where Mary Magdalene is explicitly identified among the women who witness the death of Christ. The feet of Jesus are those washed in the house of the Pharisee and those nailed to the cross, each capable of receiving the tears of the penitent or the grieving Mary. The conflation of scenes has its precedents elsewhere in literature and art on Mary Magdalene. Among the many artistic representations of Mary are numerous associations of her with the death of Christ and, even, in intimate contact with his feet, kissing or weeping over them.[13]

The poems written from the perspective of tearful women moved by the life and death of Christ are, I believe, Crashaw's most important contribution to grief expression. Their distinctiveness lies both in their recollection of and devotional response to a biblical occasion for mourning and in the extraordinary presence and power of the women mourners. His funeral elegies are not without interest and, in fact, deserve more attention than they have normally received. But Crashaw's heart and soul are surely less in his response to the deaths of Cambridge acquaintances than in the experiences of the two biblical Marys whose emotional and tearful responses he both represents and seeks to make his own.

11 • Precious Grief
Mourning and Melancholy in Andrew Marvell's "Nymph"

Phillip McCaffrey

Among the small group of Andrew Marvell's poems that seem to concern grief or mourning, "The Nymph complaining for the death of her Faun" stands out as the only one that actually deals with those topics, in however odd a fashion. Elsewhere Marvell slants his treatment of the subject or distracts himself from it. In "Mourning," for example, the mourner, Chlora, is actually no mourner at all but a narcissistic self-lover whose tears become the mirrors of her preoccupation with herself and the emblems of her hypocrisy as she readies herself for a new lover:

> Yet some affirm, pretending Art,
> Her Eyes have so her Bosome drown'd,
> Only to soften near her Heart
> A place to fix another Wound.
>
> (13–16)[1]

The decorum required of her mourning enforces a narcissistic isolation "Within her solitary Bowr" where she "courts her self in am'rous Rain; / Her self both *Danae* and the Showr" (18–20). If there is any grief in Chlora, her weeping expels it rather than expressing it: "whatsoever does but seem / Like Grief, is from her Windows thrown" (23–24). Her tears are not, in fact, consecrated to her dead lover but are "Donatives" which she "casts abroad. . . / At the installing of a new [lover]" (27–28). In the last stanza of the poem the speaker trades in his own pose of objectivity for a final, condemning irony: "But sure as oft as Women weep, / It is to be suppos'd they grieve" (35–36).

In "Eyes and Tears" there is no specific object of grief and the tears in the poem become a kind of universal veil that shields human eyes from the sorrows of the world. But in this poem the idea is much less important than the image of the tears themselves, an image that dances through a series of metaphysical mutations: by Nature's wisdom they stand ready to flow at the sight of any "object vain" (3); they "measure" the world like plummets (7–8); they replace the honey in flowers (19–20); they are the essence of the world (21–23). In their career of literary transmutations, they finally share the identity of the eyes that produce them, first by "blessing" them with blindness:

> Yet happy they whom Grief doth bless,
> That weep the more, and see the less:
> And, to preserve their Sight more true,
> Bath still their Eyes in their own Dew.
>
> (25–28)

By the last stanza of the poem eyes and tears are interchangeable:

> Thus let your Streams o'reflow your Springs,
> Till Eyes and Tears be the same things:
> And each the other's difference bears;
> These weeping Eyes, those seeing Tears.
>
> (53–56)

The grief with which this poem concerns itself is the raw material of an extended metaphysical conceit, one that is not unlike some of John Donne's experiments in the alchemy of tears.

Of Marvell's entries in "the literature of tears," "On a Drop of Dew" probably comes closest to a treatment of grief, but here, too, special considerations dominate. The dewdrop, a metaphor for the soul exiled from heaven into this life, weeps for the loss of its former home, the "clear Region" of light which it "Round in its self incloses" (5–6). Its sorrow takes the form of a kind of duplication or intensification of its own nature and shape: "But gazing back upon the Skies, / [It] Shines with a mournful Light; / Like its own Tear" until the sun pities it and "exhale[s] it back again" (11–13, 17–18). In effect, the mourner here is a tear, the dewdrop which does not reflect the mourner or the object of mourning but which becomes them both at once. And though we might be willing to say that sorrow for the lost home of the soul might well occasion true mourning, in "On a Drop of Dew" Marvell's metaphysical condensations manipulate this fictional experience of mourning rather than dramatize it. Against this background, Marvell's "The Nymph complaining for the death of her Faun" (1650–52?) stands out as a double paradox. On the one hand, it is the only of Marvell's poems that seems to feature grief as its principal subject; on the other hand, its specifics render the topic of grief more problematical than in any other poem by Marvell.

Critical confusion over Andrew Marvell's quizzical poem has become an accepted commonplace. It is not just that no one has been able to interpret the poem in a comprehensive and also convincing way, but that readers of Marvell have not even been able to decide what approach to take to the poem. Phoebe Spinrad summarizes the situation when she says, "critics have interpreted the poem as a political, religious, or romantic allegory; as a metaphorical lament for innocence, an old order, Christ, or love; and as a literal lament for a pet or — in one reading that borders on self-parody — for a child." Anthony Low had already written that "One cannot even be certain whether it is primarily a love poem, a political allegory, an ironic psychological analysis, or a religious devotion." Almost every critic of the poem has acknowledged this state of affairs; the only thing that they have been able to agree upon is that there is no agreement.[2] And perhaps it is just to say that, although almost every feature of the poem has been worried, stretched and juggled, the chimerical fawn has often been the centerpiece of the puzzle. The situation reminds one a little of Chaucer's *House of Fame*.

Whatever the poem means, and in what way or in how many ways Marvell would have had us read it, its literal subject is clear. It is about a young girl (nymph) who is mourning the death of her pet, the fawn her unfaithful Sylvio gave to her as a love-gift before she knew that he was unfaithful. Whatever else the poem means, it is a poem about grief, about an experience that can be examined in psychoanalytic terms. A reading of "The Nymph complaining" in modified Freudian terms can answer at least some questions about the poem and it can offer a perspective from which to reevaluate not only the prominent details of the poem but also some of the critical approaches that have been brought to bear on it.

In his essay on "Mourning and Melancholy" (1917) Freud distinguishes between mourning and melancholy in a way that has generally gone unchallenged.[3] In the natural and necessary process of mourning, the subject "re-cathects" his internal "imago" of the lost loved one repeatedly — that is, internal representations of the loved one are evoked, one by one, mentally cherished and then relinquished, at least from conscious preoccupation. This is done in order to accomplish contrary goals: on the one hand, the mourner must eventually be able to neutralize the power of this internal figure and, like the victim of trauma, "wear it down" by repeatedly evoking it in the imagination. On the other hand, the mourner must eventually succeed in installing an imago that may be even more powerful in the unconscious rather than the conscious in a specific process of "(re-) identification." Melancholy, however, entails quite a different internal dynamic: the griever grieves for himself or, more precisely, concerns himself with his own imago of himself and attacks and demeans it. No real, external object has been lost; what has been lost is an internal object that, for the subject, is at least as imposing as any to be found in reality. "The Nymph complaining for the death of her Faun" illustrates Freud's clear distinction between these two states, their potential relationship to each other, and also how the aggression involved in melancholic grief may delay and then finally prevent any mournful healing.

The Nymph suffers two literal losses, Sylvio's betrayal and the fawn's death, and it is important to recognize that her grief over the loss of Sylvio ought not to have been different in kind from her grief over the death of the fawn: "Grief is the characteristic response to the loss of a valued object, be it a loved person, a cherished possession, a job, status, home, country, an ideal, a part of the body, etc."[4] Thus the loss of a lover through betrayal rather than death would normally provoke a period of mourning.[5]

It is true that the Nymph gives minimal evidence of any deep reaction to Sylvio's betrayal: "And quite regardless of my Smart, / [He] Left me his Faun, but took his Heart" (35–36). Whatever she may have felt she condenses (at least at this point) into the single noun, "smart."[6] On the other hand, and without making the naive assumption that the Nymph is an analysand rather than a peculiar literary character, an absence of reaction to the loss of a loved one is not uncommon. Such an absence of overt mourning usually signifies repression, a failure to mourn because of the survivor's ambivalent attitude toward the lost object. What is repressed is not only the normal sorrow of mourning but also the anger and aggression that constitutes the other half of the ambivalence.[7]

The Nymph herself claims otherwise, of course — except in her short speculation on whether Sylvio's gift might have turned out to be as unreliable as Sylvio was (47–50). When she describes her substitution of the fawn for Sylvio after the latter has abandoned her, she seems content, almost placid, as if the substitution were of no great significance to her:

> Thenceforth I set my self to play
> My solitary time away,
> With this: and very well content,
> Could so mine idle Life have spent.
>
> (37–40)

Her calm transition with its apparent lack of emotion and its freedom from anger amounts to an absence of grief, a repression of the strong emotions necessarily involved but here hidden; it is a form of "delayed mourning."[8] When such anger finally emerges, it is often directed at the self or at some person other than the lost beloved, as we will see more clearly when we consider the end of Marvell's poem.[9] But here the element of aggression that a psychoanalytic reading seems determined to uncover is apparently lacking. Toward the "wanton Troopers" who have killed the fawn, she expresses a passive tolerance, a generic forgiveness: "I'me sure I never wisht them ill; / Nor do I for all this; nor will" (7–8). And even the implied wish for revenge that immediately follows these lines (13–24) seems moderate for the occasion, given the circumstances as seen from the Nymph's point of view.[10]

The Nymph's reactions are *too* moderate for the occasion. The 12 lines of muted vengefulness that follow the Nymph's forgiveness of the troopers signal that there may be a deeper reaction. And those 12 lines are followed by the Nymph's description of the presentation of the gift of the fawn, a description bracketed by her complaint against Sylvio:

> Unconstant *Sylvio*, when yet
> I had not found him counterfeit,
> One morning (I remember well),
> Ty'd in this silver Chain and Bell,
> Gave it to me: nay and I know
> What he said then; I'me sure I do.
> Said He, look how your Huntsman here
> Hath taught a Faun to hunt his *Dear*.
> But *Sylvio* soon had me beguil'd.
> This waxed tame, while he grew wild,
> And quite regardless of my Smart,
> Left me his Faun, but took his Heart.
>
> (25–36)

The Nymph's reactions to Sylvio's betrayal and then to the wounding of the fawn seem far more restrained than one would expect while, at the same time, they give hints of an underlying anger which the Nymph may be repressing.

It is more than a good guess that some of that repressed emotion must fuel the Nymph's extravagant relationship with the fawn, a relationship that endows the animal with a distinct and specific psychological status for the Nymph.[11] Most obvious is the Nymph's close connection to the fawn. It is linked to her by her ownership of it (25–29), by her having raised it (55–58), by the fact that she is content to spend her solitary idleness with it after Sylvio has left her (37–40), by its responsiveness to her (41–45, 65–68), and by its virtual identification with her private garden of roses and lilies (71 ff.). Her affection for it is evident in almost every couplet in the poem: "How could I less / Than love it? O I cannot be / Unkind, t'a Beast that loveth me" (44–46). Her intense attachment to the fawn is the proportional and inverted measure of her intense grief over its death.

To a significant extent, the qualities she sees in the fawn are her own or like her own (Asp, 400; Baruch, 153). Her coy refusal to compare the fawn's white "foot" directly to her own hand, for example, makes clear that pure white is a color that they share: "I blusht to see its foot more soft, / And white, (shall I say then my hand?) / NAY any Ladies of the Land" (60–62). Once the fawn has reddened its lips by eating roses, it is both red and white as is the blushing Nymph in the two lines just quoted. But the resemblances are not merely physical. The fawn, whatever its future intentions, is thus far every bit as innocent as the Nymph and so has earned its emblematic white as much as she has. They are also both innocently playful as the frolicking fawn evokes this response from the Nymph (41–44, 63–68).

It is clear that the Nymph idealizes the fawn and does so in part because of their resemblances; but she idealizes it to the point of rendering it, in her descriptions and metaphors, nearly bizarre. Whatever allegorical implications its pure white color may have,[12] the Nymph attributes an intensity of whiteness to the fawn that far exceeds the needs of allegory.[13] It is not only white but becomes more white as she feeds it white milk and sugar (55–58). Not only is its body white but its feet are whiter than any lady's hands, as we have seen (60–62). And lying among the lilies, it is so white it is completely camouflaged (77–80).[14]

The fawn is idealized in other ways as well. Its breath is sweet, presumably from its diet of milk and sugar (59), as unlikely as that would be.[15] Its feet are not only white but "more soft" than the Nymph's or any lady's in the land (60–62), and on those soft feet "it was nimbler much than Hindes; / And trod, as on the four Winds" (69–70). Some readers may also find the fawn's responses to the Nymph exaggerated in the Nymph's description of them. Not only did the fawn "invite, / Me to its game" and "challenge me the Race" (42–43, 66) but, in those famous lines,

>Upon the Roses it would feed,
>Until its Lips ev'n seem'd to bleed:
>And then to me 'twould boldly trip,
>And print those Roses on my Lip.
>
>(83–86)

Whatever sexual implications the rosy kisses might have, they unite the Nymph with both the fawn and her own garden simultaneously, thus intensifying the Nymph's connection to the fawn (and vice versa) by means of the garden.[16]

These combined attributes of the fawn suggest that it is a particular kind of psychological object for the Nymph even before it is shot, a "linking object," which Volkan and Josephthal think can be central to the mourning process. They describe the ways in which some mourners try to keep symbolic contact by focusing on some object associated with the lost one: "Another sort of contact with the dead, again one under the mourner's absolute control, is maintained by the use of some object contaminated with certain elements, some of which came from the dead while others come from the mourner himself. These have been named 'linking objects.' They differ from the ordinary keepsake since the mourner invests them with magic capable of linking him with the one he has lost."[17] To a certain extent, the fawn qualifies as a linking object for the Nymph because it is linked to Sylvio on the one hand, and to herself on the other. In describing some typical linking devices, Volkan and Josephthal further clarify the nature of this sort of psychological object: "A great variety of objects may become linking objects. The mourner chooses such an object from among (1) something once used routinely by the dead . . . (3) a symbolic or realistic representation of the dead person . . . or (4) something at hand when the mourner first learned of the death. . . . We have also known patients to cling to something less tangible, such as an elaborate fantasy" (305). Sylvio is not dead, of course, but earlier we noted that losing a loved object by almost any means can provoke grief and require mourning. Given that adjustment, the fawn was associated with Sylvio, was symbolic of him to the Nymph, and was "at hand" when the Nymph learned of his betrayal. Two other characteristics of the linking object are pertinent to the fawn: "The linking object is completely under the patient's control; he has the unconscious illusion that it makes it possible for him to kill the dead person or bring him back to life" (Volkan and Josephthal, 308). While the fawn may not be completely under the Nymph's control, it is nearly so and certainly was when she nursed it. The second magical quality of the linking object, its power to kill or revive the dead person — or in the Nymph's terms, to bring Sylvio back or send him away — refers once again to the factor of aggression and aggression against the self (based on guilt) which we have touched on several times.

In a therapeutic situation, the goal is to deprive the linking object of its magical intensity and thus "tame" the intense love and hate which it embodies for the mourner. That done, the mourner can begin to progress through the normal stages of mourning, no longer fixed on the linking object (Volkan and Josephthal, 313–15). But in the Nymph's case, her linking object is destroyed while it is at the height of its magical appeal and so the death of the fawn explodes the hidden tinderbox of the Nymph's reactions to Sylvio's betrayal. It is, in a sense, a triple loss: the old loss of Sylvio is repeated in the loss of the fawn itself and to both is added the loss of the fawn as a linking object — which is to say, the Nymph's loss of a significant part of herself. There can be no normal process of mourning for her.

But the situation is even more complicated because although the fawn's importance to the Nymph can be partly explained by its function as a linking object, the fawn exceeds this role. The ways in which the Nymph idealizes and relates to the fawn make her relationship with it narcissistic and make the fawn itself a narcissistic object, what Heinz Kohut has called a "self- object" or what I have elsewhere called a "Narcissistic Idol."[18] The self-object or Narcissistic Idol can be imagined as a kind of *tabula rasa*, a real person or object in the external world but one that is viewed by the narcissist almost entirely in terms of the narcissist's own projections. In effect, the narcissist "remakes" the idol in his or her own self-image. As a result, the idol acquires certain typical characteristics, among them those the Nymph attributes to the fawn. The supposed attractions of the idol are exaggerated and idealized, sometimes to the level of an imaginary perfection.[19] The relationship to the idol is felt to be essential for the narcissist, exclusive and profoundly mutual.[20] In fact, the relationship with the idol is a distortion of reality and is therefore fragile and superficial, managing to conceal its unconscious elements of aggression and self-aggression only temporarily. In order to maintain the supposed perfection of the idol, the narcissist necessarily must split his or her own imago, projecting only those idealized qualities the narcissist is willing to imagine. Finally, because of the close mirror relationship between the narcissist and the idol, any damage to or disappointment in the Idol is devastating to the narcissist because it reflects back on him or her, returning those "positive" projections back upon the sender in a reversed and therefore negative form. Because it is false and superficial, the idol is always potentially dangerous; it always harbors the hidden threat of betrayal.

In psychoanalytic terms, then, the Nymph's emotional dependence upon the fawn places her in a precarious and fragile relationship, one that by its very nature was unlikely to offer enduring support.[21] As a love-gift from Sylvio the fawn must remind her of him even as she makes it replace him in her attention and affections.[22] It is not an accident that in the passage quoted earlier (25–36) the Nymph brackets her account of the gift of the fawn between statements of Sylvio's unfaithfulness; this framing nicely illustrates the ambivalent value of the pet which, apparently intended to represent Sylvio's love, instead becomes a substitute for it and, therefore, an emblem of his infidelity. It is this same ambivalent value, I think, that leads the Nymph to speculate on the *fawn*'s faithfulness: "Had it liv'd long, I do not know / Whether it too might have done so / As *Sylvio* did" (47–49). And one might argue that part of the motive for the Nymph's intense involvement with the fawn is precisely its ambivalence: it is the only part of Sylvio that the Nymph can still claim. At the same time, the Nymph's substitution of the fawn for Sylvio constitutes, in effect, a good-bad split wherein, consciously at least, Sylvio understandably becomes the object of the Nymph's (muted) anger while the fawn becomes the idealized good object. It is just after toying with the idea that Sylvio's gift might have turned out to be as unfaithful as Sylvio was that the Nymph decides that, so far at least, the fawn has been otherwise: "Thy Love was far more better then / The love of false and cruel men" (53–54). Before Sylvio left, the Nymph's attitude to him and to the fawn must have been approximately the same; after Sylvio's betrayal, however, the Nymph has split her hate and her love in a typically preoedipal defense that is designed to negotiate the conflict between hate and love and to preserve something of the love object in a favorable status.[23]

It should not be surprising that any individual loss may recall the experience of a previous one and thus work in a kind of cumulative way on the griever's emotions.[24] It has been clear to many readers of Marvell's poem that the Nymph's distress over the death of the fawn somehow includes or recapitulates her distress over Sylvio's betrayal and that (without imagining that we are dealing with a realistic fiction here) the excesses of her grief for her dying pet can partly be explained by this cumulative connection. In wounding the fawn the troopers open an emotional Pandora's box for the Nymph; all the love, sorrow and aggression which the Nymph had repressed are suddenly released in exaggerated form.[25] The second loss not only reenacts the first but is made even more intense by the fact that the first loss had never been dealt with.[26] The fawn's role as a "magic" linking object had allowed the Nymph to postpone the process of mourning over Sylvio's betrayal by repressing its most painful emotions and by constructing, instead, a kind of edenic oblivion. By killing the fawn at the height of its psychological magic, the troopers have destroyed any possibility the Nymph might eventually have had for properly mourning Sylvio's betrayal. Precisely because it is now lost, the fawn cannot be "reevaluated" by the Nymph; the real "Elizium" into which the idealized fawn ascends is the Nymph's psyche where it will assume a far more durable, less negotiable form than any alabaster figure.

All of these implications are enormously compounded and deepened by the fawn's overlapping and far more elemental role as the Nymph's Narcissistic Idol. The fact that the fawn could be both — linking object and idol — concatenates both its attractions and its psychological dangers for the Nymph. In each of these two individual roles the fawn is greatly overvalued and each of the two reinforces the overvaluation due to the other. It is as if the Nymph is not only holding onto the lost Sylvio (through a linking object) but she is holding onto herself (Narcissistic Idol) and, in addition, holding onto the self that is holding onto Sylvio (both roles combined).

Not every loved person, pet or thing is a Narcissistic Idol and however painful the labor of mourning for something loved and lost, mourning proceeds apace through its predictable stages until a partial peace is attained. But when the lost object is not only loved but is loved narcissistically, the self is lost in a far more comprehensive sense than in normal mourning.[27] This entails a different kind of mourning or, more precisely, a failure of mourning, a depressive stasis from which the griever cannot progress through the stages of the normal process of mourning but is locked into its most painful phase, more or less permanently. There is much to be mourned in the loss of a loved one — the loss of another person and the loss of that part of oneself which was, in effect, an internalized version of the other person. In the destruction of a Narcissistic Idol, however, *everything* must be mourned for — the loss of the whole self of the mourner.[28] It is too much;

there is no other part of the narcissistic psyche exempt from the loss and therefore available to do the work of mourning.

The full extent of the Nymph's psychological disaster becomes bitterly explicit in the final symbolic object she deals with, the memorial statue of herself and the fawn which she imagines. As Carolyn Asp writes, "The whole trajectory of the action in the poem . . . is ordered to the stone figures with which it ends" (403). Here, too, the full measure of the Nymph's aggression and the proper index to the quality of her mourning for the fawn emerges in her description of the imaginary statue which will be as much a memorial to her grief as to the dead fawn.[29] The statue, then, replaces the Nymph's Narcissistic Idol in the poem and reverses its valence. Whereas the fawn made manifest the positive (and defensive) emotions in the Nymph's reaction to her first loss, the statue reverses these and finally makes manifest the Nymph's negative reactions to both losses. The Nymph's aggression finally reaches the surface in her description of the imaginary statue, but this aggression is directed, not toward Sylvio or the troopers (or even the fawn), but primarily against herself.[30]

The statue would memorialize the fawn, of course, representing it "in purest alabaster" which will be very white, but not as white as the fawn: "For I would have thine Image be / White as I can, though not as Thee" (121–22). The lines are somewhat ambiguous. Most simply, the Nymph recognizes that no memorial can adequately represent the fawn's qualities and so the statue necessarily will be an inadequate memorial. That is, the memorial cannot possibly express the idealized fawn's value as the Nymph has perceived it. But a second, less obvious reading suggests a different implication. The Nymph would not have the sculpture of the fawn be as white as the fawn[31]; the Nymph chooses or at least acquiesces to the fact that the memorial could not adequately represent the fawn. She would prefer that it not be adequate because, after all, the alabaster fawn will not be her real fawn and insofar as it continues to reflect her, statue echoing statue, it will have become the reflection of her losses.[32] Finally, though, this reading is not as different from the first as it might seem: in either case, the fawn's extraordinary qualities (for example, its whiteness) cannot be duplicated in a memorial sculpture because those extraordinary qualities exist in the eyes of the Nymph. Absent her projections, the fawn will have to settle for the lesser compliment of alabaster. In this, too, there is a muted element of the Nymph's aggression. Since the real fawn, her fawn, has been killed, she would not have its idealized form survive her possession of it. She will be linked with the fawn in a statuary merger which, by implication, will fail to represent *her* adequately, too.[33]

But it is the statue of the Nymph herself which has attracted greater interest, and rightly so, for it not only climaxes her grief but in doing so clarifies its nature in retrospect. It is in her decision to die with the fawn, if we are to take this literally (Wilcher, 88), and to imagine herself as a memorial that her aggression, so little in evidence before, now appears turned against herself. Since the fawn has died she can only respond by dying herself and reducing herself to a statuesque embodiment of her own grief.[34] The fawn was the externalized representation of her self-imago and so, necessarily, her death must follow his (Asp, 401). At the same time, the imaginary petrification of her grief expresses her punishment of herself for losing the fawn and this, of course, is only an extension of her punishment of herself for losing Sylvio.

The most unusual feature of the Nymph's statue has been frequently discussed. She imagines it grieving for the fawn by shedding live tears, as she is doing while she imagines it:

> First my unhappy Statue shall
> Be cut in Marble; and withal,
> Let it be weeping too: but there
> Th'Engraver sure his Art may spare,
> For I so truly thee bemoane,

> That I shall weep though I be Stone:
> Until my Tears, still dropping, wear
> My breast, themselves engraving there.
>
> (111–22)[35]

It is important to emphasize the fact that she only imagines this double memorial; the difficulty with this is precisely the fact that her internal image of the statue is only imaginary whereas the fawn was real and external, however idealized.[36] In imagining the statue, the Nymph succeeds in "internalizing" the fawn, but only as a dead(ened) object; since she has made the fawn into her own imago, she must also imagine herself as dead(ened) object. Her psychological suicide seems required, whether or not it is to be understood as a "real" possibility in the fiction of the poem. More than anything else, the Nymph's imaginary petrification of herself expresses the stultification of her emotions and her inability to mourn the double loss with which the fawn's death confronts her.[37] She has no substitutes left, not even herself. The imagined statue does, in several important senses, replace the fawn that replaced Silvio, but that is exactly its drawback; it essentially reverses the function of the fawn in that it is an entirely negative imago whereas the fawn had been made into a mirror of the Nymph's positive projections, however self-deceptive or regressive those may have been. The Nymph "dies" four times: once with the loss of Silvio, once with the loss of the fawn, and twice with the loss of herself in each of those two cases.

This reading carries a number of implications about several arguments that have been made about the poem. For example, if full emphasis is granted to the fact that the memorial statue is entirely imaginary rather than real, then the Nymph can hardly be described as an artist or a figure for the artist because she actually makes nothing. Elaine Hoffman Baruch writes that "she does not think of herself as an artist. The metamorphosis that she wants someone else to effect will lead her to create no poetry and no music" (155). It is precisely a mark of her narcissistic desolation that she is reduced to imagining the statue, to replacing her lost Narcissistic Idol with a purely mental image, and a negative one at that.[38] A second implication of this psychoanalytic reading of the poem is that it qualifies the Nymph's potential to be an allegorical figure. Insofar as the fawn is a Narcissistic Idol for the Nymph, it is by definition unavailable for allegorical duty because the essential characteristics of a Narcissistic Idol are determined by the projections of the narcissist. It is *the Nymph's* fawn, not merely by ownership but also and more fundamentally by her conception of it (Allen, 184). The fawn is a reflection of the Nymph, or at least of those qualities she chooses to have reflected. Were the fawn allegorical, it would have to represent some larger, external reality and that would be exactly contrary to the nature of a Narcissistic Idol that represents nothing but the narcissist. The two alternatives are mutually exclusive unless the larger, external reality has also been conceived in narcissistic terms, in which case it would fail to retain its objective identity and would be reduced, once again, to the narrow world of the narcissistic reflection.

A third implication of the reading offered here concerns the nature of the Nymph's relationships with both Sylvio and the fawn. These have often been interpreted sexually but understanding the fawn as a Narcissistic Idol makes a sexual reading of the fawn complicated. Whether or not the Nymph's relationship to Sylvio was sexual[39] (and it is quite impossible to read through Marvell's adaptations of pastoral conventions on this point), the Nymph's relationship to the fawn is decidedly preoedipal. That is, to the extent that her relationship to the fawn can be interpreted sexually, it must be "autoerotic" since she has "constructed" the fawn in her own self-image. If the Nymph were a realistic character, we would want to say that during the whole narrative time covered by the poem she has either regressed to or become fixed at the level of a preoedipal mentality, perhaps because of her betrayal by Silvio.[40] Her relationship with the fawn is primarily a relationship with herself. Having been abandoned by her lover, she has retreated into the convenient (narcissistic) delusion that, not only does she love the fawn, but that the fawn is an adequate "mate" for her. If the Nymph and Sylvio were lovers, as some readers suppose, then the Nymph's loss of that love has reduced her to a more elemental mentality. Her relationship to the fawn may have inspired any number of sexual symbols, but they have become only symbols, vacant references to the loss behind the loss.[41]

This description of the Nymph's experience of successive and compounding losses refines and particularizes Freud's distinction between mourning and melancholia — with the help of the more recent psychoanalysts I have cited. Insofar as they are represented in the poem, Sylvio's betrayal can be understood as an occasion for mourning and the Nymph's reaction a failure to mourn or a delay of mourning. On the surface and temporarily, the Nymph seems to escape both mourning and melancholia to a large extent. But no one understands the fickleness of surfaces better than Marvell. In order to repress her grief and its components of sorrow, disappointed love and consequent anger, the Nymph invests the fawn in double measure. As a linking object, the fawn becomes the mechanism by which the Nymph institutes that repression. As a Narcissistic Idol the fawn becomes the idealized, external reflection of the Nymph's "wished-for self" which compensates her for the psychological damage she does not or cannot deal with.[42] With the wounding and then death of the fawn, however, the fragile structure of these defenses shatters and the Nymph can no longer avoid facing the grief that has returned to her in a compounded and intensified form. The destruction of her linking object and of her Narcissistic Idol means that the delay in her mourning has been made permanent and that self (ego) which ought to have begun the process of mourning has been thoroughly disabled. The repressed aggression, therefore, is reloaded and aimed especially at herself. What the Nymph's literary experiences illustrate is the way in which mourning can be stalled, can fail altogether and can settle into self-destructive grief. Her deepest loss is of an internal part of herself, now no longer able to find its idealized reflection in the fawn; she is reduced to an imago of the self that memorializes its own insubstantiality in a monument no one will ever see.

12 • Repairing Androgyny
Eve's Tears in *Paradise Lost*

Margo Swiss

I

In his theological tract *Christian Doctrine,* Milton describes God as both anthropomorphic and anthropopathetic: "if God attributes to himself again and again a human shape and form, why should we be afraid of assigning to him something he assigns to himself."[1] Later, Milton elaborates this anthropomorphism, giving it an affective emphasis:

> If *Jehovah repented that he had created man,* Gen. vi.6, . . . let us believe that he did repent . . . If *he grieved in his heart,* Gen. vi.6, and if similarly, *his soul was grieved,* Judges x.16, let us believe that he did feel grief . . . If it is said that God, after working for six days, *rested and was refreshed,* Exod. xxxi.17, and if he *feared his enemy's displeasure,* Deut. xxxii.27, let us believe that it is not beneath God to feel what grief he does feel, to be refreshed by what refreshes him, and to fear what he does fear. For however you may try to tone down these and similar texts about God by an elaborate show of interpretative glosses, it comes to the same thing in the end. (*CP,* 6:134–35)

Such arguments for God's human-likeness help us to attend more closely to Milton's portrayal of the Creator in *Paradise Lost*. God's "high sufferance" (1.366) of human events shows him to be actively involved with Creation to the extent that the climax of Milton's presentation comes in book 11, where Adam's collapse into grief at the prospect of future annihilation (the flood) corresponds to God's own grief: "when looking down he saw / The whole Earth filled with violence, and all flesh / Corrupting each thir way."[2]

That Milton's God, like his creatures, is in part an affective being is seldom acknowledged. Whether designated "the autocratic designer of the conservative politics of heaven" or read pejoratively within the limitations of an Old Testament characterization, Milton's God has often been misinterpreted by critics. However, as Joan Webber has shown, "Milton does not accept him [such a God], nor is this God satisfied with himself. He is in process toward full realization of the higher state imagined in the images of light." Moreover, writes Webber, "[t]he only way to achieve that condition is abnegation of title and rank." Viewed from this perspective, then, Milton's God can only be fulfilled by uniting himself with Creation through the condescending Son. He will otherwise remain eternally incomplete.[3]

An essential strand of the theological fabric of the epic is therefore an anthropomorphized and affective God, derived in part from a number of sources known to Milton. Works by Tertullian and Lactantius, purported to be Milton's favorite Fathers, offer lengthy accounts of God's anthropomorphized nature.[4] With respect to an epic rendering of a God in process toward fulfillment, tracts such as Lactantius's *Ira Dei* and Tertullian's *Adversus Praxeam* and *Adversus Marcionem* provide accounts that bear directly upon Milton's characterization of God the Father.[5] As well as being constrained by the Arminian principles of Milton's portrayal, the God of *Paradise Lost* is one who, according to Tertullian's description, might almost appear to suffer loneliness, or to experience what Lactantius calls the "vicious passions."[6]

The anthropopathos of God is reflected in *Paradise Lost*'s portrayal of a sad and grieving God. In fact, God's bereavement over the loss of his first creation, which "dispeopl'd Heav'n" (7.151) of one third of the angelic host, is dramatized as a prerequisite to the act of Creation itself. In book 7 God speaks plainly concerning his reasons for acting. The reparative intention behind Creation is poised adversarily against the fractious forces of Satan whose "heart [God knows] exalt[s] him in the harm / Already done" (7.150–51). Rather than stooping to violent retaliation, God "can repair / That detriment" and "will create / Another World" (7.152–53, 154–55). As Milton relates, God knows his enemy well and sets out to perform the irrefutable spiritual act: to confound hate with love. These humanizing features of the deity (his anger, fear and grief) involved highly sensitive issues of interpretation for the readership of Milton's day, just as they have continued to influence his reception history to the present. Milton's contribution to the perennial question of the divine nature is that of an anthropopathetic God, one who suffers, to some extent in himself and fully through the Son, and whose suffering is efficacious to the providential plan and exemplary to his creatures. In short, Milton's epic argues that human grief finds its prototype in God's own grief, together with that of the Son, and their mutually compassionate response to Creation.

God's pathos for his human creatures is illustrated especially well in the opening lines of book 5. He has watched Satan's dream invasion of Eve's sleep and discerns what readers may not, that the couple is about to undergo their first domestic crisis. Eve's dream is crucial and has been much discussed. Of the various readings, three are pertinent to my concern in this essay, that is, with Eve's affectively complicated existence following her dream, notably signified by her tears. I would agree with Diane McColley that Eve's dream, though "unwilled," does, in a manner of speaking, represent "an important first step in [Adam and Eve's] education." I would, in turn, qualify the nature of that education by reaffirming Ann Astell's emphasis on its "affective" imperative. To this end, the dream is surely lesson one. As Joseph Duncan reminds us, "Eve's first major confrontation with the unconscious occurs in her dream initiated by Satan [5.28–92]. Her consciousness has been expanded by experience, 'which [her] mind / Never knew till this irksom night' (5.34–35)." Even before she wakens, Eve is described through Adam's eyes, whose "wonder was to find unwak'n'd *Eve* / With Tresses discompos'd, and glowing Cheek, / As through unquiet rest" (5.9–11). Eve's "glowing cheek," in contrast to her innocent "blushing like the Morn" (8.511) on the verge of her first lovemaking with Adam earlier, is now flushed by an appetitive urge beyond any she has ever known. She experiences her first inner conflict, between new sensations of power which her dream apparently offers and unprecedented pangs of conscience correcting that illusion. To understand this reaction from a Renaissance perspective, Timothy Bright's *A Treatise on Melancholie*, first published in 1586 and reprinted into the seventeenth century, provides a useful explanation. According to Bright, blushing is a direct expression of the conscience: "we commend blushers, because it declareth a tender heart, & easily moved with remorse of that which is done amisse, and a feare to offend, and a care least it should commit ought worthy of blame. Furthermore it sheweth a conscience quicke, and tender, and an upright sentence of the minde agreeable to this ingraven maxime of good and evill" (207). Eve's blush, even during the unconscious state of sleep, surprises Adam and suggests her inherent sense of error. Eve's consciousness, now contaminated by her dream, will, in future, prove no less than *excruciating* in its consequences. Adam and Eve's eventual sorrow for the sin into which they are now being led will become their veritable "cross," until the damage begun by this satanic dream is at last teleologically matched and healed by the "great good" (612) of that God-sent dream Eve enjoys at the end of book 12.[7]

II

The pairing of opposites (of Eve's satanic dream, portending schism, and her Godly dream, heralding reunion with husband and God) sets an appropriate context in which to re-present the long disputed androgyny of Adam and Eve's relationship. The controversy concerning androgyny in *Paradise Lost* originated in the late 1960s, possibly fired by Jungian psychology and interest in such popular works as Carolyn Heilbrun's *Toward a Recognition of Androgyny*. Despite Milton's denial of the hermaphroditic origins of the first couple in *Tetrachordon*, a number of critics have convincingly argued for androgyny as a pervasive principle in *Paradise Lost*.[8] It has been claimed that androgyny informs not only Adam and Eve's relation, but also the poet's own office as the "inspired" receptacle of God's active "infusion," and, of course, the very nature of God him or herself. I would suggest that, taking first things first, the nature of Milton's God, whose presiding, masculine presence, described in book 3 as one who "sits / High Thron'd above all highth" (3.57–58), is poignantly complemented by the various affective, often characteristically feminine qualities attributed to him. A comparatively recent advocate of God's androgynous nature, Robert A. Erickson, actually refers to the "sexual life of [Milton's] God" to the extent that "the Father's heart is the genital organ of the Son."[9] Erickson adds that Milton also "reimagines the Spirit . . . who combines the feminine inspiring and nurturing characteristics of the Greek Muses and the sister of scriptural Wisdom with the masculine impregnating power of the Son/Logos/Word" (97). Just as God the father, through the agency of the Spirit, "[i]mpregnates the vast abyss" of precreation darkness, so, argues Erickson, "Milton recreates that act in the opening lines of the poem by wedding the masculine Spirit with the feminine Muse Urania and indirectly imploring that androgynous Spirit to impregnate him so that what is dark may be illumined and he may transmit his vision to humankind" (93).

Evidence for God's androgyny presented so persuasively by Erickson has been preceded by such critics as John Shawcross and Virginia Mollenkott. In his discussion of Adam and Eve's relation, Shawcross concludes that "gender differences should be emphasized in reading *Paradise Lost* only where we see them leading to the concept of the androgyne, that form of human duality (as there is the duality of God the Father and God the Son, producing God the Holy Spirit to create the Trinity), yielding oneness."[10] Similarly, Virgina Mollenkott extends the implications of what she terms "Milton's Androgynous Muse," when she writes, "Milton's organic, deiform universe in which everything was born from God ... makes God not only the Father but very much the Mother of us all" (29-30). In the light of such arguments the account of human creation in book 7 affirms that human creatures, as reflections of the Divine Creator, must exemplify this same androgyny:

> Let us make now Man in our image, Man
> In our similitude, and let *them* [emphasis mine] rule,
> Over the Fish and Fowl of Sea and Air,
>
> . . . .
>
> This said, he form'd thee, *Adam*, thee O Man
> Dust of the ground, and in thy nostrils breath'd
> The breath of Life; in his own Image hee
> Created thee, in the Image of God
> Express, and thou becam'st a living Soul.
> Male he created thee, but thy consort
> Female for Race.
>
> (7.519-30)

The installation of God's androgynous image within male and female creatures ensures that their union of body, mind and soul will forever replicate this same complementary nature. Like God, Adam and Eve are to become ubiquitously creative: they are called to "[b]e fruitful, multiply, and fill the Earth, / Subdue it, and throughout Dominion hold" (7.531–32). In their divine androgyny man and woman will ideally procreate in goodness as the Father, Son and Spirit once cocreated the heavens and Earth, and continue to transact all godly benefits.

Meanwhile, Raphael's cosmological explanation to Adam in book 8 demonstrates that Creation itself reflects the fruitful pairing of male and female agencies. Here is an order whose wondrous complementarity is as mysterious as its Creator and that can only be partially apprehended through human reason. Man cannot understand: "Whether the Sun predominant in Heav'n / Rise on the Earth, or Earth rise on the Sun, / Hee from the East his flaming road begin, / Or Shee from West her silent course advance" (8.160–63), or whether there be "other Suns perhaps / With thir attendant Moons . . . Communicating Male and Female Light, / Which two great Sexes animate the World" (8.148–51). In the context of the androgynous principles that inform Creation, Adam and Eve's androgyny finds its natural place. I would therefore disagree with Marilyn Farwell's conclusion that "[Adam and Eve's] strength is based on existential support and responsibility rather than androgynous, ontological fusion" (15). Farwell's astute analysis, based on the separation scene of book 9, provides me as a reader with what Raphael's acute discourse on gender relations offers Adam, that is, the occasion to counter cogent discussion with "What inward thence I feel" (8.608). Adam celebrates what he *believes* to be his androgynous unity with Eve. What he "declare[s]" as "unfeigned / Union of Mind, or in us both one Soul" (8.604–05) derives not, as Raphael claims, from "carnal pleasure" (8.593), but from Adam's experience of "mysterious reverence" (8.599) arising from "those graceful acts, / Those thousand decencies that daily flow / From all her words and actions, mixt with Love / And sweet compliance"

(8.600–03). Here is perfect human love! Milton may be suggesting that even the angels in heaven cannot fully understand the complexity of such love. If we, as critics, proceed to label Adam's reply to Raphael "uxorious," then we show ourselves to be equally inexperienced (as we clearly are) in the ideal nature of prelapsarian love.

Though Adam's belief in their joyful "oneness" is tinged with irony, the trying and testing of this relationship will be ultimately justified. The human marriage of male and female, because it is created in God's image, reflects not only all variants in the providential plan, but the potentially redemptive nature of God. Just as Adam and Eve's original androgyny will be violated by Satan's influence, and their *via dolorosa* toward individuation initiated, so the cooperative intervention of the Son on the Father's behalf will provide a model of reconciliation through which man and woman's androgynous ontology will be divinely "repaired." In effect, the cooperative androgyne of the Father and Son is paradigmatic of Adam and Eve's relation. The interactive dynamic between these androgynous pairs, between the Father/Son God and his gendered creatures in the paradisiacal state, is intended to be mutually responsive, as we shall see, beyond humanity's wildest dreams.

To consider what mars Adam and Eve's relation, we must return to book 5. As they resume gardening the morning after Eve's dream, the couple is, as the narrator tells us, "beheld / With pity" by "Heav'n's high King." (5.219–20). We soon see that the equilibrium of their androgyny has been disturbed. The "distemper'd, discontented thoughts, / Vain hopes, vain aims, inordinate desires / Blown up with high conceits engend'ring pride" (4.807–09) which Eve's dream has unleashed will never be eradicated from her psyche. Eve has lost, if not her innocence, at least her primal peace of mind. As we know, the events of her dream will culminate in a variation of the temptation sequence later in book 9. Though it should have been instructive, perhaps prohibitive of events to follow, Adam's less than ideal reception of Eve's account will itself constitute a preliminary factor in the couple's downfall. The nightmare of her collusion with Satan makes Eve desperate for reassurance. It has been argued that, through her unconscious association with Satan, Eve has already partially fallen.[11] If so, we know she has not fallen on terms prescribed by the divine prerogative of book 3; she has not been "free to stand" and "free to fall" (3.80–134). To compound her problem, Adam has failed to meet the new, more pressing needs of his spouse. His rationalization of Eve's dream is perhaps the best he can do, given his continent nature, limited experience of evil, and innocent optimism concerning matters both divine and human. Just the same, Adam's dismissal of Eve's tears is a pivotal complication and Milton affords it its own verse paragraph:

> So cheer'd he his fair Spouse, and she was cheer'd,
> But silently a gentle tear let fall
> From either eye, and wip'd them with her hair;
> Two other precious drops that ready stood,
> Each in their crystal sluice, hee ere they fell
> Kiss'd as the gracious signs of sweet remorse
> And pious awe, that fear'd to have offended.
>
> (5.129–35)

Here we have the first emotional weeping in history.[12] After her disturbing dream, Eve is in a state of "tearfulness."[13] In her ritualized expression of two tears "wip'd . . . with her hair," she is the iconographic equivalent of that "penitent woman," who, as Diane McColley has observed, "began to wash [Christ's] feet with tears, and wipe them with the hairs of her head" (103). In turn, associations of the penitent woman with Mary Magdalene, so prevalent in Milton's time, would also have evoked descriptions of the saint as she was portrayed in numerous widely circulating treatises concerning her life as a weeper, convert and minister of Christ.[14] As a popular exemplar of contrition, Magdalene, like her male contemporary

Peter and their scriptural precedent David, were popular subjects of devotional treatises in the late sixteenth and earlier seventeenth centuries.[15] Like those of the Magdalene, Eve's tears arise from what Timothy Bright describes as the "affliction of conscience." A guilty conscience can bring upon the soul "all kinde of misery ioyned together with a troubled spirit" concerning "the censure executeth with the hand of God" (225). Eve's attempt at a therapeutic rehearsal of her dream initially evokes Adam's sympathy, only to be followed by his discourse on "Fancy" (5.102) and the logical deduction: "That what in sleep thou didst abhor to dream, / Waking thou never wilt consent to do" (5.120–21). Her apparent acquiescence to Adam's counsel on the matter of her dream is generally interpreted as Eve's obedient deferral to reason's voice. Yet her heroic attempts at repression (never before exercised) are followed by the "cloud[ing]" over of her "wont[ed]" "cheerful and serene" "looks" (122–23), which brings her inevitably to the brink of tears. These "disheart'n'd" (5.122) expressions are unknown to Adam. Adam and Eve are literally primitives; in their prelapsarian bliss they have still to experience those complex, more deleterious emotions known to their postlapsarian readers. Yet now anxiety and grief are being introduced, via Eve, whose "sense" of her satanic dream admits to their existence new experiential possibilities.

III

Here in book 5 Eve attempts to weep emotional tears. According to patristic accounts, woman's affective response, even within the prelapsarian state, aligns her with "sense perception," a faculty thought to compromise man's more purely rational nature. From Aristotle to Aquinas, sense perception was associated with error and sin; it was believed to contaminate woman's thinking and, by contagion, man's.[16] Sense perception, first associated with woman's affective inclinations, will lead to the so-called "evil imagination," which endures as a perennial explanation for humanity's wickedness. Read in this context, are Eve's tears then suspect, mere enticements to man's unsophisticated emotionality? Would we, therefore, second the disclaimer of Joseph Swetham's *Arraignment of Woman* (1615): "[S]he [woman] will vex thee, blubbering forth abundance of dissembling tears (for women do teach their eyes to weep) . . . the more she is entreated, she will pour forth the more abundance of deceitful tears?"[17] In refutation of this sentiment it is interesting to note that even a comparatively early Renaissance account of tears such as Bright's argues that tears, of their nature, simply cannot be "counterfeited" since "they rise not of any action or faculty voluntary, but naturall: and the weeping caused by ioy is as hearty, as that which ryseth upon conceit of sorrow" (180). Bright's designation of tears as "naturall" suggestively prefigures Milton's use of the same epithet in his final reference to tears in his epic. Indeed, Adam and Eve's shedding of some "natural tears" (12.645) as they leave Eden is the final event in a continuum of weeping that begins with Eve's tears in book 5. Furthermore, Bright's attribution of tears to the spontaneous overflowing of a full heart corresponds directly to Milton's presentation of Eve's heartfelt grief on the occasion of her dream.

When we first met Eve in book 4, her earliest self-absorbed tendencies were, for a time, masterfully suppressed by male discourse, that disembodied, corrective "voice" (4.467) which, as Christine Froula notes, soon after Eve's creation leads her to Adam's supervision.[18] Yet on this occasion of her dream, Eve's deeper instincts are aroused. As Adam surmises, her incipient tears are "gracious signs of sweet remorse," but they also signify what she senses may be the advent of her involuntarily fallen state. If we seriously doubt that Eve could not discern what Adam cannot yet fathom, we do well to recall that Eve has been created, as Adam later attests, "to enjoy" with him, "*all* [emphasis mine] rational delight" (8.391). Theirs is to be a relationship, intellectually as well as physically and spiritually fulfilling, satisfying Milton's largely egalitarian ideals of conjugal love outlined at length in the divorce tracts. Though relatively subordinate to her male partner, Eve's capacities are nonetheless qualitatively differentiated to complement and enhance those of her husband. Unlike Adam, we as readers know that Eve's ominous sense surrounding her dream is entirely accurate. By the same token, Adam's limited response to her anxiety, though appropriate to the procedures of edenic life to date, has now, by Satan's intrusion, become insufficient. If we persist in assuming the standard interpretive position, that Eve is ontologically and politically inferior to Adam and that Adam knows best in all domestic affairs, we are radically underestimating the marital relations which Milton meant to stand as no less than "mysteriously" complex, mirrored as they are in the communal life of the Father-Son androgyne.

For Milton, the Father is Logos, reason in its omniscient capacity, just as the Son is Love and creativity, through whose passionate commitment all things are created and redeemed. These reciprocal identities are fundamentally indicative of the ontology of the male-female bond. Not only do we err in minimizing the interdependent dynamic operating between Godlike rationality and its complement, divine affection, but we fail also to acknowledge the interactive role of these attributes in the evolution of human nature predicted by Raphael in book 8. A preference for manly reason over feminine affect allies us with Satan who strategically privileges Adam's "higher intellectual" (9.483), undervaluing, as always, the efficacy of affective logic, which, having himself contemptuously repudiated, he cannot possibly understand. Ironically, of course, this mystical synthesis of reason and affect, unimaginatively discounted by Satan, will prove his nemesis. The firm yet tenderhearted expression of affective logic, embodied in the Son, will enable God to refute the merely tactical intelligence of Satan. In

Milton's logocentric universe, created and administered in love, hateful subversions, however ingenious, are doomed to defeat.

The satanic prejudice that would categorically bifurcate human intelligence along gender lines, discriminating between reason and affective logic, proves as fallacious as it is divisive. Such discriminatory views are opposed by Renaissance commentators like Nicholas Breton who endorse gender equality in all respects. Milton later asserts what Breton's *In Praise of Vertuous Ladies* (1599) had earlier claimed: that man is part of woman; and that any attack on woman is an attack on man himself; "that man and woman are one 'substance'; neither can be 'discommended' except as an act of self-repudiation."[19] Eve's individuation from, and eventual reconciliation with, Adam — all that will felicitously ensue concerning humanity's redemption — is carefully founded on the tearful dilemma of book 5. If Eve's unconscious has been stirred by her nightmare, so have her deepest moral reflexes. In this first brush with evil, Eve begins to know the good, and her possible violation of it, and thus she begins to weep: again, she "let[s]" one tear "fall" "from either eye" and immediately two others ready "stood." This deployment of the predicates "stand" and "fall," which inscribe the free will defense of *Paradise Lost*, connects Eve's torment here with her agony in the garden where she will tragically fall and weep, for a time, inconsolably (9.1121–33). On both occasions, her grief cannot be immediately expunged and endures beyond Adam's rational analysis of circumstance. Eve's exercising of the affective mode here (for better or for worse) heralds humanity's passage from a conservatively cognitive experience of knowledge toward a more fully inclusive, affective understanding.

Among the questions raised by such a reading, we may ask why, from the beginning, woman's capacity for grief appears more highly developed than man's. Is it simply woman's possession of that dreaded contaminant, sense perception? On the other hand, is it possible for man — if his capacity for grief is less developed than a woman's — to experience a fully human existence? If God himself exhibits androgynous, anthropopathetic properties, how can human creatures, created in his image, do otherwise? Renaissance accounts of tears certainly address woman's apparent predisposition to weeping. For example, Laurent Joubert's *Treatise on Laughter* (1579) explains that "weeping is easier for those who by their constitution and nature, or by reason of their age, sex, or culture, are weaker and moister, which is why we see phlegmatic people tear promptly, along with children, elderly people, and women."[20] Similarly, Bright observes that "children are more apt to weepe, then those that are of greater yeares, and women more than men the one having by youth the body more moist, rare, and soft, and the other by sex" (175). Even Thomas Hobbes, writing in the mid-seventeenth century, concludes in his "On the Emotions, or Perturbations of the Mind" (1658), "that those that weep the greatest amount and more frequently are those, such as women and children, who have the least hope in themselves and the most in friends."[21]

Assuming woman's predisposition to tears and emotion, Milton explores the biblical origins of her affective inclination. Adam's dream memory of Eve's creation in book 8 pictures God humanly "stooping" over Adam as He "op'n'd [his] left side, and took / From thence a rib, with cordial spirits warm, / And Life-blood streaming fresh" (465–67). This extraction from Adam's heart region, bathed in affective fluids, becomes the matter from which Eve is "fashion'd," and defined, in turn, as "manlike, but different sex" (471). Adam's primal erotic yearning for his female counterpart, "so lovely fair, / That what seem'd fair in all the world, seem'd now / Mean, or in her summ'd up" (471–73), follows logically upon his description of Eve's being drawn from his own being. "Bone of [his] Bone, Flesh of [his] Flesh" (8.495), Eve has, by God-instituted consequence, deprived Adam of certain "cordial spirits," which he will now only access through intimate reunion with her. Together Adam and Eve stand as a perfect androgyny. Individually, the emotional component of each is different. As the narrator has said in book 4, "For contemplation hee and valor form'd, / For softness shee and sweet attractive grace" (4.297–98). Here in book 8 we actually learn firsthand from Adam the source of this differentiation. Although he believes himself to be fully healed of his "wide," life-giving "wound," Adam's donation has taken from him more than he knows. He remains, in his prelapsarian state at least, affectively challenged.

Milton's attention to feminine affect signals his acknowledgment of an emotional intelligence that adumbrates modern psychology.[22] In keeping with the imperative of his epic, Milton privileges Eve's affective response to her dream. By implication, at least, he affirms the necessity of satisfactory grief expression.[23] Despite the relaxation of strictures against grief expression in the seventeenth century, the prevailing attitude remained strongly cautionary. Anne Laurence in "Godly Grief: Individual Responses to Death in Seventeenth-Century Britain" writes: "in seventeenth century England it [grief] was ... regarded as a potentially fatal affliction" to the degree that "it was widely believed that grief could send people mad" (*DRB*, 75–76). Adam's attempt to transform Eve's sorrow into joy is therefore predictable, even culturally correct. But Milton is opposing current conventions. More simply, who better than the husband of three wives and father of two daughters to recognize the functional necessity of confronting such affective intensity as weeping, most commonly associated with woman?

Eve's grief over her dream in book 5 is so skillfully embedded in the narrative that it might serve as the decisive pivot to which Adam's thoughts could return during his torments after the fall. If Adam's do not, and they do not, ours should. Milton makes the point emphatically clear: that masculine mentality initially resists the emergence of affective intensity.

While Adam is denying the "modern" conception of tears as "participatory" and "self-transcendent,"[24] Milton is progressively authorizing this conception. Lange argues (3) for the "unexpressed assumption [during the period] that tears divide the weeper from the community, isolate her or him (more usually her) in an unhealthy way." Adam's dismissal of Eve's tears tragically illustrates his enactment of this Renaissance norm. As Milton shows, Eve's sorrow not only foreshadows her loss of innocence and Adam's with her, it also anticipates her death and the death of all her progeny to come. Her grief also shows her awareness of impending danger, even of her unarticulated sense of catastrophe. Eve's tears are more than self-indulgent. They are an expression of "Godly sorrow," a mode of expressing grief widely advocated by Protestant divines throughout the period, fulfilling, for example, William Whately's sermonic exhortation of 1623, "crie before it [misery] come, with such crying as may prevent it."[25]

Eve's grief, if authorized, might have proved prevenient; but because unauthorized, it becomes prophetical. Eve's prophecy seeks to preserve the androgyny of her first community. Though the prophetical side of Eve's nature is not developed to any practicable degree, the operation of this faculty, for which we see her naturally gifted, is inadvertently aborted by Adam's denial of her grief expression at this most crucial moment in their history. Nevertheless, there still remain in Eve's grief several features of prophetical experience, as they are enumerated, for instance, by Abraham Herschel, in his classic discussion of prophecy. Concerning the manner of the prophet, Herschel identifies first and foremost a "sensitivity to evil," together with the prophet's sense of "the importance of trivialities" and "the loneliness and misery" consequent to the prophetical vision and its often unwelcomed reception.[26] Concerning the emotional state of the prophet, Herschel writes: "[O]ne cannot understand [God's] word without sensing the pathos. And one could not impassion others and remain unstirred" (1:26). The prophet, according to Herschel, is an "[a]ssayer, messenger, or witness" who "discloses a divine pathos, not just a divine judgment" on human events. Although Eve's performance as a fully fledged prophet is only hinted at, her intense sense of evil surrounding her dream, Adam's trivializing and dismissing of what she believes to be significant, and the resultant misery and alienation she feels following the suppression of her sentiments, all distinguish her as a prophetical agent. In fact, her discourse on the possibly negative implications of her dream, directed as they are at Adam, stand as Eve's principal enactment of prophetical address to her (albeit tiny) community. Moreover, the denial provoked in her spouse also parallels the traditionally equivocal response of the community to such disclosures, which, although tolerant of the procedure itself, remains intolerant of the message expressed. Finally, a vital contingency of the prophetical function, as Herschel shows, is that of an affectively present and involved God, such as we indeed have in the anthropopathetic God of *Paradise Lost*.[27]

Meanwhile, Milton instructs us that Eve's godly sorrow, with its prophetical intentionality, is significant. Further, he indicates that, precisely because it is deliberately suppressed, her grief becomes the more tragically pitiable. In book 5, Milton positively counters the view of his day that expression of grief "can drive one mad." In fact, Eve's grief, denied and suppressed, is shown to be a demonstrable source of psychological disturbance, as potentially fatal to her as to the unreceptive audience to which it is offered. Milton is arguing that precisely because it is both self-transcending and prophetical, Eve's grief is unquestionably worthy of Adam's full attention and participation. Moreover, her attempt to share her anxiety with her husband is Eve's means of being a godly wife. As Barnaby Rich exhorts in *The Excellency of Good Women* (1613), a good wife is like a ship (Prov. 3.14): "[S]he must not sayle but by leade and line still sounding the deapth and foreseeinge the danger . . . and discovering any perill within her kenning, to give her husband warning . . . to helpe him to avoyde it."[28] Eve might also have referred her husband to the widely circulating *Ancilla Pietatis* (1626) by Daniel Featley, one of Milton's boyhood rectors. Before her God and co-creator Adam, Eve might ask: "Why hast thou given me a *tender heart*, but to receive *deepe* the impression of compassionate grief? Why hast thou given me melting eyes but to *weepe* for *my own* infirmities, and my brethrens calamities?"[29] Unfortunately, Adam's neglect of Eve's sorrow ensures her continued discomfort and increasing sense of alienation from her husband. It is therefore retributively correct that Adam should be later penalized by the fully realized grief expression of his own postlapsarian state: when he is "[to] sorrow abandoned" "[a]nd in a troubl'd Sea of passion tost" (10.717–18). Adam's grief denial also has aetiological import. What but obduracy, associated in Scripture with divorce and satanic in derivation for Milton, does Adam's rationalization impose upon Eve? She must in practice "harden" herself to what has befallen her.[30]

As book 5 continues, God sends Raphael in response to this dilemma. The charming account of Adam and Eve's reception of their angelic guest may encourage us to believe, with the narrator, that "all was clear'd" (5.136) concerning Eve's morning tearfulness. Even God's intent that Raphael should "Go . . . as friend with friend" to "[c]onverse with *Adam*" (5.229–30), Eve unmentioned, or Eve's subservient role during the visit, as "at Table [she] [m]inister'd naked" (5.443–44) before her male companions, may be conventionally accepted. It *is* significant, however, that we are never exactly told whether Eve, after completing her duties, stays or leaves. Except for fleeting reference in book 7 (50), it is not until the opening of book 8 that we actually see Eve "r[i]se" from where she has been sitting, "retir'd in sight" (8.41). This terse, equivocal reference to Eve's posture for nearly two and a half books is followed by her choosing to leave, later to audit Adam's version of the continuing tutorial. We are told that she recedes "with lowliness Majestic" (8.42) yet with such "Goddess-like demeanour" as would make any "wish her still in sight" (8.60, 64) suggesting, as never before, that Eve has become a woman to be reckoned with. A modern reader cannot accept the benign account of the male narrator without remembering Eve's sorrowful experience only hours earlier. Why does her presence after dinner remain but nominally noted, so that, in the process of first reading, students routinely ask, "where is Eve now?" Where indeed, but to employ a term used by those same readers, "marginalized," quite literally, as is later confirmed in book 8.

To make matters worse, the one-to-one "Converse" between Adam and Raphael forces Eve to witness at length the appropriation of her only relational model to date. The intimacy of this male discourse makes Eve's presence redundant. Some may prefer to reassert the traditional reading of God's gender-inclusive intentionality concerning the tutorial, that Raphael's visit and counsel were ideally offered to both Adam and Eve. Yet surely Eve's satanic association, through her unfortunate dream and her subsequent distress, which she is attempting to rationalize, must have by now profoundly altered her original sense of an ideal world. A solitude, freely chosen, allows Eve time to reflect on the day's unprecedented events. However we wish to construe her limited involvement in Raphael's tutorial, it suggests Eve's progressive individuation from Adam.[31]

Not surprisingly, when we next meet the couple in book 9, Eve proposes that they separate to work more efficiently. To add to the controversy concerning the separation scene, I suggest that Eve's proposal follows naturally upon the events of book 5, her absent presence in the latter half of book 5, books 6 and 7, and her decisive departure in book 8.[32] And although in book 9 Eve's rejection of the liturgical concept of work and her substitution of a production model is both modern and resourceful, it can only be viewed as such from a postlapsarian perspective. Satan, for obvious reasons, "wish'd his hap might find / *Eve* separate" (9.421-22) but is certain he will not. To "sp[y]" "*Eve* separate" (9.424) must surely be the opportunity of his dreams. The "Tragic . . . Notes" (9.6) of book 9 are the logical culmination of events begun with Eve's dream and her obedient repression of grief. As she sought to internalize the male imperative for rational response in book 5, she could not know that tears were by nature intended to flow until, like all other bodily emissions, they are fully voided. Eve's efforts at repression are activated by fear. Under the constraint of Adam's counsel, Eve thus attempts to do no less than swallow her sorrow. Her internalized anguish is then augmented by the new pressures of possible marital and divine recrimination. As her grief is incorporated, so too is her sense of guilt.

IV

From the earliest lines of book 5, Milton inscribes the rudiments of Eve's eternally debased notoriety. By her error, she becomes the "deviant" one of Carol Gilligan; the "abject" one of Julia Kristeva; and the "sorceress," "hysteric" and "guilty" one(s) of Hélène Cixous and Catherine Clément, by whose account, not coincidentally, "having interiorized all stolen objects, she keeps her inner desires to herself, holding back her tears and swallowing her cries."[33] Eve's tears, painfully repressed, are prototypal of those that will one day flood forth as the "deferred tears" of Freud's hysteric patients — women who, like Eve, despite their existential stamina, will eventually cry for healing. Eve's dis/eased obduracy, begun by Adam's suppression of her tears in book 5, will compel her, for a time, to suffer in her fully vulnerable humanity as a classic female hysteric. Eve's agony in a postlapsarian Eden is a feminine, human version of Christ's agony in the Garden of Gethesame. As Christ will endure *Deus Absconditus*, during the process of his Crucifixion, she also experiences the excruciating sense of her own abandonment by both God and husband.

Eve's possession by the forces of evil after the Fall, proceeding through despair toward deliverance by Adam's mercy, prefigures the Son's future Passion, when he will be "[s]eiz'd on by force, judg'd, and to death condemn'd / A shameful and accurst, nail'd to the Cross" (12.412–13), but, by the Father's grace, "soon revive[d]" (12.420). Similarly, Eve's passion must be eventually attended to by Adam whose permissive will has inadvertently allowed his wife to suffer the throes of sin. He must correct his earlier failing and minister personally to his wife's needs, receiving Eve's tears in his tripartite ministry as physican, priest and husband. As she strives to attain Adam's forgiveness, Eve performs the liturgical work of penitence and contrition. Her "humble" petition "at [Adam's] feet" (10.911–12) is parenthesized by accounts of exhaustive weeping, "with Tears that ceas'd not flowing, / And tresses all disorder'd" (10.910–11). Disheveled hair, signifying a posture of grief and utter disregard for appearances, while sterotypical of the hysteric female, is also emblematic of the penitent woman (Magdalene) who wept in contrition at her Lord's feet.[34] The associations of the female hysteric with Mary Magdalene and with Christ fuse evocatively in the concluding lines of Eve's supplication to Adam when she admits that they

> both have sinn'd, but thou
> Against God only, I against God and thee,
> And to the place of judgement will return,
> There with my cries importune Heaven, that all
> The sentence from thy head remov'd may light
> On me, sole cause to thee of all this woe,
> Mee mee only just object of his ire.
>
> (10.930–36)

Just as Mary Magdalene was demonized by her community (Luke 8.2) yet became the "Apostle to the Apostles," and the Son was crucified "by his own Nation, slain for bringing Life"

(12.414), so Eve, denounced by her own husband as a "Serpent" (10.867–908), is nevertheless prepared to assume altruistically *all* responsibility for sin. Here Eve initiates a penitential work that depends on Adam's reciprocal response. Expressly because she so requires his "Commiseration" (10.940), we see Adam's "heart relent[s] / Towards her" (10.940–41). The reconciliatory work that ensues between Adam and Eve in union with God's grace replicates the cooperative work of redemption itself enacted by the Father-Son androgyne. As Adam ministers receptively to Eve's assumption of blame, so too the Father's will becomes manifest through the Son's condescension to the redemptive plan. Like the Father and the Son in their redemptive engagement, Adam and Eve work together to perform the act of their mutual repentance. Eve "rise[s]" to Adam's wish that they "no more contend, nor blame / Each other" (10.958–59). The ritual of absolution which follows functions therapeutically to expose the root of Eve's hysteria, her delusion, that paradise must have indeed been lost. Her terror actualizes in her proposal, first, of their conjugal abstinence and, second, of their suicide (10.966–1006).

The depth of her despair, once articulated, requires the care of an affectively experienced spouse. Adam wisely advises they "repair" to the place of original mercy where the Son first "clothed" them, "pitying how they stood" (10.211). The couple's "repair[ing]" to the holy place, twice repeated at the end of book 10 (1087–92; 1099–104), doubly inscribes their return not only to a former place but to a former state of wholeness. As they kneel together to "water" the "ground" "with their tears" (10.1089–92), Adam and Eve are the first man and woman to engage in a liturgy of love that "repairs" their fractured androgyny. This colloquy of love resonates with Julia Kristeva's account of the modern psychoanalytical process. In her book, *In the Beginning Was Love*, Kristeva writes:

> This mobilization of two people's minds and bodies by the sole agency of the words that pass between them sheds light on

Freud's remark, in *The Future of an Illusion*, that the foundation of the cure is "Our God Logos." It also recalls the words of the Gospels: "In the beginning was the Word" (John 1.1) and "God is love" (1 John 4.8).³⁵

The deferral of Eve's tears in book 5 and this intimate colloquy in book 10 extend in turn to the "Sighs and Prayers" (11.23–24) offered by the Son in his priestly office of "at-one-ment" to the Father. And last but not least, the couple will express what finally becomes normalized as "[s]ome natural tears" (12.645) during their exodus from Eden. This mystical culture of tears in Milton's epic fulfills a theoretical rubric expressed decades earlier in *Of Education*. Human tears help to "repair" the "ruins" of Adam's and Eve's androgyny, ensuring their atonement with God and each other.³⁶ But the chief source of their healing will be their therapeutic practice of a "Love / By name to come call'd Charity," which, not yet dreamed of by its recipients, will become "the soul / of all the rest" (12.584–85).

13 • Afterword

Ralph Houlbrooke

The cosmic drama of man's Fall through Satan's wiles and redemption by Christ's sacrifice provided the framework for the Christian understanding of grief in all the senses comprehended in these essays. The wages of sin "is death" (Rom. 6.23). Sorrow in giving birth and sorrow in eating the fruit of intractable ground were the lot foretold by God for Eve and Adam after they had tasted the forbidden fruit. Death itself, and each individual's return to dust, fulfilled the warning that accompanied the divine prohibition against eating of the tree of knowledge of good and evil. Henceforth sin, and the gnawing of conscience, were to be inseparable from the human experience on Earth. But God, whose nature and property it was ever to have mercy, gave his Son Jesus Christ to suffer death upon the cross for the redemption of mankind; "who made there (by his one oblation of himself once offered) a full, perfect, and sufficient sacrifice, oblation, and satisfaction, for the sins of the whole world," in the words of the Prayer of Consecration in the Order of Communion of the Book of Common Prayer. Jesus had already foretold that those who believed in him would not perish, but have everlasting life. The Christian scheme presented both an explanation of the miseries apparently inseparable from human existence on Earth, and a promise that they would be far exceeded by the rewards of a realm of eternal light.

The Bible repeatedly evokes both joy and sorrow in passages of great emotional depth and power. Nowhere are evocations of sorrow clustered more thickly than in the narratives of Christ's later days, and particularly of his Passion. One of the most eloquent of all accounts occurs, however, in a passage in the Old Testament book of Isaiah, usually interpreted as a prophetic description of the sufferings of Jesus: "He is despised and rejected of men; a man of sorrows, and acquainted with grief: and we hid as it were our faces from him; he was despised, and we esteemed him not. Surely he hath borne our griefs, and carried our sorrows" (53.3–4). Although Christ was most fully a "man of sorrows" during the sequence of events which began with the agony in Gethsemane and culminated in his death on the cross, he was by then no stranger to grief. His own sorrow found memorable expression after the death of Lazarus. On seeing the tears of Mary and the Jews who were with her, "Jesus wept."

While focusing on the pivotal message and experience of Jesus, the Gospels afford glimpses of the effects of the shock waves of grief on his followers and disciples during those traumatic days between Christ's arrest and his Resurrection. Scarcely had Peter denied his master for the third time, cursing and swearing, before he heard the cock crow, and "went out, and wept bitterly." The effects of his greater act of betrayal were far more calamitous for Judas, whose abortive repentance was followed by despair and suicide. Great numbers of people, including many women, followed Jesus to Golgotha, bewailing and lamenting him. It was the women, "Daughters of Jerusalem," whom Jesus particularly addressed, telling them to weep for themselves rather than for him (Luke 23.28, 29).

Her shock, disappointment and perplexity on finding that Christ's body had disappeared from the sepulchre caused Mary Magdalene to weep (John 20.11). According to Mark's account, Mary found Christ's followers mourning and weeping when she went to tell them the news of his resurrection (Mark 16.10).

Christians learned from the Bible that grief was an inseparable element of life on Earth, pictured in an eleventh century hymn as "this vale of tears" from which the "poor banished children of Eve" sent up to compassionate Mary their "sighs, mourning and weeping." The expression of grief, furthermore, seemed to receive clear divine warrant in the Sermon on the Mount. "Blessed are they that mourn: for they shall be comforted" (Matt. 5.4). But such expression of sorrow was not to be excessive. Paul urged the Thessalonians not to mourn the dead in the same way as those who had no hope of a future life (1 Thess. 4.13). Earthly suffering was to be embraced as a sign of God's favor. The Lord loved those whom he chastened, Paul pointed out in his epistle to the Hebrews, and scourged every son whom he received: "But if ye be without chastisement, whereof all are partakers, then are ye bastards, and not sons" (Heb. 12.8). Punishment was necessary for the sinful yet loved descendants of Adam, even though no human suffering could equal what God-made-man had undergone on their behalf. In the face of bereavement, Christians were urged to contemplate the happiness of the departed rather than the pain of their own loss. The *Visitation of the Sick* in the Book of Common Prayer included an exhortation reminding the gravely ill that "there should be no greater comfort to Christian persons, than to be made like unto Christ, by suffering patiently adversities, troubles, and sicknesses." Religion provided lessons in how to cope with the loss which is at the heart of grief in all its manifold guises: loss of friends and loved ones, loss of wealth and health, loss of good name and loss of good conscience.

Religion, and above all the Scriptures, provided the bedrock upon which rested much of the writing discussed in these essays, and its prime source of inspiration. Milton's epic interpretation of the story of the Fall argues, in Margo Swiss's words, "that human grief finds its prototype in God's own grief, together with that of the Son, and their mutually compassionate response to Creation." Donne and Taylor in their funeral or commemoration sermons, Donne in his "Elegie on the Lady Markham," Jonson in his "Elegy on my Muse," Hammond in his sequence of poems on the death of Henry Sandys, and Crashaw in his elegies upon the deaths of Herrys and Stanninow, all drew on the consolation of the happiness of the departed or the prospect of the Resurrection. In the somber maternal elegies of Mary Carey, Lucy Hastings, Alice Thornton and Gertrude Thimelby, this theme is present but more muted. All these poems express their authors' struggle to submit to God's will; Carey and Thornton recognized that the cause of their losses lay in their own shortcomings. "I only now desire of my sweet God / the reason why he tooke in hand his rodd?" wrote Mary Carey, as she contemplated the sight of her miscarried infant; but God's voice and her conscience soon supplied the answer in the shape of the dead heart and affections she brought to all her religious duties.[1] No motive for human love of God could be more potent than contemplation of the suffering undergone by God-made-man. In the final version of George Herbert's "The Church," Louis L. Martz points out, the writer's "cries of grief are constantly intermingled with the memory of Christ's grief and of the opening poem in which that grief is commemorated." In "Sancta Maria Dolorum," Richard Crashaw, dry-eyed and cold of heart, prayed to the Virgin Mary at the foot of the cross, "Great Queen of greifes," to share her tears with him.[2] An Collins attributed her own chronic bodily suffering to "God's providential workings upon her soul," in Scott Howard's words.

Two closely related questions concerning grief are addressed by a number of essays in this volume: the extent to which attitudes toward it can be seen to have changed during this period, and its connection with gender. It is clear, despite Paul's strictures against excessive mourning, that the Scriptures afforded abundant examples of the acceptable expression of sorrow. This is not, however, to deny the existence of strong and deep-rooted attitudes hostile to open grief. The "angry consoler," as G. W. Pigman III characterized him in his learned and justly influential study of elegy, could draw on a stock of arguments inherited from pagan antiquity (*Elegy*, 11–26). Grief was above all a sign of *weakness*, of an irrational failure to accept the inevitable or already accomplished dictates of fate. It was futile, indeed worse than useless. It damaged the health of the individual who succumbed to it and impaired his performance of social duties. Sorrow for loss was all too often angry, self-centered, attention-seeking, even narcissistic. It was unworthy of a strong or wise man, and the higher the status of the individual who indulged in it, the more embarrassing and socially disruptive the consequences. Those who mourned most, according to the conventional wisdom of "rigorism," were the weak, the irrational and the socially inferior.

Long-established social conventions nevertheless sanctioned formal mourning for the dead in certain contexts and on the part of certain categories of people. Clothes of black or "sad" colors distinguished participants in funerals, and, for a longer period, certain individuals with a close relationship to the dead. The wearing of "mourning" in the vestimentary sense did not necessarily coincide with "mourning" in the sense of behavioral manifestations of grief, much less with grief itself. Yet Richard Hooker expressed a widespread sentiment very well when he defended the wearing of mourning by saying that "the signs are meet to shew what should be" even when sorrow itself was absent. Moderate sorrow was acceptable above all in the funeral context. Many English commentators strongly deprecated extravagant shows of grief, especially in the form of lamentations, in the funeral rites of other cultures. Friendship's testimonial of the "kind" or "courteous" tear (Crashaw) was nevertheless appropriate, indeed welcome. The tribute of grief paid by servants, followers, the people and the poor to masters, magnates, sovereigns and benefactors — by social inferiors to their superiors — was noticed with evident approval by many of those who wrote accounts of the funerals of the great during the sixteenth and early seventeenth centuries. A quiet, reserved, unostentatious sorrow of mien that matched her somber apparel was especially fitting in a widow during her customary year of mourning.[3]

It was understandable that parents should feel sorrow for the loss of children; according to the conventional ideas of the time, love flowed most vigorously "downwards" from the "stronger" partner in any relationship — from man to woman, parents to children.[4] But such a loss was a personal and private matter which touched them above all, not a source of public sorrow, and therefore not something to be mourned demonstratively, in a way that invited the substantial participation or concern of a larger group. At the same time, it behooved them, as householders and governors of families, holders of responsibility in the commonwealth, to set an example by showing that they had accepted and internalized the consolations and assurances offered by religion, which were particularly firm in the case of young children.

How did attitudes to grief change during the three-quarters of a century spanned by this volume? G. W. Pigman III has traced in elegy a major shift from anxiety about, to acceptance of, expressions of sorrow which was already well underway by 1600. He suspected that this shift was connected with wider social developments. Emblematic of the change in attitudes to mourning, in his view, is John Marston's *Antonio's Revenge*. Its "vehement rejection of stoicism" is most strikingly expressed in Pandulpho's sudden surrender to grief for his son as he is smitten by his perception of the hollowness of the arguments with which he has been attempting to console himself (*Elegy*, 2, 125–27).

Fred Tromly's essay in this volume explores a kindred aspect of the change in treatment of grief. Shakespeare, he shows, puts some of the common themes of conventional consolation in the mouths of characters whose own motives are questionable or sinister, or have interests opposed to those of the individuals they are ostensibly trying to console. These themes of consolation include the childishness, irrationality and unmanliness of grief, its life-threatening potential and the futility of repining against the inevitable, including death itself. Shakespeare makes such "comforts" look threadbare in a way that points to his own hostility toward the consolatory tradition of which they formed a part. (Hardly any of the speeches discussed by Tromly offer properly *religious* consolations, though Claudius does indeed tell Hamlet that his perseverance in "obstinate condolement" is a "fault to heaven.") These feeble, self-interested consolations fail utterly to cure the griefs to which they are addressed. Cordelia alone, in the scene of her reconciliation with her father Lear, is a comforter who "feels and tastes the grief she comforts." The conclusion that here "Shakespeare gives us a communion in suffering so powerful that the comfort it affords is indistinguishable from grace itself" is both eloquent and convincing.

The extent to which the effectiveness of attempted consolation depends upon the consoler's sharing in suffering is a question that arises elsewhere in this collection, notably in the essay by John Shawcross. In his analysis of a sequence of ten poems by William Hammond, Shawcross argues that Hammond himself felt the grief for his brother-in-law Henry Sandys which he sought to assuage in his sister Margaret. Despite his use of a standard vocabulary of grief, Hammond was sincere, Shawcross believes, in his expression of a deep sense of loss. He did, however, move through grief to an understanding and acceptance of that loss which he hoped to be able to share with Margaret Sandys through the "restorative power" of his poetry. The first three poems focusing on Henry

Sandys's death are followed by several more which work patiently at the task of consolation. The last poem in Hammond's sequence, as if in recognition of the limits of his powers, commends the starlike brightness of Margaret's tears.

One of the most important reasons for a more sympathetic, cautious, and nuanced treatment of grief during this period was the belief that its effects might be exacerbated by the excessive influence of melancholy, due to an imbalance among the individual's humours. Such an imbalance was not the individual's fault. It did not free him of the responsibility to take whatever steps he could to ensure his physical and mental health by mastering his sorrow, but it called for a more compassionate approach than that characteristic of the "angry consoler." The consultant's task was, to put it at its simplest, to disentangle as far as possible the effects of melancholy from those of some other source in external events or the patient's actions. Marjory Lange considers the particular case of the individual in whom acute consciousness of his sin combines with melancholy to create a vicious spiral toward despair. Robert Burton claimed the category of religious melancholy as his own innovation, though Timothy Bright had preceded him in discussion of the predicament of the melancholic sinner.[5] Lange shows that John Donne's approach to this problem paralleled that of Burton in sundry important respects. Despair of God's mercy was in his view a pathological disorder to which unguided examination of one's soul and conscience might contribute. Sorrowful tears were, however, a hopeful sign: often, though not always, a mark of healthy contrition. Inability to weep was a characteristic of the incorrigible sinner, Horace's *Pluto illacrymabilis.*

The "compassionate severity" that Lange perceives in Donne's handling of melancholy is also apparent in his "Elegie on the Lady Markham," considered in the immediately preceding essay by Robert C. Evans. The poem's basic argument is that passionate grief not only is sinful and morbid, but also blinds us to the happy destination of the blessed departed, who is the true victor in the encounter with death. This thoroughly conventional Christian message is, however, delivered in a series of ingenious conceits (discussed by Evans) whose very complexity invests its assimilation with an element of intellectual challenge, and thereby compels the reader to think afresh about its implications. As Evans concludes, Donne's poems of mourning "seek deliberately to master passion by controlling and redirecting thought." The other poem analyzed by Evans, Jonson's "Elegy on my muse" (Venetia Digby), derives a special interest from the fact that it was addressed by a man characterized by Pigman as an outstanding rigorist to Sir Kenelm Digby, this period's foremost performer of husbandly mourning. Evans rightly implies that the poem's preliminary sharing of Sir Kenelm's sense of loss, rising to a note of angry passion, makes it difficult to categorize as simply "rigorist." The celebratory vision of Venetia's happiness in "the court of bliss" is a prolonged essay in vigorous poetic persuasion. The poem is indeed "intensely emotional *and* intensively reasoned." There is, nevertheless, a reproach (especially in view of what we know of Digby's elaborate display of sorrow) in the rhetorical question "And will you, worthy, son, sir, knowing this, / Put black, and mourning on?"[6]

A greater readiness to engage with grief is also characteristic of many of the published funeral sermons of the early and middle years of the seventeenth century and the epistles dedicatory which preface them. Of the relatively few such sermons published before 1600, a number contain no eulogy of the deceased, or a very attenuated one. They concentrate on the exposition of the sermon text, without close personal application. As Frederic Tromly has shown, the Reformed churches were deeply suspicious of the misuse of praise of the dead.[7] Some seventeenth century preachers still tended to avoid eulogy. But the inclusion of kind words about the deceased, the direct application of the text to them, and expressions of confidence about their destination after death, were now commoner than they had been. Awareness of the grief of the bereaved, and of the ways in which the preacher's discourse might assuage that grief, was more explicit.

Some of the sermons analyzed by P. G. Stanwood provide good examples in illustration of these generalizations. "To lament a dead friend is naturall, and civill; and he is the deader of the two, the verier carcasse, that does not do so," wrote John Donne, commenting on Martha and Mary's grief at the death of Lazarus in his sermon for Sir William Cokayne in 1626. "But inordinate lamentation implies a suspition of a worse state in him that is gone." Donne's ingenious inversion of his text, "*Lord, because thou wast here, our Brother is not dead,*" leads into a demonstration that God had been with Cokayne all his life and at his death, good grounds for confident hopes of his good estate in the next world.[8] Undoubtedly the most outstanding of these sermons is, nevertheless, the one Jeremy Taylor delivered for Lady Carbery in 1650, justly described by Stanwood as "the apogee of his funeral oratory." He alludes to the way in which Taylor, who had recently lost his own wife, ministered to Lord Carbery's grief in his prefatory epistle to the published sermon. Taylor, while admitting that it would have been better to bring something that might have alleviated or diverted Carbery's sorrow, asked leave to present him with his wife's portrait. (He must in truth have known that one of the greatest comforts of the bereaved is to hear praise of the departed.) "My lord, I pray God this heap of sorrow may swell your piety till it breaks into the greatest joys of God and of religion: and remember when you pay a tear upon the grave, or to the memory of your lady . . . that you pay two more: one of repentance for those things that may have caused this breach; and another of joy for the mercies of God to your dear departed saint, that He hath taken her into a place where she can weep no more." There follows what is (for a funeral sermon) an unusually full discussion of relations between the living and the dead. Taylor's sermon confidently asserts that the blessed dead pray for those they have left behind, and sets out the duties the living owe to the dead, including prayer for their joyful resurrection and merciful judgment. It gives a notably full account of the state of the dead before the resurrection, and concludes with a eulogy of Lady Carbery so eloquent and full of relevant evidence that it can have left no doubt of her soul's happiness in its hearers' or readers' minds.[9]

An increased readiness to address grief, and a wider variety of responses to it, are evident in the literature of these decades compared with the preceding period. The connection between grief and gender is the second major theme of this volume. Open or prolonged grief was still widely regarded as unmanly, weak and "womanish." Digby's mourning for Venetia may be emblematic of its greater acceptability around that time, but he was nevertheless exceptional, especially among men, in the degree to which he indulged, displayed and discussed his sorrow. Women, the weaker sex, were conventionally regarded as being more prone to grief and more likely to display it. Half the essays in this volume explore women's experience of grief, or demonstrate that some male authors viewed aspects of female grief in a positive light.

A number of the maternal elegies discussed by Donna J. Long convey a powerful impression of the anguish and disappointment suffered by women when, as all too often happened, they miscarried or their infants died. In these situations mothers could experience a very distressing conflict between their need to express grief and their duty to submit to God's will. The presence of a plaintive note in some of these elegies is hardly surprising, and as Long remarks, Mary Carey's attempted self-consolation is "rife with ambivalence." In perhaps the bleakest of all these poems, Alice Thornton, without even naming her son William, accepted his death as punishment for her sins with no overtly expressed consolation save the painfulness of the earthly life which he had escaped.[10] (Contrast this reaction of Alice's with An Collins's readiness to interpret her physical suffering as a manifestation of God's grace at work in her, rather than as a punishment for her sins.)

Given the amount of time early modern women, in the upper classes especially, spent in pregnancy, the anxieties which childbirth inspired, and the pains of labor, many women may indeed have felt, as Donna J. Long suggests, that the deaths of young children were insufficiently recognized. Katherine Philips intimated as much in a poem upon her little son Hector which is free of overt self-reproach or religious consolation:

> Thus whilst no eye is witness of my mone,
> I grieve thy loss (Ah boy too dear to live)
> And let the unconcerned World alone,
> Who neither will, nor can refreshment give.[11]

A husband ought (we might think) to have been his wife's chief source of support in such a situation. George Payler exhorted his wife Mary Carey to join with him in learning how to submit to God's will, and Mary clearly expected him to see her little book of poems and meditations. It was perhaps some consolation to Alice Thornton to know that her husband shared her grief at the loss of their 14-day-old son William, who was "exceding like" him in person. Yet it is notable how little most of these poems say of husbands, and how intensely *personal* is the sense of loss. Some fathers did nevertheless mark the deaths of their children with elegies: Ben Jonson's "On My First Son" is justly the most famous essay of this sort. In its poignant companion, written for his six-month-old first daughter, Jonson remarked that though both parents had rued her death, "all heaven's gifts being heaven's due, / It makes the *father*, less, to rue" (my emphasis). Not all fathers felt like Jonson, however: when the London turner Nehemiah Wallington and his wife Grace lost their three-year-old daughter Elizabeth in 1625, it was Grace who had to admonish her distraught husband and remind him of

Elizabeth's present happiness and their duty to surrender her willingly to God.¹²

There may have been a connection between the relatively large number of elegies for infants and small children composed during this period and the vogue for their depiction on funeral monuments, sometimes in their mothers' arms or in their cradles. Maximilian Colt's monument to Princess Sophia, who died shortly after her birth in 1606, allegedly appealed to women particularly strongly, and probably played an important part in the spread of cradle monuments.¹³

Another especially challenging poem of female grief is Andrew Marvell's "The Nymph complaining for the death of her faun" (1650–52?). The enigmatic character of this poem has drawn commentators in the same way that the north face of the Eiger draws mountaineers. There is no consensus about its meaning or the best way of approaching it. Instead of trying to surmount the probably insoluble problems of reference and identity which the poem presents, Phillip McCaffrey scans the rock face through the glasses of a modified Freudian psychoanalysis. (His sustained use of this approach distinguishes his essay from all the others in this volume.) He suggests that the poem gives a psychologically penetrating account of the way in which the untimely death of the pet left by her unfaithful lover thwarts a young and immature girl's delayed mourning for that lover's loss. The pet has become her "linking object" with him and also her "Narcissistic Idol." Her repressed aggression is finally turned against herself as she imagines her own death. The poem illustrates, in short, "the way in which mourning can be stalled, can fail altogether and can settle into self-destructive grief." In this way it stands as an example of this period's increasingly sophisticated understanding of grief and mourning.

Two essays show how female grief could sometimes be presented in a highly positive light by male authors. Michael McClintock sees in Thomas Heywood's *Apology for Actors*

(1612) and *A Woman Killed with Kindness* (acted 1603) an understanding of theatrical affectivity as a force with a potential for integrating society "by regulating both gender identities and familial relations." "Affectivity — a character's ability to project or respond to intense emotion — is one of the primary measures of moral worth" in *A Woman Killed with Kindness*. The grief suffered by Anne Frankford and Susan Mountford brings about a deep change in John Frankford and Sir Francis Acton respectively, illustrating the tempering of "the rigidity of masculine reason and aggression . . . by the female's traditionally superior capacity for emotion." It is Wendoll, Anne Frankford's seducer, who cannot weep, a characteristic mark of the incorrigible sinner. Paul Parrish observes that Richard Crashaw, a poet who never resisted or spoke against the legitimacy of mourning, nevertheless expressed the deepest and most genuine grief through women mourners and demonstrated that his most profound attachments and insights were ones that would traditionally be judged "feminine." His most powerful poetry of mourning, in Parrish's judgment, was that in which he sought to share more fully in the response of the Virgin Mary and Mary Magdalene to the death of Christ, looking to their affectivity to help shape his own sensibility.

In contrast with these two examples, it is a perceived failure in male response to female grief that plays a crucial role in Margo Swiss's thought-provoking reading of *Paradise Lost*. Eve relates to Adam in book 5 the sinister dream in which Satan has tempted her, the previous night, to eat the forbidden fruit. Adam's answer — his assurance that her trouble affects him equally, his attempted reassurances concerning "unapprov'd" evil's entry into the mind, and expressions of confidence in his wife — constitute in Swiss's view an inadequate rejoinder to what Eve has told him. She is "cheard," yet weeps tears, the third and fourth of which Adam kisses before they fall, "as the gracious signs of sweet remorse / And pious awe, that feard to have offended."[14] So all is "cleard" only in appearance: Adam has denied her grief expression, and trivialized and dismissed what she believes significant, in Swiss's challenging intepretation. Adam's neglect of his wife's sorrow ensures her increasing sense of alienation from him and contributes to her ultimate fall. The task of repairing its consequences begins only when "Eve initiates a penitential work that depends on Adam's reciprocal response." This time it is forthcoming, and the process culminates in their kneeling together to confess their faults, and beg pardon, watering the ground with their tears. *Paradise Lost* stands, in Swiss's view, as one more work of this period affirming "the necessity of satisfactory grief expression." It is something necessary for both sexes: an element of that androgyny to which the title of her essay refers.

These essays, then, explore important themes: the role of religion in explaining grief and shaping ways of responding to it, the exposure of the inadequacy of certain stock consolations inherited from antiquity, the acceptance of the would-be consoler's need to engage with grief more closely, differences between men's and women's experiences of grief and ways of expressing it, the attribution of positive value to female affectivity, and the affirmation of the need for satisfactory grief expression on the part of both sexes. One tentative conclusion must be that while this period allowed an unprecedented range of different attitudes to grief to be articulated, no simple schema of change can be imposed upon its literary expressions of sorrow and mourning. Many inherited ideas did not simply disappear, and we often see the eclectic mingling of attitudes which to a superficial view might seem opposed, rather than the supersession of, for example, "rigorist" ways of looking at grief by more compassionate ones. Nor, as G. W. Pigman III long ago remarked, did the more open acceptance of grief necessarily make for better or more moving poetry. He found Henry King's direct expression of his grief in "An Exequy" on his wife's death less moving than the conflict arising from Ben Jonson's suppressed mourning for his first son (*Elegy*, 126–27). Indeed, an outpouring of poetical grief can seem forced, even insincere. We must not lose sight of the fact that the composition of a funeral elegy was one way for a young poet to make his name. Paul Parrish rightly reminds us of Dennis Kay's point that it was a medium that encouraged competition, a sort of laboratory for creative experiment.[15] Such competition was especially intense in academe, and Richard Crashaw's elegy on the death of George Porter, the Regius Professor of Civil Law at Cambridge, gives a vivid picture of the customary pinning of poetic tributes to mourning hangings around the biers of famous people:

> See all in mourning now; the walles are jett,
> With pearly papers carelesly besett.
> Whose snowy cheekes, least joy should be exprest,
> The weeping pen with sable teares hath drest.[16]

The poem may urge "abundant, consistent, and eloquent grieving." Yet for all its wit, ingenuity and inventiveness and the variety of its aqueous imagery, or even because of them, it is for me much less moving than Crashaw's "An Epitaph Vpon Husband and Wife, which died, and were buried together" (174). The hint that tears may disturb the sleeping pair in their cold, hard, but love-made bed, and the prospect of their ultimate awakening to an eternal day, are combined in a poem of considerable economy and great emotional power.

This collection helps the reader to see more clearly possible ways forward in the investigation of the literature and history of grief and kindred emotions. The period spanned in this volume was one of extraordinary richness in English literature. "No other time has so valued the expression of feeling," concluded Bettie Doebler, in her own study of the literature of dying in early modern England.[17] These essays, forays into rich, yet still largely unexplored territory, may encourage its more systematic mapping.

One question that deserves more thorough investigation in this context is that of the ways in which different religious beliefs or standpoints influenced the literary expression of grief. Clearly there was a stock of basic doctrines and consolations available to all Christians: a number of them have been touched on in the first paragraphs of this afterword. Equally clearly, the intellectual complexity of a writer such as Donne prevents the churchmanship reflected in his poems and sermons from being neatly labeled or pigeonholed. None of the major writers discussed in this collection (apart from Milton, whose heterodoxy makes him a special case) can be considered "puritan," though Louis Martz has touched on the matter of "Calvinist" influence on the poetry of George Herbert. Are there any distinctively puritan themes in the literature of grief? Dennis Kay noted that "demonstrations of grief were coming to be associated with Puritanism — a process accelerated (if not inaugurated) by the hyperbolic zeal with which Prince Henry had been lamented."[18] (An association which has a certain irony, in light of the fact that Puritans had been among the foremost rigorists 50 years earlier.) The outpouring of grief in verse certainly neither was nor became the preserve of Puritans. Crashaw's progress toward Catholicism needs to be taken into account in an assessment of his religious poems. The imagery of pieces such as "Sancta Maria Dolorum" reminds one very powerfully of some of the more openly expressive visual art of the continental Counter-Reformation.

The relationship between the written word and the visual arts during this period still awaits thorough exploration. It was in funeral sculpture that England made her foremost artistic contribution. It was precisely during these years, as Adam White has shown, that English funeral monuments were greatly enriched by the influence of a wide range of forms and motifs imported from the continent. Epitaphs and sculpture were meant to illustrate and complement each other. How well their marriage was achieved is a question as yet barely considered, even though the English poetic epitaph has been the subject of a notable study by Joshua Scodel. Certainly the pathos of premature death and bitter grief, together with the power of Christian consolation, were forcefully expressed by some sculptors, among whom Epiphanius Evesham stands preeminent.[19]

Continental influence on English literature as well as the visual arts also needs to be taken into account. This is a huge and complex subject. Although certain aspects of Juliana Schiesari's thesis concerning *The Gendering of Melancholia* may require adjustment or qualification in the light of these essays, her work remains an outstanding example of the placing in their European context of some English works concerned with melancholy.[20] Marjory E. Lange in her essay in this collection also mentions some of the continental writers on whom Robert Burton drew in his own treatment of melancholy. Louis Martz draws attention to Herbert's awareness of the continental literature of tears, and to that literature's influence on English Catholic poets, including Crashaw.

Some of the most important questions about the treatment of grief in English culture will require a reexamination of the years of the English Reformation and its immediate aftermath — that is the period immediately preceding the one covered in this volume. It looks as though the reception in England of the northern Renaissance and the Protestant Reformation created during the middle of the sixteenth century an atmosphere especially favorable to the articulation of what G. W. Pigman III dubbed "rigorist" attitudes to grief. Ancient wisdom, above all in the shape of Stoicism, and Protestant hostility to "hypocritical" mourning or anything that might smack of prayers for the dead, appear to have combined to produce this result. "Rigorism," Pigman wrote, "is at its height during the reign of Edward VI." He identified important landmarks in "The Shift from Anxious Elegy," most notably in the collections of elegies published in 1587 after the death of

Sir Philip Sidney. He also drew attention to brief passages in defense of mourning by Whitgift and Hooker in his discussion of "The Emergence of Compassionate Moderation" (*Elegy*, 29, 33–34, 57–59). But a much fuller examination of the poetry, polemic and sermons of these earlier years would be necessary to identify the causes of change more clearly and to establish more precisely the links between literature and churchmanship.

Perhaps a historian should close with a plea for closer cooperation between literary scholars and historians. For several years now, many literary scholars have shown a growing disposition to treat all sorts of written evidence surviving from the past as "texts," while historians have been increasingly ready to regard literary texts as "historical documents." In order to understand major shifts in emotional climate, or at least in ways of expressing emotions, we need to set art and literature securely in their social context. The resulting picture will doubtless appear a great deal more complex, even messy, than the bold scheme of seismic changes outlined in Lawrence Stone's magnificent panoramic surveys of English social history.[21] But the work of recovering it will be immensely rewarding.

Notes

Notes to Introduction/Swiss & Kent

1. All references to Shakespeare's plays are from *The Riverside Shakespeare* (Boston: Houghton Mifflin, 1974), and are hereafter cited in the text. Arnold Stein, *The House of Death: Messages from the English Renaissance* (Baltimore: The Johns Hopkins University Press, 1986), has remarked about this same passage: "It is a well-known truth that the best medicine for a sad heart is to lament aloud. . . . As a first channel of release, though not only that, words were essential to human beings" (124–25).

2. For background on the "stoical" texts of the sixteenth century and their role in shaping attitudes to grief expression, see *Elegy*, 11–19.

3. See *Elegy*, 7–8, where Pigman identifies these stages. Colin Murray Parkes, *Bereavement: Studies of Grief in Adult Life*, 3rd ed. (Madison, Conn.: International Universities Press, 1998), gives the grieving process more detailed phases (and also gives many subdivisions of each phase): the broken heart, alarm, searching, mitigation, anger and guilt, and gaining a new identity. Different individuals will respond in different ways, of course, and therefore the duration and form of each phase will vary according to personality and circumstance. "Nevertheless, there is a common pattern whose features can be observed without difficulty in most cases, and this justifies our regarding grief as a distinct psychological process" (7).

4. Julie Schiesari, *The Gendering of Melancholia: Feminism, Psychoanalysis, and the Symbiosis of Loss in Renaissance Literature* (Ithaca, N.Y.: Cornell University Press, 1992), 2.

5. "Sorrow a Cause of Melancholy," 1.2.4 in Robert Burton, *The Anatomy of Melancholy*, ed. Thomas J. Faulkner, Nicolas K. Kiessling and Rhoda L. Blair (Oxford: Clarendon Press, 1989), 1.256, 257.

6. In "Hamlet's Grief," *English Literary History* 48 (Spring 1981), Arthur Kirsch considers the relevance of Freud's essay "Mourning and Melancholia," especially the process by which grief is overcome ("the work of mourning") in relation to Hamlet's dilemma. He suggests also that Hamlet's readiness to die at the conclusion of the play signals that he has completed "the work of mourning" (32–33). Kirsch's argument is well taken but most would concede that Hamlet's oppressive circumstances prevent him from participating in the usual process of mourning. He experiences the agonies of bereavement but is trapped in a community that cares nothing for his pain.

7. James L. Calderwood, *Shakespeare and the Denial of Death* (Amherst: University of Massachusetts Press, 1987), 77–78.

8. Anne Laurence, "Godly Grief: Individual Responses to Death in Seventeenth-Century Britain," in *DRB*, 75, 76.

9. We are grateful to Frances Batycki, University of Calgary, for allowing us to read her as yet unpublished essay, "The Rhetoric of Grief in Rachel Speght's *Mortalities Memorandum*."

10. Edward Doughtie, *Lyrics from English Ayres 1596–1622* (Cambridge, Mass.: Harvard University Press, 1970), 410. See also Daniel Fischlin, *In Small Proportions: A Poetics of the English Ayre 1596–1622* (Detroit: Wayne State University Press, 1998), 341 n. 17. Fischlin's "'Sighes & Teares Make Life to Last': The Purgation of Grief and Death Through Trope," is especially relevant to our purposes, and we are indebted to his insights.

11. Fischlin has described the immense difficulty of giving an adequate account of grief: "Hyperbole ('extreame grief,' 'greatest miserie') intensifies self by suggesting an experiential world beyond the ability of a constructed self to express. The result of such a ritual of eloquence is that the self-reflexive subversion of language becomes, in fine, a means for language to achieve the enduring expression of its own desired immortality" (149).

12. George Puttenham, *The Arte of English Poesie*, ed. Gladys Doidge Willcock and Alice Walker (Cambridge: Cambridge University Press, 1936), 1.47.

13. Heather Dubrow, *Shakespeare and Domestic Loss: Forms of Deprivation, Mourning, and Recuperation* (Cambridge: Cambridge University Press, 1999), writes about the experience of loss in Shakespeare, particularly in connection with domestic concerns.

14. Quoted by Laurence, *DRB*, 62. See Lawrence Stone, *The Family, Sex and Marriage in England 1500–1800* (New York: Harper & Row, 1977), 117.

15. *DRB*, 74. Ralph Houlbrooke notes: "A great mass of intimate testimony in the form of letters, diaries, and biographies gives us a vivid sense of the intense feelings of personal loss suffered by seventeenth century people" (*DRF*, 381).

16. Cressy, *BMD*, 393, gives another helpful overview: "Grief was both a natural and cultural phenomenon. It was something people felt, but also something they performed. Failure to grieve might be seen as cold and heartless, while excess grief displayed weakness and lack of control. The subject lent itself to the Aristotelian discourse of balance and moderation." The quotation in the text is from Raymond Anselment, *The Realms of Apollo: Literature and Healing in Seventeenth-Century England* (Newark: University of Delaware Press, 1995), 89.

17. See Margo Swiss, "*Lachrymae Christi*: The Theology of Tears in Milton's *Lycidas* and Donne's Sermon 'Jesus Wept,'" in *Heirs of Fame: Milton and Writers of the English Renaissance*, ed. Margo Swiss and David A. Kent (Lewisburg, Pa.: Bucknell University Press, 1995), 135–57; and Marjory E. Lange, *Telling Tears in the English Renaissance* (Leiden: E. J. Brill, 1996), 156–85, for a full discussion of Jesus' tears.

18. The phrase is borrowed from Stephen Greenblatt, *Renaissance Self-Fashioning: From More to Shakespeare* (Chicago: University of Chicago Press, 1980). See also Bettie Anne Doebler, *Rooted Sorrow: Dying in Early Modern England* (Rutherford, N.J.: Fairleigh Dickinson University Press, 1994), 31. Doebler's title also alludes to a phrase from *Macbeth* 5.3.41.

19. Timothy Bright, *A Treastise of Melancholy* (London: Thomas Vautrollier, 1586), 193, 195.

20. Jacques Derrida, *The Gift of Death*, trans. David Wills (Chicago: University of Chicago Press, 1995). Derrida's attention to tears and grief in *The Gift of Death* and *The Politics of Friendship*, trans. George Collins (London: Verso, 1998), suggests a current intellectual preoccupation with grief and mourning which were, of course, constant and inescapable realities for the seventeenth century.

21. "Death rates normally fluctuated around 25 per 1,000 with mortality of 35 per 1,000, or even higher in the worst of seasons. (This compares to death rates of 8 to 12 per 1,000 in the modern industrial West.)" Cressy, *BMD*, 380. See also Houlbrooke, "The Face of Death," in *DRB*, 5–27, and Lawrence Stone, *The Family, Sex and Marriage*, on early modern mortality rates (66–82). Life expectancy in the period is, however, extremely hard to determine owing to unreliable or incomplete data. See Mary Abbott, *Life Cycles in England 1560–1720* (London: Routledge, 1996), 134–38. The quotation is from Anselment, *Realms of Apollo*, 91; his Chapter 3 analyzes plague literature in the period.

22. Charles Carlton, "Civilians," in *The Civil Wars: A Military History of England, Scotland, and Ireland 1638–1660*, ed. John Kenyon and Jane Ohlmeyer (Oxford: Oxford University Press, 1998), 275–76.

23. Raymond Anselment, "'The Teares of Nature': Seventeenth-Century Parental Bereavement," *Modern Philology* 91 (August 1993): 26. Chapter 2 of *The Realms of Apollo* also examines parental bereavement,

while chapters 4 and 5 are concerned with venereal disease and smallpox, respectively.

24. Carlton, "Civilians," 273, 278.

25. Daniel Featley, *Ancilla Pietatis* (London, 1626), 215.

26. William Whately, *Charitable Tears* (London, 1623), 251.

27. John Featley, *A Fountain of Tears* (London, 1646), 5.

28. *Elegy*, 45. Pigman's survey of formularies also leads him to observe how the "letter of consolation" was becoming "the letter of condolence" (20).

29. Parallel developments were occurring in funeral practices and in other art forms such as music, as Clare Gittings and Daniel Fischlin have pointed out. See Clare Gittings, "Expressions of Loss in Early Seventeenth-Century England," in *The Changing Face of Death: Historical Accounts of Death and Disposal*, ed. Peter C. Jupp and Glennys Howarth (London: Macmillan, 1997), 19, and Fischlin, *In Small Proportions*, chap. 4.

30. See also *DRF*, 374. In "The Cultural Functions of Renaissance Elegy," *English Literary Review* 28 (winter 1998), Matthew Greenfield argues that the elegy in the seventeenth century increasingly privileged "the private, the spontaneous, and the unmediated" (85). He is also concerned with the tension between the public and the private tasks of the elegist within the trend to the "privatization" of mourning.

31. In response to Kaja Silverman's claim in *The Acoustic Mirror: The Female Voice in Psychoanalysis and Cinema* (Bloomington: Indiana University Press, 1984), that "female melancholia," depression in women, originates in "the *specific* object loss, the mother" (Schiesari, *Gendering*, 75), Schiesari argues that "the loss that is mourned is . . . not merely the mother's absence, nor simply the daughter's devalued sense of self, but also and more generally the structured denial of privilege to *all* women within patriarchal societies" (Schiesari, 77). Elsewhere, Schiesari states that the culturally depressed state of women serves only to demean women, "whose association with loss or grief is expressed by less flattering allusions to widow's weeds, inarticulate weeping, or other signs of ritualistic (but intellectually unaccredited) mourning" (12).

32. Lange continues: "Normatively, men have been defined as the tearless ones leaving their written tears to become prisms to magnify some remarkable or noteworthy matter. In love lyrics male poets exploit tears to indicate the intensity — and singularity — of these feelings. They 'play' at being disempowered before their anonymous, indiscernible, primarily female audience" (*Telling Tears*, 3).

33. Two helpful collections on women writers in early modern England are *Women and Literature 1500–1700*, ed. Helen Wilcox (Cambridge: Cambridge University Press, 1996), and *Women's Life-Writing: Finding Voice/Building Community*, ed. Linda S. Coleman (Bowling Green, Ohio: Bowling Green State University Press, 1997).

34. Steven Zwicker, "Lines of Authority: Politics and Literary Culture in the Restoration," in *Politics of Discourse: The Literature and History of Seventeenth-Century England*, ed. Steven Zwicker and Kevin Sharpe (Berkeley and Los Angeles: University of California Press, 1987), 248. In *Milton: Poet of Exile* (New Haven: Yale University Press, 1980), Louis Martz also addresses Milton's creative life during the Restoration. In a public lecture in May 1986 (University of Manitoba), Balachandra Rajan linked Milton's exilic suffering with the inspiration for *Paradise Lost*.

Notes to Chapter 1/Tromly

1. *Sonnet 120*, line 10. All quotations of Shakespeare are from *The Riverside Shakespeare*, ed. G. Blakemore Evans (Boston: Houghton Mifflin, 1974). In the sonnets, which I do not discuss in this paper, the tension between the grieving and comforting impulses is usually located within the speaker. See Martha R. Lifson, "The Rhetoric of Consolation: Shakespeare's Couplets," *Assays* 2 (1983): 95–114, and Emily E. Stockard, "Patterns of Consolation in Shakespeare's Sonnets 1–126," *Studies in Philology* 94 (1997): 465–93, neither of which refers to the consolatory tradition. In contrast to the frequency of "comfort," the word "consolation" appears only twice in Shakespeare, "consolate" once, and "console" never. See Marvin Spevack, *The Harvard Concordance to Shakespeare* (Cambridge, Mass.: Harvard University Press, 1973).

2. In addition to those discussed in this essay, other scenes of rejected consolation include *The Tempest*, 2.1.1–10; *The Comedy of Errors*, 2.1.32–41; *Romeo and Juliet*, 3.3.54–70; *Othello*, 1.3.199–220; *King John*, 3.4.22–105; *Richard II*, 1.3.257–303; and *Troilus and Cressida*, 4.4.1–10. For commentary on these passages as well as those discussed in this essay, see Brian Vickers, "Shakespearian Consolations," *Proceedings of the British Academy* 82 (1993): 219–84. This valuable essay does not address what I take to be the central issue of authority and its abuses in Shakespeare's consolations. Girolamo Cardano, *Cardanus Comforte*, trans. Thomas Bedingfield (1576; reprint, Amsterdam: Da Capo Press, 1969), 1 verso. I have silently modernized archaic usages of *u* and *v* throughout this paper.

3. For the construing of not only "immoderate grief" but indeed *all* grief as a tacit denial of faith in salvation and resurrection, see *Elegy*, 27–39. For the legitimation of grief in the seventeenth century, see *BMD*, 393–95, and Anne Laurence, "Godly Grief: Individual Responses to Death in Seventeenth-Century Britain," in *DRB*, 62–76.

4. Thomas Wilson, *The Art of Rhetoric* (1560), ed. Peter E. Medine (University Park: Pennsylvania State University Press, 1994), 103. Henry Peacham, *The Garden of Eloquence* (1577; reprint, Scolar Press Facsimile,

Menston, England, 1971), sig. L2, casually observes in a discussion of *consolatio* that "cheerefull wordes be repugnaunt to a sorrowfull mynde." St. Thomas More, *A Dialogue of Comfort against Tribulation*, ed. Frank Manley (New Haven: Yale University Press, 1977), 15 (I.iii). Angel Day, *The English Secretary* (1599), ed. Robert O. Evans (Gainesville, Fla.: Scholars' Facsimiles & Reprints, 1967), 127.

5. In a speech similar to that of Leonato, Gorboduc exclaims:
Many can yield right sage and grave advice / Of patient sprite to others wrapped in woe / And can in speech both rule and conquer kind, / Who, if by proof they might feel nature's force / Would show themselves men as they are indeed, / Which now will needs be gods.

Thomas Sackville and Thomas Norton, *Gorboduc; or, Ferrex and Porrex*, ed. Irby B. Cauthen Jr. (Lincoln: University of Nebraska Press, 1970), 4.2.159–65. For an instance contemporary with Shakespeare, see John Marston, *Antonio's Revenge*, ed. W. Reavley Gair (Manchester: Manchester University Press, 1978), 1.5.34–57.

6. Consolatory writing had long argued that insistent grief is fueled by anger and narcissism. For anger, see More's *Dialogue of Comfort*, 15. For narcissism in grief, see Plutarch's influential consolatory letter to Apollonius (*Moralia*, trans. Frank Cole Babbitt, 15 vols. [London: Heinemann, 1928], 2.159–61).

7. The figure of 300 titles is from A. D. Beach Langston, "Tudor Books of Consolation," Ph.D. diss., University of North Carolina, Chapel Hill, 1940, v. It should be supplemented by the works noted in Josephine Evetts Secker, "Consolatory Literature of the English Recusants," *Renaissance and Reformation* 18 (1982): 122–41. For the tradition of consolatory letters, see Benjamin Boyce, "The Stoic *Consolatio* and Shakespeare," *PMLA* 64 (1949): 771–80, and the excellent first chapter of Pigman's *Elegy*. For elegies, see Michael West, "The *Consolatio* in Milton's Funeral Elegies," *Huntington Library Quarterly* 34 (1971): 233–49, and *Elegy*, 40–127.

8. Cicero, *Tusculan Disputations*, trans. J. K. King. Loeb edition (London: 1927), 145 (1.149.119). For an excellent account of the classical tradition of consolation (before Boethius) and its assimilation in the Renaissance, see Vickers, 218–45. On Christian countertradition, see Sister Mary Melchior Beyenka, *Consolation in Saint Augustine*, Patristic Studies 83 (Washington, D.C.: Catholic University of America Press, 1950). For an exceedingly thorough study of medieval consolation, see Peter von Moos, *Consolatio: Studien zur mittellateinischen Trostliteratur über den Tod und zum Problem der christlichen Trauer*, 4 vols. (Munich, 1971–72).

9. See George W. McClure, *Sorrow and Consolation in Italian Humanism* (Princeton: Princeton University Press, 1991). The standard surveys of Shakespeare's sources are Vickers, "Shakespearian

Consolations," Boyce, "The Stoic *Consolatio* and Shakespeare," and John L. Tison Jr., "Shakespeare's *Consolatio* for Exile," *Modern Language Quarterly* 21 (1960): 142–57. See also Rolf Soellner, "Shakespeare and the 'Consolatio,'" *Notes and Queries* 199 (1954): 108–9. Hardin Craig argues for Shakespeare's knowledge of Cardano's *De consolatione* (translated in 1573 as *Cardanus Comforte*) in "Hamlet's Book," *Huntington Library Bulletin* 6 (1934): 17–37. For other links between Shakespeare and the consolatory tradition, see the articles cited below by Presson, Elton, Duncan-Jones and Asp.

10. John T. McNeill, *A History of the Cure of Souls* (New York: Harper, 1951), 326–27. McNeill makes reference to consolatory literature throughout the volume. For the importance of the consoler's authority at the end of Boethius's *Consolation of Philosophy*, see Seth Lerer, *Boethius and Dialogue* (Princeton: Princeton University Press, 1985), 212–16.

11. Plutarch, *Moralia*, 2.165–67. Wilson, *The Art of Rhetoric*, 112. There is a similar hierarchy in Cardano, *Cardanus Comforte*, 58.

12. *The Letters of Queen Elizabeth*, ed. G. B. Harrison (Cassell: London, 1935), 251. The use of shame in the service of consolation goes back at least to the famous consolatory epistle in which Servius Sulpicius exhorts the grieving Cicero "never to forget that you are Cicero, one who has ever been wont to instruct and advise others"; see Cicero, *Letters to His Friends*, 3 vols. (London: Heinemann, 1927–28), 1.275.

13. For two examples of consolation from male social inferiors to noblewomen, see Samuel Daniel's letter to Anne Clifford, countess of Pembroke, in H. Sellers, "Samuel Daniel: Additions to the Text," *Modern Language Quarterly* 11 (1916): 29, and Wilson's letter to Katherine Brandon, duchess of Suffolk in *The Art of Rhetoric*, 103–19.

14. Burton, *The Anatomy of Melancholy*, 4 vols. (Oxford: Clarendon, 1989–98), 2:126, 181 (2.3.1.1). For commentary, see John L. Lievsay, "Robert Burton's *De Consolatione*," *South Atlantic Quarterly* 55 (1956): 329–36. In "Consolatory Topoi: Aspects of a Tradition," *Neohelicon* 12 (1985): 239–63, Richard Spuler notes that in *European Literature and the Latin Middle Ages*, Ernst Robert Curtius opens his chapter on "Topics" with a disquisition on "all who live must die."

15. Cardano's words (64 verso–65) are quoted by Burton, with the gloss that the idea derives from Plutarch's consolatory letter to Apollonius.

16. Lily B. Campbell, *Shakespeare's Tragic Heroes: Slaves of Passion* (New York: Barnes and Noble, 1959), 115. Rather narrowly, she sees "the real significance of the play in the challenge of philosophy to passion, of consolation to grief."

17. Arthur Kirsch, "Hamlet's Grief," *English Literary History* 48 (1981): 20.

18. Caspar Hueber, *A riche Storehouse, or Treasurie, for the Sicke*, trans. Thomas Godfrie (London: 1578), 62–86. For other Tudor discussions

of how clerical comforters should prepare prisoners for death, see Beach Langston, "Essex and the Art of Dying," *Huntington Library Bulletin* 13 (1950): 109–29, esp. 114–19.

19. For possible sources, see Katherine Duncan-Jones, "Stoicism in *Measure for Measure*: A New Source," *Review of English Studies* 28 (1977): 441–46, and *Measure for Measure*, ed. Mark Eccles, New Variorum Edition (New York: Modern Language Association of America, 1980), 124–31. For the *ars moriendi* in the play, see Phoebe Spinrad, "*Measure for Measure* and the Art of Not Dying," *Texas Studies in Literature and Language* 26 (1984): 74–93, and for substantial excerpts from relevant treatises, see David William Atkinson, *The English 'ars moriendi'* (New York: Peter Lang, 1992).

20. *The Countess of Pembroke's Translation of Philippe de Mornay's "Discourse of Life and Death,"* ed. Diane Bornstein, Medieval and Renaissance Monograph Series III (Detroit: Marygrove College, 1983), 57.

21. For the interesting relation to Lucretius, see L. C. Martin, "Shakespeare, Lucretius, and the Commonplaces," *Review of English Studies* 21 (1945): 174–82.

22. Robert N. Watson, "False Immortality in *Measure for Measure*: Comic Means, Tragic Ends," in *Critical Essays on Shakespeare's "Measure for Measure,"* ed. Richard P. Wheeler (New York: G. K. Hall, 1999), 100.

23. Similarly, when Cardano minimizes the loss of children, he asks, "what is more in thy sonne then the effusion of thy seede?" (53v).

24. Virginia M. Carr, "The Power of Grief in *Richard II*," *Études Anglaises* 31 (1978): 145. Carr does not refer to other Shakespearean plays or to the consolatory tradition.

25. For consolation in Sidney's *Arcadia*, see William Elton, *"King Lear" and the Gods* (San Marino, Calif.: Huntington Library, 1966), 105.

26. Harbage, introduction to *King Lear* in *Shakespeare: The Complete Works*, gen. ed. Alfred Harbage (Penguin: Baltimore, 1969), 1061. Immediately before this comment, Harbage makes the dubious point that "the implications of the play are more comforting than the data it abstracts."

27. Gerard Manley Hopkins, *Poems and Prose*, ed. W. H. Gardner (Baltimore: Penguin, 1953), 61.

28. The fullest treatment of Edgar's consolatory sources is in Elton, *"King Lear" and the Gods*, esp. 97–107. For the identification of Edgar with Christ the Consoler, see Harry Morris, *Last Things in Shakespeare* (Tallahassee: Florida State University Press, 1985), 148–52.

29. Alvin B. Kernan, *The Playwright as Magician* (New Haven: Yale University Press, 1979), 120–28, usefully discusses the morality play elements in the scene, though he misleads when he applies the same label to Cordelia's comforting of Lear in the following scene.

30. Here I disagree with Vickers, "Shakespearian Consolations," who

does not take account of Edgar's suppressed aggression toward his father and considerably exaggerates the efficacy of his comforting: "In Edgar's consoling his father the offices of philosophy are validated" (183).

31. For Gloucester as Flibbertigibbet, see Sheldon P. Zitner, "*King Lear* and Its Language," in *Some Facets of "King Lear": Essays in Prismatic Criticism*, ed. Rosalie L. Colie and F. T. Flahiff (Toronto: University of Toronto Press, 1974), 16.

32. Cardano, *Cardanus Comforte*, 58. *Gabriel Harvey's Marginalia*, ed. G. C. Moore Smith (Stratford-upon-Avon: Shakespere Head Press, 1913), 95.

33. In "Shakespeare's Paulina and the *Consolatio* Tradition," *Shakespeare Studies* 11 (1978): 145–58, Carolyn Asp links Lady Philosophy's consoling of Boethius with Paulina's healing of Leontes in *The Winter's Tale*.

34. For connections between the two works, see Paul N. Siegel, "Adversity and the Miracle of Love in *King Lear*," *Shakespeare Quarterly* 6 (1955): 325–41, and Robert K. Presson, "Boethius, King Lear, and 'Maystresse Philosophie,'" *Journal of English and Germanic Philology* 64 (1965): 406–24. While the former argues (unconvincingly) for the play's essentially Boethian vision, the latter posits a more complex relationship between the works. Neither critic discusses consolation.

35. Boethius, *The Consolation of Philosophy*, trans. Richard Green (New York: Bobbs Merrill, 1962), 31–32, book 2, prose 5.

36. Michael Ignatieff, *The Needs of Strangers* (New York: Penguin, 1986), 31.

37. Another such vision of consolation, and one that is clearly based on his experience of the reconciliation with Cordelia, is Lear's fantasy of himself and Cordelia living in prison (rather like Boethius and Lady Philosophy) and transcending the false happiness that Fortune bestows and takes away (5.3.8–18).

38. In "King Lear and His Comforters," *Essays in Criticism* 16 (1966): 135–46, John D. Rosenberg appositely argues that "Like Job's pharisaical comforters, those critics who find 'poetic justice' in *King Lear* are guilty of a morally shocking reading of the play" (139).

39. Elton, *"King Lear" and the Gods*, 257–58.

Notes to Chapter 2/Evans

1. For a thorough and convenient overview of commentary on Donne's poems prior to 1990, see *DV*, vol. 6. Some sense of the relative lack of interest in Jonson's poem can be gathered from John Burdett and Jonathan Wright, "Ben Jonson in Recent General Scholarship, 1972–1996," *Ben Jonson Journal* 4 (1997): 151–79, esp. 178.

2. Useful studies of early modern death, grief, mourning and elegiac

writing include the following: Philippe Ariès, *The Hour of Our Death* (New York: Knopf, 1981); Lawrence Babb, *The Elizabethan Malady: A Study of Melancholia in English Literature from 1580 to 1642* (East Lansing: Michigan State College Press, 1951); Lucinda McCray Beier, "The Good Death in Seventeenth-Century England," in *DRB*, 43–61; James L. Calderwood, *Shakespeare and the Denial of Death* (Amherst: University of Massachusetts Press, 1987); Cressy, *BMD*; Bettie Doebler, *Rooted Sorrow: Dying in Early Modern England* (Rutherford, N.J.: Fairleigh Dickinson University Press, 1994); John W. Draper, *The Funeral Elegy and the Rise of English Romanticism* (New York: New York University Press, 1929); William E. Engel, *Mapping Mortality: The Persistence of Memory and Melancholy in Early Modern England* (Amherst: University of Massachusetts Press, 1995); Claire Gittings, *Death, Burial and the Individual in Early Modern England* (London: Croom Helm, 1984); Matthew Greenfield, "The Cultural Functions of Renaissance Elegy," *English Literary Renaissance* 28 (1998): 75–94; O. B. Hardison Jr., *The Enduring Monument: A Study of the Idea of Praise in Renaissance Literary Theory and Practice* (Chapel Hill: University of North Carolina Press, 1962); Houlbrooke, *DRF*; Houlbrooke, ed., *DRB*; Dennis Kay, *Melodious Tears: The English Funeral Elegy from Spenser to Milton* (Oxford: Clarendon Press, 1990); Anne Laurence, "Godly Grief: Individual Responses to Death in Seventeenth-Century Britain," in *DRB*, 62–76; Barbara Kiefer Lewalski, *Donne's Anniversaries and the Poetry of Praise: The Creation of a Symbolic Mode* (Princeton: Princeton University Press, 1973); Bridget Gellert Lyons, *Voices of Melancholy: Studies in Literary Treatments of Melancholy in Renaissance England* (New York: Barnes and Noble, 1971); Pigman, *Elegy*; Juliana Schiesari, *The Gendering of Melancholia: Feminism, Psychoanalysis, and the Symbolics of Loss in Renaissance Literature* (Ithaca, N.Y.: Cornell University Press, 1992); Joshua Scodel, *The English Poetic Epitaph: Commemoration and Conflict from Jonson to Wordsworth* (Ithaca, N.Y.: Cornell University Press, 1991); Peter Spierenburg, *The Broken Spell: A Cultural and Anthropological History of Preindustrial Europe* (New Brunswick, N.J.: Rutgers University Press, 1991); Arnold Stein, *The House of Death: Messages from the English Renaissance* (Baltimore: Johns Hopkins University Press, 1986); Robert N. Watson, *The Rest Is Silence: Death as Annihilation in the English Renaissance* (Berkeley and Los Angeles: University of California Press, 1994).

Useful studies adopting a broader chronological and geographical perspective include the following: Thomas Attig, *How We Grieve: Relearning the World* (New York: Oxford University Press, 1996); Roy F. Baumeister, *Meanings of Life* (New York: Guilford, 1991); Ernst Becker, *The Denial of Death* (New York: Free Press, 1973); Kathy Charmaz, *The Social Reality of Death* (New York: Random House, 1980); Jacques Choron, *Death and Modern Man* (New York: Collier, 1964); Marc P. H. D.

Cleiren, *Bereavement and Adaptation: A Comparative Study of the Aftermath of Death* (Washington, D.C.: Hemisphere, 1993); Susan Letzler Cole, *The Absent One: Mourning Ritual, Tragedy, and the Performance of Ambivalence* (University Park: Pennsylvania State University Press, 1985); Herman Feifel, ed., *The Meaning of Death* (New York: McGraw-Hill, 1959); Robert Fulton, ed., *Death and Identity*, rev. ed. (Bowie, Md.: Charles Press, 1976); Robin Andrew Haig, *The Anatomy of Grief: Biopsychosocial and Therapeutic Perspectives* (Springfield, Ill.: Charles C. Thomas, 1990); Richard A. Kalish, *Death, Grief and Caring Relationships* (Monterey, Calif.: Brooks/Cole, 1981); Robert Kastenbaum and Ruth Aisenberg, *The Psychology of Death* (New York: Springer, 1972); Michael C. Kearl, *Endings: A Sociology of Death and Dying* (New York: Oxford University Press, 1989); Robert Jay Lifton, "On Death and Death Symbolism," in vol. 1, *The Self in Social Interaction*, ed. Chad Gordon and Kenneth J. Gergen (New York: Wiley, 1968), 251–58; Jane Littlewood, *Aspects of Grief: Bereavement in Adult Life* (London: Routledge, 1992); Peter Metcalf and Richard Huntington, *Celebrations of Death: The Anthropology of Mortuary Ritual*, 2nd ed. (Cambridge: Cambridge University Press, 1991); Donovan J. Ochs, *Consolatory Rhetoric: Grief, Symbol, and Ritual in the Greco-Roman Era* (Columbia: University of South Carolina Press, 1993); Cohn Murray Parkes, *Bereavement: Studies of Grief in Adult Life*, 2nd American ed. (Madison, Wis.: International Universities Press, 1987); Therese A. Rando, *Treatment of Complicated Mourning* (Champaign, Ill.: Research Press, 1993); Beverley Raphael, *The Anatomy of Bereavement* (New York: Basic Books, 1983); Peter M. Sacks, *The English Elegy: Studies in the Genre from Spenser to Yeats* (Baltimore: Johns Hopkins University Press, 1985); Bernard Schoenberg et al., ed., *Bereavement: Its Psychosocial Aspects* (New York: Columbia University Press, 1975); W. David Shaw, *Elegy and Paradox: Testing the Conventions* (Baltimore: Johns Hopkins University Press, 1994); Eric Smith, *By Mourning Tongues: Studies in English Elegy* (Totowa, N.J.: Rowman and Littlefield, 1977); Wolfgang Stroebe and Margaret S. Stroebe, *Bereavement and Health: The Psychological and Physical Consequences of Partner Loss* (Cambridge: Cambridge University Press, 1987); and Arnold Toynbee et al., *Man's Concern with Death* (London: Hodder and Stoughton, 1968). Hereafter cited in the text by author and page number.

3. See, however, *DV*, 538. I have chosen to use the text printed in *The Complete Poetry of John Donne*, ed. John Shawcross (New York: Anchor, 1967), 250–52. This version is a bit more reader-friendly than the one in *DV*, although the commentary and notes in the latter are superb; hereafter cited by line number in the text. Similarly helpful are the notes in Wesley Milgate, ed., *The Epithalamions, Anniversaries, and Epicedes* (Oxford: Charendon Press, 1978). For a fine recent discussion of the poem, see Claude J. Summers, "Donne's 1609 Sequence of Grief and Comfort," *Studies in Philology* 89 (1992): 211–31, esp. 219–21.

4. Claire Gittings, in *Death, Burial and the Individual*, argues that reluctance to face the unappealing physical aspects of death is one key difference between modern and early modern reactions to death; see 13, 102.

5. For the texts of the letters, see Vittorio Gabrielli, *Sir Kenelm Digby: Un Inglese Italianato nell'età della Controriforma* (Roma: Edizioni di Storia e Letteratura, 1957), 237–83. See also Gabrielli's serialized articles, "A New Digby Letter-Book: 'In Praise of Venetia.'" These articles were published in *The National Library of Wales Journal*, 9, no. 2 (1955–56): 113–48; 9, no. 4 (1955–56); 440–62; and 10, no. 1 (1956–57): 81–105. Because there is no overlapping of the page numbers in these four sources, they will be cited hereafter in the text by page numbers alone.

Claire Gittings has recently used these letters in her article "Venetia's Death and Kenelm's Mourning," in *Death, Passion and Politics: Van Dyck's Portraits of Venetia Stanley and George Digby*, ed. Ann Sumner (London: Dulwich Picture Gallery, 1995), 54–68. Although this entire volume is helpful, particularly useful are the following articles: Polly Amos and Ann Sumner, "Sir Kenelm Digby and Venetia Stanley: A Great Love Story of the Seventeenth Century," 26–31; Oliver Millar, "Sir Kenelm Digby and Van Dyck," 32–36; and Caroline Bowden, "Venetia Digby — A Perfect Wife?," 37–44. Also helpful on Digby's life is R. T. Peterson, *Sir Kenelm Digby: The Ornament of England* (London: Jonathan Cape, 1956).

6. In quoting from the poem, I cite the text printed in volume 8 of the 11-volume *Ben Jonson*, ed. C. H. Herford and Percy and Evelyn Simpson (Oxford: Clarendon Press, 1925–52). Previous comments on the poem include the following: Draper, 31; George Burke Johnston, *Ben Jonson: Poet* (New York: Columbia University Press, 1945), 55–62; W. David Kay, *Ben Jonson: A Literary Life* (New York: St. Martin's, 1995), 182–83; Dennis Kay, 209–11; Alexander Leggatt, *Ben Jonson: His Vision and His Art* (London: Methuen, 1981), 221–22; Lewalski, 339–42; Michael McCanles, *Jonsonian Discriminations: The Humanist Poet and the Praise of True Nobility* (Toronto: University of Toronto Press, 1992), 132, 136, 138; Kathryn Anderson McKuen, *Classical Influence upon the Tribe of Ben* (1939; reprint, New York: Octagon, 1968), 6–7; Richard S. Peterson, *Imitation and Praise in the Poems of Ben Jonson* (New Haven, Conn.: Yale University Press, 1981), 107–08; *Elegy*, 94; David Riggs, *Ben Jonson: A Life* (Cambridge, Mass.: Harvard University Press, 1989), 337–42; Stein, 146; Wesley Trimpi, *Ben Jonson's Poems: A Study of the Plain Style* (Stanford: Stanford University Press, 1962), 137; and Sara J. van den Berg, *The Action of Ben Jonson's Poetry* (Newark: University of Delaware Press, 1987), 178–81. Hereafter cited in the text by page number.

7. For a practical example of Venetia as a link to Kenelm and then Kenelm as a link to even higher patrons, see Jonson's "Epigram to my MUSE, the Lady Digby" (Under-wood, 78), 20–32. In a letter dated 23

May 1633, Digby describes how his grief prevents him from focusing on anything else, "so that I haue proposed my library to sale which cost me deare and I was long raking together; and all my lettered men that I had about me, I haue licensed" (447).

Notes to Chapter 3/Lange

1. John Donne, "A Sermon Preached at the Spittle, Upon Easter-Munday, 1622," in *The Sermons of John Donne*, 10 vols., ed. George R. Potter and Evelyn M. Simpson (Berkeley and Los Angeles: University of California Press, 1952–64), 4:3, 108; 4.4, 137; 4.13, 343. All subsequent references to Donne's sermons will be made from this edition, and are cited by volume number, sermon number and page.

2. Robert Burton, *The Anatomy of Melancholy*, 3 vols., ed. Thomas C. Faulkner, Nicolas K. Kiessling and Rhonda L. Blair (Oxford: Clarendon, 1989–94), 1.1.3.1. Hereafter cited in the text by part, section, member and subsection numbers.

3. On the physical-medical material, see Lawrence Babb, *Insanity in Bedlam: A Study of Robert Burton's "Anatomy of Melancholy"* (East Lansing: Michigan State University Press, 1959), 18. Michael O'Connell has pointed out that, throughout the seventeenth century, Burton's work was referred to as the *Melancholy*, not the *Anatomy*. See *Robert Burton*, Twayne English Authors Series 426 (Boston: G. K. Hall, 1986), 32. That title's emphasis on content, rather than genre, seems far more relevant, so I join O'Connell in its adoption. O'Connell's comments on the shift over its editions from melancholy as disease to "melancholy as metonymy for the human condition" are to the point: he perceives the medical concern to recede in favor of the symbolic over the course of revision — and over the course of the three parts (*Robert Burton*, chap. 3). Burton's few additions to the medical side are often due to the publication of new material. Jacques Ferrand's *De la maladie d'amour ou melancholie erotique* (1610, expanded 1623), translated as *Eratomania, or a treatise discoursing of love* by E. Chilmead for publication in Oxford in 1640, is first mentioned in Burton's 1632 edition — indicating he had access to the French edition.

4. John Donne to Goodyer, October 1622, *Letters to Severall Persons of Honour (1651)* (New York: Scholars' Facsimiles & Reprints, 1977), 134–35. Donne would have been over 50.

5. On Syminges, see R. C. Bald, *John Donne: A Life* (Oxford: Oxford University Press, 1970), 36–37, 49. Bald infers that Syminges was associated with St. Bartholomew's Hospital (38), in which case a connection could exist between him and Timothie Bright [see below], whose appointment as physician to that institution occurred — not without major opposition — in 1585. See Geoffrey Keynes, *Dr. Timothie Bright*

1550–1615: A Survey of His Life with a Bibliography of His Writings (London: Wellcome Historical Medical Library, 1962), 1, 6–7, for details of Bright's dubious career. On Donne's medical knowledge, see Don Cameron Allen, "John Donne's Knowledge of Renaissance Medicine," *Journal of English and Germanic Philology* 42 (1943): 336. Allen concludes that Donne often "talk[s] like a learned cynic in a circle of eager savants" (342), which may be true when he discusses ailments and/or remedies in his secular works; it is not the case when he employs the language of humours in sermons. See *Sermons* 3:244; 3:286; 8:188 et passim. His reliance on humours in *Devotions upon Emergent Occasions* (Ann Arbor, Mich.: University of Michigan Press, 1959) is even more direct; see below. This volume is hereafter cited by *Devotions* and page number.

6. No one, as far as I can determine, has shown that Donne ever read Burton. Certainly, only two of Donne's sermons employing melancholy (7:22, preached before the king at Whitehall, and 8:2, Lady Danvers's Commemoration) were published during Burton's life. It therefore seems wiser to speak of parallel development than of mutual influence. Both writers engaged the same authorities. Some of these, like Augustine, are to be expected. Others, particularly the somewhat heavy debt each pays to Philip Melanchthon, deserve further study.

7. "Humour" originally meant, simply, liquid. It was early adapted to the four basic bodily fluids, and spread its meaning from there, fluidly. "In the body of Man be foure principall humours, whiche contynuinge in the proportion, that nature hath lymytted, the body is free from all syckenesse" (Elyot, 3).

8. Thus the double meaning of "complexion" and why we still refer to individuals as having sanguine or phlegmatic attitudes toward life.

9. Elyot is relatively vague. Later writers exhaustively detail the mechanisms of decoction, the order in which each humour emerges during the process, and the manner by which each causes disease. There was no agreement about *how* the process worked, only that it did. Elyot consistently avoided creating ambiguities of complexity when the complications merely obscured without explaining anything conclusively.

10. Lawrence Babb, "Preface," *The Elizabethan Malady: A Study of Melancholia in English Literature from 1580–1642* (East Lansing: Michigan State University Press, 1951), vii. Michael MacDonald has analyzed the "voluminous medical practice notes of a seventeenth century astrological physician named Richard Napier"; over 2,000 descriptions of mentally troubled people (*MB*, 13). He treated patients in all walks of life, for all types of mental ailments. MacDonald claims that Bright and Burton, who "taught educated men and women to speak the language of classical medicine," affected the way Napier's patients described their illnesses. With Babb, MacDonald concludes, "[m]elancholy patients were

in good company: More than 40% of them were peers, knights, and ladies, or masters and mistresses; the ordinary ruck of mentally disturbed people included less than half that measure of gentlefolk." Looking at the specific numbers of gentry who reported suffering various ailments, "the social prestige of melancholy is even more sharply visible. Almost two-thirds (65%) of the aristocrats complained of *melancholy*, about one-fifth (18%) were *troubled in mind*, and only 4 (6%) were called *mopish*" (*MB*, 151–52).

11. Thomas Elyot, *The Castel of Helthe* (1541; reprint, New York: Scholars' Facsimiles, 1937). The edition is foliated.

12. Much of Elyot's *Proheme* responds to various perceived censures, such as that he, a knight, would be better occupied in other service, that he was ignorant of medicine and that writing in English was unworthy. His responses are entirely characteristic of the man and his age. To the first point, he asserts that he was but "studiouse about the weale of his countray," the business of every capable citizen, regardless of rank. On the second point, he writes that "whan I wrate fyrste this boke, I was not all ignorante in phisycke, for before that I was .xx. yeres olde, a worshipfull phisition, and one of the most renoumed at that tyme in England [Thomas Linacre], perceyvyng me by nature inclined to knowledge, rad unto me the workes of Galene of temperamentes, natural faculties . . . some of the Aphorismes of Hippocrates." In addition, he announces, he has studied works by Celsus, Dioscorides, the Canons of Avicenna, the Commentaries of Averroes, Isaac and many others. Thus he could justifiably say that, "all thoughe I have never ben at Montpellier, Padua, nor Salern, yet have I found some thynge in phisycke, whereby I have taken no litle profyte concernynge myne owne helthe." His are indeed impressive theoretic credentials; his critics could reply only that he lacked practice. His response to his choice of language is also highly characteristic: "remembre, that the grekes wrate in greke, the Romanes in latyne, Avicena, and the other in Arabike, whiche were their owne propre and maternal tonges." He also criticizes the avarice of his contemporaries as being the only reason they could wish to disguise their knowledge in "a strange syphre or fourme of lettres."

13. This remained true until 1628, which saw publication of William Harvey's revolutionary study of the circulation of the blood, *Exercitatio anatomica de motu cordis et sanguinis*. His work, of course, marks the beginning of the dissipation of the humoural model altogether, replacing it with the more familiar chemico-mechanical paradigm of heart/lung circulation and oxygenation of the blood.

14. Timothie Bright, *A Treatise of Melancholie, containing the causes thereof, & reasons of the strange effects it worketh . . . and spirituall consolation for such as have thereto adioyned an afflicted conscience* (London, 1586). Andreas Laurentius, *Discourse of the Preservation of the Sight: of Melancholike Diseases: Of Rheumes and of Old Age* (Paris,

1597), trans. Richard Surphlet (London, 1599), Shakespeare Association Facsimiles 15 (London: Oxford University Press, 1938). Laurentius is the Latin for Andre du Laurent, but I have chosen to follow the practice of using the Latin, both because it appears on the translated title page of the *Discourse*, and Bright and Burton use it in its Latin form. Bright and Laurentius are cited among Burton's many references — unusual in that both are near contemporaries and, in Bright's case, even more extraordinary given how few British authorities Burton recognizes.

15. The tributes in the dedication praise the patroness's physical well-being, instead of more usual styles of compliment ("Cheer up your selfe then Madame, you are but yet on the first step of your old age, which is overgrowne with flourishing greene, and affording an undaunted courage"), but this does not abrogate the writer's debt nor the attention paid to the patron.

16. In this respect, his approach — and Elyot's — contrasts with that of Robert Burton, who writes scarce a sentence without a reference. Bright alludes to several major names (like Galen, Hippocrates and Erastothenes) but never quotes them, and is more likely to refer to his own beliefs or opinions than to anyone else's: "And this I take to be the cause why certaine things will not grow" (15); "Thus you have mine opinion" (71); "I hold humours to be occasions of disorderly perturbations" (92). Such self-referentiality contrasts strongly with the more objective, impersonal tone Elyot uses, and corresponds closely to that of Michel de Montaigne in the *Essais*, and presages Burton's extreme involvement with the reader in the *Melancholy*. The characteristic becomes part of the genre, especially as the genre moves more into the religious realm: sermons are rarely effective if too abstract. In addition, Bright's reliance on his own "take" on medical melancholy provides a very idiosyncratic interpretation — important to recall when he goes off the beaten track in his readings.

17. The term "psychological" is wholly anachronistic, but no other expresses, for us, similar meaning.

18. Noel L. Brann, "The Problem of Distinguishing Religious Guilt from Religious Melancholy in the English Renaissance," *Journal of the Rocky Mountain Medieval and Renaissance Association* 1 (1980): 63–72, has identified this concern over whether one suffers from melancholy or from a conscience tormented by a wrathful God as a characteristic of the Reformed English, further suggesting that this preoccupation is most pronounced in England. However, Robert Burton's frequent references to Philip Melanchthon and his writings in the *Melancholy* make it apparent that many groups coming under the influence of reforms that removed them from the traditional, indisputable direction of a mediating priesthood, and threw sinners on their own resources, also found themselves anxious over the fear and doubt that could result. Brann skews the emphasis of Bright's *Treatise*, whose objective of establishing

the difference between melancholy and tormented conscience is not "the cardinal aim" (65) but rather one of four, and not the one to which Bright gives most attention. It is, however, the one that is most likely to interest modern readers.

19. Elyot did not make conscience an issue of humours to the degree later writers assumed it to be.

20. Laurentius thus amends earlier preferences for the unmoderated sanguine type of individual, often characterized as "jovial." Gradually, melancholy was not only associated with genius, but considered a beautiful emotion — in moderation. This view was not available to the Renaissance, for whom melancholy, however constituted, was always potentially negative.

21. Elyot finds burnt melancholy to be "in foure kyndes, eyther it is of naturall melancoly aduste, or of the more pure parte of the bloudde aduste, or of choler adust, or of salt fleume adust." More significant is his conclusion that, "fynally all aduste melancoly annoyeth the wytte and judgement of man, for whan that humour is hotte, it maketh menne madde, and whan it is extincte, it maketh menne fooles, forgetfull and dulle" (72v–73r). Even in the midst of describing its dangers, Elyot reminds his readers that melancholy was necessary: an element one could love to hate.

22. Elyot has limited the catalog to symptoms that can be traced, directly and logically, to one of the humour's traditional elements: temperature accounts for the heaviness, the fear and numbness in the limbs; the desire for light things and dark dreams both can be attributed to the blackness of the *melan*choly; as it is the most morbid humour, melancholy increases all awareness of death. Cramps and the tendency to garrulousness disappear in later treatises.

23. Elyot had written, in discussing "affects of the minde," that passions of the mind can "bringe a man from the use of reason, and sometyme in the displeasure of almighty god. Wherfore they do not only require the helpe of phisyke corporall, but also the counsell of a man wyse and well lerned in morall philosophye" (62v). Elyot addresses all mental passions, not just the effects of melancholy; nonetheless, he provides the solid foundation upon which Bright can build so readily.

24. Burton, later, claims to be the first to identify religious melancholy as a distinct species of the disease (3.4.1.1).

25. O'Connell (*Robert Burton*, 59) cites Jean Robert Simon's comprehensive work for this statistic: *Robert Burton (1577–1640) et "L'Anatomie de la Mélancholie"* (Paris: Didier, 1964), 428.

26. Burton is in excellent company: Laurentius, when he briefly touches on erotic melancholy, and Jacques Ferrand, in his *De la maladie d'amour ou melancholie erotique* (1610, expanded 1623, translated 1640), both highlight the psychological effects of love while acknowledging a host of physical signs and symptoms.

27. "Called Religious because it is still conversant about Religion and such divine object" (Burton's note).

28. "*Generall* causes, are either *supernaturall*, or *naturall. Supernaturall are from God* and *his Angells*, or *by Gods permission from the Divell*, and his ministers . . . Physitians and Physick can doe no good, *we must submit our selves under the mighty hand of God* . . . otherwise our diseases are incurable, and wee not to be relieved" (1.2.1.1.).

29. The actual ending is an epigram: "Sperate miseri, Cavete Fœlices" (Hope, ye miserable; beware, you that are happy), and a brief admonition from Augustine. It is wholly typical that Burton gives the last words to an authority.

30. The sermon was preached at Lincoln's Inn, probably during the first half of 1618 ("Introduction," *Sermons* 2:14).

31. Preached 1 July 1627 in Chelsea Church, and printed with Herbert's poems in *Memoriæ Matris Sacrum* in the same year.

32. Preached at Saint Dunstan's, Trinity Sunday, 1627.

33. Preached at Saint Paul's, 27 January 1627/28.

34. Preached at Saint Paul's Cross, 22 November 1629. When preaching outside a church, to a public congregation, Donne is much more direct and unsubtle; the melancholy here is in the eye of the beholder, who would understand, clearly, the implication.

35. Preached at Whitehall, 29 February 1627/28. This passage all but duplicates George Herbert's process in "Affliction (I)," where he writes:

> Sorrow was all my soul; I scarce beleeved, / Till grief did tell me roundly, that I lived . . . My mirth and edge was lost; / a blunted knife / Was of more use than I. / Thus thinne and lean without a fence or friend, / I was blown through with ev'ry storm and winde. // Whereas my birth and spirit rather took / The way that takes the town; / Thou didst betray me to a lingring book, / And wrap me in a gown.

See *The Works of George Herbert*, ed. F. E. Hutchinson (Oxford: Clarendon Press, 1941), 29–30, 32–40. Herbert's symptoms are undeniably melancholic; his outcry is the articulation of the affliction's grief.

36. Preached before the King at Whitehall, 5 April 1628.

37. Trinity term, 1620 or 1621, most likely.

38. The epithet comes from Horace's *Carminum Liber II*, Ode XIV, "Eheu fugaces, Postume, Postume." The lines Donne employs follow the opening statement that it is impossible to slow down the approach of indomitable death, "non si trecenis quotquot eunt dies / amice places inlacrimabilem / Plutona tauris" (Not, if with three hundred bulls daily, you seek to placate "untearable" Pluto). Modern translations make "illacrimabilis" metaphoric, using "relentless," or, more accurately, "tearless," which last still ignores the *inability* to shed tears.

Donne has called on this dry Pluto in another sermon, on John 11.35 (4:13), there to summon compassion for anyone who may be apostrophized as unable to weep. See Marjory E. Lange, *Telling Tears in the English Renaissance* (Leiden: E. J. Brill, 1996), 180, for discussion of the image in that environment.

39. This sermon was probably preached within a year or two of 4:13, in which Donne used the quotation from Horace as well. The idea of the God of the underworld being "illacrimabilis" fascinated the preacher, although one can see that, for Horace, it was not only natural, but necessary, that Pluto should be without the compassionate release of tears.

40. Probably earlier than 1625.

41. Preached at Lincoln's Inn, probably Easter term, 1620.

42. Preached at Lincoln's Inn Ascension Day, 1622.

43. Christmas, 1627. This sermon certainly represents one of Donne's more unseasonable efforts.

Notes to Chapter 4/McClintock

1. Thomas Heywood, *An Apology for Actors* (London, 1612; reprint, New York: Scholars' Facsimiles and Reprints, 1941). References for quotations from this work will be provided parenthetically.

2. The rhetorical language used to express grief in *Gorboduc* is most evident in the lament delivered by Videna at the beginning of act 4. A convenient edition of the play is the one found in Russell A. Fraser and Norman Rabkin, eds., *Drama of the English Renaissance I: The Tudor Period* (New York: Macmillan, 1976), 81–100. Definitions and examples of the rhetorical figures can be found in Richard A. Lanham, *A Handlist of Rhetorical Terms: A Guide for Students of English Literature* (Berkeley and Los Angeles: University of California Press, 1968).

3. Kier Elam, "Inelocutio: Shakespeare and the Rhetoric of the Passions," in *Shakespeare: Rhetoriques du texte et du spectacle*, ed. M. T. Jones-Davies (Paris: Belles-Lettres, 1992), 143–56. Quotation from 144.

4. See Lynn Enterline, *The Tears of Narcissus: Melancholia and Masculinity in Early Modern Writing* (Stanford, Calif.: Stanford University Press, 1995), and Juliana Schiesari, *The Gendering of Melancholia: Feminism, Psychoanalysis, and the Symbolics of Loss in Renaissance Literature* (Ithaca, N.Y.: Cornell University Press, 1992).

5. Albert H. Tricomi, *Reading Tudor-Stuart Texts Through Cultural Historicism* (Gainesville, Fla.: University Press of Florida, 1996), 155.

6. Philip Stubbes, *The Anatomie of Abuses: Contayning a Discoverie, or Briefe Summarie of Such Notable Vices and Imperfections, As Now Raigne in Many Christian Countreyes of the Worlde* . . . (London, 1583; reprint, New York: Garland, 1973), L8r–v.

7. Thomas Wright, *The Passions of the Mind* (London, 1601; reprint, Hildesheim: Georg Olms, 1973), for example, argues that passions are aroused when sensory information is processed by the imagination

and then forwarded to the heart, which is the seat of the passions:

> First then, to our imagination commeth, by sense or memorie, some obiect to be knowne, conuenient, or disconuenient to Nature, the which being knowne . . . in the imagination which resideth in the former parte of the braine, (as wee prooue when wee imagine any thing) presently the purer spirits flocke from the braine, by certaine secret channels to the heart, where they pitch at the doore, signifying what an obiect was presented, conuenient or disconuenient for it. The heart immediately bendeth, either to prosecute it, or to eschew it: and the better to effect that affection, draweth other humours to help him, and so in pleasure concurre great store of pure spirites; in payne and sadnesse, much melancholy blood[,] in ire, bloud and choller; and not only (as I sayde) the heart draweth, but also the same soule that informeth the heart residing in other partes, sendeth the humours vnto the heart, to performe their seruice in such a woorthie place. (82–83)

8. See Jean E. Howard and Phyllis Rackin, *Engendering a Nation: A Feminist Account of Shakespeare's English Histories* (London: Routledge, 1997), 101–04.

9. Jean E. Howard, "The Materiality of Ideology: Women as Spectators, Spectacles, and Paying Customers in the English Public Theater," *The Stage and Social Struggle in Early Modern England* (London: Routledge, 1994), 73–92; quotation on 77.

10. But see Howard and Rackin, *Engendering a Nation*, 100–18, on the dangers the feminizing emotions of tragedy posed to male spectators.

11. Steven Mullaney, *The Place of the Stage: License, Play, and Power in Renaissance England* (Chicago: University of Chicago Press, 1988), 97–103, in a discussion of Heywood's *Apology for Actors*, notes that the theater described by Heywood creates "apprehending" subjects in two senses: first, in the sense of understanding or comprehending something; and second, in the modern sense of shame or anxiety.

12. All quotations, scene, and line references are taken from Brian Scobie's New Mermaids edition of *A Woman Killed with Kindness* (London: A. C. Black, 1985), and will be provided parenthetically.

13. In a deliberative soliloquy in scene 6, Wendoll's attempt to control his lust for Anne is overruled by his "sad destiny," reflecting in miniature the larger Renaissance debate between free will and predestination. In the play, Heywood opts for Calvinist predestination as the motive force behind Wendoll's unkindness. Anne is similarly presented as one unable to resist sin. When Wendoll finally makes his proposition, Anne is unable to say no: "What shall I say? / My soul is wandering, and hath lost her way. / O Master Wendoll, O" (6.149–51).

14. O. B. Hardison, "Three Types of Renaissance Catharsis," *Renaissance Drama*, n.s., 2 (1969): 3–22. Two problems with using Aristotelian "catharsis" as a critical term in this discussion are, first, the fact

that Aristotle's *Poetics* was virtually unknown and unstudied in England until the Restoration, and, second, the fact that the term focuses only on the effect of theatrical emotion on an individual (here, Acton), whereas Heywood clearly sees a series of emotional effects moving from stage to audience to society at large.

15. For examples of the male characters grieving in soliloquies, see Sir Charles's speech after he murders two of Sir Francis Acton's men (3.42–56), or Wendoll's deliberation over whether or not to seduce Anne (6.1–25). This contrast between discursive masculine grief and silent feminine grief also parallels an argument found in the work of contemporary feminist theorists such as Luce Irigaray, who notes that while men have the ability to express anxiety or psychosis through language, "A woman in a state of madness does not have, for some reason, the means for elaborating a delirium. Instead of language being the medium of expression of the delirium the latter remains within the body itself.... Thus, ... women do not manage to articulate their madness: they suffer it directly in their body, without being able to transpose it in some different mode." See Irigaray's "Women's Exile," trans. Couze Venn, in *The Feminist Critique of Language: A Reader*, ed. Deborah Cameron (London: Routledge, 1990), 94.

16. Lisa Hopkins, "The False Domesticity of *A Woman Killed with Kindness*," *Connotations* 4 (1994–95): 1–7.

17. A more thorough discussion of the role of music in Heywood's play can be found in Cecile W. Cary, "'Go Breake This Lute': Music in Heywood's *A Woman Killed with Kindness*," *Huntington Library Quarterly* 37 (1974): 111–22.

18. The use of Orpheus and Amphion as mythical orator-civilizer figures by Renaissance rhetoricians is discussed by Wayne Rebhorn in *The Emperor of Men's Minds: Literature and the Renaissance Discourse of Rhetoric* (Ithaca, N.Y.: Cornell University Press, 1995), passim. In England, an early chapter in George Puttenham's *The Arte of English Poesie* (1589) presents a typical reading of the Orpheus myth: "*Orpheus* assembled the wilde beasts to come in heards to harken to his musicke, and by that meanes made them tame, implying thereby, how by his discreete and wholsome lessons vttered in harmonie and with melodious instruments, he brought the rude and sauage people to a more ciuill and orderly life, nothing, as it seemeth, more preuailing or fit to redresse and edifie the cruell and sturdie courage of man than it" (reprint ed., Edward Arber, Arber's English Reprints 15 [Westminster: Constable, 1895], 22–23).

19. In scene 13, Frankford told Anne he would "do nothing rashly" (130), and, after retiring to his study in order to discover a reasonable plan, he informs Anne of her unique punishment:

> I'll not martyr thee,
> Nor mark thee for a strumpet, but with usage

> Of more humility torment thy soul,
> And kill thee, even with kindness. (154–57)

20. That Anne's eventual death in exile was Frankford's initial intention can be seen in some of the final lines he speaks to her before sending her into exile:

> I charge thee never after this sad day
> To see me, or to meet me, or to send
> By word, or writing, gift, or otherwise
> To move me, by thyself, or by thy friends,
> Nor challenge any part in my two children.
> So farewell, Nan, for we will henceforth be
> As we had never seen, ne'er more shall see. (13.175–81)

21. Cynthia Lewis, "Heywood's *Gunaikeion* and Woman-Kind in *A Woman Killed with Kindness*," *English Language Notes* 32 (1994): 24–37, has argued that the true "kindness" of the play's title is the self-sacrifice that both Anne Frankford and Susan Mountford undergo, since this leads to a moral awakening in the men they love. Anne's theatrical grief and death teach Frankford how to empathize and relate to others on an emotional level rather than on a superficial level of appearances; similarly, Susan's grief and her willingness to play Lucrece to Sir Francis Acton's Tarquin deflate the egos of both Acton and her brother Charles. As Lewis concludes, "In all of these cases, the same principle of change is at work: each character is afforded a glimpse into another's suffering, whereby ensues a new awareness of the other's humanity. A recognition of one's kind gives rise to one's kindness" (34).

22. T. S. Eliot, "Thomas Heywood." Eliot's essay first appeared in the *Times Literary Supplement* (30 July 1931) and is critical of the affectivity of *A Woman Killed with Kindness*. This quote is taken from the version reprinted in Eliot's collection *Elizabethan Essays* (London: Faber, 1934), 101–16; quotation from 116.

Notes to Chapter 5/Martz

1. The title does not appear in the Williams manuscript. See Amy Charles, "The Williams Manuscript and *The Temple*," in *Essential Articles for the Study of George Herbert's Poetry*, ed. John R. Roberts (Hamden, Conn.: Archon Books, 1979), 427–28. Throughout this essay I will use the running title of Herbert's book, rather than *The Temple*, partly because that title may not be Herbert's own, partly because the action of grief occurs only in this section of the book, and mainly because the persistent emphasis of the running title — "The Church," "The Church" — at the top of every page — suggests that Herbert is presenting his poems, not only as the experience of an individual author, but more generally as poems that represent the varied experiences of grief,

fear, joy and praise that constitute the life of human beings in the church of Herbert's day.

2. *The Works of George Herbert*, ed. F. E. Hutchinson (Oxford: Clarendon Press, corr. edn., 1945), 304. Quotations are taken from this edition and are hereafter cited in the text by line numbers.

3. Chana Bloch, *Spelling the Word: George Herbert and the Bible* (Berkeley and Los Angeles: University of California Press, 1985), 94, 97–98, 160.

4. For the numerical significance of 63, see Sibyl Lutz Severance, "Numerical Structures in *The Temple*," in *"Too Rich to Clothe the Sunne": Essays on George Herbert*, ed. Claude J. Summers and Ted-Larry Pebworth (Pittsburgh: University of Pittsburgh Press, 1980), 230–33.

5. William Empson, *Seven Types of Ambiguity*, 2nd ed. (New York: New Directions, 1947), 228–29. For the relation of this poem to the ancient tradition of the Improperia, the reproaches spoken by Christ from the cross, see Rosemond Tuve, *A Reading of George Herbert* (Chicago: University of Chicago Press, 1952), 19–99.

6. The *OED* does not mark this usage as specifically legal, but the early examples cited are taken from legal documents: see *OED*, "resume," 1:3. The legal overtones in this stanza seem to carry the implication that this argument is a "case" between two equal parties.

7. See the essay by Richard Strier, "Ironic Humanism in *The Temple*," in *"Too Rich to Clothe the Sunne,"* 34–39, where Strier points out the "anomalous" quality of "Man" in Herbert's "The Church," when considered "from the Reformation point of view."

8. Barbara Kiefer Lewalski, *Protestant Poetics and the Seventeenth-Century Religious Lyric* (Princeton: Princeton University Press, 1979); Richard Strier, *Love Known: Theology and Experience in George Herbert's Poetry* (Chicago: University of Chicago Press, 1983); Ilona Bell, "'Setting foot into Divinity': George Herbert and the English Reformation," *Modern Language Quarterly* 38 (1977): 219–41, reprinted in *Essential Articles*, 63–83; Gene Edward Veith Jr., *Reformation Spirituality: The Religion of George Herbert* (Lewisburg, Pa.: Bucknell University Press, 1985); Elizabeth Clarke, *Theory and Theology in George Herbert's Poetry* (Oxford: Clarendon Press, 1997).

9. See my "The Generous Ambiguity of Herbert's *Temple*" in *From Renaissance to Baroque* (Columbia: University of Missouri Press, 1991), 64–83.

10. *Love Known*, 72; but Strier sees only two speakers, assuming that the "one" of line 3 and the "friend" are the same. He appears to take the "one" as referring to God; see his detailed commentary (66–72).

11. In addition to examples given in the text, see the second stanza of "Home," the conclusion of "The Dawning," the conclusion of "Dialogue," the echo of the Communion ritual in "Peace," the penultimate stanza of "Divinitie," the second stanza of "Church-rents and schisms,"

the fourth stanza of "An Offering," the sixth stanza of "Longing," the penultimate stanza of "Praise" (III), and the fifth stanza of "The Priesthood."

12. See my *The Poetry of Meditation* (New Haven: Yale University Press, 1954), 199–203, 310.

13. The first line, however, is unrhymed, suggesting an opening dissonance that is soon corrected by "will" into a regular sequence of rhyming.

Notes to Chapter 6/Shawcross

1. See Pigman, *Elegy*. See also Ellen Lambert, *Placing Sorrow: A Study of the Pastoral Elegy Convention from Theocritus to Milton* (Chapel Hill: University of North Carolina Press, 1976); Eric Smith, *By Mourning Tongues: Studies in English Elegy* (Ipswich: Boydell Press, 1977); and Peter Sacks, *The English Elegy: Studies in the Genre from Spenser to Yeats* (Baltimore: Johns Hopkins University Press, 1985).

2. Celeste Marguerite Schenck, *Mourning and Panegyric: The Poetics of Pastoral Ceremony* (University Park: Pennsylvania State University Press, 1988), 178.

3. Douglas Bush, *English Literature in the Earlier Seventeenth Century 1600–1660* (Oxford: Clarendon Press, 1962), writes, "One relative [of Thomas Stanley] was William Hammond (1614–55?), whose *Poems* (1655) are not distinctive" (127–28). Stanley married Hammond's oldest sister Mary in 1621. Little is known of Hammond past the printing of the poems in 1655; he had published commendatory verses to John Hall's *Horæ Vacivæ* in 1646. His poetry was reprinted in 1816 by Sir Samuel Egerton Brydges.

4. *Poems. By W. H.* (London: Printed for Thomas Dring, 1655) are reprinted by George Saintsbury in *Minor Poetry of the Caroline Period*, vol. 2 (Oxford: Clarendon Press, 1906), [483]–520; see 512–17.

5. The lines are ambiguous because of punctuation: "A Sun that set in floods, but, oh sad haste, / Ere the meridian of his age was past" (15–16). Saintsbury comments: "A comma seems wanted here [after 'age'], lest the subject of 'was' should be uncertain." More meaningful might have been "has" instead of "was." The "floods" may refer to the setting of the sun in the west, as if in the horizon of the ocean, for the next line invokes the east; it primarily has reference to Sandys's being drowned.

6. A modern example may suffice, Edna St. Vincent Millay's "Lament": "Life must go on; / I forget just why."

7. We might recall Wisdom in Proverbs 8.32, 35: "Now therefore hearken unto me, O ye children: for blessed are they that keep my ways. . . . For whoso findeth me findeth life, and shall obtain favor of the Lord."

8. See, for example, Peter Apian's universally accepted *Cosmographia* (1524) or Robert Fludd's *Utrinsque Cosmi Historia* (1624).

9. One is tempted to think that Sandys was around 33 when he died, the age of Jesus at his Crucifixion.

10. Saintsbury glosses this word as "'property,' or 'right of property'" as a standard usage of the seventeenth century; that meaning seems thus to say that her tears have a clearer right of ownership of light. But the original word may be what Hammond meant; that is, her tears may have a clearer "appropriateness to light" than stars or may have a more clearly "proper" relationship to light. In any case, the line underscores the erroneous statement that stars have a borrowed light (13), apparently through conflation with the moon.

Notes to Chapter 7/Long

1. Kathleen Woodward, "Freud and Barthes: Theorizing Mourning, Sustaining Grief," *Discourse* 13 (fall-winter, 1990–91): 93.

2. Sarah Savage (1664–1732), *Memoirs of the life and character of Mrs. Sarah Savage. To which are added memoirs of her sister, Mrs. Hulton*, ed. J. B. Williams (London: Holdsworth & Ball, 1828), 71.

3. *Kissing the Rod: An Anthology of Seventeenth-Century Women's Verse*, ed. Germaine Greer et al. (London: Virago Press, 1988), 155. Unless otherwise cited, quotations from Carey's poems and prose are from this anthology. See also Mary Carey, *Meditations from Her Note Book of 1649–1657* (Westminster: Printed & sold by Francis Meynell, 1918).

4. Jean R. Brink, "Royalist Correspondent: Lucy Davies Hastings, Countess of Huntingdon," *American Notes and Queries* 5 (April, July 1992): 61–63. The version of Hastings's elegy cited here is from the Brown University Women Writers' Project.

5. All quotations of Thimelby's work are from *Tixall Poetry*, ed. Arthur Clifford (Edinburgh: James Ballantyne, 1813). In "Women's Writing and the Self," in *Women and Literature in Britain*, ed. Helen Wilcox (Cambridge: Cambridge University Press, 1996), Elspeth Graham notes the difficulties of working with later editions of women's manuscripts or diaries, as particularly eighteenth and nineteenth century editors' practices may misrepresent or distort the work as they found it (211). Alice Thornton's *Autobiography*, published by the Surtees Society in 1875, is an often-cited example. The Surtees edition is a conflation of several of Thornton's manuscripts.

6. In *Women and Religion in England 1500–1720* (London: Routledge, 1993, 1996), Patricia Crawford notes, "Since the public world was very dangerous for professing Catholics, the private world of the household became extremely important, the only place in fact where faith could be practiced" (60).

7. See Paul Schlueter and June Schlueter, ed. *Encyclopedia of British Women Writers* (New Brunswick, N.J.: Rutgers University Press, 1998), 446; and Joan Goulianos, ed., *By a Woman Writ: Literature from Six Centuries by and about Women* (London: New English Library, 1974), 37–38. All quotations from the memoirs of Alice (Wandesford) Thornton (1627–1707) are from *Autobiography*, Yale University Microfilm MISC 326 (1930), and are noted by page number.

8. Elspeth Graham, Hilary Hinds, Elaine Hobby and Helen Wilcox, "Pondering All These Things in Her Heart: Aspects of Secrecy in the Autobiographical Writings of Seventeenth-Century Englishwomen," in *Women's Lives/Women's Times: New Essays on Autobiography*, ed. Trev Lynn Broughton and Linda Anderson (New York: SUNY Press, 1997), 53.

9. Anne Laurence, "Godly Grief: Individual Responses to Death in Seventeenth-Century Britain," in *DRB*, 62, 65; Ralph Houlbrooke, "Death, Church, and Family in England Between the Late Fifteenth and the Early Eighteenth Centuries," in *DRB*, 25–42; and Lucinda McCray Beier, "The Good Death in Seventeenth-Century England," in *DRB*, 44, 56.

10. Commenting on the loss of female friends, Graham suggests that "mourning for feminine or domestic suffering" was not recognized, "not identified as a specific loss in its own right" ("Aspects," 56). Of the "social purposes" of mourning rituals noted by Houlbrooke, few seem applicable in the case of an infant's death (*DRB*, 33). A sermon for an infant could not use "a quarter, or even a third, of the whole" for biography; if there was no "social position" to honor then certain rituals might be dispensed with; if no destabilization of authority threatened, then no affirmation of the deceased's role would be necessary (*DRB*, 37, 33). A child's death did not carry the same implications for familial or other forms of status and power as the death of an adult (unless the child was a national figure such as an heir to the monarch). On the other hand, that some rituals were observed for every death suggests that any death had the potential to disrupt familial and other socially constructed orders. The variety of mourning rituals and consolatory arguments suggests disorderly grief was a threat no matter what the deceased's identity.

11. Clare Gittings, *Death, Burial and the Individual in Early Modern England* (London: Routledge, 1988), 122. Van Gennep makes a similar argument for the significance of childbearing. As Adrian Wilson, "The Ceremony of Childbirth and Its Interpretation," in *Women as Mothers in Pre-Industrial England*, ed. Valerie Fildes (London: Routledge, 1990), notes, "It was necessary for such an 'event of nature' to be 'immersed in culture' since this 'made the birth a social and human act'" (84).

12. Patricia Crawford, "The Construction and Experience of Maternity in Seventeenth-Century England," in Fildes, ed. *Women as Mothers*, 29.

13. See also Avra Kouffman, "'Why feignest thou thyselfe to be another woman?': Constraints on the Construction of Subjectivity in Mary Rich's Diary," in *Women's Life Writing: Finding Voice/Building Community*, ed. Linda S. Coleman (Bowling Green, Ohio: Bowling Green State University Popular Press, 1997), 11–21; and Selby Jacobs, *Pathologic Grief: Maladaptation to Loss* (Washington, D.C.: American Psychiatric Press, 1993).

14. James Fitzmaurice, "Carew's Funerary Poetry and the Paradox of Sincerity," *Studies in English Literature* 25 (1985): 133. Napier in *MB*, 103. See also Laurence, *DRB*, 75–76.

15. Crawford, *Women and Religion*, notes that women were thought more "tender-hearted" than men (8).

16. A poem by Mary Carey's husband, George Payler, empathizes with Carey's grief, but his first two lines — "Dear wife, let's learne to get that Skill, / Of free Submission to God's holy Will" — chide her for excessive feeling (*Kissing the Rod*, 157). As Payler's poem makes clear, mourning had specific boundaries. In her husband's view, Carey was overstepping those boundaries by failing to submit to God's will.

17. William Temple, *Miscellanea* (London: Printed by J. C. for Edw. Gellibrand, 1690), 182. See also Wilson on male "hostility" to women's laying-in periods after childbirth, a period of up to a month when the husband had to take on more of his wife's household duties (77, 82).

18. Simon Patrick (1626–1707), *A consolatory discourse to prevent immoderate grief: for the death of our friends* (London: Printed for R. W. for Francis Tyton, 1671), 118.

19. Temple's reasons for this lack of recognition are, first, "because they die in innocence, and without having tasted the miseries of Life"; second, because "a Parent may have twenty Children, and so his mourning may run through all the best of his Life, if his Losses are frequent of that kind"; and, finally, because "our kindness to Children so young, is taken to proceed from common Opinions, or fond Imaginations, not Friendship or Esteem; and to be grounded upon Entertainment, rather than Use in the many Offices of Life" (177).

20. In my book-length study of maternal elegy, I also work with elegies by Elizabeth Brackley, Mary Chudleigh, Anna Cromwell, Katherine Philips, Elizabeth Russell and Anne de Vere.

21. There is a similar absence or abstraction of praise and lament in Jonson's elegies for his children. See also John Beaumont, "Of My Deare Sonne, Gervase Beaumont," and Bishop Henry King's "On two Children dying of one Disease, and buried in one Grave" and "Upon the untimely death of J. K. first borne of H. K." See *The Poems of Sir John Beaumont*, ed. Rev. Alexander B. Grosart (St. George's, Blackburn, Lancashire, 1869), 183; and *The Poems of Bishop Henry King*, ed. John Sparrow (London: The Nonesuch Press, 1925), 42–43, 152.

22. Of the maternal elegies I have found, only Carey uses this phrase

and it is in relation to her living children (which "God yett lends to Maria," 28).

23. Kate Lilley, "True State Within: Women's Elegy 1640–1740," in *Women, Writing, History 1640–1740*, ed. Isobel Grundy and Susan Wiseman (Athens, Ga.: University of Georgia Press, 1992), 87.

24. Joshua Scodel, "Genre and Occasion in Jonson's 'On My First Sonne'," *Studies in Philology* 86 (1989): 235–59. Scodel suggests that most epitaphs employ a "powerful aesthetic closure," a way to "respond . . . to the brute fact of death . . . with an end regulated by art" (239).

25. Carey's relationship with God may be contrasted with, for example, John Donne's in his *Holy Sonnets*. As R. V. Young suggests, Donne's *Holy Sonnets* "emphasize that God must take [Donne's] part and 'fight for' or 'defend' the sinner, who is helpless without such assistance." Both Carey and Donne require God's intervention, but Carey demands it, sure she is deserving of it, while Donne begs for it, unsure whether he is worth saving. See R. V. Young, "Donne's Holy Sonnets and the Theology of Grace," in *"Bright Shootes of Everlastingnesse": The Seventeenth-Century Religious Lyric*, eds. Claude J. Summers and Ted-Larry Pebworth (Columbia, Mo: University of Missouri Press, 1987), 28. See also Michael Schoenfeldt, "The Poetry of Supplication: Toward a Cultural Poetics of the Religious Lyric," in *New Perspectives on the Seventeenth-Century English Religious Lyric*, ed. John Roberts (Columbia, Mo: University of Missouri Press, 1994), 75–104, and idem, "The gender of religious devotion: Amelia Lanyer and John Donne," in *Religion and Culture in Renaissance England*, ed. Claire McEachern and Debora Shuger (Cambridge: Cambridge University Press, 1997), 209–33.

26. See Cynthia S. Pomerleau, "The Emergence of Women's Autobiography in England," in *Women's Autobiography: Essays in Criticism*, ed. Estelle C. Jelinek (Bloomington: Indiana University Press, 1980), 21–38.

27. Peter M. Sacks, *The English Elegy: Studies in the Genre from Spenser to Yeats* (Baltimore: Johns Hopkins University Press, 1985), 28.

28. In *The Hearts Ease*, Patrick similarly suggests, "If [a child] could have known the miseries of living, and it had been put to its choice, very likely it would not have chosen to live" (119).

29. These presents, listed in the poem, include "hearing; reading; Conference; Meditation; / . . . acting graces & . . . Conversation" (43–44), and are the "principal spiritual exercises of Calvinism" (*Kissing the Rod*, 162).

30. W. David Shaw, "Elegy and Theory: Is Historical and Critical Knowledge Possible?" *Modern Language Quarterly* 55 (March 1994): 11.

Notes to Chapter 8/Howard

1. An Collins, *Divine Songs and Meditacions*, ed. Sidney Gottlieb (Tempe, Ariz.: Medieval and Renaissance Texts and Studies, 1996), 9, lines 50–56. All citations from and references to the poetry and prose of An Collins follow Gottlieb's edition, hereafter identified in parenthetical format by page and/or line number. For reviews of Gottlieb's edition, see Mishtooni Bose, "Divine Songs and Meditations," *The Review of English Studies* 49 (1998): 513; and Boyd M. Berry, "An Collins: Divine Songs and Meditacions," *The Journal of English and Germanic Philology* 98 (1999): 260. Sidney Gottlieb, "Introduction," in *Divine Songs and Meditacions*, vii. Gottlieb's allusion here to John Crowe Ransom's foundational critique of "Lycidas," "A Poem Nearly Anonymous," *The American Review* 1 (1933): 179–203, warrants further reflection. Ransom held that Milton's political motivations compromise the elegy's anonymity; Stanley Stewart, "Introduction," in *Divine Songs and Meditacions*, ed. Stanley Stewart (Los Angeles: William Andrews Clark Memorial Library, 1961), iii, has made similar charges against Collins's elegy, "A Song composed in time of the Civill Warr, when the wicked did much insult over the godly," which is central to my argument in this essay.

2. See William Thomas Lowndes, *The Bibliographer's Manual of English Literature*, rev. ed. (London: Henry G. Bohn, 1862), 497; W. Carew Hazlitt, *Hand-Book to the Popular, Poetical, and Dramatic Literature of Great Britain* (London: John Russell Smith, 1867), 115; and S. Austin Allibone, *A Critical Dictionary of English Literature and British and American Authors* (Philadelphia: J. B. Lippincott Co., 1899), 411. While Lowndes, Hazlitt and Allibone each attest to a second edition printed in 1658, at present no such volume is known to be extant.

3. In an anthology of autobiographical writings by seventeenth century English women that has become a popular teaching text, Helen Wilcox, "An Collins," in *Her Own Life*, ed. Elspeth Graham et al. (London: Routledge, 1989), 54–57, tentatively introduces An Collins as "a middle-of-the-road believer who interpreted and found purpose in her uncomfortable and withdrawn life by means of biblical precedent and a vocation to poetry" (55).

4. See Stewart, "Introduction," iii, iv, n. 6, and *The Enclosed Garden* (Madison: The University of Wisconsin Press, 1966), 55; Louise Bernikow, "Introduction," *The World Split Open*, ed. Louise Bernikow (New York: Vintage Books, 1974), 22; Germaine Greer et al., eds., *Kissing the Rod* (New York: Farrar Straus Giroux, 1988), 148; Elaine Hobby, *Virtue of Necessity* (London: Virago Press, 1988), 60; and "'Discourse so unsavoury,'" in *Women, Writing, History*, eds. Isobel Grundy and Susan Wiseman (Athens: University of Georgia Press, 1992), 30; Elspeth Graham et al., eds., "Introduction," in *Her Own Life*, 55; Maureen Bell et al.,

A Biographical Dictionary of English Women Writers, 1580–1720 (Boston: G. K. Hall, 1990), 53; David Norbrook and H. R. Woudhuysen, eds., *The Penguin Book of Renaissance Verse* (London: The Penguin Press, 1992), 881; Joanne Shattock, *The Oxford Guide to British Women Writers* (Oxford: Oxford University Press, 1993), 113; Gottlieb, "Introduction," xviii; and "An Collins and the Experience of Defeat," in *Representing Women in Renaissance England*, ed. Claude J. Summers and Ted-Larry Pebworth (Columbia: University of Missouri Press, 1997), 224 n. 11.

5. On devotional writing by women, see Hobby, *Virtue*, 1–25; Phyllis Mack, *Visionary Women* (Berkeley and Los Angeles: University of California Press, 1992); Diane Purkiss, "Producing the Voice, Consuming the Body," in *Women, Writing, History*, 139–58; and Hilda L. Smith, "Humanist Education and the Renaissance Concept of Woman," in *Women and Literature in Britain*, ed. Helen Wilcox (Cambridge: Cambridge University Press, 1996), 9–29. On devotional writing by men, see Arthur L. Clements, *Poetry of Contemplation* (Albany: State University of New York Press, 1990); Eleanor J. McNees, *Eucharistic Poetry* (Lewisburg, Pa.: Bucknell University Press, 1992), 33–68; and Marjory E. Lange, *Telling Tears in the English Renaissance* (Leiden: E. J. Brill, 1996). On Christian tenets heightening women's sensitivity, see Mack, *Visionary Women*, 15–44; and Helen Wilcox, "'My Soule in Silence?'" in *Representing Women*, 9–23.

6. For a study of Collins's illness within the context of early modern views of sickness, see Sarah E. Skwire, "Women, Writers, Sufferers: Anne Conway and An Collins," *Literature and Medicine* 18 (1999): 1–23.

7. Although my argument in this essay is not psychoanalytic, I employ the phrase "work of mourning" here in recognition of the foundational theories of grief and the poetic elegy advanced by Freud, Sacks, Ramazani and Zeiger. See Sigmund Freud, "Mourning and Melancholia," *A General Selection from the Works of Sigmund Freud*, ed. John Rickman (London: Hogarth Press, 1953), 142–61; Peter M. Sacks, *The English Elegy* (Baltimore: Johns Hopkins University Press, 1985); Jahan Ramazani, *Poetry of Mourning* (Chicago: University of Chicago Press, 1994); and Melissa F. Zeiger, *Beyond Consolation* (Ithaca, N.Y.: Cornell University Press, 1997). On the relationship between mourning and religious devotion in early modern England, see Pigman, *Elegy*; Anne Laurence, "Godly Grief: Individual Responses to Death in Seventeenth-Century Britain," in *DRB*, 62–76; and *DRF*.

8. For example, see, respectively, A. F. Griffith, *Bibliotheca Anglo-Poetica* (London: Thomas Davison, 1815), 66–67; Graham et al., *Her Own Life*, 4–5; and Stewart, *Garden*, 55.

9. Twelve of the 15 poems in the *Divine Songs* section are in fact elegies. In order of their appearance, these 12 poems are: *"The Preface"; *"A Song expressing their happinesse who have Communion with

Christ"; "A Song shewing the Mercies of God to his people, by interlacing cordiall Comforts with fatherly chastisements"; "A Song demonstrating The vanities of Earthly things"; "A Song manifesting The Saints eternall Happinesse"; "A Song exciting to spirituall Alacrity"; "Another Song exciting to spirituall Mirth"; *"Another Song (The Winter of my infancy)"; *"Another Song (Having restrained Discontent)"; *"Another Song (Excessive worldly Greife)"; *"A Song composed in time of the Civill Warr, when the wicked did much insult over the godly"; and *"Another Song (Time past we understood by story)." In the above list, an asterisk indicates an elegy that places spiritual consolation within the context of secular time.

10. My formulation of grief as a private experience and mourning as the public expression of grief complements Houlbrooke's model. See Houlbrooke, "Introduction," in *DRB*, 14. The Acts of Uniformity, printed at the beginning of the Elizabethan prayer book and in all subsequent editions (1549, 1552, 1559, 1662), extended justification to Anglicans as well as to dissenters for working toward the true Reformation in the secular realm. This rhetorical emphasis in Collins's verse upon religious conversion and social reform suggests her affiliation with either Baptist or Independent congregations. See Nigel Smith, *Perfection Proclaimed* (Oxford: Clarendon Press, 1989); Mack, *Visionary Women*, 106–07; and David Cressy and Lori Anne Ferrell, *Religion and Society in Early Modern England* (London: Routledge, 1996), 56.

11. Sidney Gottlieb, "Commentary," in *Divine Songs and Meditacions*, 93 n. 3.

12. Skwire, "Women, Writers," observes that, in seventeenth century England, the experience of illness blurred distinctions between sacred and secular realms, "as pious sufferers often consulted with medical practitioners and took medicine, and scientific individuals tried prayer and magic charms for healing" (1).

13. Stewart, *Garden*, 108, and Skwire, ibid., 13–20, infer that Collins was barren; Gottlieb, "Defeat," 219, suggests that she may have suffered from smallpox.

14. Collins ironically grants us that much in her proleptic lines from "The Discourse": "Yet seeing here, the image of her mind; / They may conjecture how she was inclin'd" (53–54).

15. Louis Martz, *The Poetry of Meditation* (New Haven, Conn.: Yale University Press), 1954; Clements, *Poetry*, 1–18; Debora Kuller Shuger, *Habits of Thought in the English Renaissance* (Berkeley and Los Angeles: University of California Press, 1990); Richard Strier, "Donne and the Politics of Devotion," in *Religion, Literature, and Politics in Post-Reformation England, 1540–1688*, ed. Donna B. Hamilton and Richard Strier (Cambridge: Cambridge University Press, 1996), 93–114; Helen Wilcox, "Entering *The Temple*: Women, Reading, and Devotion in Seventeenth-Century England," in *Religion, Literature*, 187–207; and

Michael Schoenfeldt, "The Gender of Religious Devotion: Amelia Lanyer and John Donne," in *Religion and Culture in Renaissance England*, eds. Claire McEachern and Debora Shuger (Cambridge: Cambridge University Press, 1997), 209-33.

16. Arnold Stein, *The House of Death* (Baltimore: Johns Hopkins University Press, 1986); Houlbrooke, *DRB*; Robert N. Watson, *The Rest is Silence* (Berkeley and Los Angeles: University of California Press, 1994); William E. Engle, *Mapping Mortality* (Amherst: University of Massachusetts Press, 1995); Mary Abbott, *Life Cycles in England 1560-1720* (London: Routledge, 1996); Cressy and Ferrell, eds., *Religion and Society*; David Cressy, *BMD*; Peter C. Jupp and Glennys Howarth, eds., *The Changing Face of Death* (London: Macmillan, 1997); and *DRF*.

17. Lawrence Stone, *The Family, Sex and Marriage in England 1500-1800* (New York: Harper & Row, 1977), 207; Philippe Ariès, *The Hour of Our Death* (New York: Alfred A. Knopf, 1981), 297-321; Clare Gittings, *Death, Burial and the Individual in Early Modern England* (London: Croom Helm, 1984), 7-18; and Sara van den Berg, "The Passing of the Elizabethan Court," *The Ben Jonson Journal* 1 (1994): 31-61.

18. Michael Neill, *Issues of Death: Mortality and Identity in English Renaissance Tragedy* (Oxford: Clarendon Press, 1997), 3.

19. Ellen Zetzel Lambert, *Placing Sorrow* (Chapel Hill: University of North Carolina Press, 1976); Eric Smith, *By Mourning Tongues* (Ipswich: Boydell Press, 1977); Sacks, *English Elegy*; and Dennis Kay, *Melodious Tears* (Oxford: Clarendon Press, 1990).

20. Celeste M. Schenck, *Mourning and Panegyric* (University Park: The Pennsylvania State University Press, 1988); Kate Lilley, "True State Within: Women's Elegy 1640-1700," in *Women, Writing*, 72-92.

21. Mary Prior, "Women and the Urban Economy," *Women in English Society 1500-1800*, ed. Mary Prior (London: Methuen, 1985), 93-117; Hobby, *Virtue*; Mack, *Visionary Women*; and Patricia Crawford, *Women and Religion in England 1500-1720* (London: Routledge, 1993). Jacqueline Pearson, "Women Reading, Reading Women," in *Women and Literature*, 80-99.

22. Hobby, *Virtue*, 1-25; Mack, *Visionary Women*, 15-44; Purkiss, "Producing the Voice," 139-58.

23. Sidney Gottlieb, "Defeat," is the first critic to offer an extended analysis of Collins's civil war poem, and I am much indebted to his work.

24. These five texts, in order of their frequency in citations, are: "The Discourse," "To the Reader," "The Preface," "Another Song exciting to spirituall Mirth," and "Another Song (The Winter of my infancy)."

25. Stewart, *Garden*, 71, 202 n. 26, 108.

26. Gottlieb, "Defeat," 222-26.

27. Ibid., 223.

28. Nigel Smith, *Literature and Revolution in England, 1640–1660* (New Haven, Conn.: Yale University Press, 1994), 44, 182–91.

29. Christopher Hill, *The Experience of Defeat* (New York: Penguin, 1985), 130; Gottlieb, "Defeat," 224.

30. See the following standard texts for studies of the Fifth Monarchist cause: Louise Fargo Brown, *The Political Activities of the Baptists and Fifth Monarchy Men in England During the Interregnum* (New York: Burt Franklin, 1911); P. G. Rogers, *The Fifth Monarchy Men* (London: Oxford University Press, 1966); and B. S. Capp, *The Fifth Monarchy Men: A Study in Seventeenth-Century English Millenarianism* (London: Faber and Faber, 1972).

31. Since there would have been a market in 1653 for millenarian devotional verse, Richard Bishop, Collins's printer and publisher, might have thought the volume a worthwhile venture. Bishop did not publish other Fifth Monarchist texts, however.

32. St. Francis de Sales, *An Introduction to a Devoute Life*, trans. John Yakesley (London, 1609), writes that "The Bee (saith the Philosopher) sucketh honey from hearbes and flowers, without hurting or endamaging them, but leaving them as whole and as freshe, as before she found them: but true devotion doth more then so: for it not onely hurteth no state, vocation, or affaire, but contrary-Wise bettereth and adorneth it" (18). Greer, *Kissing the Rod*, notes that the "origin of the mistaken notion that spiders use the same nutrients to manufacture poison as bees do to make honey . . . was commonly used at least since 1542 (by Wyatt) to disarm malicious interpretation" (151), and cites the motto to *A Chaine of Pearle* (1630) by Diana Primrose — "Dat rosa mel apibus qua sugit aranea virus" (The rose gives honey to the bee whereas the spider sucks poison, 151) — as a possible source text for Collins's use of the idiom.

33. Walter B. Fulghum Jr., *A Dictionary of Biblical Allusions in English Literature* (New York: Holt, Rinehart and Winston, 1965), 54–55.

Notes to Chapter 9/Stanwood

1. Only a tiny number of funeral sermons found their way into print before the Restoration, most remaining in manuscript, or simply forgotten. Houlbrooke notes that about 20 funeral sermons are known to have been printed in Elizabeth's time, and that by the end of the 1630s that number had risen to well over 100. There was an important collection of 47 sermons published in 1640, called *Threnoikos: The House of Mourning*, with an expanded edition in 1660. See Ralph Houlbrooke, *DRF*, 298. Chapter 10, to which I am greatly indebted, deals entirely with "Funeral Sermons." See also the very helpful discussion of the development of

the importance of the sermon mode by Frederic B. Tromly, "'Accordinge to sounde religion': The Elizabethan Controversy over the Funeral Sermon," *Journal of Medieval and Renaissance Studies* 13 (1983): 293–312, and a corroborative discussion by Clare Gittings, *Death, Burial and the Individual in Early Modern England* (London: Croom Helm, 1984), esp. 39–59.

2. See Andreas Hyperius, *The Practice of Preaching: Otherwise Called the Pathway to the Pulpit* [with the running head, "Of framing of Diuine Sermons"], trans. John Ludham (London, 1577), and cf. Bartholomew Keckermann, *Rhetoricae Ecclesiasticae* (Hannover, 1606). The quotations from Hyperius occur in 2.14, 175v, 155. Barbara K. Lewalski surveys the seventeenth century funeral sermon, its patristic and classical influences, and the formulations of Hyperius in *Donne's Anniversaries and the Poetry of Praise: The Creation of a Symbolic Mode* (Princeton: Princeton University Press, 1973), 174–215, and she also summarizes Donne's funeral sermons. But Lewalski is primarily interested in providing a theological context for Donne's *Anniversaries*.

3. See *The Sermons of Henry King (1592–1669), Bishop of Chichester*, ed. Mary Hobbs (Rutherford, N.J.: Scolar Press, 1992), 251, 245.

4. "*Quid retribuam Domino pro omnibus quae retribuit mihi?*" [Ps. 116.12] Eo auctore ex nihilo orti sumus, ornavit nos ratione, largitus nobis est artes vitae tuendae inservientes, alimenta e terra educit, servitio nostro jumenta addixit et pecora. Propter nos imbres, propter nos sol; adornata est nostri causa regio montosa aequataque, effugia atque recessus parans nobis ad summitates montium vitandas. Propter nos fluunt flumina; propter nos fontes scaturiunt; mare patet nobis ad mercaturam exercendam; effodiuntur ex metallicis fodinis opes; undelibet commoda affluunt et deliciae, conferente nobis munera creatura omni ob locupletem uberemque benefici Dei in nos gratiam.

"Sed quid opus est parva recensere? Propter nos versatus Deus est inter homines: propter carnem corruptam *Verbum caro factum est, et habitavit in nobis*. [John 1:14] Commoratur cum ingratis beneficus; venit liberator ad captivos: illuxit sol justitiae sedentibus in tenebris, in crucem tollitur qui omnis prorsus doloris expers est, vita, morti addicitur. Lux descendit ad inferos; propter eos qui mortui erant, resurrectio, adoptionis spiritus, donorum divisiones, repromissae coronae." See J.-P. Migne, ed., *Patrologiae Graeca* (Paris, 1857), 31.238–62, for the complete Greek text; the quotation (and parallel Latin version) occurs on 254–55. The English translation is slightly adapted from W. Fraser Mitchell, *English Pulpit Oratory from Andrewes to Tillotson* (1932; reprint, New York: Russell & Russell, 1962), 142.

Evelyn M. Simpson and G. R. Potter, in their edition of Donne's *Sermons*, 10 vols. (Berkeley and Los Angeles: University of California Press, 1953–62), discuss Donne's frequent use of Basil and other early fathers in their study of "Donne's Sources," 10.345–64, esp. 358–60. Donne nearly always quotes the Greek fathers in Latin, probably from such sixteenth century translations as that by Tilmannus, 1568. For the reference to "In Martyrem Julittam," see Donne, 5.364, and Basil, in *Patrologiae Graeca*, 31.243D. There may be other references to this work which I have not noticed, but none appear in the two funeral sermons. About 12 references to Basil occur in Taylor's 64 sermons, though there are no explicit mentions of this father in his three funeral orations. Further citations to Donne's sermons appear in the text by volume and page number of the California edition.

5. Walton writes in his *Life of Dr. John Donne* (1640): "[A]fter some faint pauses in his zealous prayer [before the sermon], his strong desires enabled his weak body to discharge his memory of his preconceived meditations, which were of dying: the Text being, *To God the Lord belong the issues from death*. Many that then saw his tears, and heard his faint and hollow voice, professing they thought the Text prophetically chosen, and that Dr. Donne *had preach't his own Funeral Sermon*." See *Lives*, ed. George Saintsbury (1927; reprint, London: Oxford University Press, 1956), 75. See Lewalski, *Donne's Anniversaries*, 201–15, who writes briefly of the five sermons. Besides the two that I consider, there is also the sermon for King James, 26 April 1625 (*Sermons*, 6.280–91); *An Anniversary Sermon*, undated but 1624 or later (*Sermons* 10.178–91); and a sermon preached at Saint Dunstan's, 15 January 1626, "a general Funeral Sermon" for those who had died of the plague (*Sermons*, 6.349–64).

6. On Taylor's funeral orations, see Mitchell, *English Pulpit Oratory*, 253–54: "[Taylor's] are the only sermons in English which can in any way be compared to the great French orations of Bossuet over Condé, Père Burgoing, and Henrietta Maria. . . . [But] Taylor's models were almost certainly St. Basil and St. Gregory of Nazianzus." Taylor's sermons are quoted from *The Whole Works of . . . Jeremy Taylor*, ed. R. Heber (1822), 2nd ed. rev. C. P. Eden, 10 vols. (London: Longman, 1847–54), hereafter cited in the text by volume and page. Bossuet's *Oraisons Funèbre* may be consulted in the edition by Jacques Truchet (Paris: Garnier Frères, 1961). See especially the oration for Queen Henrietta Maria, which concludes triumphantly: "Ne plaignons plus ses disgrâces, qui font maintenant sa félicité. Si elle avait été plus fortunée, son histoire serait plus pompeuse, mais ses oeuvres seraient moins pleines, et avec des titres superbes elle aurait peutêtre paru vide devant Dieu. Maintenant qu'elle a préféré la croix au trône, et qu'elle a mis ses malheurs au nombre des plus grandes grâces, elle recevra les consolations qui sont promises à ceux qui pleurent. Puisse donc ce Dieu de miséricorde accepter ses afflictions en sacrifice agréable! Puisse-t-il la placer au sein d'Abraham et, content de ses maux, épargner désormais à sa famille et au monde de si terribles leçons!" ["Let us no longer pity her misfortunes, which are now her felicity. If she had been more fortunate, her story would have

been less grandiose, but her works would have been less full, and if she had eminent titles, she would perhaps have appeared empty before God. Now that she has preferred the cross over the throne, and that she has placed her misfortunes among her greatest graces, she will receive the consolation promised to those who mourn. May this God of Mercy accept her afflictions as a worthy sacrifice! May He place her in the bosom of Abraham, and, satisfied with her misfortunes, spare henceforth her family and the world from such frightful lessons!"] (142–43).

7. The quotation is from "Prolegomena" to *St. Basil: Letters and Select Works*, in *Nicene and Post-Nicene Fathers of the Christian Church*, 2nd ser., ed. Philip Schaff and Henry Wace (Grand Rapids, Mich.: Eerdmans, 1955), 8.64. Donne alludes to this famous passage (see note 4, above), as does John Cosin, *Collection of Private Devotions* (1627), ed. P. G. Stanwood (Oxford: Clarendon Press, 1967), 66 n. 331, and esp. 142 n. 342, an admonition set before the Order for Evening Prayer: "When thou lookest upon the Heavens, and beholdest the beautie of the Starres, adore Him that in his wisedom made them all for thee. When the day is ended, and the Night approcheth on, fall down and worship Him, who made both the day and the Night, to give thee joy and rest." Thus every day should be lived in recollection of God's grace toward us.

8. See Saint Gregory Nazianzen, "The Panegyric on S. Basil," in *Nicene and Post-Nicene Fathers of the Christian Church*, 2nd ser., ed. Philip Schaff and Henry Wace (New York: Christian Literature Company, 1894), 7.417.

9. See ibid., "Second Oration on Easter," esp. 7.424, and cf. "On the Theophany, or Birthday of Christ," 7.345–51.

10. Walton writes in his *Life of Mr. George Herbert* (1670) that he was present in Chelsea church when Donne preached this sermon: "I saw and heard this Mr. *John Donne* (who was then Dean of *St. Paul's*) weep, and preach her Funeral Sermon" (*Lives*, ed. Saintsbury, 267).

11. The quotation is from Browne's *Urne Buriall*, V. See *Religio Medici and Other Works*, ed. L. C. Martin (Oxford: Clarendon Press, 1964), 118.

12. See Jeremy Taylor, *Holy Living* and *Holy Dying*, ed. P. G. Stanwood, 2 vols. (Oxford: Clarendon Press, 1989), 2.6–7. References in the text to *Holy Dying* are from this edition. Richard Vaughan, second earl of Carbery (1600?–86), was married to Frances, daughter of Sir John Altham of Orbey, in June 1637. She died on 9 October 1650 at the age of about 33, in giving birth to her tenth child, a daughter called Althamia, who survived. Lord Vaughan was married again, to Alice, the eleventh daughter of John Egerton, first earl of Bridgewater, and the original "Lady" in Milton's *Comus* (1634). Taylor was married on 27 May 1639, to Phoebe Landisdale, or Langsdale, when he was the incumbent at Uppingham, Rutland. Phoebe predeceased Lady Carbery, dying also in 1650.

13. On "grief," Cressy (*BMD*, 393–95) cites Thomas Playfere, in his sermon of 1595, *Meane in Mourning*, who judged weeping to be permissible so long as it was not immoderate. "Early Stuart writers judged weeping to be appropriate at funerals, so long as it was done with moderation," according to Richard Brathwaite, *Remains after Death* (1618). See also Anne Laurence, "Godly Grief: Individual Responses to Death in Seventeenth-Century Britain," in *DRB*, 62–76.

14. Mitchell, *English Pulpit Oratory*, 254, observes of Taylor's funeral sermons: "If they were not preeminently calculated to bring comfort to the bereaved, they were certainly the magnificent tributes of a great artist who gave freely and unsparingly of his best in order to dignify the obsequies of the departed, and when the first pang of loss had subsided were likely, on account of their very detachment, to be all the more acceptable. In one instance [that of the Countess Carbery], also, the pearls which were dropped lavishly into the grave were formed of the preacher's tears." The sentiment, while imprecise, is close to my own sense of Taylor's achievement.

Notes to 10/Parrish

1. Jahan Ramazani, *Poetry of Mourning: The Modern Elegy from Hardy to Heaney* (Chicago: University of Chicago Press, 1994), xi.

2. Juliana Schiesari, *The Gendering of Melancholia: Feminism, Psychoanalysis, and the Symbolics of Loss in Renaissance Literature* (Ithaca, N.Y.: Cornell University Press, 1992), x.

3. Peter M. Sacks, *The English Elegy: Studies in the Genre from Spenser to Yeats* (Baltimore: The Johns Hopkins University Press, 1985), 19.

4. See, for example, Maureen Sabine, *Feminine Engendered Faith: John Donne and Richard Crashaw* (London: Macmillan, 1992); Anthony Low, *The Reinvention of Love: Poetry, Politics, and Culture from Sidney to Milton* (Cambridge: Cambridge University Press, 1993); and my essays "The Feminizing of Power: Crashaw's Life and Art," in *The Muses Commonweale: Poetry and Politics in the Earlier Seventeenth Century*, ed. Ted-Larry Pebworth and Claude J. Summers (Columbia: University of Missouri Press, 1988), 148–62; "'O Sweet Contest': Gender and Value in 'The Weeper,'" in *New Perspectives on the Life and Art of Richard Crashaw*, ed. John R. Roberts (Columbia: University of Missouri Press, 1990), 127–39; "Richard Crashaw, Mary Collet, and the 'Arminian Nunnery' of Little Gidding," in *Representing Women in Renaissance England*, ed. Claude J. Summers and Ted-Larry Pebworth (Columbia: University of Missouri Press, 1997), 187–200; and "Writing about Mother: Richard Crashaw and the Maternal Body," in *Performance for a Lifetime: Essays on Women, Religion and the Renaissance in Honor of Dorothy H. Brown*,

ed. Barbara Ewell and Mary McCay (New Orleans: Loyola University, 1997), 223–38.

5. Anthony Low, *Love's Architecture: Devotional Modes in Seventeenth-Century English Poetry* (New York: New York University Press, 1978), 130–31. See also his *The Reinvention of Love*, esp. 124–27.

6. I am citing the edition of George Walton Williams, *The Complete Poetry of Richard Crashaw* (1970; reprint, New York: Norton, 1974). Latin translations are also taken from this edition.

7. Dennis Kay, *Melodious Tears: The English Funeral Elegy from Spenser to Milton* (Oxford: Clarendon Press, 1990), 6.

8. For studies of the tradition and conventions of the funeral elegy, see, in addition to the works noted above, Ruth Wallerstein, *Studies in Seventeenth-Century Poetic* (Madison: University of Wisconsin Press, 1950); A. L. Bennett, "The Principal Rhetorical Conventions in the Renaissance Personal Elegy," *Studies in Philology* 51 (1954): 107–26; O. B. Hardison Jr., *The Enduring Monument* (Chapel Hill: University of North Carolina Press, 1962); and my "Crashaw's Funeral Elegies," in *Essays on Richard Crashaw*, ed. Robert M. Cooper, Salzburg Studies in English Literature (Salzburg: Universität Salzburg, 1979), esp. 52–56.

9. From *The Anniversaries and The Epicedes and Obsequies: The Variorum Edition of the Poetry of John Donne*, Gary A. Stringer, gen. ed. (Bloomington: Indiana University Press, 1995).

10. See, for example, Austin Warren, *Richard Crashaw: A Study in Baroque Sensibility* (Baton Rouge: Louisiana State University Press, 1939), 156–57, and Mario Praz, *The Flaming Heart* (New York: Doubleday/Anchor, 1958), 238–39.

11. Susan Haskins, *Magdalene: Myth and Metaphor* (New York: Harcourt Brace, 1993), 3.

12. Williams, *Complete Poetry*, 50, and L. C. Martin, ed., *The Poems English Latin and Greek of Richard Crashaw*, 2nd ed. (Oxford: Clarendon Press, 1957), 434.

13. See Haskins's informative account, esp. 192–228. Among other visual representations of the weeping Mary is a thirteenth century crucifix portraying Mary kissing and weeping over the nailed feet of the crucified Jesus.

Notes to Chapter 11/McCaffrey

1. All quotations from Marvell's poetry are from *The Poems and Letters of Andrew Marvell*, ed. H. M. Margoliouth (Oxford: Clarendon Press, 1971).

2. Phoebe S. Spinrad, "Death, Loss, and Marvell's Nymph," *PMLA* 97 (1982): 50; Anthony Low, *Love's Architecture: Devotional Modes in Seventeenth-Century English Poetry* (New York: New York University

Press, 1978), 248; Frank Kermode and A. J. Smith, "The Metaphysical Poets," in *English Poetry*, ed. Alan Sinfield (London: Sussex Books, 1976), 70.

3. Sigmund Freud, "Mourning and Melancholia" (1917), in *The Standard Edition of the Complete Psychological Works of Sigmund Freud*, trans. and ed. James Strachey et al. (London: The Hogarth Press, 1953-74), 14:237-58. For example, of the 18 "post-Freudian" essays in Rita Frankel's excellent anthology, 13 make favorable references to Freud's "Mourning and Melancholia," notwithstanding their varied theoretical approaches. See Rita V. Frankel, ed., *Essential Papers on Object Loss* (New York: New York University Press, 1994). Paul Lerner, "The Treatment of Early Object Loss: The Need to Search," in Frankel, writes that "Freud laid the conceptual groundwork from which most subsequent psychoanalytic theories of loss have arisen" (469).

4. George L. Engel, "Is Grief a Disease," in Frankel, *Essential Papers*, 11.

5. So Julia Kristeva, *Black Sun: Depression and Melancholia*, trans. Leon S. Roudiez (New York: Columbia University Press, 1989), writes, "Loss of the erotic object (unfaithfulness or desertion by the lover or husband, divorce, etc.) is felt by the woman as an assault on her genitality and, from that point of view, amounts to castration. At once, such a castration starts resonating with the threat of destruction of the body's integrity, the body image, and the entire psychic system as well" (81).

6. "Smart," meaning "Sharp physical pain, esp. as is caused by a stroke, sting or wound" and also "Mental pain or suffering; grief, sorrow, affliction; sometimes, suffering of the nature of punishment or retribution" nicely connects the Nymph's mental wound with the fawn's physical one (*OED*).

7. On the failure to mourn, see Helene Deutsch, "Absence of Grief," in Frankel, *Essential Papers*, 222-31, and also Erich Lindemann, "Symptomatology and Management of Acute Grief," in Frankel, 24-25. Also note Carolyn Asp, "Marvell's Nymph: Unravished Bride of Quietness," *Papers on Language and Literature* 14 (1978), who comments that "Without the poet's voice to provide a critical norm, it is easy for the reader to overlook the fact that the world the nymph creates in this enigmatic poem is permeated with negativity and the presence of death" (403). Rosalie Colie, *"My Ecchoing Song": Andrew Marvell's Poetry of Criticism* (Princeton: Princeton University Press, 1970), seems to suggest a similar idea: "The girl, the garden, and the fawn all blend into one virginal scene, white, cold, and still" (131).

8. Elaine Hoffman Baruch, "Marvell's 'Nymph': A Study of Feminine Consciousness," *Études Anglaises* 31 (1978), notes "Nor is the nymph in touch with her own feelings. She is so repressed she is incapable of expressing either anger or passion. She remains not only isolated from the world but ignorant of herself" (156).

9. See Lindemann, "Symptomatology," 25–26 and George H. Pollock, "Mourning and Adaptation" in Frankel, *Essential Papers*, 158. For a variety of clinical examples of the tendency to self-punishment, see Erna Furman, "Some Effects of the Parent's Death on the Child's Personality Development" in Frankel, 392; Christina Sekaer and Sheri Katz, "On the Concept of Mourning in Childhood: Reactions of a Two-and-One-Half-Year-Old Girl to the Death of her Father," in Frankel, 419–20; and Marie E. McCann, "Mourning Accomplished by Way of Transference," in Frankel, 455–57.

10. On the Nymph's wish for revenge, see Carolyn Asp, "Marvell's Nymph," "Careful to dissociate herself from any vengeful attitudes, she projects her desires for reprisal onto an unrelenting deity who will mete out appropriate punishments" (397).

11. Don Cameron Allen, *Image and Meaning: Metaphoric Traditions in Renaissance Poetry* (Baltimore: The Johns Hopkins University Press, 1968), considers the poem "a sensitive treatment of the loss of first love, a loss augmented by a virginal sense of deprivation and unfulfillment. The nymph has brooded so much over losing her lover that she has enlarged the token of love into a life symbol" (165–66).

12. See Yvonne L. Sandstroem, "Marvell's 'Nymph Complaining' as Historical Allegory," *Studies in English Literature* 30 (1990): 94–96. Charles I was called the White King because he wore white, rather than purple, robes at his coronation; further, popular parallels were drawn between Charles I and Richard II, "whose White Hart Badge was well known"; and finally, both roses and lilies (the fleur-de-lis) appear in Charles I's heraldry. These connections lead Sandstroem to read the fawn as a symbol for Charles I.

13. But see Graham Parry, "What is Marvell's Nymph Complaining About?," *Critical Survey* 5 (1993): 249: "In a pastoral reading of Marvell's story, it is the nymph who has been betrayed; a political reading requires the fawn to be the betrayed figure.... Pastoral poetry is opening into political poetry, but the change is not complete, and Marvell here seems to be feeling his way. The pastoral apparatus that conceals the political allegory is not consistent." Robert Wilcher, *Andrew Marvell* (Cambridge: Cambridge University Press, 1985), concludes that "None of the allegorical interpretations that have been offered by critics is wholly satisfying, and the care Marvell takes to invest the Nymph's manner of speaking with individuality encourages us to attend to the psychological rather than the symbolic significance of details" (84).

14. On the fawn's whiteness, see E. S. Le Comte, "Marvell's The Nymph Complaining for the Death of her Fawn" in *Andrew Marvell: A Critical Anthology*, ed. John Carey (Baltimore: Penguin Books, 1969), 277–78. Of the fawn in the lilies, in *Voice Terminal Echo: Postmodernism and English Renaissance Texts* (New York: Methuen, 1986), Jonathan Goldberg writes: "It can't be seen. Its very whiteness is a blank. Folded

in lilies, that whiteness is annihilative" (31). Robert Wilcher, *Andrew Marvell*, notes that "the fawn has assumed the status of an emblem" (89).

15. The point here may be not so much that Marvell has given his readers an unrealistic image but that he has given us one that is difficult to imagine and in so doing has used the image to mark the fawn's idealization. Jonathan Goldberg finds the Nymph's description of the fawn, beginning with its nursing, that of a "voice [that] begins in excess, with a superlative that marks the superabundance and fullness of this exclusive preserve.... A story of a growing perfection that has nothing to do with the processes of natural growth or ordinary time or space" (27). Julia Kristeva suggests: "Might the beautiful be the ideal object that never disappoints the libido? Or might the beautiful object appear as the absolute and indestructible restorer of the deserting object?" (*Black Sun*, 98–99).

16. "The garden of roses and lilies expresses the mind and the nature of the weeping maid, and she communes in it and through it with the fawn" (Allen, *Image*, 179). See also Colie (*"My Ecchoing Song,"* 89, 118–19). On lines 95–96 ("See how it weeps. The Tears do come / Sad, slowly dropping like a Gumme"), Joan Hartwig, "Tears as a Way of Seeing," in *On the Celebrated and Neglected Poems of Andrew Marvell*, ed. Claude J. Summers and Ted-Larry Pebworth (Columbia: University of Missouri Press, 1992), comments in passing: "The nymph ... sees, or thinks she sees, her dying fawn weeping" (84).

17. Vamik D. Volkan and Daniel Josephtal, "The Treatment of Established Pathological Mourners," in Frankel, *Essential Papers*, 305.

18. See Phillip McCaffrey, "*Le Roman de la Rose* and the Sons of Narcissus," *Mediaevalia* 11 (1985): 101–20, for the term "Narcissistic Idol." I mention Kohut's term here ("self-object," with an added hyphen) because it is well known and is vividly descriptive; see Heinz Kohut, *The Analysis of the Self* (New York: International Universities Press, 1977). However, much of my analysis here is based on theory that contradicts his in important respects. See in particular the work of Edith Jacobson, *The Self and the Object World* (New York: International Universities Press, 1964), and Otto Kernberg, *Borderline Conditions and Pathological Narcissism* (New York: Jason Aronson, 1975), and "Further Contributions to the Treatment of Narcissistic Personalities," in *Essential Papers on Narcissism*, ed. Andrew P. Morrison (New York: New York Univesity Press, 1986), 245–92.

19. Carolyn Asp, "Marvell's Nymph," phrases the idea elegantly: "Like the narcissist, in seeking the perfect reflector for her own perfection she seeks for something that exists only in her own need of it" (400). See also Arnold Rothstein, *The Narcissistic Pursuit of Perfection* (New York: International Universities Press, 1980).

20. Barbara Estrin, "The Nymph and the Revenge of Silence" in

Summers and Pebworth, *On the Celebrated,* also "idealizes" the fawn in terms that might more appropriately refer to the Nymph's distorted view of the fawn than to the creature itself: "The deer may be the inspiration of the Nymph's creativity, but he is also its audience that she molds by sensitizing him to her. The deer is her creation, a male aware of female needs, one who reads her body because he understands her text" (109).

21. Compare Julia Kristeva's description of her analysand "Isabel" who, disappointed in love, "wanted to have a child 'for herself.'. . . She had to have a 'reliable companion,' 'Someone who would need me, we would be accomplices, we would never leave each other, well, almost never'" (*Black Sun,* 88). Kristeva summarizes Isabel's expectations in this way: "Desire for a child was revealed as a narcissistic desire for lethal fusion — it was a death of desire. . . . Once she had become a mother she would be able to remain a virgin. Deserting the child's father in order to live as a single woman . . . alone with her daydreams, needing no one and threatened by none, she entered motherhood as one enters a convent" (89).

22. Peter M. Sacks, *The English Elegy: Studies in the Genre from Spenser to Shakespeare* (Baltimore: The Johns Hopkins University Press, 1985), writes, "The movement from loss to consolation thus requires a deflection of desire, with the creation of a trope both for the lost object and for the original character of the desire itself" (7).

23. The fact that the fawn has been idealized into an almost purely "good object" for the Nymph does not, however, completely exempt it from negative feelings toward the "bad object," as the Nymph's speculation about the fawn's future faithfulness hints. These negative feelings are simply repressed with the help of the "good object"; they belong to the other, hidden side of the coin.

24. Thus Erna Furman, "a current object loss through death revives earlier losses in a selective manner. . . . The revival of a specific past loss may, however, represent the telescoped experience of several losses" ("Some Effects of the Parent's Death on the Child's Personality Development," in Frankel, *Essential Papers,* 398). The fawn's connection to Sylvio virtually guarantees that its death will impose itself on the Nymph as, in part, a repetition of that earlier loss.

25. There is general agreement among psychoanalysts that the precise circumstances of a death can influence and distort the process of mourning in various ways. Thus Pollock, "Mourning and Adaptation," writes that "The response noted in this initial stage [of shock] varies in intensity according to the suddenness of the death and the degree of preparation the ego underwent prior to the death" (151). Volkan and Josephthal, "Treatment," compare the impact of a sudden death to that of trauma and go on to add that, "It is significant whether the death being mourned came about from natural causes or involved violence, as

in suicide, accident, or homicide. Violence, unconsciously connected with the mourner's aggressive feelings, fosters guilt that can preclude the expression of natural anger and aggressive reactions" (312).

26. Thus Goldberg, *Voice*, notes that "Not only is the past suppressed as this voice [that is, the Nymph's] starts speaking, not only is the history of the figures involved implicitly denied; this voice speaks as if it were discovering loss for the first time" (15–16).

27. Sacks, *English Elegy*, writes that "the deprivation of someone whose presence had supported the survivor's self-image may join the threat of death to drive the mourner back to the earlier form of narcissism" (10).

28. Volkan and Josephthal, "Treatment," speaking of mourners with "narcissistic character pathology," write: "Such patients, while seemingly trying to deal with the lost object, are actually trying to deal, whether in hidden or open ways, with the narcissistic blow itself" (312).

29. In Baruch's words, "So great is the masochism at the end of the poem that the nymph becomes her own tear. So great is her narcissism that she sees her suffering itself as a work of art" ("Marvell's 'Nymph,'" 155).

30. In Goldberg's terms, this is "Disowned vocalization, at last explicit, when the voice becomes the engraved engraver, wearing away all pretenses of a self or self-presence, offering the image in its full inadequacy" (*Voice*, 36). Sacks, *English Elegy*, approaches the problem from a slightly different angle in linking the regressive wish for merger with the death drive (15–17).

31. This does not necessarily contradict the fact that she would have it be "White as I can." On the morbid implications of white, as opposed to painted statues, in general and especially in funerary art, see Jean Clair, *Méduse* (Paris: Gallimard, 1989), 145–46, 207–08.

32. Donald M. Friedman, *Marvell's Pastoral Art* (Berkeley: University of California Press, 1970), makes the complementary point that "in describing the fawn's tears the Nymph has come upon a comparison which better fits her situation than the fawn's" (111).

33. Goldberg, *Voice*, describes this aspect of the idealized fawn in a different vocabulary and against the background of the famous *fort/da* game in Freud's *Beyond the Pleasure Principle*: "Such merging does not dissolve loss, however; it embodies it and enacts it as the location of pleasure" (31). Sacks, *English Elegy*, makes the complementary point: "Indeed, few elegies or acts of mourning succeed without seeming to place the dead, and death itself, at some cleared distance from the living" (19).

34. Barbara Estrin, "The Nymph and the Revenge of Silence," in Summers and Pebworth, *On the Celebrated*, argues that the Nymph triumphs over the troopers (as she had in quite a different way over Sylvio) by means of "the de-creation of the world she made." Estrin sees this as a

general antimale response: "When the nymph commissions a statue that will eventually corrode, she destroys the [Petrarchan] text that commemorates love" (102–03).

35. It is not insignificant that the *two* lines describing the fawn's statue *follow* these *eight* which describe the Nymph's. Both the relative lengths and the positions of the two descriptions are small, formal echoes of the self-centered nature of the Nymph's grief.

36. John Klause's reading, in *The Unfortunate Fall: Theodicy and the Moral Imagination of Andrew Marvell* (Hamden, Conn.: Archon Books, 1983), that "Marvell may have intended [the poem] to be an Ovidian aetiological myth, purporting to explain how the statue of a nymph and her pet came to be in a particular garden or wilderness" (86) would make my interpretation impossible. But within the poem itself, no actual statue exists.

37. Contra Freud, "Medusa's Head" (1922) in *Standard Edition* 18:273–74, I would argue that petrification most often represents a psychological stasis, an inability "to move" in the face of an overwhelming psychological conflict as, for example, Freud's patient Dora, in "Fragment of an Analysis of a Case of Hysteria" (1905) in *Standard Edition* 7:1–122, dreamed she was unable to move in front of a train station symbolic of her intricate conflicts or as Fraulein Elisabeth von R. reacted to her father's death: "she was *standing* by a door when her father was brought home with his heart attack, and in her fright she stood stock still as though rooted to the ground." See Sigmund Freud and Josef Brener, "Studies on Hysteria" (1895) in *Standard Edition* 2:150. J. B. Leishman, *The Art of Marvell's Poetry* (Minerva Press, 1968), collects a small anthology of analogues to the Nymph's petrification from the works of Petrarch, Donne, William Browne, Milton and "one Eldred Revett" (160– 61).

38. In Ovid's *Metamorphoses*, trans. Frank Justus Miller, vol. 1 (Cambridge, Mass.: Harvard University Press, 1921), 3:505–10, Echo's body disappears after Narcissus rejects her and his disappears after he has realized that his reflection is only a reflection; the naiads and dryads who come to mourn him find only the flower that has come to bear his name.

39. For a convenient review of opinions on this subject, see Paul R. Sellin, "'The Nymph Complaining' as a Stesichorean *Calyca*," in Summers and Pebworth, *On the Celebrated*, 94–99.

40. Wilcher, *Andrew Marvell*, attributes to the Nymph "an unsophisticated mind" and says that from the poem's opening lines, "It is evident at once that this is the voice of a child" (82–83). Baruch, "Marvell's 'Nymph,'" thinks that the Nymph "never reaches the level of adult consciousness" (156).

41. Thus Barbara Everett, "The Shooting of the Bears: Poetry and Politics in Andrew Marvell," in *Andrew Marvell: Essays on the*

Tercentenary of His Death, ed. R. L. Brett (Oxford: Oxford University Press, 1979), thinks that the poem "is *not* classical, *not* erotic; its lecherous 'faun' is merely a dying animal, its nymph is almost a child" (70); and again: "The girl is childish, the fawn after all a spoiled pet, chewing up the roses and trampling the garden; no wonder Sylvio got tired and went" (96). See also Karina Williamson, "Marvell's 'The Nymph Complaining': A Reply," in *Andrew Marvell: A Critical Anthology*, 285–86.

42. David Milrod, "The Wished-for Self Image," *The Psychoanalytic Study of the Child* 37 (1982): 95–120.

Notes to Chapter 12/Swiss

1. John Milton, *Complete Prose Works of John Milton*, ed. Don Wolfe et al, 8 vols. (New Haven: Yale University Press, 1978), 6:136. All subsequent quotations from Milton's prose will be taken from this edition and will be noted in the text by CP, volume and page number.

2. John Milton, *John Milton: Complete Poetry and Major Prose*, ed. Merritt Y. Hughes (1957; reprint, Indianapolis: Bobbs Merrill, 1983), *Paradise Lost* 11.887–89. All subsequent quotations from *Paradise Lost* are taken from Hughes's edition and are noted in the text.

3. For "autocratic designer," see Sandra Gilbert, "Patriarchal Poetry and Women Readers: Reflections on Milton's Bogey," *PMLA* 93 (1978): 368, 375. Joan Malory Webber, "The Politics of Poetry: Feminism and *Paradise Lost*," *Milton Studies* 14 (1980): 8–9.

4. Ruth Mohl, *John Milton and His Commonplace Book* (New York: Frederick Ungar Publishing, 1969), 37. Mohl writes: "[O]f the church fathers, Tertullian and Lactantius must have been the most interesting to him. It is with three entries from them, on 'Moral Evil' and 'Of the Good Man,' that the *Commonplace Book* begins." Mohl also notes that the *Commonplace Book* contains four entries from Tertullian, who is referred to 14 times in later work, while Lactantius is referenced six times in the *Commonplace Book*, with five allusions to him in later work.

5. The influence of these two Fathers on *Paradise Lost* has been thoroughly discussed by Dennis Danielson in *Milton's Good God: A Study in Literary Theodicy* (Cambridge: Cambridge University Press, 1982). Concerning contrariety as an essential element in a "Soul Making" theodicy, Danielson cites Lactantius's imperative in *Ira Dei* that good and evil must contend: "[T]herefore, unless we first know evil, we shall be unable to know good." Lactantius continues: "if evils are taken away, wisdom is in like manner taken away; and that no traces of virtue remain in man, the nature of which consists in enduring and overcoming bitterness of evils." Lactantius concludes: "[I]t is plain, therefore, that all things are proposed for the sake of man, as well evils as also goods."

See Lactantius, *A Treatise on the Anger of God*, trans. Rev. William Fletcher, in *The Ante-Nicene Fathers, Translations of the Fathers Down to A.D. 325*, ed. Rev. Alex Roberts and James Donaldson, American Reprint of Edinburgh Edition (Buffalo: Christian Literature, 1886), 7:271. For Danielson's discussion of Lactantius's informing thought in Milton's theodicy, see 172–77. Danielson also describes the self-limitation of God: "[that] the impossiblity of God's intervening to overrule Adam's free will is no slur on omnipotence, but rather follows from a choice that God himself had made and in accordance with the self-limiting character of such a choice" (Danielson, 98–99). Citing Tertullian, he notes God's "restraining within himself that foreknowledge and superior power by which he might have been able to intervene to prevent the man from presuming to use his freedom badly, and so falling into peril" (*Adversus Marcionem* 2.7, trans. Ernest Evans [Oxford: Clarendon Press, 1972]). Such self-limitation may be equated with Milton's application of the term of God's "high sufferance." Concerning the mystery of divine suffering (of the Father as well as the Son), Danielson writes: "[A]lthough the creature cannot behold it except as mediated through the Son, God's countenance, the expression of his person and character, reveals strife. Presenting as he does this conflict of mercy and justice within the Godhead, occasioned by man's sin and resolved by the sacrificial death of the Son, Milton would appear to agree with [Nicholas] Berdjaev that 'tragedy exists within the Divine life itself'" (55). See Nicholas Berdjaev, *The Destiny of Man*, trans. Natalie Duddington (1955; reprint, New York: Harper & Row, 1960), 32.

6. In *Adversus Praxeam*, Tertullian considers the aloneness of God but denies any inference of God's being actually lonely in himself. "For before all things God was alone, himself his own world and location and everything — alone, however because there was nothing external beside him. Yet not then was he alone: for he had with him that Reason which he had in himself — his own, of course." Even before Creation, God had reason with him, as it were, as a companion. Tertullian continues: "For although God had not yet uttered his Discourse, he always had it in himself along with and in his Reason, while he silently thought out and ordained with himself the things which he was shortly to say by the agency of Discourse: for while thinking out and ordaining them in company of his Reason, he converted into Discourse that Reason which he was discussing in discourse." See *Tertullian's Treatise Against Praxeas*, trans. Ernest Evans (London: S.P.C.K., 1948), 135.

Lactantius attributes various positive emotions to God, such as love, pity, kindness, and so on. God's anger in itself is viewed as yet another positive emotion. As Lactantius, *A Treatise on the Anger of God*, 7:262, explains, "[F]or if God is not angry with the impious and the unrighteous, it is clear that He does not love the pious and the righteous." His anger, or what may be interpreted as his righteous indignation against sin, is actually proof of his kindness.

7. Diane Kelsey McColley, *Milton's Eve* (Urbana: University of Illinois Press, 1983), 103, 99. Ann W. Astell, "The Medieval *Consolatio* and the Conclusion of *Paradise Lost*," *Studies in Philology* 82 (1985): 477–92. Joseph E. Duncan, "Archetypes in Milton's Earthly Paradise," *Milton Studies* 14 (1980): 41. Timothy Bright, *A Treatise of Melancholie, Containing the causes thereof . . . with the physicke cure, and spiritual consolation for such as have thereto adioyned an affected conscience* (London, 1586). Bright's treatise was subsequently corrected and amended, before being reprinted in 1613. All citations used here come from the 1613 publication and are noted in the text.

8. Carolyn Heilbrun, *Toward a Recognition of Androgyny* (1964; reprint, London: V. Gollancz, 1973). The *Tetrachordon* passage bears citing in full: "It might be doubted why he saith, *In the Image of God created he him*, not them, as well as *male and female* them; especially since that Image might be common to them both, but *male and female* could not, however the Jewes fable, and please themselvs with the accidentall concurrence of *Plato's* wit, as if man at first had bin created *Hermaphrodite*: but then it must have bin *male and female* created he him. So had the image of God been equally common to them both, it had no doubt bin said, *In the Image of God created he them*. But *St. Paul* ends the controversie by explaining that the woman is not primarily and immediately the Image of God, but in reference to the man" (*CP*, 2:589). This critical discussion of androgyny in *Paradise Lost* includes the following publications: John T. Shawcross, "The Metaphor of Inspiration in *Paradise Lost*," in *Th'Upright Heart and Pure: Essays on John Milton Commemorating the Tercentenary of the Publication of Paradise Lost*, ed. Amadeus P. Fiore (Pittsburgh, Pa.: Duquesne University Press, 1967): 75–85; Don Parry Norford, "'My Other Half': The Coincidence of Opposites in *Paradise Lost*," *Modern Language Quarterly* 36 (1975): 21–53; Virginia R. Mollenkott, "Some Implications of Milton's Androgynous Muse," *Bucknell Review: Women, Literature, and Criticism*, ed. Harry R. Garwin (Lewisburg, Pa.: Bucknell University Press, 1978), 27–36; Duncan, "Archetypes," 25–58; Webber, "The Politics of Poetry," 3–24; Marilyn R. Farwell, "Eve, the Separation Scene, and the Renaissance Idea of Androgyny," *Milton Studies* 16 (1982): 3–20; James W. Stone, "'Man's effeminate s(lack)ness': Androgyny and the Divided Unity of Adam and Eve," *Milton Quarterly* 31 (May 1997): 33–42.

9. Robert A. Erickson, *The Language of the Heart, 1600–1750* (Philadelphia: University of Pennsylvania Press, 1997), 98.

10. John T. Shawcross, *John Milton: The Self and the World* (Lexington: University Press of Kentucky, 1993), 12.

11. Critics have discussed a variety of positions concerning Eve's moral condition after her dream. The debate begins with E. M. W. Tillyard's view that, because of her dream, Eve has "passed from a state of innocence to one of sin." See *Studies in Milton* (London: Chatto & Windus, 1960), 12. Mary Ann Radzinowicz, "Eve and Dalila: Renovation

and the Hardening of the Heart," in *Reason and Imagination: Studies in the History of Ideas, 1600–1800*, ed. J. A. Mazzeo (New York: Columbia University Press, 1962), argues that in her "susceptibility" to tasting the fruit in her dream, Eve "has experienced alone the pattern of the choice she will repeat at the Fall" (170). For a detailed discussion of critical responses to the implications of guilt, or not, surrounding Eve's dream, see McColley, *Milton's Eve*, 108 n. 62.

12. William H. Frey has researched emotional weeping or what he terms "psychogenic lacrimation" (2) in *Crying: the Mystery of Tears* (Winston Press, 1985). Frey's study examines the physiology of weeping, with special attention to the biochemistry of tears. In Darwin, weeping from "a psychical stimulus" as opposed to "an irritant stimulus" evolved "phylogenetically and ontogenetically late" as a "purposive action to attract attention with the object of eliciting aid and sympathy." See Charles Darwin, *The Expression of Emotions in Man and Animals*, chap. 6, cited by E. Treacher Collins, "The Physiology of Weeping," *The British Journal of Ophthalmology* (January, 1932), 5. For additional modern considerations of weeping, see Börje L. Løfgren, "On Weeping," *International Journal of Psychoanalysis* 47 (1966): 375–81; Jerome Neu, "'A Tear Is an Intellectual Thing,'" *Representations* 19 (1987): 35–61; and Tom Lutz, *Crying: The Natural and Cultural History of Tears* (New York: W. W. Norton, 1999).

13. "Tearfulness," as a physiological step in the direction of overt weeping, is discussed by Edwin C. Wood and Constance D. Wood, "Tearfulness: A Psychoanalytic Interpretation," *Journal of the American Psychoanalytic Association*, 32 (1984): 117–36. It is explained as "a result of the phenomenon of being overwhelmed with affect because of intrapsychic conflict and a demand for needed compromise." The Woods make the point that tearfulness, the "too much phenomenon" (119), often occurs within the psychoanalytical hour. Not only is Eve's weeping in book 5 the first emotional weeping, but it may also be read as the first session of psychoanalytical consultation. Adam, in his innocence and inexperience, is ill prepared to undertake the necessary procedure.

14. Some notable treatises on Mary Magdalene during the Renaissance are the following: *Complaynt of the Lover of Cryst Saynt Mary Magdaleyn* (1520); Robert Southwell, *Marie Magdalens Funeral Teares* (1591); *Marie Magdalens Love* (1595); *Maries Exercise* (1597); *Mary Magdalens Lamentations for the Loss of her Master Jesus* (1601); *Saint Mary Magadalens Conversion* (1603); John Sweetman, *S. Mary Magdalens Pilgrimage to Paradise* (1617); Thomas Robinson, *The Life and Death of Mary Magdelene* (1620).

15. Louis L. Martz, *The Poetry of Meditation: A Study in English Religious Literature*, rev. ed. (New Haven: Yale University Press, 1962), notes that Robert Southwell's *Saint Peters Complaint* "was printed in London no less than eleven times between 1595 and 1636, to say

nothing of two continental and two Edinburgh editions during the same period." Similarly, "*Marie Magdalens Funeral Teares* . . . saw eight editions in London and two on the Continent between 1591 and 1636" (184).

16. J. M. Evans, *Paradise Lost and the Genesis Tradition* (Oxford: Clarendon Press, 1968), considers the allegorical readings of the Genesis narrative, beginning with Philo (c. 20 B.C.–c. A.D. 45). According to Philo, Evans writes, "[t]he master of the rational soul . . . was the mind, represented by Adam, whose task it was to take care of the plants, that is, to guard his virtues. Eve stood for the soul's sense or sense-perception of the physical world: 'In the allegorical sense, however, woman is a symbol of sense, and man, of mind.' Sense-perception was born when the mind relaxed its attention, when, as Genesis had it, Adam fell asleep, and his waking words meant that: 'For the sake of sense-perception the Mind, when it has become her slave, abandons both God the Father of the universe, and God's excellence and wisdom, the Mother of all things, and cleaves to and becomes one with sense-perception.'" Evans concludes that "Adam's recognition of Eve, then, constituted the beginning of the Fall, revealing that the Mind was ready to abandon its natural authority for the sake of physical sensation" (72). Subsequent writers (Ambrose, Augustine, Isidore of Seville, Pseudo-Bede, John Scotus Erigena, and Gregory of Nyssa) continue to expand allegorical interpretations in several directions, all of which tend to support the pejorative bifurcation of reason and sense perception along gender lines (see Evans, 69–77).

17. Joseph Swetnam, "The Arraignment of Lewd, Idle, Froward, and Unconstant Women," in *Half Humankind: Contexts and Texts of the Controversy about Women in England, 1540–1640*, ed. Katherine Usher Henderson and Barbara F. McManus (Urbana: University of Illinois Press, 1985), 197.

18. Christine Froula, "When Eve Reads Milton: Undoing the Canonical Economy," *Critical Inquiry* 10 (September 1983): 328–29.

19. Nicholas Breton, *In Praise of Vertuous Ladies* (1599), quoted in Constance Jordan, *Renaissance Feminism: Literary Texts and Political Models* (Ithaca, N.Y.: Cornell University Press, 1990), 240–42.

20. Laurent Joubert, *Treatise on Laughter* (1579), trans. Gregory David de Rocher (University of Alabama, 1980), 98.

21. Thomas Hobbes, "On the Emotions, and Perturbations of the Mind," in *Man and Citizen* (1658), trans. Charles T. Wood, T. S. K. Scott-Craig and Bernard Gert (Garden City, New York: Anchor Books, 1972), 59. For an excellent study of the philosophy of emotion as understood by seventeenth century thinkers, see Susan James, *Passion and Action: The Emotions in Seventeenth-Century Philosophy* (Oxford: Clarendon Press, 1997).

22. During the past 20 years, psychologists have recognized the

importance of the emotions in intelligence functioning. Neuropsychologists have detailed the processes of the amygdala or "storehouse of emotional memory" in cooperation with the neocortex which governs cognition. Interestingly, much of this research validates the correctness of Freud's theories of the unconscious and related mechanisms of repression. Daniel Goleman, *Emotional Intelligence* (New York: Bantam Books, 1994), writes: "the amygdala and its interplay with the neocortex are at the heart of emotional intelligence" (16). For a closer consideration of the neurology of emotion and its implications, see also Joseph LeDoux, *The Emotional Brain: The Mysterious Underpinnings of Emotional Life* (New York: Simon & Schuster, 1996). For the evolutionary theory of emotion, see Charles Darwin, *The Expression of Emotions in Man and Animals*, ed. Paul Ekman (New York: Oxford University Press, 1998). A useful summary of various theories of emotion is Randolph R. Cornelius, *The Science of Emotion: Research and Tradition in the Psychology of Emotion* (Upper Saddle River, N.J.: Prentice Hall, 1996).

23. Marjory E. Lange, *Telling Tears in the English Renaissance* (Leiden: E. J. Brill, 1996), 3. Although I would agree with Marjory Lange's perspective that in the general Renaissance conception of tears "a good cry" was simply not accessible and that "[tears] were perceive[d] as debilitating, life-shortening, dangerous," I believe, nevertheless, that in *Paradise Lost* Milton is taking exception to the convention.

24. Arthur Koestler, *The Act of Creation* (New York: Arkana/Viking-Penguin, 1964), 54.

25. William Whately, *Charitable Teares* (London, 1623), 3.

26. Abraham Herschel, *The Prophets* (New York: Harper & Row, 1955), 1:3–26.

27. Herschel discusses pathos with respect to its theology, philosophy, and anthropopathy; see 2:1–58.

28. Barnaby Rich, *The Excellency of Good Women* (London, 1613), 8.

29. Daniel Featley, *Ancilla Pietatis* (London, 1626), 337. Featley's handbook was widely popular in the seventeenth century and was reprinted in 1630, 1633, 1639, 1647, 1656 and 1675.

30. For a consideration of the tragic consequences of Eve's obduracy contracted from Satan, see Margo Swiss, "Satan's Obduracy in *Paradise Lost*," *Milton Quarterly* 28 (October 1994): 98–103.

31. Arguing from a Jungian perspective, Hermine J. van Nuis assumes the "androgynous natures" of Adam and Eve. She notes that Eve's restless, disinterested presence during the angelic tutorial and her subsequent desire to work separately facilitate their individuation as maturing partners. See "Animated Eve Confronting Her Animus: A Jungian Approach to the Division of Labor Debate in *Paradise Lost*," *Milton Quarterly* 2 (May 2000): 48–56.

32. For a full summary of the various explanations as to what prompts Eve to propose their separation in book 9, see Deborah A. Interdonato,

"'Render Me More Equal': Gender Inequality and the Fall in *Paradise Lost*, 9," *Milton Quarterly* 29 (December 1995): 95–106. I would agree with Interdonato's thesis that "Eve's gender-based 'inferiority complex' is rooted in the time before the Fall." She continues: "it might be suggested that these feelings of gender inequality have informed a state of mind that is implicated in her decision to work apart from Adam" (95). I second this interpretation and would attribute Eve's growing sense of inferiority, at least in part, to the suppression of her dream-disturbed sentiments which begin in book 5.

33. Carol Gilligan, *In a Different Voice: Psychological Theory and Women's Development* (Cambridge, Mass.: Harvard University Press, 1983), writes: "[I]t all goes back, of course, to Adam and Eve — a story which shows, among other things, that if you make a woman out of a man, you are bound to get into trouble. In the life cycle, as in the Garden of Eden, the woman has been the deviant" (6).

Julia Kristeva, *Powers of Horror: An Essay on Abjection*, trans. Leon S. Roudiez (New York: Columbia University Press, 1982), writes with passionate precision about the abject notoriety of Eve: "The brimming flesh of sin belongs, of course, to both sexes; but its root and basic representation is nothing other than feminine temptation. That was already stated in *Ecclesiasticus*: 'Sin originated with woman and because of her we all perish.' The reference to Eve's enticement of Adam is clear, but in other respects it is certain that Paul stigmatizes a much more physical corporeality, one closer to the Greek notions of it, when he implants the power of sin within the flesh. And yet, the tale of Adam's fall opens up two additional channels of interpretation throwing light on the ambivalence of sin. The one locates it in relation to God's will and in that sense causes it to be not only original but coexistent with the very act of signification; the other places it within the femininity-desire-food-abjection series" (126).

Cixous and Clément's discussion of the witch and hysteric, the latter of whom deliberately and willfully withholds or "swallows" her tears in defiance of the men who would make her weep, is an interestingly modern variation of Milton's narrative. Unlike Adam in Milton's story, men in general "have wanted to make tears come out of women's eyes; we understand that the refusal to emit seems a crime to them. Not to cry: refuse *jouissance*, to emit the precious secretions that are partial objects for the other's desire. Cry to show that I love you, the man says to the woman, the inquisitor says to the sorceress and, somewhere, Freud must say to the hysteric." See "The Guilty One," in *The Newly Born Woman*, trans. Betsy Wing (Minneapolis: University of Minnesota Press, 1986), 35–36. There can be no question that under such circumstances woman's continence is heroic. She stands her ground, dry-eyed, against male intrusion, and resists divulging her affective content. In a secular world, such as Cixous and Clément assume, such resistance is woman's raison d'être. In Milton's Christian universe, however, such autonomy is not in itself existentially valid though it may be, as it is for Eve, an important phase in her spiritual journey.

34. Daniel W. Doerksen, "'Let There Be Peace': Eve as Redemptive Peacemaker in *Paradise Lost*, Book 10," *Milton Quarterly* 31 (December 1997): 127. According to Doerksen, Eve's role is that of a "Redemptive Peacemaker." As he further observes, "*tresses* in a state of disarray — hair that has previously been described as attractively 'golden' [4.305]" occur in connection with other female peacemakers in contexts known to Milton. For a recent note on Eve's postlapsarian tears, see Francis O'Gorman, "Milton's *Paradise Lost* 10.937," *Explicator* 57 (Fall 1998): 23–24.

35. Julia Kristeva, *In the Beginning Was Love: Psychoanalysis and Faith*, trans. Arthur Goldhammer (New York: Columbia University Press, 1987), 3.

36. In his treatise *Of Education* (1644), Milton writes: "[T]he end, then, of learning is to repair the ruins of our first parents by regaining to know God aright, and out of that knowledge to love him, to imitate him, to be like him, as we may the neerest by possessing our souls of true vertue, which being united to the heavenly grace of faith makes up the highest perfection," (*CP*, 2:366–67). This reconciliatory re-union through grace, especially as it pertains to imitation of God's sorrow at the loss of his first creation, is precisely the process through which Adam and Eve must pass in the healing of their schismatic androgyny in *Paradise Lost*.

Notes to Chapter 13/Houlbrooke

1. Mary Carey, "Upon ye Sight of my abortive Birth ye 31th: of December 1657," in *Kissing the Rod: An Anthology of Seventeenth-Century Women's Verse*, ed. Germaine Greer, Susan Hastings, Jeslyn Medoff and Melinda Sansone (New York: Noonday Press, 1989), 159.

2. Richard Crashaw, *The Poems English Latin and Greek of Richard Crashaw*, ed. L. C. Martin (Oxford: Clarendon Press, 1927), 285–86.

3. Houlbrooke, *DRF*, 230–45, 253–54, 257–59, 261–64, 267–73, 383; idem, "Civility and Civil Observances in the Early Modern English Funeral," in *Civil Histories: Essays Presented to Sir Keith Thomas*, ed. Peter Burke, Brian Harrison and Paul Slack (Oxford: Oxford University Press, 2000), 71–73; Richard Hooker, *Of the Laws of Ecclesiastical Polity*, in *The Works of that Learned and Judicious Divine, Mr Richard Hooker* (Oxford: Oxford University Press, 1841), 2:153; Crashaw, *Poems*, 168, 395.

4. Daniel Rogers, *Matrimoniall Honour; or, The Mutuall Crowne and comfort of godly, loyall, and chaste Marriage* (London, 1642), 92–93, 152–53.

5. Timothy Bright, *A Treatise of Melancholie* (London, 1586), prefatory letter, cited by Lawrence Babb, *The Elizabethan Malady: A Study of Melancholia in English Literature from 1580 to 1642* (East Lansing: Michigan State University Press, 1951), 51–52.

6. Ben Jonson, *The Complete Poems*, ed. George Parfitt (London: Penguin Books, 1975, reprinted with revisions 1988), 243, lines 97–98.

7. Frederic B. Tromly, "'Accordinge to Sounde Religion': The Elizabethan Controversy over the Funeral Sermon," *Journal of Medieval and Renaissance Studies* 13 (1983): 293–312, esp. 294–96.

8. John Donne, *The Sermons of John Donne*, ed. Evelyn M. Simpson and George R. Potter (Berkeley and Los Angeles: University of California Press, 1953–62), 7:269, 273–78.

9. Jeremy Taylor, *The Whole Works of the Right Reverend Jeremy Taylor, D.D.*, ed. C. P. Eden (London: Longman, 1847–54), 8.427, 435–50.

10. Alice Thornton, *The Autobiography of Mrs. Alice Thornton of East Newton, Co. York, Surtees Society*, 62 (1875): 125.

11. Greer, ed., *Kissing the Rod*, 196–97.

12. Ibid. 157; Thornton, *Autobiography*, 125; Jonson, *Complete Poems*, 48, 41 (the commas before and after "less" in this edition seem redundant); Ralph Houlbrooke, *English Family Life, 1576–1716: An Anthology from Diaries* (Oxford: Basil Blackwell, 1988), 142–43.

13. Thomas Fuller, *The History of the Worthies of England* (London, 1811), 1:490; Adam White, "Westminster Abbey in the Early Seventeenth Century: A Powerhouse of Ideas," *Church Monuments* 4 (1989): 29, 32.

14. John Milton, *Paradise Lost*, 5.95–128.

15. Dennis Kay, *Melodious Tears: The English Funeral Elegy from Spenser to Milton* (Oxford: Clarendon Press, 1990), 6, 231–32.

16. Crashaw, *Poems*, 395.

17. Bettie A. Doebler, *"Rooted Sorrow": Dying in Early Modern England* (Cranbury, N.J.: Associated University Presses, 1994), 241.

18. Kay, *Melodious Tears*, 208 n. 10.

19. Adam White, "England c. 1560–c. 1660: A Hundred Years of Continental Influence," *Church Monuments* 7 (1992): 34–74; Joshua Scodel, *The English Poetic Epitaph: Commemoration and Conflict from Jonson to Wordsworth* (Ithaca, N.Y.: Cornell University Press, 1991); and Brian Kemp, *English Church Monuments* (London: Batsford, 1980), esp. 105–07.

20. Juliana Schiesari, *The Gendering of Melancholia: Feminism, Psychoanalysis and the Symbolics of Loss in Renaissance Literature* (Ithaca, N.Y.: Cornell University Press, 1992).

21. See especially Lawrence Stone, *The Family, Sex and Marriage in England 1500–1800* (London: Weidenfeld and Nicolson, 1977).

About the Contributors

ROBERT C. EVANS is professor of English at Auburn University Montgomery. An editor of the *Ben Jonson Journal* and *Comparative Drama*, he has published various books and articles on Jonson as well as several articles on Donne. Most recently he has written about Elizabeth With, whose grief-filled collection of poems entitled *Elizabeth Fools Warning* provides detailed insights into the breakdown of a seventeenth century marriage.

RALPH HOULBROOKE teaches at the University of Reading, England, where he is professor of early modern history and director of the Early Modern Research Centre. His books include *Church Courts and the People during the English Reformation, 1520–1570*, *The English Family, 1450–1700*, and *Death, Religion and Family in England, 1500–1750*.

W. SCOTT HOWARD is assistant professor of English at The University of Denver. With essays forthcoming in *Studying Cultural Landscapes*, *Grief and Gender*, and *Printed Voices*, he is also working on two books: *Fantastic Surmise*, a study of early modern English elegies and historiography; and, with Sara van den Berg, *John Milton's Divorce Tracts*, an edition of Milton's complete writings on divorce.

About the Contributors

DAVID A. KENT teaches at Centennial College in Toronto. He coedited *Heirs of Fame: Milton and Writers of the English Renaissance* with Margo Swiss and has edited other collections of essays on Christina Rossetti and Canadian poet Margaret Avison. He has also coedited *Romantic Parodies, 1797–1831, Selected Prose of Christina Rossetti* and *Regency Radical: Selected Writings of William Hone.*

MARJORY E. LANGE is associate professor of English at Western Oregon University, where she explores and teaches a wide range of material. She has previously published *Telling Tears in the English Renaissance,* and is working on a study of early English doctors and healing, as well as researching in the area of the *ars bene moriendi.*

DONNA J. LONG is assistant professor of English at Fairmont State College, where she teaches early modern literature and creative writing. She has an essay on Mary Carey in *Discovering and (Re) Covering the Seventeenth Century Religious Lyric.* Most recently, she taught "Cultural Power, Cultural Performance: Reading Early Modern Women," a course developed in collaboration with Dr. Rhonda Lemke Sanford and with the assistance of a Grant for Faculty Research from Fairmont State.

LOUIS L. MARTZ was Sterling Professor of English at Yale University. He is the author of five books on seventeenth century literature, including *The Poetry of Meditation* and *Milton, Poet of Exile.* He served as chairman of the editorial board for the recently completed *Yale Edition of the Complete Works of St. Thomas More* and has published *Thomas More: The Search for the Inner Man.* He also published widely in the field of twentieth century, with editions of both the *Collected Poems* and the *Selected Poems* of H. D., and an edition of D. H. Lawrence's *Quetzacoatl,* the early version of *The Plumed Serpent.* His studies in this field have been summed up in his book *Many Gods and Many Voices: The Role of the Prophet in English and American Modernism.*

PHILLIP MCCAFFREY is professor of English at Loyola College in Maryland. He has published articles on medieval and Renaissance literature and a book on Freud's case history of Dora. He is currently completing a book on female doubles in literature and film.

MICHAEL MCCLINTOCK is assistant professor of English at McKendree College in Illinois where he teaches courses in early English literature, drama and composition. He is working on a study of language, emotion and Renaissance drama as well as on early English rhetoric books.

PAUL A. PARRISH is professor of English at Texas A&M University. He is the author of *Richard Crashaw* and a number of articles, especially on Crashaw, Milton, Donne and other seventeenth-century poets. He is the volume commentary editor for volume 6 (*The Anniversaries and the Epicedes and Obsequies*) of *The Variorum Edition of the Poetry of John Donne* and is the chief editor of the Commentary for the Donne Variorum project.

JOHN T. SHAWCROSS, professor of English, emeritus, University of Kentucky, is the author of *John Milton: The Self and the World* and *The Uncertain World of Samson Agonistes*, as well as "The Virtue and Discipline of Wrestling with God," in *Wrestling with God: Literature & Theology in the English Renaissance. Essays to Honour Paul Grant Stanwood*, eds. Mary Ellen Henley and W. Speed Hill.

PAUL G. STANWOOD, who is professor emeritus of English at the University of British Columbia, has published widely on Renaissance and later English literature. Among his editions are the posthumous books of Richard Hooker's *Of the Laws of Ecclesiastical Polity* and Jeremy Taylor's *Holy Living* and *Holy Dying*, and (as coeditor) *John Donne and the Theology of Language* and *Selected Prose of Christina Rossetti*. He is the author of a book-length study of Izaak Walton and also *The Sempiternal Season: Studies in Seventeenth-Century Devotional Literature*. A past president of the John Donne

Society, he is currently president of the International Association of University Professors of English.

MARGO SWISS teaches Renaissance studies and creative writing in the Division of Humanities at York University, Toronto. She has published articles on Milton and Donne and coedited *Heirs of Fame: Milton and Writers of the English Renaissance*. Her poetry has been anthologized on three occasions, and she published a collection in 1996, *Crossword: A Woman's Narrative*.

FRED B. TROMLY is professor of English at Trent University, where he teaches Renaissance literature. Among his publications on Renaissance topics are articles on English elegies and on the Elizabethan funeral sermon. He is the author of *Playing with Desire: Christopher Marlowe and the Art of Tantalization* and is currently working on a book-length study of fathers and sons in Shakespeare.

Index

Anselment, Raymond, 8, 12, 13
Astell, Ann, 264

Baker, Augustine, 221
Baruch, Elaine Hoffman, 257–58
Basil, Saint (of Caesarea), 200–2, 207
Batycki, Frances, 6
Beier, Lucinda, 158
Boethius: The Consolation of Philosophy, 37
Breton, Nicholas, 273
Bossuet, 207
Bright, Timothy: *A Treatise on Melancholie*, 10, 264, 270, 271, 274, 318 n 13; on melancholy, 78–79, 81–83
Burton, Robert: *The Anatomy of Melancholy*, 3, 9–10, 16, 26–27, 70–71, 81, 83–86, 91

Carey, Mary, 155, 165–67, 169, 173, 295
Cixous, Helene, 280
Clarke, Elizabeth, 132–33
Clement, Catherine, 280
Collins, An: "The Discourse," 177, 181; *Divine Songs and Meditacions*, 177–79, 191; as a Particular Baptist, 190–91; "The Preface," 194–96; "To the Reader," 180, 181–82; "A Song composed in time of the Civill Warr," 179, 187–94; "Another Song (The Winter of my infancy)," 179–80, 185–87
Consolation tradition, 23–26; strategies, 21–22; language, 26–27; conventions, 163–64; William Hammond's *consolatio* sequence, 143–45
Crashaw, Richard, 297; occasions for mourning, 219–21; "Death's Lecture at the Funeral of a Young Gentleman," 227–28: "Elegia," 225; "Elegy upon the death of Mr. Stanninow," 227; elegy for George Porter, 232–33, 299; "Epitaph" [William Herrys], 224–25; "An Epitaph Upon Mr. Ashton," 222; "An Epitaph upon a Young Married Couple," 223, 299; "Epitaphium" [William Herrys], 224–25; epitaphs for

362   Index

Samuel Brooke, 222–23; "In Eundem Scazan," 225; "The Teare," 233–34, 238–39; "Sancta Maria Dolorum," 233–36; "Upon the death of a freind," 223; "Upon the Death of a Gentleman" [Michael Chambers], 231–32; "Upon the Death of Mr. Herrys," 226–27; "Upon the Death of the most desired Mr. Herrys," 229; "Another," 230–31; "The Weeper," 233–34, 238–40
Crawford, Patricia, 159
Cressy, David, 8, 12, 14–15, 160, 183

Danielson, Dennis, 347–48 n 5
Derrida, Jacques, 10
Digby, Sir Kenelm, letters (to Lady Venetia Digby), 55–58, 292
Doebler, Betty Anne, 11, 299
Donne, John, 137; *Anniversary* poems, 230; "Elegie" (on the death of Lady Bridget Markham), 43–55, 291–92; compared with Jonson's "Elegie on My Muse," 65–68; funeral sermons, 197–98; funeral sermon for Lady Danvers, 89–91, 204–6; funeral sermon for Sir William Cockayne, 202–4, 293; melancholy, 69–74, 87–97; melancholic despair, 91–92; melancholy and superstition, 95; Roman Catholicism, 96–97
Duncan, Joseph, 264

Elam, Kier, 99
Elegy, 14–15, 184–85; maternal elegies, 155, 162–64, 294–95

Elyot, Thomas: *Castel of Helthe*, 76–78, 79–81, 316 n 9, 317 n 12, 318 n 6, 319 n 21, n 22, n 23
Enterline, Lynn, 100–1
Erickson, Robert A., 265–66
Evans, J. M., 351 n 16
Evans, Robert C., 291–92

Farwell, Marilyn, 267
Featley, Daniel, 14, 278
Featley, John, 14
Fischlin, Daniel, 6, 304 n 11
Freud, Sigmund, 280; "Mourning and Melancholy," 245–46, 304 n 6
Funeral sculpture, 300–1
Funeral sermons, 197–99, 211–12, 292–93, 335–36 n 1

Gilligan, Carol, 280
Gittings, Clare, 158
Godly sorrow, 9, 14, 183–84, 276, 277
Goodyer, Henry, 73
Gottlieb, Sidney, 189, 331 n 1
Graham, Elspeth, 157
Greenfield, Matthew, 306 n 30
Gregory, Saint (of Nazianzen), 199–200, 207
Grief, 159–60; bibliographical list of works about, 311–13 n 2; causes of grief: 7, 12, (plague), 12–13 (infant and child mortality), 13 (death of spouse), 13–14 (war); changing attitudes toward, 287–88, 289; Christian understanding of grief, 284–87; Eve's grief in *Paradise Lost*, 276–78; gender and grief, 15–16, 160–61, 294–95; grief for children, 12–13, 289; maternal grief, 158–59, 175–76; grief as melancholy,

Index 363

72; process of grief, 303 n 3; sincerity of grief, 17–18, 136–38; woman's grief, 15, 17, 160–61, 294–95

Hammond, William: "The Chamber," 143–44 (printed 151); "On the Death of my Brother, Mr. H. S., drowned: The Tomb," 138–40, 142 (printed 150); "On the Same: The Boat," 140–41, 142–43; "On the Same: The Tempers," 141–43; "The Excuse," 146; "Man's Life," 145–46, 149; "The Reasons," 146–47; "The Rose," 145, 149–50; "The Tears," 147–49 (printed 151–52); "Thursday," 144–45
Haskins, Susan, 237
Hastings, Lucy, 155–56, 165, 167–69, 172
Herbert, George, Calvinism, 126–27, 129–30; "Affliction (I)," 119–20; "Affliction (III)," 121–22; "Affliction (IV)," 124–25; "Assurance," 128–29; "The Bag," 131–32; "Bitter-Sweet," 134; "Conscience," 130; "The Crosse," 133–34; "Deniall," 125; "The Flower," 130, 134; "Grief," 132–33; "The Holdfast," 127–28; "Josephs Coat," 134–35; "Longing," 131; "Love Unknown," 126–27; "Man," 125; "Obedience," 123–24; "The Pearl," 124; "Prayer II," 125; "The Sacrifice," 120–21; "The Search," 132; "Submission," 122–23; "The Water-course," 129–30
Herbert, Mary (Countess of Pembroke), 137
Herschel, Abraham, 276–77

Heywood, Thomas: *Apology for Actors*, 98–100, 102–6; *A Woman Killed with Kindness*, 100, 106–18, 296–97
Hobbes, Thomas, 274
Houlbrooke, Ralph, 10–11, 12–13, 157–58, 183
Howard, Jean, 104
Hyperius, Andreas, 198–99

Jonson, Ben, 217–18; "Elegie on My Muse," 42–43, 58–65, 292; compared with Donne's "Elegie" (on the death of Lady Markham), 65–68; "On My First Son," 295
Joubert, Laurent, 274

Kay, Dennis, 224, 299, 300
King, Henry, 199–200
Kirsch, Arthur, 3, 304 n 6
Kristeva, Julia, 280, 282–83

Lactantius, 262–63, 347 n 4, 347–48 n 5, 348 n 6
Lange, Marjory, 10, 16, 276, 291, 301
Laurence, Anne, 5, 7–8, 11, 12, 157, 159, 160 183, 275
Laurentius, Andreas, 78–80, 82
Lewalski, Barbara, 130
Long, Donna, 294–95
Low, Anthony, 221, 245

MacDonald, Michael, 2, 13, 316–17 n 10
Magdalen, Mary, 236–38, 269–70, 281, list of treatises, 350 n 14
Martz, Louis, 300, 301
Marvell, Andrew: "On a Drop of Dew," 244; "Eyes and Tears," 243–44; "Mourning," 242–43; "The Nymph

complaining for the death of her faun," 244–60, 296
McCaffrey, Phillip, 296
McColley, Diane, 263–64, 269
McLintock, Michael, 296–97
Melancholy, 3, 291; causes of disease, 87–88; as destructive, 94–97; as disease in Donne, 86–87; as grief, 72; as humour, 74–76, 79–80; religious melancholy, 84–85 (and despair, 85–86, 91–92); as Renaissance fashion, 76–77
Milton, John, 18–19, 137; *On Christian Doctrine*, 261–62; *Of Education*, 283; *Paradise Lost*: androgyny in, 265–68; Eve's dream, 263–64, 268–69; Eve's tears, 269–70, 270–71, 273–76, 281–83; Milton's God, 261–63; relationship between Adam and Eve, 268–69, 271–72, 282–83; separation scene, 279–80
Mollenkott, Virginia, 266
Mourning, 3, 11; changes in practice, 182–83; formal, 288–89; ritual, 158–59

Napier, Richard, 13, 160, 316 n 7

Orpheus, 112–14, 323 n 18

Parkes, Colin Murray, 303 n 3
Patrick, Simon, 161–62
Parrish, Paul, 297
Philips, Katherine, 295
Pigman, G. W. III, 2, 8, 14, 58, 136, 183, 217–18, 288, 289, 301–2
Puttenham, George, 7, 9

Ramazani, Jahan, 218–19
Rich, Barnaby, 277–78

Sandys, Henry, 138, 139
Savage, Sarah, 154
Schenck, Celeste, 136–37
Schiesari, Juliana, 15, 100–1, 219, 301, 306 n 31
Shakespeare, William: *Hamlet*, 2–5, 27–28; *King Lear*, 32–41, 99; *Macbeth*, 1–2, 5; *Measure for Measure*, 29–32, 35; *Much Ado About Nothing*, 20–21, 22–24; *Richard II*, 32–33; *Two Gentlemen of Verona*, 24–25
Shawcross, John, 266, 290–91
Spinrad, Phoebe, 244–5
Stanwood, P. G., 293
Stewart, Stanley, 185–87
Strier, Richard, 128
Stubbes, Philip, 101–2
Syminges, John, 73
Stone, Lawrence, 7, 302
Swetham, Joseph, 271
Swiss, Margo, 297–98

Taylor, Jeremy, 197–98, 206–8, 215–16; funeral sermon for John Bramwell, 209–11; for Sir George Dalstone, 208–9; for the Countess of Carbery, 212–16, 293–94; *Holy Dying*, 212–14
Tears, 9–10, 93; Eve's tears in *Paradise Lost*, 269–71, 273–74, 280–81, 350 n 12, n 13
Temple, William, 161–62
Tertullian, 262–63, 347 n 4, 348 n 6
Thimelby, Gertrude, 156, 164, 167, 169–70, 173–75
Thornton, Alice, 156–57, 164–65, 167, 169, 170–72
Travers, Rebecca, 159
Tricomi, Albert, 101
Tromly, Fred, 290, 292

Volkan, Vamik D. (and Daniel Josephtal), 250–51

Walton, Izaak, 87
Webber, Joan , 262

Whatley, William, 14, 276
Wright, Thomas, 321–22 n 7

Zwicker, Steven, 19